Was Greek Thought Religious?

Was Greek Thought Religious?

ON THE USE AND ABUSE OF HELLENISM
FROM ROME TO ROMANTICISM

LOUIS A. RUPRECHT, JR.

palgrave

First published 2002 by PALGRAVE™
175 Fifth Avenue, New York, N.Y. 10010 and
Houndmills, Basingstoke, Hampshire, England RG21 6XS.
Companies and representatives throughout the world.

PALGRAVE is the new global publishing imprint of St. Martin's Press LLC Scholarly
and Reference Division and Palgrave Publishers Ltd. (formerly Macmillan Press Ltd.).

ISBN 0–312–29562–6 (hardback)
ISBN 0–312–29563–4 (paperback)

Library of Congress Cataloging-in-Publication Data
Ruprecht, Louis A.
Was Greek thought religious? : on the use and abuse of Hellenism, from Rome to
romanticism / by Louis A. Ruprecht, Jr.
   p.   cm.
   Includes bibliographical references.
   ISBN 0–312–29562–6 – ISBN 0–312–29563–4 (pbk.)
   1. Hellenism.   2. Philosophy, Ancient.   3. Philosophy and religion—Greece.
4. Philosophy and religion—History.   I. Title.

B945.R853 W37   2002
180—dc21   200225178

A catalogue record for this book is available from the British Library.

Design by Letra Libre, Inc.

First edition: June 2002
10 9 8 7 6 5 4 3 2 1

Printed in the United States of America.

This book is dedicated
to my mother
Nancy Holt Ruprecht

and there came to me
      just now
            the knowledge of
the tyranny of the image
      and how
            men
in their designs
      have learned
            to shatter it
whatever it may be,
      that the trouble
            in their minds
shall be quieted
      put to bed
            again.

—William Carlos Williams,
"Tribute to the Painters" (1955)

Contents

Acknowledgments

The metaphor of journeying is an especially prominent one in this book. I will spend nearly as much time, albeit peripherally and somewhat episodically, talking about the pilgrimage practices of several religions as I do discussing the nature of their devotional symbols, images, and icons. This is due, in part, to my dawning interest in displaying the recent interest in *material* culture and the practices associated with such material, interests that have so decisively transformed the collective brainscape of religious studies and classics in the past decade. Turn your sights on new arenas, and you will inevitably see new and different things. That is one very large rationale for journeying, of course.

But there is more than this. This book is also the product of a journey—my own travels, which at times verged on becoming pilgrimages themselves, in these same long years. I traveled to Greece for the first time in 1986, under the auspices of the American School of Classical Studies in Athens. Their remarkable summer program in Aegean archaeology provides those lucky enough to be accepted into it with a way to see more of the country—the *modern* country, as well as her wealth of antiquities, whether Bronze Age, Classical, or Byzantine—than would be possible in any other way in the short space of one summer. That experience was doubtlessly the most transformative one of my graduate career, and I have returned to Greece every year since then, both to work on an exciting Hellenistic excavation on the northwest tip of Crete, as well as to avail myself of the marvelous resources of the American School's Blegen Library—not to mention the Gennadius Library's unique holdings in Byzantine and Modern Greek materials, housed just across the street. Bridging the divide that separates these two collections—our subtle perception that the ancient and the modern Greeks do not and should not meet—is one of my chief goals in this book. Special thanks are due to Robert Bridges, tireless secretary of the American School, to Nancy Winter, the Blegen Librarian who retired just this year, and to Sophia Papagiorgiou, curator of the Gennadius collection, all of whom have been faithful and generous supporters of my work, as well as sources of abiding insights and suggestions along the way without which this book would not have found its way to completion, however tentative.

This project finally began to come into sharper focus last year, when I was fortunate enough to be accepted for participation in an NEH Summer Seminar devoted to a comparative study of ethnography and maps in the ancient world. How did the ancients define themselves? How did they locate themselves in space, and in relation to other peoples? These are all preeminently travelers' questions. The seminar had the grand good fortune of being housed at the spectacular facilities of the American Academy in Rome, sister to the institution to which I'd grown so very attached in Athens. I am especially indebted to Michael Maas and Richard Talbert, codirectors of that seminar, who so kindly offered me a seat at their rich intellectual banquet. I am equally and deeply indebted to Pina Pasquantonio, Assistant Director for Operations and our institutional host, to Lester Little, Director of the Academy, and to Christina Huemer, the Academy's head librarian. Each of these good people made my two-month sojourn in Rome an uncannily productive one, intellectually speaking, but their warmth and unerring sense of Roman hospitality also laced the visit with a very special kind of warmth and joy. Those who have had the good fortune to dine in the Academy courtyard on a summer evening, and to linger afterward in the Garden, will smile in whimsical recognition of the gratitude I am attempting to describe.

If this is true of the Academy as a whole, and it is, then it is doubly true of the Academy's manager of daily affairs, Anne Coulson. Anne held my hand through all of the bureaucratic intricacies and challenges associated with academic life in the Eternal-but-slow-moving City, securing permissions for the photographic images I have put to great use on the cover of this book. Along the way, Anne also became a trusted and much-treasured friend.

My academic career, since the completion of my degree, has been every bit as peripatetic as some of the characters I will endeavor to describe in the pages that follow. In what continue to be the trying circumstances for all of us who endeavor to do such work, I have been richly blessed by the kind sponsorship of a number of extraordinary institutions, among them: Barnard College, Princeton University, Duke University, the Georgia State University, and Mercer University. Still more, my own work would be unthinkable apart from the generous support I continue to receive from Emory University, the program that awarded me my degree, and that has continued to support my work. I am indebted to two former professors, Jon Gunnemann and Stephen Tipton, who, as successive directors of Emory's Graduate Division of Religion, have continued to grant me a kind of adjunct status that has allowed me access to Emory's rich library holdings and computer facilities, among many other things. This book could quite literally never have been written apart from this institutional support. I trust my former colleagues in the Department of Religion at Emory to know how much I have learned from them, and how present they continue to be (for better and for worse) in what I write and think. Such are the risks and responsibilities of academic friendship.

Friendship of other forms has also been instrumental in the conception and completion of this project. Far and away the most significant intellectual discovery of my postgraduate career has been the institution of Modern Greek Studies, especially as it was presented to me at the Ohio State University. Vassilis Lambropoulos, Artemis Leontis and Gregory Jusdanis invited me to a three-day symposium on the large topic of Hellenic appropriation, and they have been critical conversation-partners ever since. Equally significant has been my friendship with Peter Murphy, now of the Victoria University in Wellington, New Zealand. As I look back on the shape of my thought before I was graced with these friendships, I am struck by the dramatic scope of the change. My mental landscape, as well as the texture of the journey in which I then understood myself to be engaged, has been significantly changed by all of them. I trust them, too, to understand the nature and extent of my debt.

With some sense of that landscape before me, I joined Princeton's Department of Religion and its Program in Hellenic Studies in the Fall of 1998. It was there that Jeff Stout, Alexander Nehamas, and Dimitri Gondicas added their own acute insights to the dazzling mental mixture with which I was then grappling. Their presence in my footnotes here provides only the scantiest picture of the depth of my indebtedness, both personally and professionally. I've never been happier anywhere than I was at Princeton, and they were a large reason for that. Jeff once mentioned to me, casually enough, that "piety" is the virtue which names how we deal with debts we cannot manage to repay—like the ones we owe our mothers. Or God. In that spirit, I feel pretty pious about Princeton; I trust my friends there to fill in the significant blanks in what I have not said here.

As I have traveled to serve in various academic posts, I have always maintained my own home in Atlanta, choosing to commute even as far away as New York City rather than to leave a city to which I have grown attached. The extraordinary circle of friends with which I've been blessed remains the primary reason for this. A remarkable range of medical doctors and philosophers, epidemiologists and historians and studio artists, they provide me with the intellectual foundation and the love that continue to make this job seem every bit as fantastic as it is real. Jim Winchester and Eve Lackritz, Tim Craker and Mary Potter, Arturo Lindsay and Melanie Pavich-Lindsay have all been subjected to more of my stories, more of my speculations, and more of my limericks, than anyone should be. That they bear this, as they bear all things, with a special grace is but one of the reasons I love them so. Two other members of our circle have recently embarked on a dramatic journey of their own. Larry Slutsker and Barbara Marsden moved to Kenya in August 2001, where they will serve at a CDC field station in Kisumu for three years, or more. They have been equally unflagging in their support of my work; they made me a gift of the computer on which I have composed every word of this manuscript. And they made me a still more spectacular gift by asking me to stand godfather to their first child, Emma Elizabeth. As they have trusted us to fill in the blanks left by their departure, I trust them to know how much they, and their departure, have meant to me.

This book has been literally ten years in the making. But it was only last year, in Rome, that the shape of the project began to come into focus, carved into higher relief. As I pursued tangent interests that ranged from a survey of the ways religion is conceived and discussed in constitutional law, to an analysis of the erotic metaphors in mature Platonic philosophy, and finally to the history of the birth of the modern Olympics—all of these interests prompted initially by requests from Emory University and Barnard College to design new courses ("Religion in the Law," "Religion and Sexuality," and "The Olympic Ideal: Ancient and Modern")—I often felt as if I were wandering more than journeying. I felt uncertain of a destination, and the poignant absence of a scholarly "plan"; I wondered if such a thing were even possible. It has been primarily the generous support of various colleges and academic institutions that enabled me to take up various parts of this project anew, and to begin to think in a more disciplined way about how they relate to one another, how they may in fact actually fit.

Chapter One was birthed at the invitation of Michael Dorf of the Columbia University Law School, who invited me to present an informal and disjointed set of reflections on the way the Greeks are used in contemporary constitutional law. These still scrambled thoughts gradually achieved sharper form, as I lectured on this material subsequently: at the annual meetings of the American Academy of Religion in November 2000; at Alfred University, where I was invited to deliver their annual Sibley Lecture in February of 2001; once again at the University of Tennessee in Knoxville in the following month, at a conference on "Art and the Public Sphere"; then yet again at Emory University in November of 2001, when I was invited by the Graduate Division of Religion to return as the initiator of their Annual Distinguished Alumni Lecture Series. A thorough review of this material in the guise of an

Independent Study I shared with Mr. Scott Michelman (now at Harvard University Law School) in the Spring of 2001 at Duke University was a source of tremendous insight and real intellectual joy; Scott's friendship has been another happy coincidence of my constant traveling.

Chapter Two received a thorough reading from Mr. Mike Lippman, another former student from my Emory days, one who is now completing a dissertation in Duke University's Department of Classics. Mike's friendship has been equally generous and important; his comic sensibilities have been as instructive and nourishing to me as his intellect has been. A true Don Quixote of the mind, he has walked through all phases of this project with me, helping me to see which ideas were windmills and which ones not. By making my journey a part of his own, he embodies much of what is best in the classical understanding of the virtue of friendship.

Chapter Three received generous readings from Richard Talbert and Michael Maas when we were in Rome together in the summer of 2000. Both of them made critical suggestions for writing and reorganization which have significantly improved my manner of saying what I had hoped to say. David Konstan also read the manuscript in the months following my return from Italy; his kindness and support of my work, both professional and personal, has been one of the more unexpected blessings of my own academic *periegesis,* all the more precious to me for being so unexpected and unearned.

During my time at Duke University, I profited from regular conversations over lunch with Kalman Bland, as well as over midday runs through the university golf course with Stanley Hauerwas and Alex Sider. Kalman and Alex just so happened to be working on religious iconography at the time, and Kalman's book, *The Artless Jew,* was just then going to press. Chapter Five would not have the shape and texture it now has—and probably would never have been written at all—without their kind support and intelligent prodding. Kalman consented to read no fewer than four drafts of this material. Only they can know how thoroughly I stand in their debt, as I wrestled with material of which I am neither master nor disciple.

As I moved into the muddied cultural morass of the nineteenth century, two remarkable women helped me find new ways to let the dirt settle a bit, and thus to allow some things to sift out into clearer form. Sarah Ferguson-Wagstaffe, a remarkable poet and graduate student now in the Comparative Literature program at Cornell University, and Lauren Todd Taylor, a Comparative Literature candidate at the University of Tennessee at Knoxville, both provided me with wonderful readings of Chapters Seven and Eight, helping me to make connections I had been unable to make, as well as helping me to see some others that it would never have occurred to me to see at all.

If the Modern Olympics constitute the modern pilgrimage-play *par excellence,* then Chapter Nine is the place where the journey inscribed in this book has been aimed. The Society for Values in Higher Education provided the setting for my first tentative presentation of these ideas, whereas Emory University's fledgling Center for Ethics in Public Policy and the Professions provided the second, both in the spring of 1996. Ralph Norman subsequently accepted a version of this work for publication in *Soundings,* a remarkable interdisciplinary journal that has consistently been a gracious booster of my written work, no matter how quirky it may seem at times. The *Soundings* editorial board has kindly agreed to the reprinting of some of that material in what is now a significantly different and a significantly longer chapter. As I was proofing galley pages for the original appearance of that article, I was also preparing another version of this material for presentation at the first Ursula Niebuhr Memorial Lecture at Barnard College; Helene Foley's formal response to that lecture was particularly illuminating and helpful to me. I have also profited enormously from conversations with many students who have enrolled in a course ("The Olympic Ideal: Ancient and Modern") I designed first at Emory in 1996, in anticipation of the 1996 Atlanta Games. I have subsequently been invited to offer this course at Barnard College, Princeton University, Duke University, and Mercer University. I trust my students at each of these institutions to recognize what I owe to them.

Finally, several people have taken friendship to new and unexpected levels, by consenting to read this entire manuscript. Brenda Fineberg, whom I met initially on that wonderful NEH Seminar in Rome, became a much-respected conversation partner and, as the summer progressed, a dear friend. Bruce Lawrence, Chair of Duke's Department of Religion, has been a devoted friend and booster of my work since my undergraduate days at Duke. I know that I did not earn this in college; I have long since stopped trying to find reasons for it all. I content myself in both cases with the sure knowledge that the undeserved boon of their love and care needs no reasons. Such love is a free gift or it is not at all. And such friendship is a virtue; this the Greeks knew. Finally, my editor at Palgrave, Gayatri Patnaik, has worked tirelessly to help me find ways to pull the project together in a tighter and more compact form, though no doubt if I'd listened to her more clearly and closely, I'd have managed to do so still better. Some gaps, as no one knows better than I, remain unfilled. Gayatri's assistant, Jennifer Stais, has managed to do much of that good work with patience and aplomb. But there is always more to do, always a further stretch of road to travel.

After nine years of episodic gestation, this book was finally written in one burst, in the summer and fall of 2000. In that same period, my mother embarked on a long and often lonely journey of her own. Diagnosed with a cancer of unspecific origin in the fall, she embarked on that singularly modern pilgrimage route we call "chemotherapy." It was a transformative journey for her and, at an admitted emotional remove, for me as well. I was as moved by her quiet grace in those long months as I have been instructed by her experience as to the true nature of pilgrimage itself. They are, in an important sense, journeys more than destinations. Our therapies allow us to live with illness now, not necessarily to escape from it. And remission is as much a state of mind as it is a state of grace. In celebration of that newfound state, we took a trip to Rome together (her first, my second) in June of last year. And so it is that my mother has instructed me about the true nature, and the real texture, of religious pilgrimage, the very thing with which I had long been preoccupied in books. She helped me to notice better both the continuities in the life that a pilgrimage is ideally designed to celebrate, as well as the radical breaks and disjunctions in the life that the journey inevitably creates. Pilgrimage draws a line that divides us in two, a line separating who we were before and who we are in the process of becoming now. It is for this reason, as well as others too precious and numerous to name, that I dedicate this book to my mother, Nancy Holt Ruprecht.

LAR
Serifos, Greece

Preface

Comparative religion—at least in my own understanding of what this curious practice involves—is intended to help us notice religion where we don't normally think to look for it. It also encourages us to notice things *as* religious that we do not normally think of in these terms at all. In this book, I want to suggest some new ways of thinking about the Greeks, ways that may help to make their own curious kinds of religiosity a bit clearer to us. It is fitting, as I will attempt to demonstrate later, that two *images* have been of great assistance to me in so doing. I introduce this larger project with and through them.

The first image resides in the justly famous "Room of Constantine," in the Vatican Museums. The walls of that room are decorated with several scenes depicting important moments in the emperor's career, moments when his own religious role was clearest to him, involving him in what I take to be a half-hearted and only lukewarm opposition to the traditional religion of the Empire. Many of these images will be familiar to many of us. Taking our eyes off of the walls, however, and raising them toward the ceiling, we are confronted by another image, one far more arresting, to my eyes, and perhaps also more appropriate to the broader message contained within this room.

This ceiling fresco is entitled "The Triumph of Christianity over Paganism," and was painted by Tomaso Laureti Siciliano in roughly 1530, at the very inception of the Protestant Reformation, as we shall see in more detail in Chapter Six. "Paganism" is depicted here, as it so often is, as a religion of *images,* more specifically, as a religion that is presumed to have "worshiped statues." These pagan statues have been defeated and, in this particular case, one of them has actually been decapitated. Ironically, then—and in order for Christianity to "triumph"—it must admit the power of these pagan images, must take them seriously on their own terms. Christianity is compelled to treat these statues as if they are real, and in a paradox still more worthy of our attention, must treat them almost as if they are real bodies.[1] The religious ironies run deeper still: For the *thing* that has defeated these pagan images is, itself, yet another image, another three-dimensional image that is distinguished from the first only by being Christian, and cruciform.

It was Nietzsche who spoke perhaps most eloquently to this paradox. And it was certainly Nietzsche who saw that the forces of good use the *same* tactics, and many of the *same* weapons, as evil does. "The victory of a moral ideal," he tells us, "will be achieved by the same 'immoral' means as every other victory."[2] We have a clear representation of Nietzsche's point here, in this painting. Christianity uses paganseeming tools to undo paganism. It takes a statue to destroy a statue. A religion of images is replaced—not by an aniconic religion (as we will see in Chapter Five, there are no such things)—but rather by a religion that uses *different* images, and claims to use them in a different way.

We know where Nietzsche was destined with this insight. In order to highlight profound paradoxes that no one else seemed to notice, he felt the need to turn everything upside-down. Not content to say that Christianity and paganism use the same instruments, Nietzsche felt compelled to show how "Greek religion" used better and more compelling instruments than a religion he consistently referred to as "Judaeo-Christian."[3] It may seem odd to speak of Nietzsche as a moralist, but so he was, in moments such as this one. And that is ironically where I part company with him. The religionist should be interested in the comparison of religions, not in creating a false and unnecessary competition between them. Of course, Nietzsche blamed Christianity for turning its relationship to other religions into a competition. But, as we will see in the fourth chapter, pagans did this as well. This Nietzsche seems not to see, or say.

In deliberate juxtaposition to this stunning visual image, I have included a short portion of a poem written by William Carlos Williams in 1955, his "Tribute to the Painters." The poem seems a fitting, if unintended, commentary on Siciliano's painting, as well as an astute comment on the larger topic of Hellenic appropriation, which will be my curious and wide-ranging topic in this book. I do not pretend that this book will put anyone's disquiet to bed, but I *do* intend to point out what seems to me a very deep trouble in many of our scholarly minds. The trouble has to do with the Greeks, figuring out where they belong—in our curriculum, as well as in our culture. True to my own methodological commitments, I will begin by noticing the presence of the Greeks in some strange and unlikely places—perhaps most surprisingly, at the U.S. Supreme Court. Let me explain the reasons behind what may appear to be a strange-seeming choice of venue before turning to that unexpectedly Hellenic locale.

The field of religious studies, which was the field in which I received my own training, has been seized with a mania for a curious set of conceptual twins in the last decade: the concept of "comparison," on the one hand; and the concept of "material culture," on the other. This book intends to display the practice of both conceptual interests, and it will be one of the book's chief arguments that there are subtle relations between the two. I will say less about "material culture" here in the Preface, in part because there is no easy way of saying it.[4] Tracking what might almost be called "the new materialism" in religious studies would require the skills of an intellectual historian that I lack.

Ironically, while I will say less about the comparatively newfound interest in "material culture" here, the book itself will go a long way, I hope, toward *displaying* what I think is best and most exciting about the study of material culture as a strategy for thinking about, and talking about, that curious rag-bag category called "religion." I content myself here with some initial observations about the equally curious companion-concept of "comparison," since I will seem to touch on it far more obliquely in the body of the book.

Of the two, the concept of "comparative studies" should seem the more peculiar. When we endeavor to "compare" two or more religious traditions, presumably what we are *not* out to do is to evaluate them hierarchically, as Nietzsche did, nor to say how one of them is actually superior to another. What, then, *is* it that we intend to do when we make cultural "comparisons?" It is far easier to say what we do *not* intend when we engage in the practice of "comparison" than it is to say what we mean to do.

Happily enough, she was a poet who first helped me to see another way of for-
mulating and comprehending the nature of my own practices, a poet who also just
so happens to be a first-rate classical scholar. Anne Carson was the deserved recipient of a MacArthur Fellowship last year; her poetry and prose have both had a major
impact on my own thinking in this and in other books. She offers us a lovely explanation of her own decision to compare two poets, one who is ancient and one who
was modern. They are Simonides of Keos and Paul Celan, and here is how Carson
defends her initially silly-seeming idea:

> Attention is a task we share, you and I. To keep attention strong means to keep it from
> settling. Partly for this reason I have chosen to talk about two men at once. They keep
> each other from settling, they are side by side in a conversation and yet no conversa-
> tion takes place. . . . With and against, aligned and adverse, each is placed like a surface
> on which the other may come into focus. Sometimes you can see a celestial object bet-
> ter by looking at something else, with it, in the sky.[5]

I admire this image very much, and have tried to pay it sufficient attention in this
book. "Comparison keeps things from settling." Surely one important goal for the
comparative study of religious traditions is the attempt to keep *them* from settling.
And while our goal ought not to be the normative task of organizing the world's religions into some sort of encyclopedic hierarchy, normative evaluations surely do
continue to have some place in what we do. The question is, What place? and, Defined by whom?

Even the poet wishes "to see *better*." And so do I. I take this to be one of the premier dilemmas in ethical theory today, the lingering question about the status of
normative judgments in a morally pluralistic world. "Comparison," I believe, is one
term we have latched onto, hoping that it will offer us a way out of our intellectual
impasse.

In this book, then, I propose to hold two terms together—to "compare" them, in
a way—to see if I can keep the slippage to a minimum. Those terms are "religion"
and "Greece." In the end, I cannot say whether I have succeeded in keeping them
from slipping, but I *have* seen to it that they overlap in what are, to me, some astonishing ways. What I will be tracking is another kind of slippage, the kind in which
the Greek identity was gradually transformed during the Roman period into something resembling what we today might call a religious identity. "Hellenism" became
a religion. As so it has been ever since—subtly so, and often just beneath the surface—until Romanticism brought this assumption into plain view.

The Romantics occupy an unusually prominent place in this book. Two chapters,
the seventh and the eighth, are devoted to Romantic poets and travelers and art historians, men and women who poked and prodded around Greece's antiquities in the
two decades prior to her War for Independence (1821–1830). Lord Byron takes his
rightful place of preeminence here, as do some other lesser-known Greek pilgrims
and poets.

But I am interested in the Romantics for another reason—in short, because I
have come to believe that we are still trained to think like Romantics, even when we
are reacting most negatively, and most ambitiously, *against* Romanticism. I will argue
many times in these pages that we are not done with Romanticism, that, in fact, we
are all still deeply invested in Romanticism and in Romantic categories—nowhere

more so than when we endeavor to talk about Greece, and about religion. I do not see that as necessarily a good or bad thing; I do see it as an inescapable cultural and curricular fact.

One reason for this is that we who have the marvelous luxury of calling ourselves "teachers" inhabit universities and curricula that are deeply indebted to Romantic models. The University of Berlin, whose curriculum was decisively reorganized in 1809, has had an enormous influence on the subsequent reorganization of modern disciplines and modern knowledge throughout EuroAmerica. And, to the degree that we still attempt to offer our students some sense of what "the west" is, and how it came to be that way, then to that same degree we are (often unwittingly) engaging in Hegel's grand project of narrating ourselves to ourselves. We are telling the *story* of Europe, a story in which ancient Greece—of all places, and of all times—is consistently invoked as Chapter One. That is a curiosity to which I will return many times in the pages that follow. I return to it because it seems such an implausible notion, if we merely consult the map. It seems all the more interesting for that very reason. How could the claim that Greece is "European" ever have been saleable? I will return to that question many times, I suppose, because I am still trying to make better sense of it myself. Of all the questions I am posing here, this one—about "the place of Greece"—threatens to slip the most.

The genealogy of this project has a more proximate history as well. It came into focus just over one year ago, when I found myself working with some early Christian documents, ones that were clearly concerned with self-definition, primarily. As many contemporary thinkers in many competing fields remind us, such self-definition usually comes at the expense of some other, a person or group whose negation becomes your position. Hegel made this insight the mainstay of his phenomenology. But in the early Christian period, two groups of others stand out: heretics, on the one hand; pagans and Jews, on the other. This is unsurprising: We would *expect* Christians to position themselves against what they viewed as an improper understanding of the faith from within; as well as against those older forms of "traditional religion" that Christianity had allegedly come into the world to correct and to replace.

But what, it finally occurred to me to ask, is the Greek word for "pagan?" I was shocked, then intrigued, then compelled to discover that the Greek term that is consistently translated into English and other Romance languages as "pagan" is *Hellên*. The Greek word for "pagan" is, amazingly, "Greek." I found myself in the presence of a paradox demanding further explanation.

This book is the tentative result. "Hellenism" came to be seen as a religion of sorts, in my judgment, at some point in the Hellenistic or Roman period. And thus, from the early Christian perspective, Hellenism—very much like Judaism, and for similar reasons—became a heresy. This idea has had a very long and surprising history, as we shall see. While a great deal of modern scholarly attention has been paid to the highly charged anti-Jewish rhetoric of the early churches, and the way in which this language helped to manufacture an important polemical fiction called "semitism," there has been a deafening silence concerning the early church's concoction of Hellenism in this same era.[6] I have felt, at times, as if I were excavating a site few others have recognized as ancient, or even as worthy of further investigation.

The result of this digging is a book in which I attempt to walk through a fairly traditional "western civilizations" curriculum, paying careful attention to what "religion" and "Hellenism" seemed to mean in each era. What I have discovered is that the two terms do indeed overlap—that "Greekness," at some point after its Classical heyday, came to constitute what we might refer to as a *religious* identity. This is the thread that ties together a body of comparative studies that will lead us "from Rome to Romanticism."

The book is intended less as an intervention in what now seems to me a rather tired, and tiring, debate about the so-called curricular canon, the question of how much classics and philosophy any well-trained modern citizen needs to know. This debate has never been a very illuminating one, and (like most people, I suspect), I am increasingly put off by those who perceive a need to sound off on the matter. It is one of those "cultural" debates in which you end up detesting all sides equally. And this seems a pity, an entirely unnecessary pity, to me.

This book freely, and quite happily, hangs itself upon the framework of a fairly traditional "western civilizations" curriculum. Thus, it continues to rely on Hegel's determinative *Lectures on the Philosophy of History*. Hegel was meant to have been a brilliant lecturer. His conceptual range is undeniable. His scholarly instincts, like Nietzsche's, also seem to have been extraordinary. In an age that seems hellbent on denying the authority of the fathers, it seems important to remind ourselves that Hegel was singularly interested in religion, in comparison, and interested in keeping things from slipping too much. I've always admired that in his thought.

One trope, which I borrow from Plato and develop in the second chapter, is the mythological image of sons who supplant their fathers. Kronos replaced Uranus. Zeus replaced Kronos. Some other god is destined to replace Zeus. That god may have been a Christian one. But Hegel, also borrowing from Plato, consistently referred to the childishness of the Greeks. For him, Greece is "the period of [the world's] adolescence," and "presents to us the cheerful aspect of youthful freshness." All Greek accomplishments are "truly youthful achievement[s]."[7] If the Greeks are also sons, I began to wonder, then who are the fathers *they* supplanted? Plato, and a great deal of ancient mythology with him, suggested Egypt as one possible answer. But the Romantics proposed another. Utilizing a temporal paradox of striking originality, their answer is: the ancient Greeks supplant the moderns. That is the secret assumption of Romanticism, resulting in a sort of "second coming" of the Hellenic. We will have much to say about this back-and-forth between the ancients and the moderns.

In this book, I deliberately chose to look in some admittedly odd-seeming, and rather *non*-Hegelian, places. Thus, I am working within Hegel's temporal framework, but I am doing so in order to bring some hidden things closer to the light, to keep them from slipping any further, if you will. I am trying to notice "religion" in places one does not normally think to look for it, and I am trying to notice "the Greeks," so it may seem, virtually everywhere.

When I turn to the Classical Greek period, I elect to look at Socrates, a man who is customarily thought of as an emphatically *non*religious figure. When I turn to the Romans, I discuss Pausanias, a much-neglected Roman citizen of the eastern Greek-speaking empire, one whose own attitudes to that empire, and especially to the religion of that empire, are complex and ambivalent. When I turn to the Christian period, I opt to discuss the Emperor Julian, not his half-uncle Constantine, a man who attempted almost single-handedly to overturn Christian developments and to dismantle Christian privileges that must have seemed pretty entrenched in his own day. When I turn to the Middle Ages, I opt to look, not at Charlemagne and the European world he helped to secure, but rather at the two empires that have always fit uneasily into the "western" worldview: the Greco-Byzantine empire, with its capital in Constantinople; and the Islamic Caliphate headquartered first in Damascus, then later in Baghdad. When I turn to the Renaissance, I choose to discuss the Puritans, and their worries about the theater, every bit as much as I discuss Shakespeare and his contemporaries. And when I turn to the nineteenth century—whose legacy is still so very much with us—I turn to the Romantics rather than the Victorians, privileging the first half of the century over its nearer neighbor, privileging the poets and travelers over the civil servants and empire-builders. In many ways, Romanticism is where this book is ultimately headed, although it will take me some time to explain fully just why I think that is so.

When I turn at last to more contemporary developments—in the first chapter and in the last—I treat two institutions that often seem to make intellectuals nervous: courts of law, on the one hand; and the Olympic Games, on the other. These two institutions, which bear more serious and sympathetic attention than they customarily receive, serve as the conceptual anchors for everything else I am trying to do and say. They provide the lenses through which I will try to look at the past. And they are also the anchors that hopefully will help to keep it all from slipping away.

But slip things surely will, both because I am not equipped fully to deal with all of the various materials of which I am trying to make sense here, and also because it is in the very nature of such material to move, to change, and thus to slip. Dealing with concepts as slippery as "Greekness" and "religion," how could my analysis do anything other than slip?

The first and last chapters also provide this book with a paradigm and a parable. I begin at the U.S. Supreme Court. I am tracking the way in which the Court has seen its way clear to *use* Greek thought, precisely by assuming that it was not "religious." In a startling array of contemporary decisions—ranging from abortion, to assisted suicide, to gay sexuality—the Court has returned repeatedly to the Greek well, but has only rarely thought to question its reigning assumption: namely, that a "philosopher" such as Plato was innocent of "religion."

I juxtapose this widespread modern way of thinking about the Greeks with another powerful version: the modern Olympic movement. Here we find the flip side of the Neohellenic coin. Pierre de Coubertin deliberately referred to his Olympics as a "revival." Ancient Olympia was a religious sanctuary, he reasoned, and a modern Olympia should be, too. He referred to "Olympism" repeatedly as the *religio athletae,* and while the contours of this religion were never articulated very clearly, one need only view a contemporary advertisement for Nike, or Gatorade, to witness the mingled asceticism and spiritual aspiration toward transcendence that has attached itself so thoroughly, and so unconsciously, to the cult of modern athletics.

There may seem to be a certain "disconnect" between these two chapters on contemporary topics that serve as bookends to this project, and the rest of the historical material that comes between them. It is one of my chief contentions that there is no such disconnection. It is simply the case that people in other ages have been as interested in, and even obsessed by, these various social institutions as modern people are fascinated by courts of law and the modern Olympics. The disconnect, such as it is, lies elsewhere—in *religion.* My question—"was Greek thought religious?"—is a fairly recent question, as I hope to make clear. It would not have occurred to anyone to ask it—at least not in this fashion—until the eighteenth century. I am trying to provide a genealogy of that question, some sense of where it came from, and why.

A final introductory point is worth raising, if not quite establishing, here at the outset. Some readers may want to accuse me of cheating in the title I have selected for this project: "Was Greek *Thought* Religious?" It will be noticed that, apart from the first two chapters, I do not deal very much with Greek "thought"—by which we normally mean "philosophy." I speak a great deal about Greek altars, and Greek temples, and Greek sanctuaries. I speak a great deal about some important dramatic rituals such as tragic and comic drama, and the ancient Olympics. I also speak a great deal about "Greek art."

There are two ways of addressing this important question, and they are related. First, this book intends to trace out a wide arc of strategies for dealing with and making sense of these ancient Greek materials. I have quite deliberately moved from the philosophers I discuss in the first and second chapters to the priests and poets, the artisans and athletes, with whom I deal in the rest of the book. One very common, and highly influential, way of talking about "the Greeks" has been to deal almost exclusively with their philosophers, as if that were all there were to the vast Greek cultural achievement. That is what makes the U.S. Supreme Court's treatment so recognizable to many of us. But another way, an eminently *Romantic* way, of dealing with the Greeks has been to focus on their artists and their art. It was religious art, by and large, and thus to reclaim it means in some measure, however half-consciously, to reclaim Greek religion as well. This is what the modern Olympic revival attempted to do, and I suspect that this is what makes the Olympics seem a bit strange to a modern audience. Yet this way of thinking about the Greeks is also closer to us and our modern sensibilities than we realize. This book attempts to provide some historical explanation of why that is so.

Answering the question I pose here at the outset requires attending to an ironic second implication of the title: "was 'Greek' thought *to be* religious?" The answer to that vexing question is "yes and no," "to varying degrees," and "it depends on when we're talking about." But it was only in the modern period that this question was ask-able in something like our present terms. Greek thought may well have been secularized, and sanitized, by Enlightenment scholars who needed Greece to serve as a beacon signaling their own kind of secular and democratic homecoming. So much so that, even when we deal with Greece's most prominent religious institutions—like her temples—we tend to view them as if they were not. That is the paradox I am interested in examining, the ways in which we have been blinded to the Greeks' vast difference from us, the ways in which we have been blinded to the Greeks' enduring religiosity.

Religious, or not religious? That really is the question. But it is an eminently *modern* question, one that would have made little sense to anyone prior to the nineteenth century. In the case of the Greeks, the courts have cast a deliberate No, yet our athleticism says Yes just as emphatically. The truth doubtless lies somewhere in the middle, somewhere along that vast spectrum of beliefs and practices that has constituted the subtle lineaments of the religion of Hellenism, from its first, halting Roman appropriations until the overwhelmingly influential Romantic appropriations that are, in some important ways, still our own. This book, then, really is an essay, an essay in Hellenic appropriations that span two millennia, or more. It takes us from Rome to Romanticism, and attempts to situate these complex cultural questions in the contemporary fabric of modern times. It was the Romantics, after all, who taught us to speak of "the ancients and the moderns," in a single breath, almost as if they belonged to the same intellectual universe. Naturally, they do. *And* they do not. Comparing them better, perhaps we can keep them both from slipping.

LAR
Rome-Athens-Istanbul-Atlanta
October 2001

CHAPTER ONE

Was Greek Thought Religious?
THE VIEW FROM THE COURTS

PRELIMINARIES

The U.S. Supreme Court has been much in the news in recent years. "Court watchers" are a permanent fixture at most major news organizations, and Court decisions have become the stuff of dinner-table conversation. The High Court has been asked to serve the very complex, and highly public, function of mediating some of the most divisive moral debates in the land. Functionally speaking, then, the Court increasingly serves as an "Ethics Center" for the nation as a whole, and yet it is institutionally ill-constructed to serve in this capacity. This Court, which has traditionally relied on its air of august removal from the everyday concerns of electoral politics (its justices enjoy lifelong, nonelective tenure), has been ever more thoroughly embroiled in the fractious and increasingly partisan politics of the post-Reagan era.[1] These developments have played out in the Court in various ways: the highly politicized nature of several recent Supreme Court nomination proceedings, from Robert Bork's rejection, to Clarence Thomas's agonized confirmation; the complex matrix of nearly continuous legal challenges to decisive older rulings, most notably to *Roe v. Wade,* which we shall examine in some detail here in this chapter; public demonstrations and protests outside of the Court building itself, which have become a commonplace drama accompanying its agreement to hear, and then to adjudicate, more recent abortion and death penalty cases; and, more recently still, the Court's dramatic intervention in modern electoral procedures. It may be precisely the illusion of political innocence, of *removal* from the everyday concerns of the political, which was lost in November and December of 2000.

Of more enduring relevance to constitutional history, however, will be the Rehnquist Court's fairly systematic attempt to dismantle the Warren Court's legacy of judicial activism, especially where it concerns states' rights, affirmative action, the death penalty, and abortion. These issues are fraught with paradox. Complaining about the overzealous "activism" of the Warren Court—"judicial legislating," or "lawmaking from the Bench," are the most common complaints—the Rehnquist Court has turned ironically activist in its turn. Most of the legal action hinges on the history of the interpretation of the Fourteenth Amendment, its wider application to race-related questions in the mid-twentieth century, and the latitude one is prepared to grant to *federal* courts in the evaluation and overturning of *state* court decisions and *state* legislatures. This is all still framed as a debate that pits states' rights against the assertion of a core of common cultural values. It is thus a piece of the larger paradox of federalism itself, and ethno-racial categories continue to be one of its moral touchstones.

In this increasingly polemical judicial environment, Associate Justice Antonin Scalia (who was appointed to the Court in 1986) has been the most vocal, and surely the most polemical thinker on the Bench. He has charted out a remarkably influential trajectory of jurisprudence, one that calls for a stricter textualism,[2] coupled with a suspicion of interpretive appeals to legislative intention or reconstructions of subsequent cultural and judicial history. It is precisely here—the claim that what Scalia amazingly refers to as the "science" of *textual* exegesis of the U.S. Constitution trumps all other historical and cultural claims—that the battle has been joined most violently. And, to all appearances, it will continue to be so joined in the foreseeable future. This is a war with a history lying behind it, as most wars have, and so we must turn ironically to history, if we are to comprehend the nuances of this only apparently textualist debate.

THE COURT AS IMAGE

But before doing so, before analyzing the Supreme Court any further as a cultural phenomenon, and before turning to its history, I want to look at the U.S. Supreme Court *as a building*. That is to say, I want to look at the Court as an important piece of the material culture of the nation's capital—as it came to be only in the twentieth century.

It is a significant but little-known fact that our Supreme Court justices did not have "a room of their own" until the twentieth century. The High Court met for the first time in the New York Merchants Exchange, in 1790, then moved to Philadelphia, where it was quartered first in the State House in early 1791, and then in the Old City Hall from August 1791 to February 1800.[3] In 1800, the federal government was moved to the District of Columbia, but these buildings, such as they were, were badly damaged by the British in 1812. Between 1819 and 1860, the Supreme Court met in the southeast *basement* of the Capital Building. Then, between 1860 and 1935, the Court was installed in the *Old* Senate Chamber, after that presumably more senior *legislative* body had moved into its newer facilities.[4]

When the U.S. Supreme Court was finally awarded a building of its own (1929–1935), that building took the shape of a Greek temple. And not just any Greek temple; this Court consciously emulates that most preeminent of all Classical Greek temples: the Athenian Parthenon. In fact, the chief architect of the U.S. Supreme Court building, Cass Gilbert (1867–1934), was so impressed by the neoclassicism of the so-called White City at the 1893 Chicago World's Fair, that he consciously modeled *his* Court complex on *their* version of the Parthenon.[5]

As even the casual student of Classical art may recall, a Greek temple was elaborately adorned with religious art. *Pedimental* sculptural groups inhabited the triangular spaces above the east- and west-facing porticoes. Raised reliefs called *metopes* adorned the space between each column. And a continuous running *frieze* graced the interior. The same is true here, roughly speaking, on this *temple* dedicated to our nominally secular democracy (See Figure 1.1). The U.S. Supreme Court building has an elaborate sculptural group on the West pediment which was carved by Robert I. Aiken (1878–1949). Instead of metopes, the building displays a dramatic democratic slogan: "Equal Justice Under Law." And it boasts an impressive array of seated figures, monumental bronze doorways, and elaborate Corinthian columns at the entrance.

Perhaps more dazzling, and especially intriguing for my purposes, is the Court's interior, decorated with two running friezes carved by Adolph A. Weinman (1870–1952) (See Figure 1.2), relief sculptures that depict Moses (See Figure 1.3), Confucius (See Figure 1.4), Muhammad (See Figure 1.5), and Solon the Athenian (See Figure 1.6), among others. This ought already to seem a peculiar list. Clearly religious figures, such as the first three I have mentioned, would seem to have no place in a temple dedicated to preserving what Thomas Jefferson referred to in 1802 as a "wall of separation" between religion and politics. The apparent justification for their inclusion here was that each of these figures is a *lawgiver,* and that *law* provides us with a nonreligious (perhaps even antireligious, at times) root metaphor for the ordering of our civic lives. Yet this ought to seem a still more peculiar justification. After all, the Ten Commandments may not be displayed on the walls of a public school classroom, and their display in any U.S. courtroom is problematic, at best.[6] How is it, then, that the image of the commandment-*giver* may be so displayed here, on the walls of the highest court in the land?[7] Moses, be sure to note, is depicted holding the Ten Commandments in his hands.

Moses, Confucius and Muhammad . . . present within this mighty religious pantheon is *Solon,* a somewhat more obscure Athenian lawgiver of the sixth century BCE, a man who was also considered to be one of the Seven Sages of the ancient world.[8] What, I began to wonder, was he doing here, in this admittedly Greek-seeming temple? Ironically enough, a recent rereading of the famous 1973 decision, *Roe v. Wade,* helped me begin to formulate an answer to that perplexing question. But in order to explain why, a short digression is in order. For there is a second question hidden inside of this one, I think, a question that bears substantially on the entire project I have laid out for myself in this book.

AN ASIDE ON NARRATIVE AND MORAL ARGUMENT

What in the world can the ancient Greeks have to do with contemporary constitutional law? A great deal indeed, as we shall see. The "strict textualists" like Justice

Figure 1.1. Photograph of West Pediment of the Supreme Court, sculpted by Robert I. Aitken. Photographed by Franz Jantzen. Collection of the Supreme Court of the United States.

Figure 1.2. Photograph of the North Courtroom Frieze by Adolph Weinman, titled Great Lawgivers of History: Lawgivers of Modern Times. Photographed by Franz Jantzen. Collection of the Supreme Court of the United States.

Figure 1.3. Photograph of the sculpture of Moses on the South Frieze of the Courtroom. Photographed by Franz Jantzen. Collection of the Supreme Court of the United States.

Figure 1.4. Photograph of the sculpture of Confucius on the South Frieze of the Courtroom. Photographed by Franz Jantzen. Collection of the Supreme Court of the United States.

Figure 1.5. Photograph of the sculpture of Mohammad on the North Frieze of the Courtroom. Photographed by Franz Jantzen. Collection of the Supreme Court of the United States.

Figure 1.6. Photograph of the sculpture of Solon on the South Frieze of the Courtroom. Photographed by Franz Jantzen. Collection of the Supreme Court of the United States.

Scalia are suspicious of making history—rather than the law, pure and simple—a resource for rendering legal decisions. But when they speak of "history," what they
have in mind are two jurisprudential strategies that compete directly with their own:
the attempt to reconstruct a *cultural* history on the one hand (with an eye to reconstructing the "original intent" of the lawmakers); and the reconstruction of a *legislative* history on the other (primarily through an investigation of the congressional
record, transcripts of floor debates, committee reports, and the like). Parallel to
these forms of historical investigation, however, runs another quite independent
sort of historical enquiry, one that has had a surprising and largely neglected place in
a number of critical Supreme Court cases. This is the historical reconstruction of
Greek (and Roman) attitudes to moral questions of special contemporary concern.

I want to relate this latter kind of classicizing "history" to a more recent philosophical development, one that is also a phenomenon of, if not actually a product of,
the Reagan Era. In 1981, the Anglo-American moral philosopher Alasdair MacIntyre published a book entitled *After Virtue*. A second edition of the book was released
in 1984,[9] after it had enjoyed an uncannily positive initial reception, at least as academic books go. In the second edition, MacIntyre attempted to answer some of his
critics—Jeffrey Stout, among them[10]—as well as to advance his own positive philosophical project. That work has continued in two subsequent books.[11]

MacIntyre's argument is very difficult to summarize; the good news is that there
is no real need for me to do so here. For my purposes, a simple conceptual overview
will suffice. MacIntyre is trying to rehabilitate what he calls "the [Aristotelian] tradition of the virtues," insisting that it coheres better morally than any of the more
modern philosophical options (among them, he troubles to mention Existentialism,
Phenomenology, and Analytic philosophy, whereas North American Pragmatism is
glaringly absent). Working within a tried and true Romantic distinction—one that
distinguishes between "the ancients and the moderns"—MacIntyre wishes to *use* the
ancient tradition of Greek moral speculation to launch a frontal assault on what he
calls "the self-images" of our own age.[12] This is an age that he labels disparagingly as
"liberal" and "modern." These are especially charged words in MacIntyre's philosophical lexicon, occasionally almost terms of abuse. MacIntyre wishes, we soon
learn, to be *pre*modern, precisely because he is so scathingly *anti*liberal. So, he insists,
would Aristotle have been.[13]

Polemics aside, one thing MacIntyre especially likes about his version of the Aristotelian tradition is its frank admission that all moral arguments have a subtly *narrative*
character. Human beings are creatures who make meaning, among many other things.
And to make meaning, MacIntyre insists, one must communicate narratively. Stories,
it turns out, are the very stuff of the moral life. "Narrative history of a certain kind," he
concludes, "turns out to be the basic and essential genre for the characterization of
human actions."[14] MacIntyre then proceeds, in his subsequent books, *to demonstrate the
way in which an historical narrative that begins with the ancient Greeks may work best as a philosophical
argument,* and in the context of such a display, to show *why* it works so well.

I have quarreled extensively with MacIntyre about this.[15] I worry very much that
an important distinction—the one between philosophical *arguments* and historical
narratives—may be lost altogether in the course of such polemics. There are a great
many contemporary debates, it seems to me—debates over the ownership of land,
and over the right to give a name to such land, are two especially salient political examples[16]—in which narrative is pitted against narrative. This is precisely what makes

such arguments so intractable. Appealing to *non*narrative standards of something called "rationality" seems a worthy aspiration in such cases. But it is MacIntyre's contention that such nonnarrative standards simply do not exist, and he equates belief in them to "a belief in witches and unicorns."[17] The idea of "rationality" itself, he suggests, takes on substance and meaning only within the context of some prior narrative tradition.

I want to leave the quarrel to one side in this chapter, and to acknowledge, instead, the real *descriptive* power of MacIntyre's claim. What I have discovered, in my own amateur forays into constitutional law, is that several significant Supreme Court cases have been resolved through an appeal, whether implicit or explicit, to an historical narrative, very much along the lines that MacIntyre has sketched out. More specifically, I have noticed what I take to be a surprisingly consistent story told in three rather different cultural arenas: the debate over abortion, which came to a head in the 1970s; the debate about same-sex sexuality, which seized the cultural imagination in the 1980s; and the debate over physician-assisted suicide, which raised a pointedly moral question in the 1990s. The story that one meets in these various court decisions is one that has gained a remarkable currency in our own society, I think, yet it is grounded in one lurking premise that I have been trying very hard to question in my own recent thinking. The question is whether Greek thought—what we think of more commonly as "philosophy"—wasn't actually *religious* thought. Put another way, I am wondering if our own post-Kantian distinction between something called "religion" and something else called "philosophy"—so central to the project of liberal democracy that MacIntyre decries—can hold up under what the courts refer to as "strict scrutiny." I am not convinced that this distinction can survive such a critical intellectual challenge.

So, with that as a sort of prefatory context for these remarks, let me return to my original task: An elucidation of the historical narrative that has served, however subtly, to fuel the argument in some of this century's most far-reaching court decisions.[18] I will try to sketch out the *implicit historical narrative* that I see at work in three areas of especially divisive contemporary moral debate, a narrative that becomes especially visible when these debates reach the courts. They are Abortion, Same-Sex Sexuality, and Physician-Assisted Suicide. And they tell a surprisingly similar story; one related to the perplexing presence of Solon the Athenian in a line that joins Moses to Confucius to Muhammad.

ABORTION: ROE V. WADE[19]

In the early 1960s, and largely due to lingering questions regarding how much federal uniformity to impose on the cultural regionalism of the various states—more specifically, with an eye to then-prevailing racial attitudes and their incompatability with court-mandated integration—the U.S. Supreme Court undertook a massive reinvestigation of the Fourteenth Amendment, that constitutional artifact of the Civil War that addresses this question specifically. The question is: What kind of "rights" are guaranteed to every citizen in the nation, regardless of the state in which he or she just so happens to live? A new body of case law gradually emerged that suggested the Constitution recognizes "zones of privacy," zones that overlap in complex but interesting ways.

One matter of note here is the way in which legal attention shifted from race to gender and sexuality, with comparative rapidity, in the later 1960s and early 1970s. In 1965, the Court struck down a Connecticut law that had criminalized any form of birth control.[20] The Court made a great deal of the fact that the couples receiving information about such reproductive technologies were *married,* and that their *marital* decisions had to be "protected" and "private." In the early 1970s, that presumption of marital unions began to break down, legally speaking. In 1972, the Court extended these same reproductive rights to unmarried persons.[21]

At the same time, a pseudonymous woman, "Jane Roe," discovered herself to be *un*married and pregnant in late 1969/early 1970. She brought suit against the Attorney General of the State of Texas in March 1970, then filed her alias affidavit to the U.S. Supreme Court in May. Ms. Roe questioned the constitutionality of a Texas law that prohibited abortion in *any* circumstance, save where the life of the mother was clearly threatened. (That law had been on the books in rough form since 1854; by contrast, a Georgia law, which was deemed more forward-looking, was upheld by the Court in a related decision.) A Texas physician named Hallford joined Roe's suit, since he had already been arrested and tried twice under this same law. Finally, another pseudonymous married couple, the Does, joined the suit on the theory that they might inadvertently become pregnant one day and would be prohibited by the law of the state from procuring an abortion, for medical and/ or personal reasons.

The Supreme Court denied the rights of Dr. Hallford and the Does to join this lawsuit, but did grant Ms. Roe's petition. The Court struck down the Texas statute as too inflexible and as an unconstitutional intrusion into Ms. Roe's rights both to privacy and to reproductive choices. This is the part of the story most of us already know, to a degree, even if we have never read the decision in this case. This was a case about "privacy" and the "right to choose." But let us look a little more closely at the decision, to see what *else* it is about. In my judgment, this case turned more subtly on a pervasive preconception of religion in general and a *mis*perception of Greek religion in particular.

Even then-Associate Justice Rehnquist, in a spirited dissenting opinion, acknowledged his respect for what he called "the extensive historical fact" and the "wealth of legal scholarship" in Justice Blackmun's majority opinion.[22] Of course, wondering where such "historical fact" comes from is one question that bedevils most outsiders' attempts to come to terms with constitutional law, my own included. The role of the so-called expert is an extremely complicated one in legal deliberation, much as it is in academe. There is, in fact, a new body of case-law that is being built around the still more devilish problem of "junk science," that is, the pronouncements of so-called experts whose expertise, and whose credentials, need to be more carefully examined.[23] What I want to be sure to underline here at the outset is not the relative "junkiness" of the science or the scholarship, since *Roe v. Wade* was not really decided on scientific grounds, except insofar as it relied upon a general trimester framework for articulating the state's emerging interest in developing fetal life, and marked viability outside of the womb as the figurative "point of no return" in abortion law. Rather, it was an *historical narrative*—not science at all—that played a really decisive role in this landmark Court decision.

In Section VI of the majority decision, the late Justice Blackmun[24] argued that the kinds of anti-abortion laws the Court was examining in 1973 were "of relatively recent vintage." He added that they were "not of ancient or even of common-law origin."[25] Instead, the laws we are worrying over today—much like the Hegelian nar-

rative[26] we will presumably use to resolve them—are all a product of the nineteenth
century. It was Blackmun's nod to antiquity—to what we, for a variety of complex
reasons, refer to as "*classical* antiquity"—that intrigued me initially as I began thinking about the strange range of Neohellenic topics that have grown into this book.

Blackmun's historical narrative is surprisingly brief, and the few sources that appear in the notes are *not* the work of Classical scholars.

> *Ancient attitudes.* These are not capable of precise determination. We are told that at the
> time of the Persian Empire abortifacients were known and that criminal abortions were
> severely punished. We are also told, however, that abortion was practiced in Greek
> times as well as in the Roman Era, and that "it was resorted to without scruple." The
> Ephesian Soranos, often described as the greatest of the ancient gynecologists, appears
> to have been generally opposed to Rome's prevailing free-abortion practices. He found
> it necessary to think first of the life of the mother, and he resorted to abortion when,
> upon this standard, he felt the procedure advisable. Greek and Roman law afforded lit-
> tle protection to the unborn. If abortion was prosecuted in some places, it seems to
> have been based on a concept of a violation of the father's right to his offspring. An-
> cient religion did not bar abortion.[27]

What has Justice Blackmun told us here? We learn that the Persians knew of abortion, but that they criminalized the practice. We are never told why. Blackmun immediately adds that abortion was widely practiced in Greek, and in Roman, society
without significant evidence of "religious" concern. Where abortion was proscribed,
this seems to have had more to do with notions of (male) property rights than with
concern for the sanctity of life, especially given a context in which infanticide was
also allegedly a common practice.

Now there is, of course, the problem of the Hippocratic Oath, a problem that
Blackmun cannot afford to ignore. This is a medical oath [an *horkos,* apparently
sworn by ancient physicians to Apollo and Asklepius, among other deities][28] that
specifically prohibits the administration of abortive remedies (or poisons, as we shall
see below) by any "Hippocratic" physician.[29] Here, then, is the relevant section of
the Oath, quoted by Blackmun in this same section.

> I will use treatment to help the sick according to my ability and judgment, but never
> with a view to injury or wrongdoing. Neither will I administer a poison [*pharmakon*] to
> anyone if asked to do so, nor will I suggest such a prescription. Similarly, I will not give
> any woman a potion to cause abortion [*pesson phthorion*]. I will maintain the purity [*hag-
> nôs*] of my life [*bios*] and art [*technê*].[30]

The question is: How are we to read this important piece of apparent counterevi-
dence? Here, after all, is a spokesperson for the "Greek" tradition who seems clearly
to be expressing a moral concern about abortion, pretty much across the board. Justice Blackmun offers an intriguing suggestion. He tells us that the Oath was extremely controversial even in Hippocrates's day, and that it relied on primarily
Pythagorean doctrines.[31]

Now, Pythagoras, be sure to note, is the one "philosopher" who, as nearly everyone acknowledges, *was* "religious."[32] His vegetarianism, his adamant opposition to
suicide, his esoteric interest in numerology, his beliefs about the reincarnation of the
human soul—all of these things smell of what Blackmun calls "dogma" (never mind

that Plato shared all but the first of these convictions, and probably owed them to his contact with Pythagoreans in Sicily). The dominant medical viewpoint was *not* Hippocratic in antiquity, Blackmun claims; rather, Hippocrates represents a significantly marginal opinion grounded in more recognizably "religious" scruples.

Having made a first pass at "religion" in this way, Blackmun now turns his sights on the next chapter in this brief historical narrative. It is an emphatically "religious" chapter. For it involves Christianity.

But with the end of antiquity[33] a decided change took place. Resistance against suicide and against abortion became common. The Oath became popular. The emerging teachings of Christianity were in agreement with the Pythagorean ethic.[34]

In Blackmun's telling of this story, the Pythagoreans have come back with a vengeance, clothed now in the robes of Christian conviction,[35] as well as of the Roman imperium, and this results in the first coherent and thoroughgoing ancient prohibitions of abortion. So ends the Court's historical narrative, at least the one with an ancient face.[36]

What have we been told? We have been told, curiously enough, that the Persians criminalized abortion, although we are not told why. The Greeks, and then the Romans, were comparatively untroubled by the practice. Then Christianity came on the scene, rendering it problematic in an entirely new way,[37] by popularizing the otherwise marginal Hippocratic Oath as one important strategy in its larger cultural war against mainstream imperial practices like abortion and suicide. It has also been suggested, between the lines as it were, that the Persians were probably "religious," the early Christians definitely were, but the Greeks and Romans were not. That is an interesting, but rather confusing, claim. It relies on a subtly normative account of what "counts" as a religion in the first place, an account that has never been fully articulated by this Court. I will trace out the contours of Greek thought more directly in subsequent chapters. But for now we may note that Greek thought, barring the Pythagorean of course, clearly does not so count. That is one reason why the Supreme Court building also can be a Parthenon. We have been trained not to see this temple as a temple. We have been taught to view the Greeks as a blithely secular people, to see their culture as preeminently this-wordly, and even to see their pieces of religion as pieces of art. There has been abundant subsequent courtroom evidence testifying to this same strange constellation of beliefs.

SAME-SEX SEXUALITY: ROMER V. EVANS [38]

In November 1992, Coloradans voted on a referendum that amended the State Constitution by prohibiting gays, lesbians, and bisexuals from appealing to the relevant housing and other authorities for relief from discrimination on the basis of their sexual orientation. The legislation was prompted by several large cities (Aspen, Boulder and Denver) that had implemented such institutional redress. Amendment 2, which passed with 53 percent of the popular vote, made it illegal for any state organization

> to adopt or enforce any statute, regulation, ordinance or policy whereby homosexual, lesbian or bisexual orientation, conduct, practices or relationships shall constitute or otherwise be the basis of, or entitle any person or class of persons to have, any claim of minority status, quota preference, protected status or claim of discrimination.

Institutionalization of the amendment was delayed, pending constitutional review. The Colorado State Supreme Court declared the amendment unconstitutional in October 1993, and the U.S. Supreme Court affirmed that decision in May 1996.

Now, this case is somewhat more complex, because what I have been referring to as the historical narrative that makes the essential argument in this case lies behind the curtain, as it were, in much the same way that the Wizard operated Oz. The historical narrative was not a part of the U.S. Supreme Court decision. But it lay ironically at the heart of the Colorado *State* Supreme Court's reasoning, which was reaffirmed by the High Court two years later. The Colorado State Supreme Court heard three days of testimony, in fact, from a battery of classicists and moral philosophers, debating the nature, the public perception, and the extent of homosexuality and/or bisexuality in Classical Greek antiquity and throughout the ancient world.

This debate, and the political fallout from the debate, has been widely published and commented on.[39] What has not been sufficiently addressed is the more fundamental question: What does *any* of this Greek material have to do with Colorado law? Martha C. Nussbaum[40] spent nearly a full day on the stand. She published a long 150-page article about the experience in the *Virginia Law Review* in 1994 (referenced above at endnote 37). Now, most of the article is an extended, and really rather polemical, review of the substantive scholarly questions at stake in the case ("did they or didn't they in ancient Greece?"). But there are two additional questions that Nussbaum addressed in her first article that are singularly relevant to the concerns of this chapter.

The first is an academic question of competence and "expertise." Nussbaum lays out fairly elaborate guidelines for what should count toward establishing "expertise" in her own scholarly discipline (classics, in this case),[41] the sorts of things anyone who wants to appear in Court as an "expert" in the classical tradition needs to know. It is a debate about credentialing, primarily, and I suppose I find it troubling not only because of the way it obfuscates the question of bad science and corrupt expertise, but also because I remain suspicious of most such scholarly appeals to "expertise." Ironically or no, it was *Socrates* who taught me to be suspicious of that. Unsurprisingly, the relationship of his own expertise to the law was a vexed one, and ultimately cost him dearly. I will return to that issue later in this chapter and again in the next.

Second, and far more interesting, Nussbaum explicitly asks what, if anything, *ancient* Greek sexual attitudes have to do with *contemporary* Colorado law. She lays out several answers to this question, none of them really adequate to its complexity, in my judgment.[42] The first is what we might simply call "the argument from difference." Greek sexual attitudes are so vastly different from our own that this very difference itself makes a pertinent philosophical point. "[W]e will be shaken into seeing that many things we think neutral and natural are actually parochial,"[43] she cautions. This insight, she adds somewhat parenthetically, marks the enduring legacy of Nietzsche and Foucault. The second argument is an historical argument, boldly asserted but almost entirely un-nuanced. Granted the assumption that ancient Greek culture is one we in the west "admire" and consider "successful," she says, it is surely relevant to note that acceptance of same-sex sexuality in both Athens and Sparta "did not have the result so frequently mentioned in modern debate: erosion of the social fabric."[44] In the third case, Nussbaum offers what might best be thought of as the argument from irony. She insists here that accusations of "shamefulness, abomination and destructiveness to the social fabric"[45] were readily evident in Roman antiquity—as charges leveled against *Christians,* not gays, with the same lack of moral substance.[46] It is an ironic and troubling turnabout, Nussbaum suggests, for the dominant Protestant culture in this country to level such charges against its own most vulnerable countercultural minorities (denying gays the status of a "minority" was, of course, one strategy embedded in Amendment 2).[47] Fourth, Nussbaum suggests that the Greek speculative tradition may serve to sharpen our own contemporary discussions of sexuality, and its role in shaping our aspirations toward the good life, precisely because it provides a more frank vocabulary that is excised in many EuroAmerican cultures, given their overt prejudice against such same-sex predilection. What Nussbaum seems to be after here is, I suppose, the argument for a kind of liberal "tolerance"—though, as in too much of her recent work, the point is asserted rather than argued. Reading narratives such as the ones in Plato's *Symposium,* she suggests, open our minds to kinds of empathic response that embody "the very characteristics of receptivity and sympathetic imagination that homophobia seeks to cordon off and to avoid."[48]

In fact, her real argument may be glimpsed now, percolating just beneath the surface of these Hellenic suggestions, I think. Professor Nussbaum offers—in much the same way the Supreme Court did in *Roe v. Wade*—an extended *historical narrative* that tells us that "the Greeks"—from Archilochus and Sappho[49] in the early Archaic period, through Socrates and Plato and Aristotle in the Classical to post-Classical periods, and on well into the first or second century CE[50]—did not think same-sex eroticism particularly problematic. When did it become problematic, then? When Christianity emerged as a decisive religio-cultural force in the pan-Mediterranean Roman Empire.

This is roughly the same story we met in the Abortion debate in 1973.[51] "The Greeks" were untroubled by something that troubled the early Christians a great deal. And we continue to be so troubled, today. "The ancients and the moderns"—as we have seen before, and will see again—frame a decisive cultural transformation of the eastern Mediterranean world in the first centuries of the Common Era, whether one asserts the emergence of Christianity as the cause of this or not.

PHYSICIAN-ASSISTED SUICIDE: WASHINGTON V. GLUCKSBERG[52] AND VACCO V. QUILL[53]

The question of Physician-Assisted Suicide became a significantly *public* issue in March 1991, when a New York physician named Timothy E. Quill published an essay[54] in *The New England Journal of Medicine* that described, among other things, his knowing prescription of painkillers to a middle-aged woman in the final stages of leukemia, a woman who later intentionally overdosed on this medication, thereby committing suicide with Quill's implicit cooperation and consent. He also confessed to lying in the report he filed subsequent to her death, listing the cause of death as "acute leukemia," an assessment that "though . . . the truth, . . . was not the whole story." Quill fudged his report in this way, he tells us, to avoid a possible inquest, the mandatory attempt to resuscitate "Diane," and, in all likelihood, nonpayment of insurance claims to her survivors. The letter touched off a firestorm of debate in *The New England Journal of Medicine* for the next six years, and contributed ammunition to the polemics in a debate that soon moved into the federal courts. The highly public work of Dr. Jack Kevorkian contributed, albeit less helpfully, to public debate in these same years, as did the increasing visibility of groups such as the Hemlock Society in Los Angeles.[55] Finally, legislation passed in New York and in Washington that explicitly prohibited a physician's (or anyone's) assistance in suicide for whatever reason, brought this matter before the federal courts.

Three separate suits were brought to the U.S. Supreme Court: a New York case, that named Quill himself;[56] a similar Washington case that will be of particular interest to me here;[57] and an Oregon case[58] that grew in response to the "Death With Dignity Act" (Measure 16) that had been passed, like the Colorado law, as an electoral referendum in 1994. For my present purposes, the Washington case is of particular interest, for several reasons. It was by far the longest decision rendered by any of the three federal appellate courts. It also *affirmed* the terminal patient's right to seek such "assistance."[59] And still more remarkable, it included an *historical narrative* as a central piece of its legal reasoning.

Judge Reinhardt, writing for the majority, introduced a long section entitled "Historical Attitudes Toward Suicide" as Section C of the original decision.[60] Omitting all mention of the pesky Persians, but invoking the very Abortion decision that had done so, Reinhardt states: "Like the Court in *Roe*, we begin with ancient attitudes." These "ancient" attitudes are strictly Greek and Roman, and they are effectively treated as if they were the same thing.[61]

This historical narrative, while admitting that matters are "far more checkered than the majority would have us believe," chooses to begin, curiously enough, with Oedipus's mother, Jocasta, "the first of all literary suicides."[62] Reinhardt emphasizes that she is portrayed favorably for responding to her crisis in this way. Of course, the account of King Saul's suicide (I Samuel 31:4–6), which is mentioned later in a footnote,[63] pretty clearly predates Sophocles's play by several centuries at least. And certainly the Homeric poems, which are cited next, are in fact significantly older than Sophocles as well. Why, then, should Jocasta serve as the starting point for this analysis? The Court's point in beginning this way is to suggest that Greek popular morality did not worry about suicide as such, and it uses what is arguably the best-known Classical story to make its case. In fact, the Court goes on to claim that several Greek *poleis* (Athens, Keos,[64] Marseilles) *sponsored* the practice in certain circumstances, keeping a store of hemlock available for its citizens (suggesting the existence of a proto-Hemlock Society, perhaps).

Socrates, Reinhardt continues, counseled against suicide (we are not told where, nor why), but he also willingly drank hemlock when ordered to do so. And this is where matters become far more complicated than the courts seem willing, or able, to allow. For Socrates, as we shall see in the next chapter, was portrayed by Plato as a *martyr,* not a suicide. This significant, if complex, distinction—relatively clear in antiquity, and fairly obvious to the student of Plato, *or* of the Bible, *or* of comparative religion[65]—is nowhere acknowledged in the Federal Court's decision. We should probably also remember in this same regard that Socrates was prosecuted on an Athenian version of a "religion and morals charge." His martyrdom to "philosophy," if you will, was "religiously" motivated—on both sides.[66]

Plato is mentioned in passing as a supporter of suicide (the court's primary source for these allegedly Hellenic claims is Emile Durkheim's first exercise in sociology[67]), whereas Aristotle is not mentioned at all, and neither is the martyrdom of Jesus.

Pythagoras, however, *is* discussed at some length. His opposition both to suicide and to abortion is called "a distinctly minority view" in much the same way, and for much the same reason, that Justice Blackmun did in *Roe v. Wade*. That decision, in fact, is cited as the source, the only source, for this remarkable point of view.[68] Such is the power of legal precedent. It renders the Hippocratic Oath, and a major Greek philosophical school, both "minor" and "marginal."

The Stoics are treated next, in somewhat greater detail—the Stoics who, Nietzsche quipped, "have but a single sacrament: suicide."[69] Justice Reinhardt suggests that the Stoics "glorified suicide as an act of pure rational will." And so, perhaps, they did—in certain circumstances. But they also "did sometimes punish suicide," as even this Court is forced to admit.[70] It is instructive in this regard that the Roman Emperor Hadrian (d. 138 CE), asked for assistance in suicide from his own personal physician, Iollas, who allegedly committed suicide himself rather than provide it.[71] Hadrian's adoptive grandson, Marcus Aurelius, the last and perhaps most eloquent spokesperson for late Roman Stoicism, also seems to have condemned suicide as an improper response to fate and this-worldly duty.[72] It was the Stoic popularizer, Seneca, who presented the clearest Stoic case *for* suicide in the previous generation, in epistolary form.[73] So, the Stoic record, like most of the record from classical antiquity, is indeed "checkered."

The Court now makes a curious assertion that seems to cut against its own case, and that seems significantly to alter the flow of the historical narrative we have met in previous cases. The early Christians, Reinhardt suggests, actually sought death out as a means of escape from this worldly vale of tears. The Early Church was full of suicides of various stripes, he insists.[74] Now, the Court's authority for this rather jarring claim is Edward Gibbon's *Decline and Fall of the Roman Empire*.[75] That book presents a wonderful historical narrative, of course, but it engages in a dubious kind of history, one that may tell us ultimately more about its own age than about antiquity. And here again, the court's failure to make the vital distinction between martyrdom and suicide—a distinction that was crucial to the various religious communities of the Hellenistic Jewish period—is determinative. It is admittedly a "checkered" and difficult distinction, yet for this very reason it is an exceedingly important one to admit into the fabric of our reflections.

The Court, in any case, suggests that it was largely Augustine's response to the overweening suicidal tendencies of heretical groups like the Donatists, and their really astonishing "will to death," that reified Christian *opposition* to suicide across the board. That is to say, the Christian mainstream gradually became opposed to suicide, in large measure as a response to an internal conflict with its own most tempting heresies. And so Christian attitudes have remained ever since, consistently so since the Council of Braga (a rather minor Council that took place in northern Portugal in 562 CE), at which the western churches "denied funeral rites to anyone who killed himself." And that consensus view, the court asserts, was not seriously challenged until the early modern period, presumably by philosophers who were trying to detach "philosophy" from "religion" (the decision specifically mentions Montesqieu, Voltaire, Diderot, Bacon, Hume, Donne, and Thomas More).[76]

Here, then, with some curious twists and turns, and some interesting philosophical complexities, is a still familiar and by now quite recognizable story: The Greeks and Romans were largely untroubled by suicide as a philosophical (read: *not* a religious) issue. Suicidal energies were, if anything, exacerbated by the early Christian movement, but pretty quickly condemned by the majoritarian (and pragmatic) Latin-speaking churches. That cultural condemnation stands—if not intact, then at least still dominant—to this day. To impose it, then, is to impose a religious, rather than a secular, value. Secular values, so it seems, are the *Greek* ones.

LEGAL REASONING AND THIS PROJECT: SOME RELIGIO-HELLENIC TRAJECTORIES

What is the moral of this thrice-told tale, and what is its relation to my titular question: "Was Greek thought religious?" How does a close reading of several highly public and contentious court cases impact upon the debatable religiosity of the ancient Greeks? Clearly, legal debates about Abortion, Same-Sex Sexuality, or Assisted Suicide are always "in danger" of being framed as *religious* issues. And this the courts— committed as they are to the Jeffersonian metaphor of a "wall" separating a place called the state from another place called the church—allegedly cannot do.

But what are the courts to do instead? It seems that several state and federal and supreme courts have hoped that they may provide an *historical narrative* that tells us how allegedly *non*-religious "philosophers" framed the moral issues in question, and then how the emergence of a scriptural religion of revelation decisively *changed* those widespread and long-standing cultural attitudes. On this view, the imposition of anti-abortion legislation, of antigay referenda, and of legislation prohibiting medical assistance in suicide thus count *functionally* as the "establishment" of a "religious" attitude and may be countered in the courts on that basis—countered, that is to say, with *Greek* thought. That is what I take to be the collective moral of this oft-told historical tale: from the Greeks and the Romans, through Christianity, then on to ourselves and our modernity. Curiously enough, in this tale's telling, the Early Church continues to be the fulcrum around which subsequent cultural and moral history revolves. We simply assert a profound cultural *dis*continuity between the late antique Roman world and the practical worldview of the earliest Christian churches.

The problem is: We must acknowledge the complex continuity-*and*-discontinuity which characterizes these tumultuous transitional centuries throughout the Mediterranean basin. I will devote *two* chapters, the third and the fourth, to this topic for this reason. "The Greeks" and "the Christians" (neither of these terms is really singular, of course) may not be so easily or so casually opposed.[77] Christianity, in fact, begins with the assumption that "Greeks" are indeed a part of this new world order and its worldview. The New Testament letters mark that belief as a central cultural and religious preoccupation.

So there are several problems with this legal-historical reconstruction, of which the most pressing is the following: a great deal of Greek thought seems pretty clearly "religious"—not Christian, to be sure, but religious nonetheless. The Court in *Roe v. Wade* suggested that Pythagoras was "religious" in a way that Plato was not. We were not told why. The way in which Greek philosophy has been desacralized may tell us a great deal about modern, post-Kantian attitudes toward philosophy and its proper relation to Christian theology, but they tell us precious little about the Greeks or the Romans themselves.[78] Whether the courts can long sustain these problematic assertions about antiquity, and its alleged innocence of religious attitudes, is another question. Doing so will require far more substantive reflection on the normative assumptions about "religion" that lie behind the curious language of the First Amendment,[79] as well as behind a great deal of more contemporary legal reasoning.

There are several points I would like to raise in passing at this point. Some of them are matters of general interest to those, like myself, who work in the area of comparative religion. Others may be of interest to any thoughtful inhabitant of North American society at the beginning of a new millennium. All are aimed, in various ways, at my larger question, concerning the image of Solon the Athenian on the wall of a temple of Athena that is also the United States of America's Supreme Court. And they are aimed ultimately at the complex religiosity of the ancient Greeks.

1. There are canons and there are scriptures, and they are not quite the same thing. I suspect that maintaining that distinction is the real, if hidden, interest of a great many judges and lawyers, not to mention other thoughtful citizens of this democracy. The Bible has nothing to say directly about abortion, nothing at all. Only a handful of texts speak about same-sex eroticism, and none of them demonstrate any familiarity with the concept of a "sexual identity," which is of course the source of all our contemporary concern. Suicide *is* addressed in several biblical texts, but mostly in narrative, rather than in legal, form, and in any case there seems always to be a subtle distinction between suicide and martyrdom at work in these same texts.

So we could not build a constitutional perspective on these issues out of the Bible even if we wanted to. As presumably we do not want to do. But why, then, has so much time and energy been devoted to developing the implicit moral point-of-view of ancient *Greek* popular morality, out of ancient *Greek* literary traditions, a really rather fluid body of poems and speeches, laws and inscriptions? Marking the vaguely "canonical" status of Hellenism in the modern world and in its secular courts is something I feel strongly compelled to do. This is, in any case, neither the first nor the last time that Greek literature has been utilized as a sort of "nonsectarian canon." This is precisely how many Romantics chose to use it, and we are heir to many of their Hellenic assumptions, as I will try to demonstrate in the last three chapters of this book.

2. This project implicitly raises another question, without even attempting to answer it—namely, why do members of North American society seem increasingly inclined to turn to courts of law for assistance in sorting out their most complex and divisive moral debates? The Court, as I suggested at the outset, now serves as an Ethics Center to the nation. Perhaps the self-understanding of this nation really has changed in the way some sociologists suggest: from the overarching metaphor of a "biblical republicanism," to that of a "democracy of laws."[80] It is surely telling that the third branch of the federal government, the U.S. Supreme Court, did not have a building of its own until 1935. And it is surely significant that, when the Court finally was awarded "a room of its own," that building took the form of a Greek temple, modeled on the Parthenon, and sporting such figures as Moses, Confucius, Muhammad, and Solon the Athenian, in its pediments and friezes. None of these persons are thought to be "religious" figures in this setting, of course. They are *lawgivers,* and—Judaism or Islam notwithstanding—that can't be religious activity, can it? Nor can this temple *really* be a temple. Therein lies the irony of these images, as well as the source of a more serious intellectual quandary. Is Greek religious architecture or Greek religious art still "religious" in any way when it is located on the Washington mall, or else housed in an urban museum? I will have much more to say about Greek art in subsequent chapters. But is Greek *thought* still "religious," in any significant way, when it is being used by "secular" courts?

3. It is surely significant that the historical narrative I have traced through these various decisions has gone increasingly underground, as it were. This story was a central, if not quite crucial, piece of the majority decision in *Roe v. Wade*, written in the early 1970s. By the mid-to-late 1980s, that narrative began to move behind the curtain. In 1992, debates about Greek sexuality mattered enormously to the Colorado State Supreme Court, but did not figure in its published decision, nor in the U.S. Supreme Court's affirmation of that decision. The same held true in 1997. Debates about Greek and Roman cultural attitudes toward death and dignity figured prominently in the Ninth Circuit Court of Appeals, but not in the U.S. Supreme Court's decision, which contented itself with an analysis of North American cultural attitudes over the past three centuries, by and large.[81] I suspect that this may well reflect a troubled intellectual and legal conscience, the dawning realization that Greek or Roman cultural norms are *not* directly relevant to the increasingly pluralist and multicultural context of the Americas. We are having debates about the curricular "canon" that echo some of these same concerns.[82] To paraphrase Martha Nussbaum's probing question, Greek norms *may not be* relevant to Colorado law. Not at all.

Most of the *visible* argument in the courts today hinges on interpretation of the Fourteenth Amendment, as I suggested at the outset, with its guarantees of "equal protection" and "due process" to all citizens. The Court has made clear that any moral "discrimination" this society wishes to make will be subject to some form of "scrutiny," and that the state may fairly be asked to demonstrate "a compelling interest" (or, at a minimum, a "legitimate interest") in making such a discrimination in the first place. The state demonstrated no such compelling interest in making a discrimination on the basis of its citizens' sexual orientation; so the Court ruled in 1996.[83] Nor were the courts convinced that the state had made such a case in defense of discrimination between the terminally ill citizen and the rest of the body politic in 1997. The state, after all, tries to *protect* its citizens from death, even a self-inflicted death. That protection must extend to all citizens, regardless of their health status, the Court reasoned. Here once again, the picture of a society that shares an historical narrative regarding its own cultural identity is giving way to the picture of a society that has the law, and perhaps only the law, genuinely in common. Alasdair MacIntyre makes this observation—that we have little more than our *procedural* commitments in common—the mainstay of his indictment of liberal society, yet it remains unclear to me how this is anything more than a descriptive statement of a profound pluralistic fact[84] . . . and therefore, the very heart of the vast cultural challenge of self-definition presently before us.

4. I recognize that my argument may be taken to support a "conservative" political agenda, since I am arguing *against* the historical-narrative-as-rationale in several recent court decisions. I take no joy in underlining what I take to be significant problems in the majority opinion in *Roe v. Wade*, since that decision has been under seige for so long from so many different quarters. This seems grossly unfair to the spirit of that decision, which was entirely tentative and provisional in Justice Blackmun's own mind. I mean only to quarrel with the way in which the courts arrived at their decision—through the use of a distorting, if enduring, historical reconstruction of Greek thought. But such specious choices as "liberal" and "conservative" are of increasingly limited value in these cases, especially the suicide cases. (What, after all, would a liberal or a conservative view of suicide actually look like? embedded in what prior values?)

That said, I should also confess that I find arguments made recently by several fundamentalist groups in the courts—and they, too, have moved decisively into the courts and into the political process[85]—both thought-provoking and profoundly challenging. As nearly as I have been able to understand it, their most recent arguments run as follows. The First Amendment claims to want to keep "religion" tightly bounded, and to keep it out of public, "political" space. Yet the normative definition of "religion"—or rather, the root metaphors used to capture it—describe a "religion" that looks suspiciously like Protestant Christianity, privileging as it does "scripture and sermon"—a body of sacred writings, and a code of moral behavior—over other significant matters of religious practice. The Ten Commandments may not appear on the wall in English, but Moses is free to carry a sacred tablet written in Hebrew, and Muhammad to carry a Qur'anic inscription written in Arabic, presumably because the viewer will not recognize these, never mind recognize their clear and abiding religiosity. What "counts" as a religion is a question of the first importance in these constitutional quandaries. In fact, gaining recognition *as* a religion is one crucial step in the task of gaining legal protection for such a religion's free exercise.[86]

Religions that are the most recognizable inherit a very different problem. Given Liberalism's commitment to the metaphors of limits and boundaries, we are working to build a wall between "politics" and what we understand "religion" to be. Protestant Christianity is out. Judaism is out. But the Greeks—some of them, at any rate—are still decidedly in. Thus, these religious groups argue, Protestant Christianity has been *more* politically marginalized than several other religions, ironically enough, because it is so clearly recognized *as* a religion. Yet the state can offer no compelling state interest in a practical discrimination between "Hebraism and Hellenism,"[87] between Protestants or Jews, let us say, and most other religious groups. I must confess to finding a great deal of insight in this argument. And I am not alone in so doing. Constitutional lawyers have done so as well, in far more elegant terms, and at far greater length than I.[88]

5. My frustration emerges here, embodied in my own inability to answer such a range of questions, and such a challenge to the constitutional status of Greece and the Greeks. For the logical challenge to everything I've said thus far is pretty much the challenge with which the field of comparative religion is currently beleaguered: "All right, if that is an inadequate way to talk about religion in the courts, then what do you want us to do, instead?" My hunch is that there is no possibility of real neutrality in religious matters, that some forms of religion will be privileged over others, granted recognition more or less easily, protected in practice with greater or lesser vigor. This might suggest that such conflicts actually are best viewed as "wars of religion," with real winners and real losers. But in a contemporary context, I am less concerned over the losses perceived so eloquently by any number of Protestant groups, than I am the losses suffered by the Greeks—losses that have been perceived by virtually no one at all since Tomaso Laureti painted his ceiling fresco at the Vatican.

This book intends to offer a series of meditations on the complexity of the perception of "Greek religion." It offers itself as a history, a history of the ways in which people have talked about "the Greeks" and about "religion." It is offered with an eye to admitting that things are far more fluid and far more complex than the outmoded metaphor of a "wall of separation" allows them to be. The 1990s witnessed the razing of several especially cantankerous political walls, yet others have been raised in their place with astonishing speed. Thinking outside of these walls, thinking outside of the *metaphor* of walls and boundaries, already becomes an act of resistance in such a setting, and an important moral challenge.

This was a point made recently by Jacques Derrida, a French philosopher whose strategies for the "deconstruction" of literary texts—and other texts, such as laws and constitutions, which he believes behave more like literary texts than most are willing to admit—present a considerable challenge to stricter textualists of the Scalia school. In a now famous address to the Cardozo Law School, fittingly entitled "Force of Law,"[89] Derrida likens his task to Socrates's own. He submits to the authority of the law, and to its force, but he refuses to use its language for his own thinking. In fact, Derrida plays craftily on the necessity of leaving his own language, to speak an alien tongue [English] in an alien land [North America] throughout this presentation. Accepting the law's authority is a very different matter from accepting its categories. In fact, resisting its categories has been philosophy's business, at least since the time of Socrates. So there may be a tension actually *built in* to philosophy's relationship to the law . . . as I suspect there is a tension built in to the Greeks' relationship to North American law, as I have tried to demonstrate in this chapter. This insight may help to set the stage for my examination of Socratic piety, and its own problematic relationship to the legal community, in the next chapter.

Living within the rule of law, shall we jettison the Greeks, as well as the Christians and the Jews, from our legal and moral reasoning? That seems to be the direction in which contemporary courts are headed. Is there perhaps another way to proceed, I wonder, a way especially well suited to the work of comparative religion? We students of comparative religion inhabit a distinction that is so obvious to us that we often fail to realize how astonishing it may be to the wider public—at least according to my remarkably consistent experience at cocktail parties, whenever the tiring topic of "what I do for a living" comes up. Those of us who work in departments of comparative religion know that we do not "teach religion." We teach *about* religions. We are not priests, or preachers. We are teachers. And if we model ourselves on anyone, it is Socrates.

Perhaps, then, we may be of assistance in finding more intelligent (which is to say, more historically subtle, and not strictly narrative) ways of talking *about* the Greeks, as well as about Christians and Jews, as religious persons—and also as significant and enduring resources for our continued thinking about human aspiration and moral value. Perhaps there are creative ways to begin blurring that too-sharp line between church and state, between Greeks and Jews, as well as between teachers and students, which is to say, between philosophers and the rest of us.

In this book, two chapters about modern appropriations of the ancient Greeks frame the dilemma posed by my original question. The courts insist that the Greeks were *not* religious, and that the tradition of Greek speculative enquiry does not "count" as religion (save in its Pythagorean incarnation). By contrast, Pierre de Coubertin and the other founders of the modern Olympic revival were attracted to ancient Greek traditions precisely *because* they were religious traditions, as we shall see in the ninth chapter. These *renovateurs* claimed to be creating a new religion—the *religio athletae*—as an important spiritual resource for distinctively modern times. Their Neohellenic endeavors have borne rich fruit.

Religious or not religious? This will prove to be a more complex question than it appears to be at first glance. The answer doubtless lies somewhere in between these posited extremes; it is a pendular notion, and it is a perennial problem. "The Greeks" were "religious," some of them at any rate, in different ways, in different places, in different historical epochs. What I will try to do in the middle chapters of this book is to excavate a number of historical layers within the site of historical Hellenism. I will also be looking for "religion" there, in places we do not normally expect to find it, and in so doing, I hope to illuminate what I take to be the fascinating complex of ancient religion, and the various ways in which its story has been told in the past 150 years. This ancient, and profoundly Socratic, complexity has, surprisingly—or perhaps not so surprising—now become our own.

CHAPTER TWO

The Son Supplants the Father

SEDUCTION, SOCRATIC PIETY, AND THE LIFE OF VIRTUE

If we are to give credence to his spouse-sister, Hera, Zeus "was interested in only one thing, going to bed with women, mortal and immortal alike." But at least one woman rejected him, and, what was worse, an immortal: Thetis. . . . [H]er union with Zeus would have led to the birth of a son destined to displace his father: "a son stronger than his father," say both Pindar and Aeschylus, using exactly the same words. . . .

Thus Zeus's womanizing takes on a new light. Each affair might conceal the supreme danger. Every time he approached a woman, Zeus knew he might be about to provoke his own downfall. Thus far the stories take us: but for every myth told, there is another, unnamable, that is not told, another which beckons from the shadows, surfacing only through allusions, fragments, coincidences, with nobody ever daring to tell all in a single story. And here the "son stronger than the father" is not to be born yet, because he is already present: he is Apollo. Over the never-ending Olympian banquet, a father and son are watching each other, while between them, invisible to all but themselves, sparkles the serrated sickle Kronos used to slice off the testicles of his father. . . .

—Roberto Calasso, *The Marriage of Cadmus and Harmony*, 91–93

PRELIMINARIES

When as a college undergraduate I was first instructed about Socrates, I was taught to believe that he lived in an age when the "traditional Greek religion" was in full retreat. The mythopoetic worldview of the Greeks had collapsed, or was in the process of collapsing. And philosophy was actually born out of this collapse, contributing to and arguably hastening the end of Greek religion. Philosophy, that is to say, was a kind of epitaphic swan song, offered in memoriam of the poets' dying Olympians. What I was not taught at the time was how very modern this notion of philosophy-as-one-thing-and-religion-as-another actually is; it would have made little sense to the Greeks themselves.

This question—regarding the relationship between "philosophy" and "religion"—is an enormously complex one, as Søren Kierkegaard illustrated with rare dialectical power and unrivaled eloquence. The difficulty that this questionable relation poses is heightened by the regnant contemporary confusion about what precisely philosophy and religion actually are. These terms are tossed around far too casually in popular discussion, and this terminological confusion has found its way into our courts. Since the nineteenth century—and Hegel clearly had something to do with this, which is one important reason why Kierkegaard devoted most of his life to a sustained conversation with Hegelian thought—philosophy has had greater authority, and broader intellectual caché, than religious thought. We see the legacy of this attitude, too, in the legal reasoning I analyzed in the previous chapter.

And yet, none of this applies directly to "the Greeks." To assume that philosophy and religion are two different things is already to think in categories rather foreign to ancient thought. The problem now is that we cannot think *without* these categories; we must use a different strategy if we are to think our way back into the Classical world. The best strategy may be to grant the distinction between religion and philosophy, but to take religion more seriously, by examining it in new ways and on its own terms, by paying more careful attention to the anthropological and archaeological dimension of ancient religion. In paying attention to what we call the "material culture" of ancient religion, we acquire valuable resources for treating religion as something quite different from speculative or systematic philosophy, precisely because we use very different methods to study it.

There have been two schools of modern Classics that have been especially good representatives of this approach: the so-called Cambridge Ritualists (Francis M. Cornford, Jane E. Harrison, and Gilbert Murray), British scholars who applied sociological (and primarily Durkheimian) categories to the study of ancient religion at the turn of the twentieth century; and an interesting group of contemporary French classicists at the Centre Louis Gernet in Paris (the codirectors of the center are Jean-Pierre Vernant and Pierre Vidal-Naquet), men and women who use a variety of anthropological methods, starting with Leví-Strauss, to better comprehend the nature and social scope of ancient religion. Their work has proven to be of special usefulness to me in thinking about the material I am attempting to present in this book.[1]

Ironically enough, both of these movements—the British and the French—are indebted to two renegade Classicists of the nineteenth century, both of whom wrote in German. Jacob Burkhardt (1818–1897) and Friedrich Nietzsche (1844–1900) taught together at the University of Basel for a decade, and while lines of influence are notoriously difficult to trace, their mutual appreciation and the clear perception of a common classical project are clear enough. Both men sought to "think Greek against the grain," to paraphrase Walter Benjamin, that is, to counter the then-dominant perception of Classical Greece as a land of laughter, sunshine, and perpetual childhood. Burkhardt and Nietzsche, both of them under the influence of Arthur Schopenhauer's philosophy, discovered a brooding, melancholic depth in Greek culture, a nearly obsessive competitiveness, and a frank brutality that belied the premises of the more optimistic forms of academic antiquarianism. Nietzsche's first book, *The Birth of Tragedy Out of the Spirit of Music* (1872),[2] represents a shot fired across the bow of this kind of scholarly optimism and fantastic wish-fulfillment. I have drunk deeply at Nietzsche's well, despite my abiding disagreements with his later polemics, throughout my own decade-long immersion in this material. Burkhardt's *The Greeks and Greek Civilization* (published posthumously in 1898–1902)[3] was a similar exercise in unmasking what Nietzsche later called the *pudenda origo,* or "dirty origins," of ancient thought.[4] But

Burkhardt's work was also an exercise in what we would today refer to as "cultural studies," and in that endeavor, he recognized the place of prominence that religion must necessarily occupy. So it is that Burkhardt and Nietzsche, haunted as they both were by the residue of Christianity in their own times, located an alternative, if not quite an antidote to it, in Greek religion. It is my assumption throughout this book that these religious needs and spiritual desires have never left us, least of all when we return, as we do ever and again, to the Greeks.

SITUATING SOCRATES

There is no denying the fact that Greek-speaking wisdom-lovers in the fifth century BCE were prepared to ask difficult questions about the traditional portrait of their gods, as presented in the Homeric poems as well as in most subsequent poetry— whether tragic or comic or lyric. Socrates, for his part, may seem to have made such questions the very stuff of the philosophical life. But the selfsame Socrates who clung so doggedly to his unfettered search for truth—the same man who, on his last day, warned his fellows to pay especially close attention to his arguments regarding the soul's immortality, lest his own personal desires be written unwittingly into what he felt should be an objective and disinterested form of enquiry—this same Socrates on this same day also reminded his fellows that he owed a relatively small sacrifice to an up-and-coming member of the mature Greek pantheon.[5]

"Crito, we owe a cock to Asklepius; be sure to pay it and not to neglect it" (*Phaedo* 118a).[6] These are the last words of Socrates as Plato records them, and they are decidedly *not* to be read the way Nietzsche read them,[7] as the grateful expression of an antihumanist who was happy to be freed finally from his body and the world. Plato, for his part, carefully marks his own conviction that Socrates fully embodied the life of free and critical rational enquiry. His Socrates follows where thought, not a body of sacred writings, leads. But this same Socrates *practices* his religion without compromise—and with no apparent perception of contradiction, no sense of a disconnection between his theory and his practice. As the previous chapter made clear, it is only when one assumes the normative definition of religion to involve matters of doctrinal belief primarily, rather than a set of material practices, that there exists a problem with Socrates at all. There is no warrant, constitutional or otherwise, for such a definition of religion.

We seem, rather, to be in the presence of a paradox, a paradox to most modern sensibilities at any rate. Socrates was a man who could and did reject certain doctrinal beliefs as presented in certain poetic portraits of the gods. Nonetheless, he continued to practice his religion, as most Athenians did. "Religion," for them, seems to have been *more* a matter of practice than a matter of doctrine or scripture. Its fluid, polytheistic character may have had something to do with this.

It is for this same reason that Plato considers the "religion and morals" charges leveled against Socrates to be so wrong-headed. The Athenian demos failed to make this distinction between theory and practice, between religion as doctrinal belief and religion as the material stuff of the devotional life—of libation and prayer and sacrifice and pilgrimage, primarily. Socrates engages in all of these practices, while at the same time asking difficult questions about the pictures poets paint with their words[8]—whether of the gods, or of morality, or what have you. But there is no necessary conflict here. In fact,

Plato will go so far as to insist on the Socratic belief that "piety" (*eusebeia*), properly understood, is best captured by the renegade metaphor of a son who *supplants* his father. Piety and blasphemy are ironically joined in this image,[9] which may be one reason why Aristotle considered Oedipus to be such a paradigmatic figure in his account of Greek drama and the myths it enacts, the *Poetics*. The irony in all of this is that such pious sons will continue to maintain and to honor their father's traditional practices. And that, I suspect, is the key. I am suggesting that Socrates is depicted, by Plato at least, as a man fully at home in traditional Athenian religion. If by piety we understand "the worship of ancestral gods according to ancestral customs,"[10] then Socrates seems a pious man, indeed. Scrupulous in the practices of Athenian religion, he never fails to offer libations and prayers to the appropriate gods and goddesses at the appropriate times (*Symposium* 176a). He fairly leaps at the chance to discuss divine matters, and is eager to correct the errors of omission that bedevil the worship of minor members of an elastic pantheon, like Eros (*Symposium* 177a–e). He has little time or patience for the exercises of rationalizing and demythologizing in which many of the Sophists delight, "accepting instead what is customary" (*Phaedrus* 229c–230a). And while he is never eager to leave his beloved city (*Phaedrus* 230d–e, *Theaetetus* 143d), save when assigned to military service (most notably at Potidaea and Delium, *Charmides* 153a–d, *Symposium* 219e–221c), he is willing to leave to make religious pilgrimage—to consult the oracle at Delphi (although it seems to have been a childhood friend who made this trip on his behalf in the most famous instance, *Apology* 20e–21a, *Protagoras* 342e–343b), and, still more telling, to the Piraeus Harbor, to witness the installation of a new goddess and her worship there (*Republic* 327a,354a).[11] In short, Socrates *practices* his religion traditionally enough. He offers libations, prayers, and sacrifices. He makes pilgrimages.[12]

But Socrates can also be drawn outside the city walls of Athens by the beautiful young men of Athens (*Phaedrus* 229a, 230b–e). He makes pilgrimage on behalf of the Olympians, to be sure, but Socrates also views human life as itself a kind of inspired pilgrimage toward beauty, both human and divine. And along that enchanted way, he is a regular pilgrim to the *palaestrae* and *gymnasia*,[13] those paradigmatically Greek (*Symposium* 182b–c) exercise places (and, in the case of the gymnasium, it is literally a "naked place") in which such beauty was celebrated (*Lysis* 203a–204a, *Laches* 178a, *Charmides* 153a, and see *Laws* 625c, *passim*).[14] This fact requires us to make a circuitous detour, prior to making an authentically Hellenic pilgrimage of our own—to the vast topic of Platonic *erôs*, and his depiction of the best human life as one committed to a sort of erotic (and ironic) philosophical enquiry. Attending to the erotic dimension in Plato's portrait of Socrates[15] can assist us in situating Socrates, helping us to clarify one of the more vexing aspects of his Platonic portrait—namely, "where Socrates is standing" when he ventures his criticisms of others and their ungrounded beliefs about the virtues and the gods.

SOCRATIC PASSION

As we saw in the previous chapter, powerful antimodern criticisms—most notably Alasdair MacIntyre's[16]—have succeeded in making most contemporary thinkers suspicious of the claim to rational objectivity, the allegedly Liberal claim to be "standing nowhere." Even one's conception of rationality, MacIntyre insists, is situated, located at its best in a *tradition* of rational and moral enquiry. The first task before us, then, is largely an historical one: that of *situating* the thought with which we wish to deal. And MacIntyre, of course, initiates his situation of modern EuroAmerican thought with the Greeks, more specifically, with Homer.[17]

Using MacIntyre's cautionary tale as my guide, then, I would like to attempt to situate Socrates before examining the specific claims he makes about piety. By beginning in this way, and by attending to several more "traditionalist" concerns, we note several important aspects of Socrates's character. First, he does *not* claim to be standing nowhere, as MacIntyre and others allege that modern Liberals do. Second, Socrates does *not* claim to know nothing. Socrates, in fact, claims to understand the erotic life as well as anyone alive (*Symposium* 177e, 198d, see also Endnote #23). He also claims to be standing within a fairly traditional kind of Athenian "piety." In this chapter, I will attempt to sketch out a connection between these two rather jarring aspects of Socratic thought and Socratic practice.

I emphasize this at the outset because I am aware of the portrait most of us have inherited of Socrates, even if we cannot say precisely where we saw it first. We think we know that he was especially wise because he, alone of all Athenians, knew that he did not know anything. Casting about within the Platonic corpus, however, it is difficult to understand how such an idea ever emerged to begin with. For Socrates can be astonishingly bold, even overweening in his claims to various sorts of knowledge. There is a kind of hybristic self-confidence lying at the very heart of his way of life.[18] He makes, in fact, the very kind of knowledge-claims that will seem ironically and unintentionally funny when Euthyphro makes them: Namely, that he is the *most* knowledgable man alive in his own areas of expertise. Euthyphro claimed to be an expert in matters relating to the gods (*ta theia*). Socrates claims to be an expert in matters relating to the erotic life (*ta erôtika*), and to be the proud possessor of a very *human* sort of wisdom (*anthrôpinê sophia, Apology* 20d). This seems simple enough, but also quite strange.

Now, in good Platonic fashion, I want to remind us of some Socratic things we presumably already know.[19] In an early dialogue on friendship, Socrates makes a rather surprising observation. His uniqueness, much like his wisdom, is tied directly to his erotic sensitivity. He is "able to recognize almost immediately when someone is in love (*erônta*), as well as who it is that they want (*erômenon*)" (*Lysis* 204c). In another early discussion, Socrates recalls one fateful day in the gymnasium, when he first met Charmides. Socrates had just returned from the disastrous experience at Potidaea. But the turmoil of that war disrupted this philosopher's soul far less than the power of the erotic does: "when everyone in the palaestra pressed in on us in a tight circle—then, just then, my noble friend—I saw inside his robes. I caught fire (*ephlegomên*) and could not control myself" (*Charmides* 155d). Socrates adds that he is completely indiscriminate in such love-matters: "I am as useless as a white line on marble when it comes to measuring beauty," he grins. "Every boy who is on the verge of manhood (*en têi hêlikiai*) seems beautiful to me" (*Charmides* 154b). Next, in an importantly transitional dialogue (transitional precisely from the Early to the Middle Period[20] of Plato's career), Socrates further elucidates his own convictions about human loving. *Erôs* is the great equalizer. It makes the weak strong, the strong weak, and it often makes the wise man turn stupid. And yet, as Socrates consistently maintains, desire also can turn the simple man into a wise one. *Erôs,* then, is fast becoming the fuel that drives the engine of the dialectic, and every other kind of wisdom-loving (*Gorgías* 481d).

That point is reiterated in another of the most important of Plato's transitional pieces, the *Meno*. The homerotic economy of leisured Athenian elites is signaled literally on the very first page. Meno, the young man who poses the central question for this dialogue—is virtue teachable?—is from Larisa, in the region of Thessaly, a region noted for its horsemanship (apparently referenced at *Antigone* 311–315), but noted now for wisdom as well (*Meno* 70a-b). Meno himself has a lover (*erastês*) from there, a man who has instructed him in the love of wisdom and quick speaking (*Meno* 70b). Slightly later in their exchange, Socrates notes that the boy has learned well—not so much to philosophize, as to trade on his good looks. When the characteristically Socratic quest for the unity of the virtues threatens to stall—all they can seem to find are examples of various virtues, not virtue itself—then Socrates notes that things could easily turn contentious, or even ugly. That they will not degenerate in this case is due in part to the fact that the two dialogue partners are friends. Furthermore, Socrates playfully submits to the beauty of the boy, since he knows that he has "a weakness for all beautiful people (*eimi hêttôn tôn kalôn*)" (*Meno* 76c). Meno is beautiful indeed (*Meno* 80c); as with Charmides before him, Socrates loses control in his presence (*Meno* 86d–e). Thus there seems to be an erotic subtext to every philosophical exchange in the Platonic key.

In making the transition to Plato's so-called Middle Period, we notice that this philosophical attention paid to *erôs* is emphasized still more clearly. I have suggested that we refer to this as Plato's *Erotic* Period for precisely this reason.[21] In the selfsame period when Plato began to put his own philosophic voice into Socrates's mouth, Plato also initiated a bold attempt to define two essential Greek terms: *erôs* and *ta erôtika*. He initiated a project that was to remain with him for the remainder of his wisdom-loving life. This profound encounter, and the meditation it prompted, ultimately altered his very conception of the requirements of a life characterized by such philosophical and romantic aspirations.

It is also in the Erotic Period that Plato begins to ask his intriguing character sketches to do real work for him. Plato devoted no less than four dialogues to this constellation of erotic ideas, and they are without a doubt his most influential mature works: *Symposium, Republic, Phaedo,* and *Phaedrus.* The *Symposium,* of course, is all about *erôs,* pure and simple. It concludes that there is nothing pure or simple about human loving—that there is, in fact, no more complex, nor more significant, human experience. How to allow a degree of passionate attachment into a life that aspires to autonomy and serene detachment here becomes a matter of the first importance. Socrates's erotic expertise is due both to his passionate attachments as well as to the fact that he has opened himself—or else he has been opened (the metaphors vary in ways that are significant)—to the risks, the vulnerabilities, and the essential non-solitariness that the erotic life demands. But the process *begins* with an erotic intuition, one beautifully captured in an image crafted by Anne Carson, whom we met first in the Preface of this book:

> As Sokrates tells it, your story begins the moment Eros enters you. That incursion is the biggest risk of your life. How you handle it is an index of the quality, wisdom and decorum of the things inside you. As you handle it you come into contact with what is inside you, in a sudden and startling way. You perceive what you are, what you lack, what you could be. What is this mode of perception, so different from ordinary perception that it is well described as madness? How is it that when you fall in love you

feel as if suddenly you are seeing the world as it really is? A mood of knowledge floats over your life. . . . This mood is no delusion, in Sokrates' belief. It is a glance down into time, at realities you once knew, as staggeringly beautiful as the glance of your beloved. . . . Sokrates says it is a glimpse of a god.[22]

If it were possible to eroticize the old Cartesian dualism, then we might almost say that Socrates loves, therefore he knows. And what he knows, while it *is* emphatically human, is equally and paradoxically divine in origin. Socratic *erôs* is thus linked essentially to Socratic piety, as Plato understands these terms.

Further evidence of this connection comes in the *Republic,* where Plato's famous quarrel with poetry is not presented as a simple ban, nor as a case of simple poetic censorship. Rather, Socrates uses an erotic metaphor (*Republic* 607e) to signal that he is "breaking up" with poetry, as it were, even though he still loves it, and probably always will. He loves poetry, but he fears that it may ultimately be bad for him. In the *Phaedo,* too, much of the argument turns oddly on an ambiguous link between pleasure and pain (*Phaedo* 59a–60b, *passim*), a link that, on the surface, seems rather hard to comprehend. These things are supposed to be opposites; Aristotle makes this opposition the very starting point for his *Ethics.* Yet pleasure and pain, erotically construed, are not opposites at all; the one blurs inescapably into its opposite throughout this strained yet winsome dialogue. Smiling in their tears, Socrates's friends discover themselves laughing and experiencing a strange kind of pleasure here, of all places, in anticipation of their friend's own demise. There is a pleasure in this pain. It is all very, very strange, as they are the first ones to admit—strange in much the way that *erôs* is.

Finally, the *Phaedrus* returns explicitly to the erotic themes first laid out in the *Symposium.* But then the dialogue turns to a metaphorical analysis of the human soul, and concludes with a long meditation on the craft of rhetoric and written composition. We are confronted in the *Phaedrus* with the curious portrait of a Socrates who is singularly capable of letting himself go. Self-control, he now suggests, may be an overrated virtue (*Phaedrus* 244d); the ability to let go, to be open to the control of another, is now highlighted as an essential task for the philosophical life. Later in this same dialogue, Socrates alludes to his own peculiar erotic gifts, referring to "that erotic skill" (*erôtikên technên*) that the god, Eros, has granted to him (*Phaedrus* 257a). This important Platonic term, *technê,* may also refer to "crafts" and to "practices," everything from stone-cutting and cobbling to medicine. So the ironic double reference here is to an erotic craft that Socrates has inherited from the gods. That craft is philosophy, of course, what we moderns call "religion" and "philosophy" being seamlessly joined in ancient Athens.

In the *Theaetetus,* Socrates confesses to a deep commitment to his city, signified first and foremost in his playful commitment to the young beauties who live within its walls (*Theaetetus* 143d). Socratic philosophy, then, is consistently presented by Plato almost as a seducer's art. Already in the *Protagoras,* we were presented with a picture of philosophy as a contest, an *agôn* housed in the gymnasium, one whose chief door prizes are the affections and attentions of the city's most promising young men. In every way, Socrates is the seducer *par excellence.*[23]

Clearly, Socratic and Platonic *erôs* are sketched on a very large canvas. But what is it exactly that Plato means to illustrate on our behalf? One clue appears in what is surely the most striking feature of Socrates's erotic career. Plato emphasizes it for us through a detailed and repeated examination of his relationship with Alcibiades. This relationship is one of the things that got Socrates into trouble later on, as we shall see.

Their relationship is backwards, according to the implicit canons of Greek ho-
mophilia and everyday Greek speech. There seems to have been a fairly strict age-
distinction built in to Athenian homoeroticism in the fifth century BCE.[24] An older
man, the *erastês,* communicates his interest in, and desire for, a younger boy, the *erômenos.* There is thus a pursuer and a pursued, conceived very loosely as active and
passive partners. These lovers' roles are never mixed, and this seems to be the
scheme that is presupposed in both the *Symposium* and the *Phaedrus.*

But Socrates is an older man who is actively pursued by many of the young beauties of Athens. Alcibiades, in particular, inverts all of the standard erotic categories
in his notoriously failed attempts to seduce him. He acts as *erastês* in order to secure
Socrates's attentions and, so he hopes, his subsequent adoption of that role, himself.
But it does not work out that way (this is all agonizingly chronicled at *Symposium*
215b–219e). Socrates decides that their relationship will evolve along other, more
ambiguous, philosophical lines. In all of this, Alcibiades is depicted as a young man
who behaves like an older man, a potential *erômenos* who acts the part of an *erastês.*
And Socrates is an old man who acts like a younger man, a potential *erastês* who seems
to be the ironic *erômenos* of all Athens. One clear message of Plato's Erotic Period dialogues is that the *erastês–erômenos* framework will not work, that it is a far too rigid
taxonomy for capturing the fluidity and inescapable nuances of erotic desire.[25] *Erôs*
is fraught with self-contradiction. Thus Plato, using Socrates as his philosophic alter
ego perhaps, intends to subvert the traditional Athenian categories of age. And this
is the point at which Socratic piety and Socratic virtue join hands, at last.

SOCRATIC PIETY

What in the world does he feel pious about, this arch ironist and philosophic gadfly?
The charter text for discerning an answer to this question is, of course, the *Euthyphro.*
What strikes one immediately about this dialogue, however, is the repeated attention paid to the age of its participants: Socrates is an older man, roughly 70 years old
now, whereas Euthyphro is clearly new to his maturity, finally in a position now to
supplant his own father—in a court of law, if necessary.

Now, certain Platonic "dialogues" are aptly named; they are virtually all dialogue—
or else one extended speech, such as the *Apology,* or the *Menexenus.* But when Plato
takes evident pains to construct a narrative frame for his speeches—as he does here,
where the narrative frame is nearly as long as the elenchus itself—then we are well ad-
vised to pay attention to that frame. Related to this is a commonplace Platonic strategy—that of "beginning in the middle" (most notably, at *Symposium* 172a).
Acknowledging how difficult it is to secure a sure philosophical starting point,[26] Plato
more often than not simply elects to begin arbitrarily, drawing us into the middle of
a discussion already in process.

Here, in the *Euthyphro,* the very first words we hear clue us in to some of the larger
concerns of Socrates at the time, as well as offering a clue as to the nature of his conception of piety.

What's new, Socrates? Or rather, what's new enough to drag you out of your old haunts
in the Lyceum and to bring you here to the Royal Stoa for conversation? (*Euthyphro* 2a)

Literally, Euthyphro asks Socrates "what newer thing has happened" (*ti neôteron gego-nen*), and the Greek word for "new" (*neos*) is the same as the word for "youth." So, this innocuous phrase—"What's new?"—has an inescapably sinister undertone—"What is young?" or "Who is younger?" Recall that it will be the accusation of having introduced "new things" into "old-time" Athenian religion that will result in Socrates's execution in the very near future, as we who read this dialogue presumably already know. But there is more at stake in this beginning. It is almost as if Euthyphro is asking Socrates something else, presenting him with an altogether different sort of challenge: "What *younger man* has happened upon you, Socrates?"—more precisely, what younger man has presumed to bring Socrates to court?

In fact, this entire dialogue is seasoned with stories about upstart younger sons who supplant their older fathers. Euthyphro, to begin with, is bringing suit against his own father, on a murder charge no less (*Euthyphro* 3e–4e). Zeus supplanted his father, Kronos, after the latter attempted to murder him, as he had so many other of his children, by ingesting him (*Euthyphro* 6a–c, 7e–8b). And now Socrates is being challenged by a rather young man who is, in fact, so young that Socrates has not had the opportunity to get to know him. Given Socrates's scrupulous interest in the youth of Athens, this is in itself remarkable. "He seems young (*neos*) and unknown (*agnôs*)," Socrates frowns (*Euthyphro* 2b). There are not many such young men in Athens.

There is an even subtler sort of supplanting at work later in this dialogue, when Socrates refers to the mythic figure of Daidalos as his own "ancestor" (literally a "progenitor," *tou hêmeterou progonou*) (*Euthyphro* 11a–e, 15b–c).[27] He reminds us that Daidalos was famous for creating statues of such lifelike quality that they seemed to move their eyes, and even to walk (*Meno* 97d). Socrates equates his own "works in words" (*ta en tois logois erga*) to Daidalos's statues (*Euthyphro* 11c). The image, then, is that of the profoundest type of artistic creativity, the creation of something which then escapes from one's creative control. The creature becomes free and autonomous, a point developed to such devastating affect in Shakespeare's *The Tempest*. Socrates suggests, a little ironically, that Euthyphro's arguments are reminiscent of this artistic dilemma; they get away from him in much the same way that Daidalos's statues get up and walk. At the end of the dialogue, in fact, Socrates tells Euthyphro that his words have walked around in a complete circle, returning us to our starting point, so that now we must undertake the whole elenchic investigation again (*Euthyphro* 15c). Euthyphro begs off, claiming that he has no more time, and so the dialogue ends, aporetically.[28]

Yet there is something stranger than this at work here. For Socrates chooses to emphasize the wisdom (*sophos*) of his ancestor, Daidalos, not merely the inventive skill that eventually resulted in the death of his son, Icarus. And he emphasizes the wealth (*ta chrêmata*) of Tantalus, rather than the bizarre crime of serving up his own child, Pelops, to the gods at a feast (*Euthyphro* 11e). Socrates is deliberately misremembering, or else deliberately and selectively narrating, the myths of his own ancestors. (This same strategy leads to the apparent censorship of such stories in *Republic* 377a–378e). While Socrates makes a great deal of sons who supplant their fathers, he seems to wish to avoid any mention of fathers who have killed their sons, intentionally or otherwise.[29]

Specifically, Socrates says that he would rather have his own words stand still (*tous logous menein kai akinêtôs*), than to have all of the wisdom of Daidalos, all the wealth of Tantalus, or anything else we might care to name (*Euthyphro* 11e). There is thus much about his alledged ancestor that Socrates does not say.[30] He chooses not to mention (or does he fail to remember?) that Daidalos manufactured the labyrinth for the Minotaur on Crete, that monstrous half-human who consumed the flesh of 12 Athenian youths each year, until Theseus traveled south to Crete and killed him. He chooses not to remember that it was Daidalos who manufactured the machinery that allowed Pasiphaë to copulate with a bull, thereby conceiving the Minotaur in the first place. He chooses not to remember that Daidalos came to Crete originally as an exile, fleeing a charge of homicide in Athens. And it was in attempting to flee his exile on Crete, with wings, that he inadvertently lost his son.

Theseus, on his own return from Crete, and his symbolic triumph over Daidalos's machinery, failed to raise the white sail on his own ship, which was the symbol his father had chosen as an indication that the son was safe and sound. So Theseus inadvertently killed his father, who suicided in his grief. Theseus was clearly preoccupied with other matters, having just abandoned Ariadne, whom he had brought with him from Crete, on the island of Naxos prior to his Athenian homecoming. It was there on that island that Dionysus later came to her, and became her lover, in turn. And it was on Naxos, quite recently, that one of Euthyphro's servants (*pelatês*) became drunk on Dionysian drink (*paroinêsas*), and killed one of the household servants (*tôn oiketôn tini*), thereby initiating the long, strange sequence of events that has now ranged the son against his father in a court of law, here, in Athens (*Euthyphro* 4a–c). For Euthyphro's father bound this accused murderer, dragged him in chains to Athens, and left him to die unattended in a prison there. It is for this curious "murder" that Euthyphro has brought his suit. So our story—much like Euthyphro's words—takes us in a peculiarly Athenian circle, following Daidalos and his progeny: from Athens, to Crete, to Naxos, then back to Athens again (see Figure 2.1).

I suspect that it is this *Cretan* connection—Crete being Zeus's birthplace, and of perennial interest to Plato[31]—that we are intended to recall on Naxos. Naxos was allegedly colonized by the Cretans, just as neighboring Paros was colonized by men from Asia Minor. And Crete was legendary for several of the innovations that made a Classical city like Athens possible: Most notably, the "mysteries" of its ancient religious practice, the written alphabet, and thus a more "graphic" concept of the law. It was the upstart cultural children of Crete, in places like Athens, who were later to supplant their southern Cretan father, by putting such essential innovations to dramatic new uses. Clearly, there are many layers to these myths; their words do not, and can not, "stand still."

The archaeological and written record suggests that Daidalos was never described as a *sculptor* until the fifth century BCE—an interesting example of deliberate Athenian myth-making for political purposes.[32] Prior to that, his inventiveness was celebrated in other areas, many of which I have already referenced. Daidalos is first mentioned in the *Iliad* (18.590–592), tellingly enough, as the inventor of a dance *for Ariadne*. Later he would become famous as the inventor of an impossible range of other things: From Pasiphaë's bestial wooden suit; to the labyrinthine architecture that imprisoned her monstrous offspring; to wings and human flight. "Wings" were a common Greek euphemism for sails, and "sailing" was to become a charter Socratic metaphor for the philosophical life (*Phaedo* 99c). Theseus's sails were the source of his father's undoing, and Daidalos's wings cost him the life of his son.

The myth of Icarus is in fact subtly referenced as soon as Euthyphro's lawsuit is mentioned. Euthyphro admits that others think him "crazy" (*mainesthai*) for what he

THE DAIDALEAN TRIANGLE
Athens-Naxos-Crete

Figure 2.1

is doing. Why? Socrates wonders. "Does the man you are suing have wings?" (*Euthyphro* 4a). Daidalos also would be associated later, like Crete, with the written alphabet, that technology most often forgotten or lost by Greeks throughout the Aegean. And finally, in the end, Daidalos would be associated with these curious sculptures that move. True heir to his ancestor, then, Socrates also is a creator (*poiêtês*) of sorts—only Meletus is so obtuse as to assume that what he makes are "gods" (*Euthyphro* 3b).

Younger sons who supplant their older fathers.[33] Ironically enough, Socrates will be accused with this very crime, himself. He has been accused of manufacturing younger gods to supplant their elders in the traditional Olympian pantheon (*Euthyphro* 3b). He is also charged with corrupting the youth of Athens by so doing. In fact, there are three formal charges leveled against Socrates in all, and they all are alleged to hang together by Meletus and his youthful companions:

1. Socrates corrupts the youth (*diaphtheirontai tous neous, Euthyphro* 2c);
2. Socrates has manufactured new gods (or new concepts of divinity) (*phêsi gar me poiêtên einai theôn, kai hôs kainous poiounta theous, Euthyphro* 3b]; and

3. Socrates stands accused of not believing in[34] the traditional gods, and hence, of undermining the traditional religion of Athens (*tous d'archaious ou nomizonta, Euthyphro* 3b).

It turns out that Meletus has brought suit (literally, he has "written him up," *egrapsato, Euthyphro* 3b) on behalf and in the name of these older and more traditional (*archaious*) gods.

Part of Plato's defense of Socrates is to suggest that these charges cannot be made to hang together, that some of them are correct descriptions of actual Socratic practices, while others are nonsense charges, the stuff of which ostracism and exile, not philosophy, are made. Socrates clearly *has* introduced new gods into the city, as Euthyphro knows well, his own *daimonion* (*Euthyphro* 3b) most clearly. But Socrates just as clearly continues to observe the *practices* of the traditional religious cults of Athens (*Euthyphro* 14b–15a, *Phaedo* 118a).

And as for corrupting the youth . . . Plato's entire literary career was dedicated to illustrating what a nonsense charge he believed this to have been. A teacher cannot *make* you better, morally or otherwise, so a teacher cannot be held responsible if you become worse along the way. It is not Socrates's fault if Alcibiades turned away from his moral example, for instance (*Symposium* 216a–c). A teacher cannot *force* learning on the young. To illustrate this point, Socrates threatens to have Euthyphro, his new-found "teacher" of piety, taken to court on his behalf, to answer the charge for which he, as Socrates's teacher, may now be held accountable (*Euthyphro* 5a–b). But Socrates, of course, was joking.

The problem here is the problem of infinite regress: If you blame me as a teacher for my students' behavior, then why should you not actually blame the teachers who taught me . . . and so on, until we are left blaming the gods themselves, or the most ancient stories about them that we know. Now, if a moral teacher takes *money* for his or her teaching, then it begins to appear as if a promise has been made, and a contractual relationship established.[35] This much we can say: Where moral knowledge has been turned into a *commodity,* there you have the right to expect "delivery on payment." That is precisely why Socrates refuses to accept payment for his teaching, and why Plato makes such a point of emphasizing this fact in Socrates's defense (*Apology* 19e–20c). Socrates teaches human, not divine, wisdom and does so "without pay" (*aneu misthou*), simply out of a general—although, be sure to note, a divinely inspired—concern for people (*hypo philanthrôpias, Euthyphro* 3d).

So Socrates teaches, but he has nothing to sell. It does not follow from this that he has nothing that he knows. He is simply uncertain how best to pass that knowledge along. How, for instance, might one sell the knowledge of *erôs*? One can sell sex, to be sure, but this is *porneía,* prostitution, of which there were many subtle gradations in Athens.[36] *Erôs,* like philosophy and philanthropy, is something else again.

Two crucial elements of the Platonic portrait of Socrates's character emerge in the *Euthyphro* with special clarity, and they help us move toward an admittedly partial resolution of our initial dilemma regarding "where Socrates is standing." First, Socrates is portrayed as a rather unusual and deeply interesting man: An elderly gentleman who is far more open to questioning the tired truisms of the traditional religion than the young people who have presented themselves as the defenders of orthodoxy. Socrates, that is to say, is an old man who thinks like a young man, a man who has grown more liberal and open-minded with age (*Euthyphro* 6a-b). Second,

Socrates is presented as an older man who is deeply concerned with, and deeply involved with, the young. He happily admits that if Meletus, "young as he is" (*to gar neon onta, Euthyphro* 2c–d), is right about the effect of his own behavior, then he is fully justified in bringing the suit. Nothing can be more important than the state of the souls of the youth in a healthy city.

But Socrates, unlike the Sophists and Simonidean poets, never takes money for his teaching. This is not because he has nothing to teach; it is rather to do with his subject matter. Socrates does not think it odd to pay for certain skills and certain sorts of training. But he seemed to gravitate toward the metaphor of apprenticeship, not salesmanship, as a better and more fitting description of his own practice (*Euthyphro* 13a–b). To learn how to cut stone, you apprentice yourself to a stonecutter. To learn how to heal (and *therapeia* is one of the most important words in this dialogue, *Euthyphro* 12e), you apprentice yourself to a doctor. (Athens might arguably think about apprenticing herself to Crete again.) But this is not Socratic work. Socrates's work is *moral* work, and he confines himself almost exclusively to moral questions. He is interested in cosmology only if it has an ethical valence (*Phaedo* 97c–99d). He immediately turns the talk about piety into moral talk as well (*Euthyphro* 7b–d). The erotic realm, in his careful hands, becomes emblematic of the premier moral gesture of which human beings are capable: The gift of passionate attachment and enduring attention.

Theology in the abstract appears not to interest Socrates. He is concerned with the question of how people come into enmity, and what they disagree most strongly about: Not mathematics, not measurement, not science, not anything quantifiable. We come to blows over matters of *moral* evaluation, things for which there are no such clear standards. The way to learn from Socrates, then, may be to apprentice yourself to his way of life.[37] And to do that, one must have learned to *desire* it, first. This is what Plato understood as *erôs,* a kind of passionate philosophical desire. Without it, the philosophical life will never get underway. Socrates did *seduce* the youth of Athens, to be sure. Whether that involved him in their *corruption* or not is another matter. It presumably appeared to be so most clearly to a youth, like Meletus, "who did not really know him" (*Euthyphro* 2b).

BACK TO THE FUTURE

This dialogue—like this chapter, I'm afraid—is classically aporetic; in some important ways, it refuses to end, because it refuses any kind of simple conclusion. The *Euthyphro,* like Socrates himself, insists on asking questions that it (and he) cannot answer. Each question it poses becomes the stalk on which other questions flower. While traditionally read as a dialogue about "piety" (*hê eusebeia*), the Classical compiler of the Platonic corpus (an Aristotelian named Theophrastus, who would presumably have been in a position to know) labeled it as a dialogue about "holiness" (*to osion*). In fact, it is about both ideas, since these terms are deliberately linked at the beginning of the dialogue (*Euthyphro* 5d). Given Plato's deep suspicion of falsifying dichotomous choices,[38] this dialogue is not about religious practice *or* religious belief, but rather about both, about the need to combine them, and about that curious amalgam they produce in combination, what we (but probably not the Greeks) might call "religion."

The dialogue is unusual in that it speaks more about beliefs than it does about practices. It is, in this sense, eminently "philosophical." Echoing Socrates's famously complicated quarrel with poetry, he underlines his own belief that the gods are good, and just, and that they do not fight with one another. This very commitment to Olympic harmony is ironically impious, if piety is understood to be the blind acceptance of ancestral stories, customs, and the elaborate practices which they commemorate (*Euthyphro* 6a–c). The younger gods supplanted their elders, just as Meletus and Euthyphro are trying to do now.

Socrates is more than merely impious; he is also a philosopher. And—irony being the very stuff of the Socratic life[39]—these same facts render him altogether pious in another sense: He is a father, placed now in the ironically renegade position of displacing the religion of his upstart sons—sons who responded, in the name of piety perhaps, by killing him. So the entire dialogue revolves around the theme of parricide, and the confused perceptions of age. The same act may be just *and* impious, or else pious *and* unjust. There is no one-to-one correspondence between religion and morality, as Kierkegaard, yet another Socratic apprentice, knew well. We should recall that the Eleatic Stranger suggested that he would be forced to be a "parricide," if he were to undercut father Parmenides's arguments (*Sophist* 241d). Philosophy, for Plato, is well on the way to becoming a nearly inevitable exercise in parricide.

Sons who supplant fathers, sons who kill their fathers: I want to underline this image here, first, because it is the image that got Plato's project underway. His entire career is an attempt to come to terms with the killing of Socrates, a murder that left he and his friends feeling "like children who had lost their father, and who were condemned to live out their lives as orphans" (*Phaedo* 116a). They were, as Socrates himself made clear in his own defense, referring to himself as the father and elder brother of Athens (*Apology* 31b).

I underline this metaphor also because I wish to use it myself, to a slightly different purpose. This metaphor will also serve as the root metaphor for all the subsequent chapters of this book, which is intended as an essay in the history of the appropriation of Hellenism. This is as much a book about the history of hellenisms as it is about Hellenism *per se*. What I want to mark is the ironic way in which the sons who appropriate the traditions of their fathers[40] are involved, perhaps inevitably, in the murderous project of unstringing them. This irony has been a major preoccupation in deconstructive circles, of late. But such has been the hidden effect of *most* Greek appropriations in the past 2,500 years. And this all began in Rome.

CHAPTER THREE

Pausanias at Olympia
THE GREECE INSIDE ROME

In turning the pages of a volume of Flaubert's correspondence, dog-eared and heavily underlined by me about the year 1927, I came upon the following unforgettable phrase: "Just when the old gods had ceased to be and the Christ had not yet come, between Cicero and Marcus Aurelius, when man stood alone." A great portion of my life was going to be spent in trying to define, and then to portray, such a man, existing alone and yet closely related to all others.

—Marguerite Yourcenar, *"Reflections on the Composition of Memoirs of Hadrian"*

Ma com'era cominciato tutto?
——*So, how did it all begin?*

—Roberto Calasso, *The Marriage of Cadmus and Harmony*

PRELIMINARIES

The way we name an issue often serves to frame the issue. This is as true in speculative philosophy and history as it is in politics. As I suggested briefly in a note in the first chapter, "Greco-Roman" is a highly suspect name, as I think it ought to be to any well-meaning Classicist. It is a term that significantly distorts the ancient record, a term that is laden with all-too-hidden assumptions and value judgments. There is yet another historical narrative subtly embedded in this terminology. And unmasking such narratives, trying to tell these stories in different terms, using different names, is a major preoccupation of this book.

The term "Greco-Roman" not-so-subtly suggests that Greek things and Roman things are a piece of the same thing—and that is the problem. We assume this in spite of the fact that we are speaking, for the most part, about civilizations separated by several hundred miles of open sea, several hundred years of quite independent political and cultural development, not to mention the vast gulf created by a linguistic divide whose terms are not cognate. Latin has no direct relationship to Greek.

The discipline of classics, as it developed over the past 200 years, has done much to promote this false perception. One need only consult a critical edition of any ancient *Greek* text, and the first thing one will notice is . . . all the *Latin.* Whether it be the editors' preface or the critical apparatus at the bottom of the page, all of this material is presented in Latin alone. The ironic message in all of this is clear: to gain access to *Greek* material at all, one must know *Latin* as well. That is a powerful, and perplexing, symbolic statement.

The term "Greco-Roman" is as much a fiction as it is a fact, reliant on the kinds of historical-narratives-as-arguments that we met in the first chapter, and will meet again in nearly every subsequent one. The term is every bit as distorting as another common enough cultural category: the term "Judeo-Christian." The problem that appeals to "Judeo-Christian" culture and its values is that they claim to equate terms that are decidedly not equivalent; terms that are rendered ironically *un*equal by the very notion that proposes to equate them. For "Judeo-Christian" is a subtly Christian category; it makes little sense as a Jewish term. Christians have to do with the Hebrew scriptures and with Jewish history in a way that Jews do *not* have to do with the New Testament or subsequent Christian theological developments. Christians made Judaism a part of their story, but Christianity need not be a part of the Jewish story at all. Given the New Testament's emphatic belief that two disparate (and often opposed) cultural categories—Greek and Jew, or *Hellên kai Ioudaios*—were joined now, it fell to the professing Christian to find a way to marry these worlds, somehow. This proved to be a complex transaction indeed, as we shall see in the next chapter and most subsequent ones. But one result of the attempted synthesis we call "Judeo-Christian" was the dawning realization that these terms could not be definitively joined. As Christianity detached itself slowly and spasmodically from Judaism, Judaism itself came to be read as a Christian heresy. So, we shall see, did Hellenism. The hyphen that attempted to link these terms eventually drove a wedge between them.

To claim—as is done all too often today, even in the U.S. Supreme Court—that North American culture is a "Judeo-Christian" culture is thus both a misnomer and the product of a deep failure of religious understanding. Ours is a culture deeply informed by, and still under the lingering influence of, a *Christian* culture—specifically, the Protestant culture of northern Europe. That culture may have been deliberately Hebraizing itself, but there is little directly Jewish about it.

Let us now consider the ambivalent place of Greece in things "Greco-Roman." "Greco-Roman" is a subtly Roman term, for much the same set of reasons. Even the name—*Graecia,* or Greece—was an uncommon Greek name that the *Romans* popularized. While the name first appears in Aristotle's corpus, he refers to it as an oddity.[1] The Greeks' name for themselves was generally *Hellên* (pl. *Hellênes*), and their homeland was called *Hellas.* It was the Romans who later located this place on their mental map as *Graecia,*[2] and it was Rome that referred to her inhabitants almost exclusively as *Graeci* (sg. *Graecus*).

The Romans, to be sure, in the era of their most dramatic expansion, elected to think of themselves in terms that incorporated a great deal of Greekness into it. Rome appropriated Greek culture and made it over in her own, Latin image. Given the story the Romans told themselves about themselves in the imperial period, Romans had to do with Greek culture in a way that Greeks of the same time did not have to do with Roman culture. The Greeks, by and large, had to deal with Roman armies and Roman civil authorities (so, roughly a century later, did the Jews), but they did not have to do with Roman culture.[3] Those who did so were presumably the literary and philosophical figures who were forced increasingly to rely on Roman patronage for their livelihood. The philistine tastes of such "Roman" *patrones* was lampooned by Lucian in the second century CE. And, in their turn, Latin poets like Juvenal made a point of mocking the effete intellectualism of "the Greeks."[4] Greeks and Romans in the imperial period, it seems, loved to hate each other—whether playfully, or in earnest, or both.

So when we speak of "Greco-Roman" culture, or religion, we have unwittingly elected to read Greek texts through the lens the later Romans provide. Let me be clear about how I choose to view this matter. I do *not* mean to be roundly condemnatory either of Romanity or of Christianity. These terms—whether Judeo-Christian or Greco-Roman—are not wrong, but it is wrong, and importantly wrong, to assume that they are neutral. This is the mistake the U.S. Supreme Court perpetuates, in rendering its own subtle forms of religious judgments, as we saw in the first chapter.

The Christian appropriation of Jewish history and theology is not inappropriate; it simply is not Jewish. Muslim appropriations of Jewish and Christian symbols are not inappropriate; they simply are not Jewish or Christian. If we are to use such terms well, if we are to tell the story they mean to tell in ways that illuminate rather than occlude, it is important to keep these issues in mind. In their best moments, Christian thinkers have seen things in Judaism, and have noticed things about the Hebrew scriptures and subsequent Jewish theology, which have had a lasting and dramatic impact on Judaism as well as on Christianity. The reverse has also been true. The dialogue between one evolving tradition called Judaism and another called Christianity *can* be a fruitful one, although its failures have probably been more dramatic, historically speaking. The fruits of this labor are, in any case, directly dependent on our ability to keep the two terms separate. It is only a dialogue, after all, if we admit that there are two distinct conversation-partners, both of whom have an equal right to speak, in their own language, in their own categories. This is what the hyphenation threatens to erase; it suggests that Judaism and Christianity are two versions of the same thing, not two entirely separate traditions that may be linked in a *cross*-cultural conversation.

In the same way, I do not mean to condemn Roman (nor, as we shall see in the next chapter, Christian) appropriations of Greek things. Any number of Roman appropriations of Greek cultural artifacts have contributed enormously to our understanding of the original Greek material, as well as having shaped it in new and unexpected forms. The tradition of Italian philology—ancient *and* modern, which is how Nietzsche understood it[5]—was arguably the most creative and insightful the world had yet seen. It continues to bear rich fruit in Italy, as it does, for instance, in the loving hands of Roberto Calasso, whose insights will contribute a fitting commentary to this chapter at several points. All I mean to point out here is that such an appropriation is *creative,* necessitating a curious *refashioning* of the Classical. "Classicism," in this sense, becomes one more ironic instance of sons who supplant their fathers.

Classical art offers us an excellent illustration of this. The vast majority of Greek art we possess actually exists in the form of Roman copies, in marble, of Greek originals—most, although hardly all, of which were originally cast in bronze. The discipline of Greek archaeology was not really born until the nineteenth century, shortly after such Roman-Greek art came into vogue. When we look at Greek art, then—and this has been true since Johannes Winckelmann (1717–1768) first created the modern project of art history, and the modern taste for Greek art—we are almost invariably viewing it through the lens of its Roman (or later) appropriations, as well as its sometime commodification. The Romans, after all, were probably the first imperial art collectors in the world. We look at Greek art through Roman eyes, in much the same way that most of us are trained to look at Jewish theology with subtly Christian assumptions. We saw this paradox amply illustrated inside the Supreme Court building of the United States.

The trick, then, lies in allowing the Greeks to be Greek *before* we Romanize them, allowing them to narrate themselves in their own terms. Then and only then may we bring that self-narration into dialogue with the way the Romans, among others, came to see the Greeks and learned to tell their story. In this chapter, I suggest that we have a singular and largely unexamined resource for doing precisely this, a book that also brings us to the very heart of the mystery of Greek religion. It is Pausanias's extraordinary second-century *Periêgêsis Hellados,* commonly translated as the *Guide to Greece,* or else as the *Description of Greece.*[6] Reference to this title first appears in a work by Stephanus of Byzantium, the first ancient author to refer to Pausanias's text at all, fully three centuries after its composition. The translation of this title presents us with our first problem. For there was, in Pausanias's own day, a 600-year literary tradition of ethnographic and descriptive writing about trips by sea (*periploi*) and by land (*periêgêseis*).[7] Interest in these genres was inspired first by exploration, then by colonization, and then again by conquest—whether Greek or Roman. I have chosen to refer to Pausanias's text as *A Greek Walkabout,* for the purposes of my analysis.

PAUSANIAS AT OLYMPIA

Surprisingly enough, two out of the ten books in Pausanias's *Walkabout* are dedicated to the region of Eleia, an indistinct corner of the northwestern Peloponnese under titular control of the city-state of Elis. The lion's share of both books is restricted to an exhaustive description of the sanctuary at Olympia. And in a memorable passage at the outset of Book Five, Pausanias tells us why. The first sentence is normally quoted by itself—Sir James Frazer, in fact, makes it the frontispiece for his entire six-volume work, in order to point out that there are indeed "many wonderful things to see in Greece." But the *entire* passage bears citation, and warrants further reflection than it has normally received. It defines Pausanias's *religious* project in a nutshell.

> There are many wonderful (*thaumatos*) things to see and hear about in Greece. But there is more divine care (*ek theou phrontidos*) bestowed upon the rites at Eleusis (*tois Eleusini drômenois*) and the contest at Olympia (*agôni tôi en Olympiai*) than on anything else in the world. (V.10.1)

Olympia and Eleusis: the two most divine sanctuaries in a land already remarkable for its haunted divinity. To this list of especially charged sanctuary-spaces, we should probably add the name of Delphi, but no others.[8]

We may not always know precisely what Pausanias meant by "religion."[9] It is not that kind of term, as we saw in Chapter One; Pausanias, for his part, does not even *have* such a term—but clearly it had something to do, already in the Homeric and Pindaric mind, with articulating those complicated transactions between the divine world and the human one, and the *places* in which this complex dance has been acted out.[10] At Olympia, the premier rituals were presumably designed to map transcendence, the manner in which the hero (or the athlete) can participate in the divine, even if only the attenuated divinity accessible to us, as "creatures of a day." At Eleusis, the reverse is true. Here, the gods are subject to the human and mortal condition. A mother loses her daughter to the underworld. But then, through a rather complicated set of divine negotiations, the daughter is returned for six months out of each year, dooming this family to an annual cycle of grief and loss, followed by fateful reunion. What is clear is that, for Pausanias, "Greek religion" serves to map these very transactions, all of them drawn on a sliding scale of transcendence.

OLYMPIA AND THE QUEST FOR ORIGINS

Pausanias describes Olympia at great length in his Eleian chapters, comprising Books V and VI of *A Greek Walkabout*. This is the single most extensive discussion of a single site in the entire manuscript, comprising fully 20 percent of the total. The only sanctuary that receives anywhere near as much attention is Delphi (X.5.3–32.5). The city of Athens is also described at some length (I.2.1–30.4). Pausanias describes Eleusis in much sketchier terms, in a book devoted to the regions of Attika and Megara (I.36–38).[11] He seems hesitant to speak about it too much, lest he unwittingly reveal aspects of the sacred rites that are supposed to remain mysterious. He does remark offhandedly that the Eleusinian initiate will already know the places that he cannot properly put in print:

> Whoever has seen the rite of Eleusis (*teletên Eleusíni*), or has read through the so-called 'Orphics' (*Orphíka*), already knows what I am talking about. (I.37.4)

He then informs us that a *dream*[12] instructed him not to describe this sanctuary in any detail, a prohibition that is all the more startling when we consider his impressive catalogue of the monuments and temple structures at Olympia.

> The dream (*to te oneiron*) forbade me to write down (*graphein*) the things inside the wall of the sanctuary (*ta de entos tou teichous tou hierou*), since those who have not been initiated (*tois ou telestheisin*) are clearly forbidden to learn about what they have not seen. (I.38.7)

It seems clear that Pausanias was an initiate at Eleusis himself.[13] He was thus one of those who presumably knew more than he was permitted to write about. So what *does* Pausanias describe at Eleusis, if he cannot describe the sites? At Eleusis, Pausanias contents himself with a description of "the way," that 25-mile corridor from Athens to Eleusis, along a well-worn, alternately serious and outrageously sexualized pilgrimage route called the Sacred Way (*Hodos Hiera* [I.36.3]). Most of this route was liberally decorated with monuments of various kinds, actual grave markers (*taphoi*) as well as simpler memorials (*mnêmai*), marking the identity of some notable Atticans of the past: a famous tragic actor named Theodorus here (I.37.3); a student of Aristotle named Theodektus of Phylatos there (I.37.4); a famous healer named Mnesitheos a little further on (I.37.4). There also seem to be tombs of famous kings and warriors, virtually everywhere.

In fact, Pausanias's descriptive account of the Sacred Way to Eleusis is actually *framed by* the story of an ancient war between the kingdoms of Eleusis and that of Athens. This war pitted the Eleusinian king, Eumolpos (who was also high priest at the sacred rite), and his sons, against King Erechtheus of Athens (1.36.4 and 38.1–3).[14] The war seems to have been fought to resolve a dispute about the boundary (*horos*) that separated the land of the Athenians from that of the Eleusinians. And the end result of this conflict is still more interesting: There *is* no clear boundary between Athens and Eleusis but, rather, a somewhat blurry administrative line. After Erechtheus and Eumolpos's son, Immarados, have both been killed in battle, Pausanias tells us:

> This is how they put an end to the war: the Eleusinians were to keep the sacred rite (*tên teletên*) as their own, but in all other matters they were to be incorporated (*katêköous*) into the Athenian state. (1.38.3)

So much, and no more, may he tell us about Eleusis.

Which brings us, at last, to Olympia. While a general pattern of using his sources and displaying his rhetorical skills is evident in all of Pausanias's writings, his long discussion of Olympia has some unique and intriguing added features. In general, Pausanias was interested in Greek antiquity, of course—both in historical terms, as well as in terms of the surviving physical remains. He tended to organize his *Greek Walkabout* by utilizing the major Greek wars as topical benchmarks. So he normally begins by telling us how large a contingent the city in question sent to Troy, then how it lined up in the Persian Wars and the Peloponnesian War, and finally what became of it after the Macedonian (and, only very occasionally, the Roman[15]) conquests. There is plenty of such information to be gathered here, in Eleia.

But the chapters on Olympia are notorious, even among friends of Pausanias, as a jumble of all-too-often discordant facts. We look for an order in the mish-mash, and we often cannot find it.[16] I suspect that one of the problems here is similar to the problem Pausanias faced in Athens, where his descriptions also tend to ramble, even to bog down in places. Pausanias suffers from the embarrassment of riches in such places. There are simply too many monuments, too much information, for him to construct a neat and tidy narrative of the place. The jumble of information is not primarily a mingle-mangle of his own making. In fact, I suspect that if we take the trouble to read Pausanias with some care, we will see that he has actually done a masterful job of cobbling together a coherent account out of a mess of ambient detail. He is especially good at fixing the order of the generations in his accounts (see Figure 3.1). He wants to tell us about local myths and legends, he wants to share what he has learned from his local guides, and he also wants to tell us, in greater detail, what physical remains he has seen himself, and what they mean to his now-practiced traveler's eye. Finally, he smiles, "I rely more than most on the poetry of Homer" (II.31.1). And so he does.

In Olympia, then, there is much with which Pausanias has to contend. There was a superabundance of personal interest stories at the Olympics, then as now. In addition, there was a plethora of local hero cults[17] on the site. The lion's share of Book VI of Pausanias's *Greek Walkabout* will be devoted to telling such (often tall) tales (VI.1.1). But Book V is all monuments and mythology. What I propose to do here is to present this material in a manner hopefully a bit more accessible to the narrative sensibilities of a

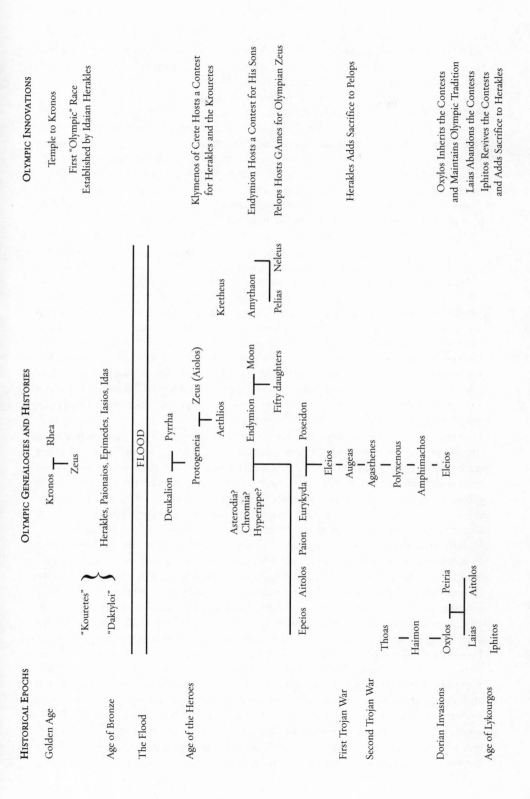

HISTORICAL EPOCHS

- Golden Age
- Age of Bronze
- The Flood
- Age of the Heroes
- First Trojan War
- Second Trojan War
- Dorian Invasions
- Age of Lykourgos

OLYMPIC GENEALOGIES AND HISTORIES

Kronos — Rhea
Zeus

Herakles, Paionaios, Epimedes, Iasios, Idas

"Kouretes"
"Daktyloi"

FLOOD

Deukalion — Pyrrha
Protogeneia — Zeus (Aiolos)
Aethlios
Endymion — Moon
Fifty daughters
Poseidon

Asterodia? / Chromia? / Hyperippe?
Epeios   Aitolos   Paion   Eurykyda
Eleios
Augeas
Agasthenes
Polyxenous
Amphimachos
Eleios

Kretheus
Amythaon
Pelias   Neleus

Thoas
Haimon
Oxylos — Peiria
Laias   Aitolos
Iphitos

OLYMPIC INNOVATIONS

- Temple to Kronos
- First "Olympic" Race Established by Idaian Herakles
- Klymenos of Crete Hosts a Contest for Herakles and the Krouretes
- Endymion Hosts a Contest for His Sons
- Pelops Hosts GAmes for Olympian Zeus
- Herakles Adds Sacrifice to Pelops
- Oxylos Inherits the Contests and Maintains Olympic Tradition
- Laias Abandons the Contests
- Iphitos Revives the Contests and Adds Sacrifice to Herakles

modern audience. Then I will discuss the relevance of Pausanias's achievement to the questions about Greek identity and Greek religion, which are my major preoccupations in this book. There are, as we shall see, some critical and representative insights in these complex chapters of Pausanias's *Greek Walkabout*.

The first surprise to the modern reader of Pausanias is his startling claim that the Greek Olympics are, themselves, a *revival* of older contests. Pierre de Coubertin's Olympic "Revival," to which we will turn in the last chapter, was not the first. Apparently, "Greek" Olympics are *always* a revival. And reconstructing their hidden history takes us back inevitably, so it would seem, to the mythic realm of originary beginnings. "It is the very image of the Platonic process of learning," Roberto Calasso notes; "nothing is new, remembering is all. What is new is the most ancient thing we have."[18]

Let us look, then, at the novelty in Pausanias's ancient musings. *A Greek Walkabout* begins in Eleia with a nod to the regional diversity of the Peloponnese.

> Those Greeks who say that the Peloponnese has five divisions, and no more, will have to admit that both Eleians and Arkadians live in Arkadia, whereas the second division is all Achaian, and the other three are all Dorian. (V.I.I).

The Peloponnese is an "island" of sorts, inhabited by five separate tribes. Why begin this account in this way? It may seem obvious that Pausanias would want to refer in the beginning to the very organizational principles (tribal names, by and large) that have given his book its structure. The four other regions to which he refers (Lakonia, Messenia, Achaia, and Arkadia) each have a book devoted to them; Eleia, in fact, gets two. And yet the unusual ethnic diversity of the borderland between Eleia and Arkadia makes borders and tribal identity a matter of special concern, as it had been once before in Attika.

It is one of the less remarked aspects of the four major panhellenic sanctuaries in the Greek world—Olympia, Delphi, Nemea, and Isthmia[19]—that none of them were cities in the proper sense.[20] They were enormous, often elaborate sanctuaries with a permanent residential community of priests, officiants, and, presumably, groundskeepers. At Olympia, Pausanias tells us that there was a permanent residential body that offered a continuous monthly circuit of vegetarian sacrifices[21] at each altar within the sanctuary (V.13.10–11, and 15.10–12). They also worked assiduously to maintain the sculptures, being especially careful in their treatment of the cryselephantine statue of Zeus carved by Pheidias, still one of the ancient world's greatest wonders (V.11.10–11). Such sanctuaries tended to be governed by a neighboring city: Delphi fell within the orbit of Krisa, until it was taken over by the Amphictionic League; Nemea was in the control of Argos; Isthmia was organized by Corinth.

Olympia, however, was as divided as the ethnic population of the region was: the sanctuary had been a source of repeated contention between the cities of Elis and Pisa (or Pisaia), which vied for control of the contests and the sanctuary over a period of several centuries. As the regional name attests in Pausanias's own day, Elis eventually won out (V.4.7–8 and VI.22.1–4). The site had been significantly rebuilt and reorganized when it fell into Pisatan control in the fifth century,[22] and there was evidence still in Pausanias's own day of the battles that had raged even within the sanctuary itself. Pausanias relates one story that he learned from a sacred guide (literally a cultic "exegete," *exêgêtês*) at Olympia named Aristarchus. Apparently, when the roof of the temple to Hera was subject to some long-overdue repair, the preserved body of a dead soldier in full armor was found in the attic space separating the ceiling from the roof tiles (V.20.4–5 and 27.11). The Eleans had been engaged inside the sacred Olympian Altis in 364 BCE,[23] and had apparently made a last stand on the very rooves of the temples—thus giving the lie to the permanence or inviolate nature of a sacred panhellenic truce in or around these precincts.[24]

Presumably, when Pausanias begins his narrative with such a nod to ethnic regionalism, he means to call this complex historical rivalry to mind. Further reflection shows this not to be the case, however, at least not directly. While Pausanias *is* interested in political history, and uses the same sorts of war lists (V.4.7ff) he uses to describe a number of other sites in his *Greek Walkabout,* his beginning here at Olympia serves another purpose altogether. *His* beginning serves to underline the problem of beginnings, in fact. Pausanias is interested in discussing who the *original* peoples in the region were, and he concludes that here, in the Peloponnese, the truly aboriginal people (*genê autochthones*) were Arkadians and Achaians (V.I.I). The Achaians were later forced west under pressure of Dorian invaders, but the Arkadians have always lived in Arkadia, *ex archês kai es tode,* "from the beginning 'til today" (V.I.2). All the rest, Pausanias notes, is inhabited by later immigrants (*epêlydôn*), most notably at Corinth, which was sacked, looted, and converted into public land (*ager publicus*) by the Roman general, Mummius[25] (V.10.5, VII.15.1–16.10) in 146 BCE,[26] then later reestablished as a Roman colony under Julius Caesar in 44 BCE, and reconstituted under Vespasian in 70–77 CE.[27]

As I have said, it is not politics or military history that concerns Pausanias here at the outset in Eleia; it is the question of origins. He wants to know who has moved where, and when, and occasionally even *why* they did so. He wants to know "how it all began." But he knows that he cannot know this. And so he elects to begin his mythopoetic peregrination in the middle of things, with the first king of Elis, a man named Aethlios, who, significantly, does *not* lend his name to this region. Aethlios was the son of Zeus and Protogeneia, Deukalion's daughter, born shortly after the Flood. And so, almost without our being aware of it, we find ourselves returned once again to the troubled trope of fathers and their renegade sons.

Zeus himself was a son before he was a father, of course, a son who very nearly did not live to sire offspring. For Kronos had received a prophecy (as would Zeus later, in turn[28]) that his own son would supplant him in power. He thus took to the curious practice of ingesting each child after it was born. But Rhea substituted her son for a stone, and left the infant Zeus in the care of the Daktyloi, also called the Kouretes, on Mount Ida in Crete.

This is well enough known, but it is not precisely the story Pausanias tells. Instead, he is on the lookout for origins, hard on the heels of sacred beginnings. He notes that "the most ancient chroniclers" (literally they are called "rememberers," *hoi ta archaiotata mnêmoneuontes*) knew Kronos as "the first king of heaven" (*tên en ouranôi schein basileian prôton*), and that a golden race (*chrysoun genos*) built a temple (*naon*) to him at Olympia (V.7.6). Then the Kouretes came, and the oldest among them, Herakles by name, organized a footrace for his brothers (Paionaios, Epimedes, Iasios, and Idas) there. He crowned the winner (who is not recorded) with a wreath of olive leaves, collected from trees that he himself brought to the region from the mythic northern lands of the Hyperboreans (V.7.7).[29] Now once again, and without our being fully aware of it, we happen on the singular innovation of Olympia[30]: the marrying of athletic contest to religious sacrifice and sanctuary. Its creator is yet another mysterious Cretan, the Idaian Herakles, he who cared for the infant Zeus.

More than this we really cannot say. Herakles has the honor (*doxa*) of being the first to add an *agôn*[31] (it is interesting that Pausanias refers to "the Olympic contest" exclusively in the singular) to a religious sanctuary, and he is also the one who named the place "Olympia" (V.7.9)—no doubt in honor of the upstart Olympians, this later race of gods. Some traditions suggest that these upstarts supplanted their fathers just here, at Olympia, when Zeus defeated Kronos in a wrestling match. Others say that Zeus held contests here as a way of celebrating what was by then already *fait accompli.* This second account then chronicles Apollo's career as an Olympic victor (*Olympíkas níkas*), since he defeated Hermes in a footrace and Ares in a boxing match at the same time (V.7.10).

There is a break at this point in Pausanias's chronicle, corresponding to Deukalion's Flood. Fifty years thereafter, a man named Klymenos returns to Olympia, arriving once again from Crete (where else? V.8.1). He was related to the Idaian Herakles through his father, Kardys, and he contributed the next significant layer to this dizzying Olympian stratigraphy. He hosted the *agônes* at Olympia in honor of Herakles and the other Kouretes, and he erected an altar (*bômon*) for them there. Now we notice still another crucial religious pattern, distinct to Olympia: New ritual contests, new dedications, and new altars—a hero adds all of these things to the vast spiritual encyclopedia called "Olympia." New contests will be added; new altars and temples will be built. You can add to the Olympics easily enough (V.8.5), but it is infinitely harder to subtract from them (although this *has* been done, rarely, V.9.1). So the fathers are supplanted, perhaps inevitably in time, but they are commemorated long after they are gone. Pausanias, one cannot help feeling, is especially moved by that.

Despite Pausanias's obvious interest in Olympic religion, politics has an inescapable role to play as well. Since Olympia and Delphi were such early and prestigious panhellenic sanctuaries, they became magnets that attracted the cultural attentions and the political munificence of every subsequent age. A hero would quite naturally strive to leave a mark on the sanctuary, or in the contests, and customarily in both: in the Altis, as well as in the Stadium. Host the contests, add new events, build onto the sanctuary: This religio-cultic *bricolage* quite literally explains how the sanctuary at Olympia came to comprise the vast tangle of images it had become in Pausanias's day.

It evolved in stops and starts. There was a temple to Kronos at Olympia already in the Golden Age (V.7.6). Klymenos erected an altar to Idaian Herakles and the other Kouretes (V.8.1). Pelops founded the first Peloponnesian temple to Hermes there (V.1.7). Herakles added an altar to Pelops (V.13.1–2). Oxylos added sacrificial altars both to Augeas (V.4.2) as well as to his ill-omened son, Aitolos (V.4.4). And Iphitos added an altar to Herakles (V.4.6). There is even a strange-seeming ritual conducted by women at sundown on the first day in honor of Achilles, a *drôsis* that is framed as a ritual lament (VI.23.2–3).[32] It just goes on like that. And paradoxically, there are also times when the sanctuary can grind to a halt, stopping (at least potentially) for good. This is presumably what happened after the Flood.

What they did at Olympia after the Flood precisely mirrored what had been done before. There is another footrace run among brothers: Endymion, Zeus's grandson, usurped the Elean crown from Klymenos, and *he* hosted a footrace among his own sons for the rights of inheritance. His eldest son, Epeios, won this race, and thus the prize of the Elean kingdom, but his reign was short-lived. While the region was called "Epeia" for a time, it ultimately came to be named after his nephew, instead

(V.1.4). For Epeios was usurped by Pelops, who dedicated the Olympic contests to Zeus for the first time, and hosted them on a grander scale (*axiologôtata*) than anyone had ever seen before (V.8.2). Still, Pelops's dynasty was never firmly established, either at Elis or Olympia; he had initially seized control of Pisa, not Elis (V.1.6–7).[33] And his sons scattered all over the Peloponnese, a region that is for this very reason known euphemistically as "Pelops's Isle." It was a cousin of Endymion, Amythaon by name, who hosted the Olympian contests next, followed by two brothers, Pelias and Neleus, who hosted them together (*en koinôi*). Then the kingdom of Elis returned to Endymion's line, in the guise of his daughter Eurykyda's son, Eleios (allegedly fathered by Poseidon, although Pausanias seems to doubt the tale, V.1.6–8). Augeas then reigned in his father's stead, but Herakles hosted the contests when he invaded Augeas's territory (during that strange period in which he also violated the Sacred Corinthian Truce).

Four generations and two Trojan wars later, Endymion's great-great-great-great-great grandson, yet another man named Eleios, was king at Elis. And now we can see why Pausanias began his account with a nod to Greek regionalism and concluded it with the Dorian invasion (itself an ironic model for the later Roman expulsion of these same Dorians, in Pausanias's judgment). His Elean Walkabout doubles back on itself here, for it was these same Dorians who killed the Olympics. It was in Eleios's day that the Dorians invaded the Peloponnese, and they rewarded a local informant who had assisted them with the kingdom of Elis. This upstart king, Oxylos, maintained the Olympic traditions he inherited, down to the very details of the sacrifice. All the Homeric heroes were commemorated, even Aeneas (V.4.2), as were local heroes like Pelops and Aitolos (V.4.4). Then "a new king came to [Elis] who did not know,"[34] and the Olympic contest died out. Oxylos's son, Laias, failed to host the contests, and thus they were abandoned, forgotten in time.

But not forgotten forever. In the age of Lykourgos of Sparta, Iphitos had control of both Elis and the sanctuary of Olympia. In his times, the greater part of Greece (*malista tês Hellados*) was riven by civil wars (*hypo emphyliôn staseôn*) and by plague (*hypo nosou loimôdous* [V.4.6]). Iphitos consulted the oracle at Delphi to determine the cause; the Pythia ordered Iphitos and the Eleans to take charge of reviving the Olympic contest (*tôn Olympikôn agôna ananeôsasthai* [V.4.6]). And so they did.

But by now, Olympia was a tangle of altars, a confusion of names, and a vast complex of competing genealogies. This is the material through which Pausanias was forced to wade and sift. Olympia is an easy place in which to be confused, just as Greece is an easy place in which to feel lost. Olympia's ritual structure seems especially easy to forget. And that, I think, is the real message of Pausanias's *Greek Walkabout* at Olympia. Like Herodotus, he has a unique horror of people or of things being lost. "When Iphitos revived the contest," he tells us,

> forgetfulness of the ancient past (*tôn archaiôn lêthê*) already reigned. The past would be recalled (*es hypomnêsin*) only a little at a time (*kat' oligon*) and whenever the people remembered something (*anamnêstheien*) they would reestablish it as a part of the contest (*epoiounto tôi agôni prosthêtên*). (V.8.5)

Pausanias goes on to catalogue the history of the Olympic contests in the historical era of actual Elean record-keeping, and he brings this account all the way up to his own day (V.8.6–9.6). Next, he turns to a description of the monuments themselves, those "wonderful things to see," and after that, to a discussion of the heroes and their memorials. The site of Olympia is itself one massive memorial, an apt and moving miscellany of all the myths, and all the heroes, and all the wars, and especially all the gods, of Greece.

DISCERNING PAUSANIAS

Pausanias, like the past he is so intent on describing, remains something of a mystery to us. He may have been a medical doctor; he may have been a Homerist; he may well have been both. He may or may not have been a Roman citizen (VIII.43.5–6); he was surely wealthy.[35] His work has come to be referred to as "the Bible of Greek Archaeology"—and so, in much contemporary practice, it is. What we know about its author is limited almost exclusively to the sparing personal references he makes in *A Greek Walkabout*. We do not know precisely why he wrote, nor is it clear who his intended audience would have been. It is especially unclear to me why this manuscript—which, seasoned as it is with unforgettable stories and wonderfully astute casual observations, is also desert-dry in places—why *this* text has survived when so many other works in similarly geographical and descriptive genres have not. Through my studies, I have gradually acquired a very special fondness for Pausanias's book. I have learned to admire his uncanny skill as a cobbler of ancient myths, as well as his quieter, and largely unsung, gifts as a storyteller when he wishes to be one.[36] By coming to terms more consciously with *why* I admire Pausanias and his work, I have identified what makes him arguably the most significant single figure with whom I deal in this book. For it was Pausanias, in my judgment, and people who thought like him, who helped turn "Greek" into a "religion."

I cannot rest content with singing Pausanias's praises in this chapter, nor with explaining what I think he accomplished through his lengthy descriptions of Eleia. Instead, I want to underline four aspects of his craft that I believe clearly demonstrate the way in which these two terms—"Greece" and "religion"—seem to be in play in an entirely new way. Pausanias is fairly late as "classical" writers go, writing more than half a millennium after Socrates grappled with the youth of Athens in his own erotic, elenchic, and peculiarly pious way. Pausanias is a "Greek," but he is not "from Greece," at least not from Socrates's or Plato's Greece—and that, I suspect, provides us with one significant key to discerning the method in his madness. Pausanias was a fairly well-traveled writer, as so many literary and philosophical figures of the Hellenistic and Roman era were, but traveling to Greece was special for him. The reason is that Pausanias was especially interested in religion, a complex kind of religiosity that he feared was on the way out in his own day. This fear he shares with the Romantics, with the founders of modern Olympism, not to mention with a great many contemporary spiritual questers in North America in our own day.

"Religion" and "Greece" are thus linked in Pausanias's mental economy with singular profit: "Greece" seems to be a singularly "religious" place, at least as Pausanias understood these terms. And so—not surprisingly, at this point in this book—I want to suggest that by highlighting these two terms—"Greece" and "religion"—we can make fresh sense of what Pausanias accomplished in *A Greek Walkabout*. Doing so turns this rather dry and encyclopedic ancient author into a source of nearly endless fascination. Let me return to my four initial observations about him, in order to begin to explain why.

He was a comparatively late "Greek" writer, fully at home in the pan-Mediterranean culture of the Roman imperium.

Pausanias composed his *Greek Walkabout* at the height of a literary movement known to Classicists as the "Second Sophistic."[37] As a narrow, technical term, this refers to a body of writings produced in the imperial Roman period—roughly speaking, from the death of Augustus in 14 CE to the death of Marcus Aurelius in 180 CE. In many ways, the reign of Hadrian (118–138 CE) represents the crest of this cultural wave.[38] Certainly the Villa whose construction he supervised so carefully after laying its foundation in 130 CE well illustrates the taste[39]: It is a massive and confusing amalgamation of all the various artistic styles Hadrian has learned to admire from the various eastern regions of his vast empire. It is a physical testimony to a then-emerging, and imperially sanctioned, elite cultural taste.

The writers in this movement were unusually self-conscious stylists who deliberately aped the rhetorical style, and even the dialect, of the fifth-century Attic rhetoricians. The very complexity of the Attic dialect contributed to the exclusivity of the movement. Deliberate antiquarians, these writers placed themselves within the tradition of the selfsame sophistic culture that was of such concern to Plato throughout his own writerly career. These sophists-at-one-remove, however, were primarily citizens of the eastern provinces of the Roman Empire, writing in Greek and deliberately refashioning both their Greek and their Greekness for a Roman (which is to say, a largely non-Greek) age.

In this narrower sense, Pausanias is hardly representative of the Second Sophistic.[40] But this literature, so much of it so odd-seeming to modern sensibilities and modern literary tastes, is representative of a far more widespread aesthetic development, one that long survives the technical end of the Second Sophistic, and one that is of special relevance to understanding Pausanias's project. Pausanias, I suggest, is fully participant in this "Sophistic" aesthetic, one best characterized as a sort of encyclopedic,[41] collector's taste. This taste is alive and well in the late third century, long after Pausanias, and the self-styled Second Sophists, are gone. Christians themselves, some of them at any rate, will be heir to this taste as well.

Roman writers—both in Latin *and* in Greek—strove to display their virtuosity and impressive command of a half-millennial literary and artistic Mediterranean inheritance. Many of these authors are probably also responsible for creating the literary culture in which the term "Greco-Roman" begins to make a kind of sense. Many of them strove explicitly, and at length, to compare-and-contrast the vagaries of Greek and Latin cultural history.

This is perhaps clearest in Plutarch of Chaironea (c. 47–120 CE) who, among countless topics examined in essay form, composed a fascinating set of *Parallel Lives* (*Bíoi Parallêloi*) in which biographies of notable political and military figures from Greek and from Roman history are presented in pairs and told in tandem. Diogenes Laertius (whom I assume to be a citizen of the early-to-mid-third century) also worked in the popular genre of biography, as a way to represent philosophical, rather than historical, matters. His *Lives of the Philosophers* (*Bíôn kai Gnômôn tôn en Philosophía*) devotes short chapters to the biographies of nearly everyone of importance from Thales to Epicurus, a text which is less interesting for the skepticism of its philosophical approach than for the delight it displays in apothegmatic storytelling.

Philostratus's *Lives of the Sophists* (*Bíoi Sophistôn*), from which we get the term "Second Sophistic,"[42] is a strikingly similar document written in this same period, somewhere between 230 and 238 CE. Aelian (Claudius Aelianus, c. 170–235 CE), who was reputed to be a marvelous exemplar of the simple and pure Attic style, was also an obsessive collector. Two books, *The Characteristics of Animals* (*Zôion Idiotêtos*) and *Various Histories* (*Poikilê Histôria*) are vast collections of tidbits and truisms culled from various authors. Strabo of Pontus (c. 63 BCE–21 CE) is a fascinating early character for the way in which his *Geography* attempts to do Greek cartographic speculation one better, in light of subsequent Roman conquests and the preeminence of a more cosmopolitan Stoic worldview. The question for Strabo is, at least in part, the manner in which the empire's expansion has confirmed or disconfirmed an older Greek picture of the world. And Vitruvius, an architect and military engineer under the Triumvirate, and later under Augustus, has left us a fascinating compendium, *De Architectura,* which summarizes the Classical and post-Classical inheritance in the plastic arts—cataloguing the materials, the decorative styles, and various strategies of city planning in one massive comparative endeavor. Interestingly, he is the only author I have mentioned thus far who wrote in Latin.

To this list many other names might easily be added,[43] not least of them the Latin-speaking Juvenal and the Greek-speaking Lucian, whom I mentioned at the outset of this chapter. But two Greek authors in particular represent this curious kind of hybridism best—the manic obsession with literary minutiae, with rhetorical collections, and their oddly slapdash manner of presentation. It is not every age that recognizes the miscellany as a legitimate genre, much less a popular one. The first of these collectors is Athenaeus of Naucratis (fl. c. 200 CE) whose sole surviving work, *Witty Table-Talk* (*Deipnosophistai*) uses the loose artistic pretense of a large banquet setting to frame longish discussions on various topics, ranging from literature and philosophy, to medicine, to law, all of them richly supported with quotations from no fewer than 1250 ancient authors. Dense and self-important, the book is nonetheless a gold mine of classical allusions and bibliography.

The second of these authors is Pausanias, and his *Greek Walkabout* is as much of an oddball genre as Athenaeus's *Table-talk*. But it is a piece of the same aesthetic, a massive encyclopedic collection of the still vaster Hellenic inheritance. To be sure, these men were not the first such encyclopediasts. Pindar, for his part, was every bit as invested in the project of collecting various mythologies as Pausanias proves to be. But there is something else at work in Athenaeus and Pausanias, something that compels them to set it all down, as if in horror that something from the past might be lost. Antiquarians they may be, but Pausanias's commitments and concerns run far deeper than this. In a world where sons supplant fathers as an act of quirky piety, it is important for someone to commit the lost fathers' legacy to print. In his own age, where Roman sons have supplanted their Greek fathers, Pausanias makes a point of erecting a literary memorial to these forlorn Hellenic fathers. And the form that this memorial will take is a lengthy discursive presentation, for the most part, of the ancient memorials themselves.

Pausanias was not from "Greece," but he was still "a Greek."

To be sure, the complex relationship of a person and a place, between geography and the construction of that allegedly modern concept we call an "identity," is a fraught one. Pausanias is not "from Greece," at least not in the way he appears to conceive of *Hellas*. Pausanias was a Roman citizen from Asia Minor, presumably born or else raised near Mount Sipylos, possibly in the neighboring city of Magnesia (I.21.5; II.22.4; V.13.7; VII.24.7; VIII.2.5–7 and 8.10).[44] This makes him a Greek-speaking citizen of the eastern Roman Empire, as were the majority of the figures whom I mentioned in connection to the Second Sophistic. *A Greek Walkabout* is actually an exhaustive account of travel on the Greek *mainland.* Pausanias never does more than mention the Hellenic coast of Asia Minor in passing, his own home included, and he is virtually silent about the Greek islands—with the notable exception of Aegina (II.29.2–30.5), to which I will turn in the eighth chapter, and a longish digression about Sardinia (X.17.1–7) included, he says, "because this is an island the Greeks (*hoi Hellênes*) know virtually nothing about" (X.17.13).[45] Delos is largely ruined in his own day, as he explains (III.23.2–6; VIII.33.2), and he says not one word about Crete, except when it relates to a mainland story he is telling—as was notably the case at Olympia.

Pausanias's "Greece," then, is a matter of the mainland,[46] comprising the entire Peloponnese (Lakonia [Book III], Arkadia [Book VIII], Messenia [Book IV], Eleia [Books V–VI], Achaia [Book VII]), and the Argolid (Book II), as well as the northern regions of Boeotia (Book IX), Phokis (Book X), and Attica (Book I).[47] No islands, no mention of Crete, and little about former Greek colonies whether to the east, west, or south. Pausanias's *Periêgêsis* begins, in fact, with the image of landfall on the mainland, in Athens' Piraeus harbor, and "mainland" is the very first word in the *Walkabout:*

> On the Greek mainland (*tês êpeirou tês Hellênikês*) facing the Cycladic islands and the Aegean Sea, the promontory (*akra*) of Sunium juts out from the land of Attika. (I.1.1)

Sunium . . . the mines at Laurium . . . the Island of Patroclus . . . the Piraeus Harbor . . . we are seeing what Pausanias sees, presumably, as he makes his own landfall here, in "Greece."

We do not know where he has come from, where he has been, nor why he has come here. Like Plato, he begins his description of this journey in the middle of it—with his arrival at Athens. What we can say is that Pausanias's Greece, while rather truncated from our perspective, also embodies the real cultural heartland, housing the essential (and always classical) spirit of the place.[48] Speaking in terms of the most important *sanctuaries* in Pausanias's own day—these being Eleusis and Olympia, and most likely Delphi as well—*A Greek Walkabout* does indeed serve to map out the essential lineaments of Greek religion. This is a description of the most important regions in Greece, from a *religious* perspective. Now, in religious terms, pilgrimages are often framed as returns to some imagined center. Delphi is considered the *omphalos,* the center of the earth, for instance, on this religionist's map (X.16.2).[49] Pausanias's pilgrimage—for such it surely was in his own mind[50]—is framed as a pilgrimage to the center, animated by some of the same free-floating spirituality I mentioned earlier. I will return to this idea many times in this book.

Pausanias was widely traveled, but "Greece" was somehow special to him.

Pausanias was clearly well-educated and well-versed in Greek literature over a period of centuries. He also seems to have been relatively well-traveled: He is familiar, at a minimum, with Egypt (I.42.3) and the Euphrates (X.29.4), Israel (V.7.4–6) and Italy (V.12.3, 6)—as well as with Asia Minor and Greece, of course.[51] He makes a point of telling us that he has been to Roman Palestine fairly early in his discussion of

Olympia. The point is made in connection with the Alpheios River, "a very great river in its volume of water, and the very sweetest (*hêdiston*) to look upon" (V.7.1). Olympia was famous in antiquity for being green, shady, and well-watered—not entirely unlike its physical qualities today, although the Alpheios is gone. Pausanias attributes this to the fact that seven independent rivers combine to make up the flow of it (V.7.1–2), but then he passes immediately on to the fabulous realm of myth. Alpheios, it seems, was a huntsman who fell in love with Arethusa. She, unwilling to marry, crossed over to the island of Ortygia, then metamorphosed into a spring of water. In response, Alpheios was also transformed by *erôs*, then crossed the Ionian Sea in order to mingle his waters with hers. "I cannot disbelieve this story," Pausanias concludes, "knowing as I do that the god in Delphi confirms (*homologounta*) it" (V.7.3).[52]

Pausanias may not disbelieve the story, but he is at pains to explain it. For here we have a river running out to sea, yet miraculously maintaining its integrity over many miles of underwater passage. To be sure, one can do almost anything on account of love (*hypo tou erotos*); the Alpheios River is famous throughout Greece for this (V.7.2). But Pausanias lives in an age of excited exploration, and his own traveler's experience lends credibility to the tale. He has been to Egypt, although he has not been all the way up the Nile past the Ethiopian city of Meroë. But he has spoken to people who have been, and they assure him that the Nile flows through a large lake there, maintaining the integrity of its waters throughout its subterranean journey (V.7.4).

Pausanias has also seen the same thing himself, a river that disappears mysteriously into the earth. This is in the Jewish country, where he has traveled extensively.[53]

> The Jordan River, in the land of the Hebrews (*en de têi gêi potamon têi Hebraiôn Iardanon*), which I have seen myself, passes through a lake called Tiberias, and then it passes into still another one called the Dead Sea (*Thalassan Nekran*), into which it disappears altogether. (V.7.4)[54]

This is remarkable. It means that Pausanias must have traveled pretty extensively in Judea, where Hadrian had crushed a bruising revolt in Pausanias's own lifetime (132–135 CE). That event is also much on our traveler's mind.

> In my own times, the Emperor Hadrian was profoundly committed to honoring the divine (*es to theion timês*) as well as to ruling with an eye out for the happiness (*es eudaimonian*) of all his various subjects. He made no war voluntarily, but he did reduce the Hebrews who live beyond Syria when they rebelled. And as for the sanctuaries of the gods (*theôn hiera*), he built some of them up from the beginning and adorned others which already existed. He gave many gifts to the cities in Greece, and in some cases to barbarian cities as well. All of this beneficence is duly inscribed in the sanctuary to all the gods in Athens (*estin hoi panta gegrammena Athênêisin en tôi koinôi tôn theôn hierôi*). (I.5.5)[55]

If Pausanias composed his *Greek Walkabout* roughly between 150 and 180 CE (or some portion thereof), which seems likely, then this suggests that he made it a point to travel the length and breadth of the eastern Roman Empire in its post-Hadrianic heyday: from Judaea (Israel) to Achaia (Greece), and then all the way to Italy. He knows about Jews at first hand. He never so much as mentions Christianity, although it is scarcely plausible to assume that he never encountered it, traveling as widely in Judea and in Corinthia as he did. Pausanias knew about Jews, and perhaps Christians, about Egyptians and Italians and Greeks, but he took the time to write a book about "Greeks." Mainland Greece, I am suggesting, had become a point of pilgrimage to him,[56] in a way that Israel or Italy never would or could have been. We are confronted with what has proven to be a recurrent Mediterranean question: Why Greece? With Pausanias, we begin to discern the contours of a possible answer.

Pausanias was deeply interested in religion, that body of mythopoetic beliefs and stories—but especially the practices—which were uniquely at home in "Greece." These are, in many cases, the selfsame stories with which we saw Socrates struggling in the last chapter. The *practices,* however, remain unchanged.

The traditional way of reading Pausanias in the nineteenth century was to view him as working in a recognizably modern genre, that of the literary travel guide. Pausanias becomes a sort of "Greek Baedeker," on this view. This seems to have been Frazer's view of Pausanias, up to a point. And certainly there are modern archaeologists who continue to use him in this fashion—often with dramatic results, most notably at Olympia itself. When Pausanias describes a site in detail, he often walks the attentive reader over the remains in the precise order in which he viewed them: We are moving, then, from pilgrimage, to traveler's diary, to published account, in something like a straight line. The well-known Praxitelean statue of Hermes holding the infant Dionysus, housed now in the National Museum at Olympia,[57] was uncovered by German excavators in 1877, *precisely* in the corner where Pausanias mentioned having seen it, himself (V.17.3).[58]

But there is something else in Pausanias, a somber sense of what Greece has lost, and a lingering melancholy embodied nowhere more poignantly than in ancient ruins that were ruins in his own day, the sort of thing that would so move the Romantics during their own, considerably later, Greek sojourns.[59] It has something to do with his interest in origins, and something to do with the vagaries of time. After Olympia, when he comes finally to Megalopolis, the ruins there inspire Pausanias to one of his more memorable meditations on the transience of all human endeavor.

Megalopolis was founded with the greatest enthusiasm (*prothymia*) during the political reorganization of the Arkadians and with the greatest hope of all the Greeks (*tôn Hellênôn elpisin*), but now all of its ancient glory (*eudaimonian tên archaian*) is gone, and most of the city is in ruins (*ereipia*). This causes me no great surprise (*thauma*), since the divine (*to daimonion*) always desires to make something new.[60] Similarly, all things—the strong (*echyra*) and the weak (*asthenê*), things at their beginning and at their end (*ginomena te kai hoposa*)—are transformed by chance (*tên tychên*), and led by strong necessity (*ischyras anankês*) wherever she wishes them to go. (VIII.33.1–2)[61]

Pausanias cites several examples of the greatest cities of antiquity to prove his point: Agamemnon's Mycenae, Assyrian Nineveh, Boeotian Thebes, Egyptian Thebes, Minyan Orchomenos, Delos, Babylon, Tiryns—all, now, in ruins. "God (*ho daimôn*) has reduced all of these places to nothing (*mêden*)" (VIII.33.3). "That is how temporary (*proskaira*) human matters really are," Pausanias grimly concludes, "none of them really strong (*echyra*) at all" (VIII.34.1). New cities, he suggests, are forever supplanting the faded glory of the past: Egyptian Alexandria and Syrian Seleucis are the "modern" cities he troubles to mention. But of course lying behind all of this—silent and largely unnoticed—is Rome herself.

It is easy to read the *political* message in all of this—even Rome may not claim an eternity for herself—but there is a *religious* message here as well. "The collapse of ancient religion or some deeper collapse was the unspoken object of [all Pausanias's] studies."[62] One gets a taste of this especially here in Book VIII, the one Pausanias dedicated to Arkadia, that primitive and isolated region well to the interior of the Peloponnese—the one with which he began his Olympic musings, the same region that Vergil helped turn into an idyll, in Rome, in the literary generation just prior to Pausanias's own.

> For the men of old were the guests (*xenoi*) of the gods, and sat at table with them (*homotrapezoi*), on account of their justice and deep reverence (*hypo díkaiosynês kai eusebeías*). Honor (*tímê*) was bestowed upon the good (*agathoís*) by the gods themselves, and wrath (*orgê*) rained down upon the unjust (*adíkêsasin*). In those days, mortals were even transformed into gods, some of whom have honor (*gera*) paid to them even still. . . . But now, in my own day and age (*ep' emou de*)—since evil (*kakía*) has spread over the entire earth and penetrated every city—no mortal is ever transformed into a god, except in the fawning words bestowed upon despots, and the punishment of the gods is invisible, coming upon people only after their deaths. (VIII.2.4–5)[63]

This is all a rather far cry from the panegyric to Hadrianic piety we met earlier. But then, these Arkadian musings took place well *after* Pausanias's enthusiastic visit to Olympia. Arkadia made a Romantic of Pausanias, as it would many a subsequent Greek traveler.

ROMANTICS, ANCIENT AND MODERN

So how did it all begin? And why did it begin in this way rather than in some other? Pausanias cannot answer such questions. He knows that he cannot, makes this fact a crucial piece of his mythological sensibility. I am no longer convinced that he even *wants* to know, really. Rather, he knew that "[s]tories never live alone: they are branches of a family that we have to trace back, and forward."[64] And in that tracing, the subtle fingering of the still subtler lineaments of Greek mythology and archaeology, one never reaches a firm conclusion. We cannot return to origins; we cannot discern the meaning of the end.

How, then, did it all begin? At Olympia, the archaeological record suggests that religious activity began there sometime around 1000 BCE. Olympia was not a Bronze Age sanctuary, despite early German archaeologists' successive desires to see it as one.[65] And the religious *sanctuary* at Olympia predates the athletic cult now so indelibly linked to the place by fully 200 years.[66] Yet it was precisely that linkage—of the Stadium to the Altis, of *agôn* and *drômenos* to ritual sacrifice—which transformed Olympia, along with Delphi and Eleusis, into the premier pilgrimage sites of the ancient Greek-speaking world.

But these are scientific dabblings. And the answer to a question posed by the Romantic quest for origins ultimately cannot be a scientific one. Archaeology is a decidedly Romantic kind of "science," so it suits my purposes well. Pausanias was familiar with the happenstance ancient phenomenon of rescue excavation (V.20.8–9), and he was eager enough to engage in his own casual forms of rationalization and demythologizing. Yet he is just as clear about those myths it would *never* do to question, and those sanctuaries it would never do to dishonor. He is neither a scientist nor an archaeologist, in the final analysis, despite many modern readers' desires to read him as one. He knows that there is no science of religion, just as he knows that there is no cartography of the human soul.

What there is, is a body of myth—and ritual, and pilgrimage, and an almost dizzying sense of historical place. So, how did this all begin? Arguably Pausanias's greatest contemporary contribution lies in the way he can turn the kaleidoscope of our perception on the nature of that question. He does not ask *how* it all began, but *where*. He seems quite convinced that the answer to this latter question is "Greece," and he attends especially to the material culture of ancient religion in making his case. His goal, as he announces it at the outset of *A Greek Walkabout*, is to describe *ta panta Hellēnika*, "all things Greek" (I.26.4), and his manner of doing so is to focus our attention on temples, sanctuaries, and holy sites, those physical remains in which traces of ancient myth may still be discerned. In his own mental-mythical topography, all roads lead back to Greece.

And yet the pilgrimage Pausanias made to Greece, the one he writes about in such loving detail, does not and cannot *end* there. For myth does not, and cannot, stand still. One of the most surprising features of Greek myth to us is its fluidity, the way it pushes us inescapably away from the very center toward which it draws us. How did Olympia "begin?" Or rather, *where* did it begin? Oddly enough, it all began in Crete, which, according to the way Pausanias sets up his *Greek Walkabout*, is not even a part of "Greece." The Olympic *agôn* began decisively in Crete, under the aegis of Zeus and the Idaian Herakles. This confirms a far wider Classical and post-Classical Greek perception—namely, that a great deal of mainland religion and culture derived from Cretan archetypes. "Crete, with its hundred cities and not a single defensive wall around them,"[67] was believed to be the great Greek innovator, home to the invention of written language, of law, of the Daedalean statues we met in the previous chapter (and will meet again many times), as well as of that mysterious miscellany we have learned to think of as "religion." *Greek* religion.

Much has been made of the nineteenth century's obsession with the question of origins—more specifically, the broadly Romantic interest in originary peoples, originary language, originary religion. Both the disciplines of Classics and of Comparative Religion were a product, in part, of this scholarly and spiritual aspiration.[68] They earned their place at the curricular table first in the reorganized scholastic program at the University of Berlin in 1809,[69] and they served a complex purpose there. Not the least of these was the task of underwriting modern national identity-formation. New nation-states (and Germany, like Italy, was not unified until 1870–1871) in search of cultural and ethnic self-definition required new narratives, of which the most determinative proved to be Hegel's.[70] His categories continue to be the ones we use to orient ourselves within most standard "western civilization" courses, and they provide the easiest conceptual frame for this book's narrative, too: from Greece, through Rome, to Europe. There is, of course, a *temporal* frame that accompanies this spatial one: from Classical, to Hellenistic, to Roman, to Late Antique, to Medieval, to Renaissance, to Reformation, to Enlightenment, to Romantic (if not also on to the Modern and the Postmodern).[71]

These Hegelian categories are not wrong, any more than Greco-Roman categories are wrong, but they do warrant more careful examination. By underlining the place of Greece, and of religion, in the Romantics' global narratives, I think that we may see some surprising implications in the sorts of stories they were then in the habit of telling themselves. Mapping our shifting moral and mental landscape is one of the chief purposes of this book.

As I have tried to show here, Pausanias is deliberately asking a question he knows he cannot answer: How did it all begin? It seems fair to say that Greek religion is built on the premise that this question is unanswerable, that the quest it places before us is inevitably an unfinished one.[72] I can think of no Greek text that makes so bold as to begin "in the beginning." Greek texts rest content with beginning in the middle—like Plato, like Pausanias. There is a famous Jewish text which begins in this way: b'reshit, "in the beginning." We know it by its Greek name, as *Genesis*.[73] And there is a Christian text that also presumes to begin in much the same way: *en archê*, "in the beginning." We know this one by another Greek name, and a proper name at that, as *John*.

Too much has been made, I think, of the seismic discontinuities that take us from the late pagan world of Pausanias to the Christian world of Constantine, and of imperial Christianity. Differences there surely were. The pedagogical challenge before us is to mark the simultaneous continuity-*and*-discontinuity in Mediterranean cultures across those tumultuous second-to-fourth centuries CE, when the battle between "paganism" and "orthodoxy" was joined most dramatically. To that complex debate, and a crucial moment in that ill-serviced historical era, I turn in the next chapter.

CHAPTER FOUR

The Short Pagan Career of Julian, the Apostate

HELLENISM AS CULTURE

*One question arose before any other and after any other: that of definitively transforming the **rta**—the connection between heaven and earth that makes life possible and gives it order. It had all started one day when the gods, perhaps weary of the dense, opaque anguish of the primordial chaos, expressed a profound desire: "How could these worlds of ours become farther apart from one another? How could there be more space for us?* . . . *And later for human beings.* . . . *[T]here was no longer any point in discussing the issue; indeed, no one even remembered it clearly. But all the same, there was an urgent need to resolve once and for all a family matter which in fact dated back to the **rta**: the matter of legitimizing legitimacy as the **rta**'s heir. Even law proved itself a troublesome topic.*

—Roberto Calasso, *The Ruin of Kasch*, 2

Why then, o gods and spirits, did you not will it so? . . . *Did he not raise altars? Did he not build temples? Did he not serve with all due magnanimity the gods and heroes, the ether and the heavens, the earth and sea, the fountains and rivers?* . . . *Did he not restore to health a world which had come to the brink of death?*

—Libanius, *Epitaph for Julian* 18.281

PRELIMINARIES

If, as I suggested in the last chapter, "Greek" was originally a *Greek* name which was granted a second and much longer life by the Romans, then "pagan" is a *Latin* term that became, at some as yet indeterminate point, virtually a Latin *translation* for the name of "Greek." The term originally derived from the late Latin word *pagus,* which refers to a village or rural district. Thus the term *paganus* seems to refer to a rural villager or peasant—the religious equivalent of a country-bumpkin, perhaps, despite how odd this must necessarily sound to the student of classical religions today. Worship of the Greek Olympians came eventually to be seen as the "folk religion" of the countryside, a throwback to a more "primitive" way of thinking about and worshipping the divine. This selfsame terminology was invented, then later deployed, by *Christianized* Romans in that vast complex of debates throughout the fourth century about the relative spiritual status of the traditional religion of the empire *vis à vis* its comparatively latecoming eastern rival: Orthodox (and not-so-orthodox) Christianity.

We meet an intriguing reference to this intellectual development already in the work of the presbyter, Orosius, a student of both Augustine and Jerome who originally hailed from Braga in latter-day Portugal, but who fled the Iberian peninsula in the face of the Vandal invasions of 414 CE. His *Historiae adversus paganos,* compiled in seven books in roughly 416–417 CE, lays this issue out quite clearly in its preface: *Ex locorum agrestium conpitis et pagis pagani vocantur;* "they are called 'pagans' (*pagani*) because they live in the countryside (*pagis*) and in other rustic settings."[1] We have returned yet again to a world in which upstart sons supplant their fathers; the suggestion seems to be that, while the urban centers of the empire have been successfully Christianized in Orosius's day, putting away the false religion of their fathers, the rural outback continues to flirt with the polytheistic practices of the ancestors. They are consistently cultural *practices,* rather than dogmas, which were emphasized in this period, as will be amply illustrated in this chapter.

I want to begin by puzzling over that name, "pagan," what it was intended to mean initially, and what it has come to mean over time. And in order to do so, I will need to puzzle over *another* name as well. It has been a commonplace, at least since the Romantic Era, to speak of "the ancients and the moderns"—not, to be sure, as if they were the *same* thing, but rather to point out how very *different* the ancient era, and its cultural assumptions, allegedly was from our own.

Some turned to the ancients in order to illuminate the vast cultural superiority of the moderns. They were evolutionists of a sort, progressivists in many cases, best symbolized in the grand tradition of Victorian anthropology and ethnography of which Sir James Frazer (whose edition of Pausanias we met in the last chapter) is amply representative.[2]

But in a previous generation, well before the Victorian event, the Romantics had turned to their fictions of antiquity for access to certain subtler truths, ancient insights, and attitudes that the "modern" age had allegedly lost. They believed in decadence more than they did in progress. I will have a great deal more to say about the lingering grip of such Romantic nostalgia on a variety of modern disciplines, from Classics to Comparative Religion, in the final three chapters of this book.[3]

What is missing from an historical narrative that takes us from the ancients to the moderns is enormous and telling. It is important to keep in mind that this *is* a narrative, with all of the dangers of distortion and misappropriation that this entails, as we saw in the first chapter. What is most conspicuously absent from this narrative framework is that enormous swath of temporal territory that stands *in between* antiquity and modernity, a period scholars commonly call "Late Antiquity" (the paradox of being simultaneously "late" and "ancient" surely bears noting). Missing, too, are what we call the "Dark Ages" (darker by far to us than to their inhabitants, to be sure), and the "Middle Ages" (in the middle of *what,* we should want to know?), and the "Renaissance" (what, we ought also to be in the habit of asking, had allegedly been reborn?). Given the interests of this book—namely, in "religion" and "the Greeks," which is to say, that wide-ranging arc of religiosity that spans a

vast divide between the ancients *and* the moderns—one obvious reason for this surprising elision of the period in between antiquity and the modern is precisely the
existence of a phenomenon that has never been satisfactorily explained: The seismic cultural transformation of the Mediterranean civilizations that made Christianity possible, and on one view even made it necessary. Since I have fretted before
about the excessive uses of periodization in the attempt to make narratives out of
history, perhaps some further ruminations about the narrative of "western civilization" is in order here. Names matter, as I have said many times already and will say
again, and some of the names that recur in these narrations are instructive.

"Late Antiquity" is the name we have inherited for that crucial transitional period,[4] itself surprisingly late,[5] in which the traditional religions of the Roman Empire gave way at last to the spiritual impetus of some initially strange-seeming and
decidedly "eastern" religious forces. The rhythmic echo of this continual see-saw between paganism and Christianity may be heard even in our own day, as I will attempt
to show in the last chapter.

"Christianity," of course, did not begin with Christ's birth or death. And Christendom did not begin with Paul's mission to the Gentiles. The Christian church did
not really begin to take shape in a form we would recognize as such for fully 300
years or more.[6] "Dark Ages," thus, is the name we have given to the final collapse of
the traditional religion and culture of the late Roman Empire—at least in its western provinces. It tells us that "paganism" came to an end—even, presumably, in the
countryside. And "Middle Ages" is the name we give to that remarkable synthesis of
ancient fragments and emerging Christendom that contributed so much to the
western Empire's sense of its own identity, under Charlemagne and thereafter. It
tells us that Christianity decisively triumphed. The "Renaissance," at least in *this* narrative retelling, may be viewed as a "pagan" swansong, a profound nod to classical antiquity—one form of it, at any rate—which took root for a variety of reasons in
northern Italy, and that produced, among other things, the strangely ambivalent
image on the cover of this book. Then came yet another Christian reaction, located
further to the north this time, an initially Teutonic phenomenon that Protestants
have learned to think of as a "Reformation." From that decisive event and its political implications, the "modern" world—with its democratic commitments to *liberté,
égalité,* and *fraternité*—was allegedly born.

In this chapter, I want to focus on the most poorly understood aspect of this religio-cultural transformation, one we may date more precisely to the fourth century
CE. On the front end of this period comes the "conversion"[7] of the Emperor Constantine, in or around 312 CE. On the tail end comes the establishment of Christianity as the state religion of the Empire under Theodosius I, in or around 380 CE.
Then comes the subsequent shutdown[8] of the most important surviving pagan
sanctuaries of the ancient world—among them, all of Pausanias's favorites, at
Olympia, Delphi, and Eleusis—in or around 395 CE. Standing symbolically in the
middle of these profound transformations, both subtle and seismic, is the Emperor
Julian (331–363 CE),[9] known to subsequent history rather misleadingly as "the
Apostate" (or "backslider," *tou parabatou*). For one to be an apostate, one must first
have been an authentic convert. And Julian, it would seem, was neither. Much has
been written about the suppleness with which the young Julian dissembled, pretending to religious[10] *and* political[11] convictions he clearly did not hold. Perhaps we
should begin there.

He was an unusual character, even by the unusual standards of an unusually tumultuous age. In an empire that had landed on the vaguely theological undergirding of
an established cult of the divine imperium, as well as the still more vague and volatile
principle of dynastic succession, Julian was condemned to being a member of Constantine's immediate family.[12] (See Figure 4.1)

I say "condemned," because of the times in which he lived, times in which such
familial associations could be fatal. Most of Julian's immediate family (his father, his
eldest brother, and six cousins) were eliminated by disaffected military officers in
337 CE; the six-year-old Julian was spared, along with his half-brother, Gallus. The
reasons are unclear. The boy grew up in a bizarre mixture of exile and occasional
house arrest, almost constantly concerned for his own political and personal survival.
He was cautiously invited into public life and service to the empire in the rebellious
province of Gaul, at the ripe old age of 25.[13] Five years later, he was declared emperor
by a northern army that was devoted to him. Hesitantly at first and then decisively,
he marched off to face his rival, Constantius, who died mercifully in 361 CE before
their armies actually engaged.[14] Nineteen months later, Julian was dead, campaign-
ing with still another Roman army, less devoted perhaps, at the outset of an ill-
conceived campaign against the Sasanian Empire in Persia. He was killed there, in
circumstances which were, to say the least, unusual and highly suspect.[15]

In an age of expansive government bureaucracy—and its inevitable marriage-
partner, expanded literacy—he was a prolific essayist, legislator and correspondent.
"Even while waging war, he left behind written works in every genre (*pasas morphas*),"
says Libanius, "surpassing all others, and in his correspondence (*tôn epistolôn*) surpassing even himself."[16] He left behind a curious literary legacy and, as was the case
with Pausanias, it is somewhat difficult to account for its survival.[17] He wrote an
enormous amount in a philosophical and religious vein, for a Roman emperor; only
Marcus Aurelius's literary career[18] can compare to Julian's in quality and in sheer
output. Presumably those monks who copied over Julian's numerous literary leavings
did so as a reminder, a reminder of how bad things once had been, and as a summary
statement of the institutional prejudices that they had successfully overcome in the
years after Julian's untimely death.

Julian's early years of house arrest were devoted largely to study and to philosophical self-cultivation; when he later came to a sense of his own larger historical
and imperial purpose, he modeled himself quite deliberately on the philosopher-
king of Plato's *Republic*. One sees evidence of this quite clearly in his surviving essays.[19] And yet, while Julian's own interests clearly inclined to the philosophical, his
self-understanding was significantly different from that of a nineteenth-century
student of Comparative Religion or Anthropology. Let me pause here to explain why
in some greater detail.

Much has been made recently, primarily under the influence of Michel Foucault's
so-called archaeology of the "human sciences,"[20] of the need for all modern disciplines—in the Humanities, if not in the natural sciences—to write their own histories. We need to be able to tell the *story* of the creation of our own core ideas, and to
trace the institutional developments that originally brought them into being. We
need historians who can write the history of the idea of History and of historical research—from Herodotus to Hegel, let us say.[21] We also need Classicists who can

Figure 4.1

THE FAMILY OF JULIAN

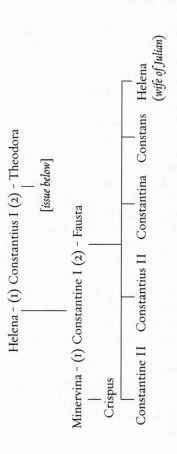
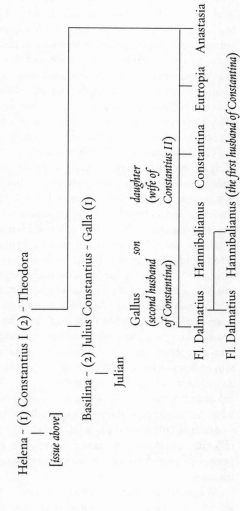

write the history of the construction of a decisive and enduring fiction called "Classical Greece."[22] And we need students of Comparative Religion who can write the history of the creation of the decidedly modern concept of "religion" as a cross-cultural and emphatically *non*theological idea.[23] That work has been significantly advanced in recent years,[24] and I suspect that this is one of the things that has made that strange period we call "late antiquity" somewhat more accessible and popular to many of our contemporaries. For the sheer fluidity of the category of "religion," which was so very much an issue in the fourth century in the Roman Empire, becomes evermore apparent again now in contemporary North American society—especially in its jurisprudence, as we saw in Chapter One.

The vast majority of early scholars in the field of Comparative Religion in the early nineteenth century were Protestants by confession. Even those who professed agnosticism, atheism, or no creed at all, had nonetheless rejected a profoundly *Protestant* notion of what is encompassed by the terms "God" and "religion."[25] Religion, in their subtle and largely unstated opinion, was a matter of "scripture and sermon" primarily, constituted by a body of sacred writings and a body of, at best, only partially coherent moral and doctrinal beliefs. Religion was something on which one meditated, something in which one believed, not something one *did*. There is a profound symbolic truth in the fact that we may speak of *practicing* Jews and *practicing* Catholics, but not of *practicing* Protestants. The term makes little sense; Protestants do not "practice" in that sense. If we must add an appellation to the name "Protestant," then it has customarily been "Bible-believing" or "fundamentalist"—emphasizing, once again, the primacy of scriptural tradition and dogmatic belief in this religious worldview. The shortcomings of this approach to the comparative study of religion have been amply documented in recent years.[26] While much of this critique does indeed signify a new approach to the comparative analysis of something called "religion"—by locating it more thoroughly in a community and a culture—it has not yet fully digested what we might call "the new materialism" in religious studies, its increasing interest in material culture and physical artifacts that emerged in the 1990s. It is this latter intellectual development that I am attempting to display more clearly in this book. The period of Late Antiquity is an especially auspicious place in which to work on these matters.

When Julian attempted to intervene in the religious wars then raging in his own world, he did not engage primarily in philosophical polemic, despite the fact that his own inclinations probably lay in this direction. Rather, Julian *legislated*. And his legislative eye was trained, as presumably *every* religious (and legal) eye was then trained, on the material culture of religion and the practices they inscribed. When Christian sons attempted to supplant their pagan fathers, they attacked the temples, first. The legislation of creedal confession would not emerge as a significant fact of Roman *law* for two centuries or more. We see some evidence of this in the law codes of Justinian in the sixth century, but far less so in those of Theodosius, compiled earlier in the fourth.[27] In Julian's century, Christians and pagans alike understood that the battlegrounds were the sanctuaries, that the primary targets were altars and statues, and that from decisive victory in this arena, all the rest would follow. A single example of this mentality[28] must suffice here, to illustrate a far larger—and, to my mind, far more lasting—cultural point.

In 29 BCE, the now-established Caesar, Augustus, held a three-day triumph in Rome, at which time he erected an Altar of Victory in the new Senate House.[29] By

the time of Constantine, the Altar was already an ancient monument, and a prominent symbol of civic administration and the much-touted *pax Romana*. Later in the
fourth century—after Constantine had established their own rights and mandated
socio-cultural tolerance on their behalf—Christian agitators quickly turned to their
own brand of iconoclastic activism and intolerance. They sought to remove this decidedly pagan structure from the central legislative body of the Empire. And so the
battle—what amounted to a vast tug-of-war over monuments, statues, and their cultural meaning—was joined.

The details of this contest are of less concern to me than the overall results, the
pendular pattern of a debate over images and visual representation that has had such
a long and strange career within Christendom. The pendulum swung with unusual
swiftness, and in an unusually erratic manner, in the fourth century CE. And Julian
lived in the midst of all this turmoil. Constantine's son, Constantius II—*not* Constantine himself, be sure to note—was the first to remove the Altar from the Senate
House. It was Julian who returned the Altar to what he considered its rightful place
in 362 CE, immediately after Constantius's death. But Julian's attempts at a repagani-
zation of the Roman Empire were notoriously short-lived, here as everywhere else.
While the co-emperors, Valentinian and Valens I, were on the whole fairly compro-
mising with the traditional religio-civic institutions of the Empire, their successor
was not. Gratian, the first Roman emperor in history to refuse the title of *pontifex maximus,* insisted once again on the Altar's removal in 382 CE.

The very extremity of Gratian's position prompted the most coherent response by
committed pagans, for whom the association of the state with a state religion was, and
ought to be, indissoluble. The leader of the cadre of traditional paganism was L. Aurelius Avianus Symmachus Phosphorius, member of a senatorial family of long standing (Julian thought very highly of his father),[30] and one of the premier Roman
aristocrats of his day. As *praefectus urbi* at Rome, Symmachus enjoyed an unusual relationship to imperial power. There was even a special genre, the *Relatione,* which might
be thought of as a regular bulletin (if such a thing existed) composed by the mayor of
Washington, DC, and sent regularly to the President of the United States on matters
concerning the health and well-being of the capital city. When Symmachus attempted
to gain an audience with Gratian on the matter of the Altar of Victory, he was denied.
When the young Valentinian II ascended to the throne in the following year (383 CE),
Symmachus composed a longish letter addressed to him, as well as to Theodosius and
Arcadius, concerning the return of the Altar, and by implication, what Symmachus saw
as devolving imperial policies regarding paganism. This manuscript came to be known
as the "Plea for Toleration."[31] When Ambrose, the bishop of Milan, heard that Symmachus had written this letter, he demanded to see a copy of it, and threatened excommunication if Symmachus's request were granted. Letter in hand, he then
composed a more formal response to Symmachus's *Plea* in the Autumn of 384 CE,[32]
which addressed Symmachus's essay point by point, and took special care to mock the
error of Julian's ways with cruel satisfaction. Symmachus's request was once again denied. Symmachus tried several more times to address the issue of the Altar, but by then
his pagan colleagues' time had clearly passed. Nothing came of a letter sent by him to
Theodosius in 391 CE, nor again in 392 CE, when the political winds had initially
seemed to be blowing more favorably in a pagan-leaning direction. Between 393 and
395 CE, the emperor Theodosius came to his own firm conclusions regarding the traditional religion of the ancient Romans,[33] and he, along with Arcadius and Honorius,

proscribed what little of it then remained. I will return to this legislative record at the end of this chapter. In any case, after Theodosius, the Altar of Victory disappears from the historical record . . . as one might have expected the Emperor Julian and his writings to have done, although such has decidedly *not* been the case.

JULIAN AND PAUSANIAS

If Late Antiquity is a period that has recently come under more acute scholarly scrutiny, then no reign has enjoyed more excited attention than Julian's, then as now.[34] His brief reign (361–363 CE) witnessed the last systematic attempt to regain pagan ground lost to a kind of Christianity that had enjoyed increasing imperial support and sponsorship since the conversion of his step-uncle, Constantine, in 312 CE, after his decisive victory over Maxentius at the Battle of the Milvian Bridge, just to the north of the ancient capital of Rome. Julian's reign is thus read as paganism's swansong, whatever that might actually have meant at the time. It is far from a simple matter, and it was not a simple song, as we shall see.

Since so much has been written about Julian, I will say a good deal less about him. I felt the need to explain more about Pausanias, simply because our sources say so little, by and large—to say nothing of his extraordinary religio-aesthetic legacy. What I propose, in any case, is to join my discussion of Pausanias in the last chapter to my understanding of Julian's career and its significance in this one. In a fascinating way, I think that Julian's intellectual career may be matched up, virtually point for point, with the themes I identified as distinctively Pausanian in the last chapter. Both men were the product of a strikingly similar religious landscape, committed to a spiritual sensibility which was perceived to be decidedly on the wane. They are both concerned about decadence and collapse, the collapse of the traditional worship of the old gods. I return to the four themes I laid out in the last chapter, since, taken together, Pausanias and Julian present an illuminating, and a surprisingly consistent, picture of what "Hellenism" had come to mean in the late imperial period. It was *their* version of Greekness against which Christianity ultimately ranged its own considerable intellectual and cultural weapons. And it was *their* version of "Greekness" that Christianity had accepted initially as a "cultural" matter, but then later condemned as "heretical."

I will trace those developments in greater detail in the next chapter, but first let me reiterate what I said about Pausanias in the last chapter. I indicated that he was a fairly late Greek author, and that while he was not technically from Greece, he was indeed a Greek. Widely traveled, Greece laid a special claim on him. And the reasons for that had something essentially to do with Pausanias's understanding of religion. Let us now apply these same insights to Julian's career.

If Pausanias was a "Greek" who was not from "Greece," then Julian was a Roman who was not really from Rome. At one level, this is the merest statement of the obvious. The Emperor Constantine, while his trip to Rome to engage Maxentius's army was one of the determinative facts of his life, did not stay there. Constantine reigned at the beginning of the formal administrative division of the eastern and western provinces of the empire, shortly after the establishment of the principle of co-rule and eventual tetrarchy by his immediate predecessors. The empire now admitted its clear division into unequal halves. Constantine's transformation of the

Greek city of Byzantium into a personal namesake—Constantinople (which is the only way Julian ever refers to it)[35]—as well as into the second imperial capital, intended literally to be a second Rome, signaled a decisive change in the imperial center of gravity, and in the imperial mind-set. Rome was no longer a singular entity, and the *eastern* provinces were where the action was.

This had enormous importance for Julian's intellectual and moral development. After surviving the massacre of his family in Constantinople, Julian's half-cousin, Constantius II, spirited him off to Nicomedia, where he was tutored by several Christian and pagan intellectuals, in turn.[36] From there, he was sent to the mountains of Cappadocia, until he was recalled to Constantinople by his half-brother, Gallus, when the latter came briefly into power in 348 CE. Julian once again took up his studies in Nicomedia. Then came the golden year of 354 CE, when Julian was sent, against all expectation, to Athens, "the holy city of Hellenism,"[37] for a blissful reprieve both from his impending imperial duties and from the house arrest he had anticipated in Milan. It was only after this Athenian sojourn that Julian was called more fully into public life, in the west. Five years of service in Gaul, punctuated by a march on Rome and Constantinople in order to seize imperial power . . . this trajectory marks his own symbolic and decisive return to the east. Then, after residing in Constantinople, Julian spent nine tumultuous and dispiriting months in Antioch, still further to the east—after which he departed for the Persian campaigns, and his own ill-augured end.

We are witnessing the same imperial back-and-forth we meet in many Roman careers after Hadrian's: from the east, to the west, then returning to the east; from Greece, to Rome, and back again. We see the same privileging of the east over the west—of Greek matters over Latin ones[38]—in Julian's writings, which we met consistently in Pausanias's work as well. Julian's early writings are cast in a deliberately archaizing Sophistic style,[39] whereas the later satires and polemics have a much rougher cut. It is, in any case, in one of the satirical works that Julian's own apparent awareness of these issues is most clearly indicated. In his *Symposium at the Saturnalia* (also referred to simply as *The Caesars,* and written in Constantinople in 361 CE, shortly after his accession), Julian makes much of the now time-honored distinction between Romans and Greeks. At a banquet hosted by the gods, a range of Roman emperors is paraded before the assembly, each vying for the title of the greatest world conqueror and ruler. Herakles points out that the contest will be meaningless without the participation of Alexander, and all agree: "Let us see if these Romans are any match for this one Greek (*henos tou Graíkou*)."[40] And Alexander, in making his reply to Julius Caesar's barbed insults, reiterates the same distinction:

> You, while waging war against Germans and Gauls, were preparing to fight your own fatherland (*patrída*)—what could possibly be worse, or more poisonous (*miaróteron*) than this? And now, since you have referred insultingly to "the ten thousand Greeks" (*tôn myríôn Graíkôn*),[41] I remind you that you Romans are descended from us, and that most of Italy was colonized (*ôíkêsan*) by the Greeks (*hoi Graíkoi*).[42]

Julian places this odd-sounding Latinism—referring to Hellenes as *Graíkoi*—at the heart of his satirical look at the Roman imperium and its excessive cultural self-satisfaction. I suggested the significance of this term in the last chapter. The most Latin of the Latins, like Caesar, refer to "Greeks" in Latin terms, not Hellenic ones. They are imperials, colonizers in their mentality. And Julian deliberately separates himself from this Romanizing mentality. He refers to Greeks consistently as *Hellênes*. In his *Hymn to King Helios* (153a), the emperor observes:

> For the Romans not only belong to the Greek race (*genos Hellênikon*), but in addition the sacred ordinances (*thesmous hierous*) and the proper belief in the gods (*peri tous theous eupistian*) are, from beginning to end, all Greek. . . . Thus I believe that the city [Rome] is a Greek city, both by descent and in its constitution (*genos te kai politeian*).[43]

Clearly for Julian, as for Pausanias, some overarching conception of "Greece"—primarily the Greek mainland, whose cultural capital was consistently perceived to be Athens[44]—was determinative. It would be difficult to exaggerate the importance that Julian later assigned to that decisive and idyllic year in Athens.[45] This was due partly to the personal significance he attached to his initiation in the Mysteries of Eleusis (yet one more connection to Pausanias), much as his Mithraic initiation in Ephesus some years previously possessed for him. Athens, Eleusis, and Delphi continue to occupy a central position on Julian's mental and spiritual map, much as they did on Pausanias's. Only Olympia has become marginal, for reasons that remain unclear.[46]

"Greece" was a major preoccupation for both men, and a decisive piece of their mutual mental furniture. Julian will go so far as to say, in an admittedly polemical and ironic context, that the Greeks have a far better claim to being the chosen people of God than the Jews do.[47] The aesthetic and religious beliefs which underwrite this viewpoint are the same ones we met in Pausanias's *Greek Walkabout*: Greece is a vast museum now, a hodge-podge of only partially assembled altars, sanctuaries, and antiquities, a place in which cults may be added easily enough, but from which nothing ought ever to be taken away . . . until the Christians come, of course.[48] Confronted with the mass of material at Olympia, we saw how Pausanias attempted to organize it, to make sense of it all in one massive encyclopedic compendium and an overarching narrative account. It seems to me that Julian is doing the same thing with "paganism." Even as he tried to reinstate its lost rituals and much-compromised prestige, Julian is forced to refashion it, by lending it a Roman structure, and perhaps even a theological coherence, which it had never needed before. This is all eminently Roman, somehow, perhaps the real prelude to the Byzantine event: "[Julian's] originality consists in having substituted the empire for the *polis,* the oriental cults for the Olympians and *Romanitas* for Greek civic patriotism."[49]

"Unity" is the religious buzzword in each of Julian's writings, in every oddball genre that Julian deployed to make his case *against* Christianity and *for* paganism. In his judgment, "Greek religion" (and the term so translated is consistently *Hellênismos*)[50]—and it is always, insistently if ambiguously, *Greek*—has continued to evolve in the two centuries that separate Pausanias's antiquity from Julian's. Thus, while Julian claims to be reasserting the Greeks' traditional religious privilege, he is ironically making this religion more Roman, less and less identifiable with the authentically Greek religion that Pausanias had been so committed to describing. While some well-known ancient cults, like those of Demeter at Eleusis,[51] still rank high in Julian's hierarchy of sacred spaces, other major sites are nearly absent, most notably Olympia.[52] A number of newer elements are apparent as well, especially Julian's personal commitment to the relatively late-coming cult of Mithras.[53] Asklepius is also mentioned as a significant rival to Christ,[54] Herakles is a paradigm of the recurring movement between worlds,[55] and Helios the sun-god enjoys a prominence in Julian's epistemology,[56] which must be a real surprise to anyone who has come to Julian's writings fresh from Pausanias.

If we ask, then, what has changed in the two centuries that separate Pausanias's Roman world from Julian's, the most obvious answer is *Christianity*. But it is the very obviousness of this answer that should counsel us to pause and reflect. By comparing Julian's writings to Pausanias's *Greek Walkabout*, we can see this crucial difference more clearly, and we can see how Pausanias's studied refusal[57] so much as to mention Christianity makes his authorial task far different from Julian's. For Christianity—at least the more aggressive kind, with which Julian would have been forced to deal—represented a threat far more serious than the ones Pausanias faced in the late second century. Pausanias expresses the repeated concern that people in his own day are not serving the gods appropriately, or else with sufficient piety. He is concerned that the sons are *neglecting* the faith of their fathers. It is only now, with the rise of a more aggressive and well-organized Christianity, that these adoptive Christian sons actually strive to *supplant* the faith of their Roman fathers. The Altar of Victory was but the tip of a devastating iceberg that Julian had ample reason to fear might yet sink the ship of state he was trying, in his own halting way, to steer well.[58] Julian could not afford to ignore Christianity, as Pausanias presumably could. This is why the emperor's final answer to the threat posed to the traditional religion of the Roman Empire by Christianity bears a closer look. We are returned once again to the complicated world of renegade Socratic piety, as well as to a related Socratic concern: the question of proper pedagogy. The education of Roman sons became a matter of such enormous concern to this young-old imperial father, that the schools were to become battlefields every bit as contentious as the sanctuaries had proven to be already in Pausanias's day.

THE EDICT ON EDUCATION

In the Spring and Summer of 362 CE, while still in residence in Constantinople and about to depart for Antioch, Julian landed on an intriguing strategy for marginalizing Christian beliefs and Christian practitioners. He would close the premier teaching posts to all rhetoricians and literary critics who professed the Christian faith. This so-called Edict on Education has easily been the most remembered aspect of his short and troubled reign.[59] The Edict, as preserved in the Theodosian Code (where it is dated to June 17, 362) seems innocuous enough: "Masters of studies and teachers must excel first in character, and then in eloquence," it begins. Julian then establishes a process of imperial review, whereby rhetoricians, grammarians, and philosophers may be certified, since "if any man should wish to teach, he should not leap forth suddenly and rashly to the task."[60] The local municipal senate is granted authority to nominate interested persons to teaching posts, subject to review by the regional decurions, "the best citizens" of the city, and finally on appeal, by Julian himself.

What, then, constitutes the "character" that Julian considers so indispensible to the teacher? He insists that it is ultimately more critical even than eloquence. Julian's answer, which is also the real subtext of the Edict, comes in an intriguing document he penned at the time, in Greek.[61] "Character," for Julian, is an especially moral[62] category, having everything to do with the heroic virtues of self-constancy and clarity of purpose. Proper education (*orthên paideían*)—and this is the very first thing he says—has more to do with possessing a "sound mind" (*hygiê noun*) than it does with eloquence and fine phrases (422a). The great danger is that our teachers, who inescapably teach morals (*êthôn*) and never mere facility with words (422d), should be duplicitous or cynical and disbelieving themselves. "When someone thinks one thing but teaches something else to his charges, then he seems to me to fall short of true culture (*tês paideías*) to the same degree that he fails to be an honest man (*tou chrêstos*[63] *anêr*)" (422b).

We can see where the Edict is headed. It leads to nothing less than the establishment of religious tests for teachers. For pagan literature, like its Jewish and Christian rivals, is ironically grounded in a scheme of revelation.

> Well then? It was the gods who provided all of this *paideia*, first to Homer, and then to Hesiod, Demosthenes, Herodotus, Thucydides, Isocrates and Lysias.[64] Did they not see themselves as priests (*hierous*), some dedicated to Hermes and others to the Muses? It seems wrong-headed (*atopon*)[65] to me that interpreters (*exêgoumenous*) of these writings from the gods should dishonor (*atimazein*) those selfsame gods. And yet even though it seems wrong-headed (*atopon*) to me, I do not say that they must change their minds and then teach the youth. Instead, I offer them a choice (*didômi de hairesin*)[66]: Do not teach things which you do not consider worthwhile (*spoudaia*); or else, if you do wish to teach them, then first persuade your students that neither Homer nor Hesiod nor any of the others of whom you are interpreters were guilty of impiety (*asebeian*) or stupidity (*anoian*) or error (*planên*) concerning the gods, such as you have claimed in the past. (423 a–b)

Julian is in deadly earnest about the need to choose. He has gone out of his way to inaugurate pagan temples, pagan culture, and pagan schools. They are pagans who should teach and officiate there. If Christian scholars consider Homer's worldview to be folly, then they can always serve as teachers in their own *alternative* institutions, what Julian refers to as "the churches of the Galileans," where they may serve as "interpreters of Matthew and Luke," instead (423a). The emperor is offering people a choice: The whole point of his pagan program has been to reconstitute this choice, and to place its pagan component on a more equal footing with Christianity, by refurbishing the most significant pagan institutions he knew. It is in this sense that the Edict on Education is the logical culmination of Julian's fairly systematic attempt to reestablish the institutions of temple and initiation, cult and sacrifice.

To any modern student of comparative religion, Julian's Edict cannot fail to disturb. It is more than the existence of state-sponsored religious tests for teachers. No, the problematic assumption here is the declaration that one must *be* what one *teaches*, religiously speaking. Only Jews can teach about Judaism, only Christians can teach about Christianity, and only pagans can teach "Hellenism," the sum total of all classical literature and philosophy.[67] All teachers are exegetes and interpreters; but the texts they are permitted to interpret may be regulated. It is this excessive textualism, along with the indelible joining of religion and culture as pieces of one seamless Hellenic worldview, that is probably most odd-seeming to the contemporary student of Julian's would-be reformation.

Yet this seems to have been Julian's preoccupation from the beginning. In one of the most fascinating of the many letters that survive from his correspondence with local officials and newly installed pagan priests,[68] Julian relates a fascinating story

about his own troubled religious youth in Nicomedia, when he was forced to participate in the pretense of Christianness, all the while wishing merely to serve his own ancestral gods.[69] Specifically, he is defending the pagan credentials of an otherwise
unknown priest named Pegasius. To do so, Julian relates the story of how they first met.

In the winter of 354 CE, while making his way to Athens (and then, so he believed,
Milan), and shortly after the murder of his half-brother Gallus, Julian passed over
from Troas to Ilion, theoretically to see the ancient battlefield at Troy. But in reality,
this trip is a pretense, inspired by Julian's desire to visit the ancient temples (*ta hiera*)
there. At a shrine dedicated to Hektor,[70] Julian is intrigued to see that the lamps and
altars (*lamprous etí tous bômous*) still possess their old fire, and the statue of Hektor is
exceedingly well maintained, freshly oiled and gleaming like the sun. Julian attempts
to sound out Pegasius about this, cautiously at the first: Are there perhaps still pagans hereabouts? "Do the people of Ilium still sacrifice (*thyousín*)?" He receives an
ambivalent reply: "Why is it odd-seeming (*atopon*) that they serve (*therapeuousín*) a
good man who was also their citizen (*polítên*), just as we serve the martyrs?" Julian is
only half-pleased with the reply: he bristles at the Christian comparison, but he ap-
proves of the attention to ritual, *and* to the divine *therapeia*. "The image (*eíkôn*) this
man used was unsound (*ouch hygiês*)," he frowns, "but the reasoning (*prohairesis*) was
cultured (*asteía*) and subtle (*exetazomena*), considering the times (*toís kairoís*) in which
we lived then." Complicated times call for subtle questions and even subtler, more
evasive answers. This man, much like Julian himself, was a closeted pagan. And the
proof was in the *practices,* innocuous enough details like well-lit lamps and gleaming,
polished bronze.

We witness many aspects of Julian's core religious attitudes in this story, especially when it is read in tandem with the Edict on Education. Julian was a city-
emperor, a man who understood that, as goes the imperial city, so goes the empire.
If Christianity had made its most serious inroads in the major cities of the eastern
empire, then this was the very territory Julian intended to reclaim. Julian considered Pegasius a man of *culture* because he was a man of the *city* (*asteía*). As a politi-
cian and an emperor, Julian devoted most of his attentions to urban religion and
urban reform.[71] And yet it was the very cosmopolitanism of such urban fleshpots as
Antioch which made his more rigorous moral reforms hard to sell. So, in these instances, he styles himself as something of a country-bumpkin (*agroíkos*), famous for
his unkempt appearance and general boorishness (*agroíkia*).[72] As an intellectual, Julian could not resist the temptation to make pagan doctrines cohere, to engage
Christian theology[73] in the field and to defend certain core principles of his own
pagan cosmology. In a way that should no longer surprise us, one of these essential
matters concerns the eternity of the world.[74] Like Pausanias before him, Julian
knows that the question of origins does not allow an answer. It is only Christian hy-
bris, in his judgment, that dares to present such a totalizing picture of the world, replete with a Beginning and an End. Julian prefers Pausanias's more cautious—and,
to his mind, more reasonable—approach.

But Julian's emphases are preeminently practical. He reserves theological debate
largely for his discussions with philosophers and church leaders (the strange, and admittedly fragmentary, *Against the Galileans* is the glaring exception to this rule, full of
both strategic and rhetorical mistakes). And Julian's most famous satires—especially
The Caesars[75] and *The Misopogon*[76]—are moralizing tracts, not pieces of speculative theology. This emperor reopens temples, rebuilds altars, reinstitutes sacrifices and other

rituals, oversees a vast bureaucracy of imperial paganism to provide the *ritual* without which no religion can long hope to survive.[77] Julian may well have been an ascetically minded moralist, himself;[78] he freely admitted that Christians had done a better job of caring for the poor and infirm than pagans had done,[79] as well as of regulating their personal and sexual lives.[80] He modeled much of his reform of pagan administrative hierarchies on the best examples the churches had to offer.[81] But his religious reforms repeatedly emphasized the material, not the moral, culture of antiquity—the institutions of the priesthood,[82] as well as certain essential ritual practices, like prayer and sacrifice, and certain essential monuments, like statues and altars and temples. Ritual activity was the key. For Julian, and this is probably a piece of his Neoplatonic inheritance,[83] is as impressed by rituals (*drômena*) as Pausanias was. We should recall that what Pausanias admired so much about Eleusis and Olympia were their rituals, what he referred to as *drômena* and *agôn*. This religion was *performative*. In this sense, too, Julian lived in, and tried unsuccessfully to recreate, a lost world—the very Greece that had moved Pausanias to set it all down some two centuries earlier.

LAW AND LEGITIMACY

Julian's intervention in educational institutions was considered wrong-headed and overzealous even by the friends of his pagan reforms.[84] In fact, the nine-month sojourn in Antioch that followed directly on the Edict, was the most divisive and disappointing period in Julian's short career. His attempts to reassert the traditional religious practices of the empire met with, at best, lukewarm support, and the Emperor himself became the butt of many jokes and satires (*skômmata*) among Antiochene cultured despisers, who saw in his seemingly endless calendar of sacrifices only a heedless bath of unnecessary blood.[85] This, in turn, prompted the bitterest and most unfortunate response from Julian, the alternatively plaintive and bombastic *Beard-Hater*, in which the emperor attempts to defend himself against the criticisms and pillorying he had received at the hands of the local populace. It was one more symbol of how badly things had turned, and how quickly. Despondent, Julian left the city on an ill-conceived and hastily prepared expedition, one that would cost his empire dearly and would cost him his life. All of his former suppleness of mind seems to have deserted him. His ability to dissemble, to say nothing of compromise, seems to have disappeared. He refused even to negotiate with Persian ambassadors, promising instead only that they "will see him soon enough."[86] He refused to acknowledge a distressing series of poor omens, which unanimously counseled *against* the Persian venture. And he turned his back on a city to which he was destined never to return.

The dead are prey to the living, of course, and this was especially true in Julian's case. Writers almost immediately vied with one another for authorial control of his legacy, "the right to write it," if you will. Libanius composed several encomia for his dead friend, one that defended his policies and lent appropriate glory and prestige to his curiously nostalgic picture of the empire and its religio-cultural meaning.[87] Christians were quick to ridicule the man, seeing in his death at the hands of an Arab spearsman[88] the clear and unambiguous judgment of God. In addition, they were to develop a rather subtle philosophical position that helped to explain what had been wrong with Julian's ideas in the first place, his Edict on Education most notoriously.[89]

In a nutshell, they argued that Hellenism was a cultural, not a religious, category. That is why Christians *could* credibly teach the classical canon; Christians believed in the *culture* of Hellenism, within certain limits, as well as any other citizen of the empire. Only by granting the assumption—which was Pausanias's *and* Julian's assumption—that "Hellenism" was a fundamentally *religious* tag did Julian's Edict make sense. This crucial distinction between a "religious" and a "cultural" identity was to have a long afterlife in imperial Roman law (as it has in our own!), nicely summarized in that vast legal encyclopedia compiled by the emperor Theodosius in the early fifth century, when these battles had been pretty well resolved. This Code tells an interesting tale, one that serves as an ironic epitaph to Julian's career, and a fitting conclusion to this chapter.

The story of the ultimate legal position of Rome on the question of Christianity is fairly easily told. But for the momentary hiccup of Julian's reign, the fourth century witnesses the steady advance of privileges, prestige, and power available to Christian clerics and Christian citizens. The real action emerges in relation to two other religious groups, *against* which Christianity was busily defining itself at the time: Jews and Greeks, the latter of whom we may now begin to refer to as "pagans." There is evidence of some significant restriction on Jewish legal rights in the Code: they are prohibited from owning Christian slaves;[90] they are prohibited from marrying Christian women;[91] they are prohibited from stoning Jewish converts to Christianity.[92] But Jewish *practices* are unassailable[93]: their priests continue to enjoy the same financial and executive exemptions that other religious officials enjoy; they are explicitly protected from Christian harassment and violence; and their synagogues are inviolable. These protections are reiterated by several emperors on several different occasions.[94]

The pagan story is a bit more complicated. Here, more attention is paid to ritual practices and public monuments than to mob violence or to social hierarchy, as we might well expect. While the emperor Constantine had maintained the traditional soothsaying practices of the traditional imperial cults,[95] his son, Constantius II, abolished animal sacrifices altogether in 341 CE.[96] A law passed 12 years later suggests that such rituals had been permitted in some places at night (the distinction between appropriate daytime and nighttime practices was a major Neoplatonic preoccupation[97]), but now, in 353 CE, these rituals are also proscribed.[98] In 356 CE, a death penalty is imposed on those found guilty of continuing to offer such sacrifices; these proscriptions are reiterated twice more by Gratian in 385 and 391 CE.[99] It is Theodosius, ironically enough, who reduces pagan sacrifice from a capital crime, reducing the penalty to a simple confiscation of property in 392 CE.[100]

Here again, we have entered a world rather different from Julian's own. There is little in the Theodosian Code about the enormous doctrinal divide separating Christianity from what it now routinely calls "paganism." There is, instead, sustained attention paid to the public *institutions* and the ritual *practices* of the pagan cults. Roman law pays special attention to oracular activity, to animal sacrifice, and to the temples around which such activities were centrally organized. There is a whole body of law specifically aimed at the temples, and this is especially interesting for my purposes, since it serves to underline the larger idea of this book: that "Hellenism" has functioned as *both* a cultural *and* a religious category throughout the past two millennia.

This distinction is already implicit in a law of Constantius II passed in 342 CE, which specifically protects the temples in and around the cities from vandalism and destruction.[101] Four years later, he seems to change his position,[102] and orders that these temples be closed. Gratian, Valentinian, and Theodosius, amazingly, reopen the pagan temples, but in an instructive way. They clearly think of these things as public monuments—almost as public museums, pieces of the urban landscape and the public trust. So long as sacrifices are not permitted to take place inside, the buildings themselves are to be protected and accorded due honor.

> We decree that the temple[103] shall continually be open that was formerly dedicated to the assemblage of throngs of people and now also is for the common use of the people, and in which *images are reported to have been placed which must be measured by the value of their art rather than by their divinity*. . . . In order that this temple may be seen by the assemblages of the city and by frequent crowds, Your Experience shall preserve all celebrations of festivities and by the authority of Our divine imperial response, you shall permit the temple to be open, but in such a way that the performance of sacrifices forbidden therein may not be supposed to be permitted under the pretext of such access to the temple.[104]

We begin to see the outlines of the compromise that was eventually achieved. Certain popular festivals would persist, so long as they were denuded of their lingering paganism. Temples could be open, and their decorative art admired, in much the way that Pausanias had done, so long as sacrifices were not performed or oracular pronouncements sought out. Many of these festivals would apparently persist for centuries,[105] until their very Hellenism was perceived as problematic in the sixth and seventh centuries, a Byzantine transformation to which we shall turn in the next chapter.

And then comes the final engagement. In 395 CE, the emperors Arcadius and Honorius close the pagan sanctuaries altogether.[106] Presumably, this is when the sites that have been of special concern to me—at Eleusis, Olympia, and Delphi—were formally closed.[107] Pagan priesthoods were canceled in the following year,[108] and yet, even still, the public monuments were specifically set aside for imperial protection: "Just as we forbid sacrifices so it is Our will that the ornaments of public works shall be preserved. If any person should attempt to destroy such works, he shall not have the right to flatter himself as relying on any authority."[109]

The major sanctuary-spaces that had moved Pausanias and Julian alike were now well on their way to becoming the overgrown ruins that would inspire the Romantics to their own flights of poetic fancy a millennium later. While allegedly protected from iconoclastic vandalism, these same sites were also robbed of their staff of groundskeepers, and presumably fell victim to spoliation, disintegration and eventual ruin.

Moreover—and this should seem strange, if we pause to reflect on the rhetoric that preceded it—each of these three sanctuaries was destined to house a Christian basilica of some importance, if not in the first century CE, or the third,[110] then certainly by the early fifth. There is a surprisingly early Christian basilica, remains of which have been found at Epidauros, the great Asklepian sanctuary, which may be securely dated to the fourth century—remarkably early, given the complex developments from that same century that I have been tracking in this chapter.[111] Other basilicae of note would appear in the next 50 years: at Athens, at Dodona, at Eleusis, at Delphi, and at Olympia. These are all a piece of one massive campaign of Christianization. We are standing on the cusp of a veritable explosion of church construction in Greece, much of it aimed at, and located very near to, the ancient sanctuaries which seem to have been closed. It makes for an odd kind of closure, this orgy of new church construction, all of it datable to the early-to-mid fifth century CE.[112]

The so-called Workshop of Pheidias, immediately adjacent to the massive Temple of Zeus at Olympia (whose cult statue was considered one of the seven wonders of the ancient world), was converted into a Church of unknown dedication in the early-to-mid fifth century,[113] and "Olympia" is mentioned as an ecclesiastical domain as early as the Fourth Ecumenical Council of 451 CE, held at Chalcedon, just across the water from Constantinople.[114]

The Hellenistic gymnasium at Delphi,[115] lying roughly halfway between the Temple to Athena Pronaios and the Oracle of Apollo—hard by the Castellian Spring, which later Roman poets were to make especially famous—was transformed into the Church of the Holy Virgin (*Panagía*), and a monastery later grew up around her name. The dating of this sanctuary is admittedly uncertain, but column drums and funerary ornaments of a decidedly Christian kind have been unearthed in large numbers by French archaeologists, and they all point to the same change in orientation, a fundamental "Christianization" of the entire site in the early-to-mid fifth century.[116] The Monastery of the Panagia became a staple of the Grand Tour of Greece in the nineteenth century, as we will see more clearly in Chapter Seven,[117] and this Romantic pilgrimage-point *par excellence* (since it was pagan *and* Christian, at once) was not demolished until 1898 . . . to make room for further French excavation of the antiquities.

Finally, the Telesterion—the heart and soul of the ritual performance in the sanctuary at Eleusis, and the culminating point of the very *drômenos* that so inspired Pausanias and Julian, that point which brought the initiate to the very heart of the Mysteries—this site also was graced, or cursed, with a church immediately to the northwest. Now dedicated to Saint Zacharios, the modern shrine is built decisively atop earlier Christian remains inside the sanctuary at Eleusis, marking the presence of a basilica that may also be dated to the fifth century.[118] Still more intriguing, there is some evidence that this church, immediately adjacent to Demeter's Telesterion (just as the Olympic basilica abuts the Temple of Zeus)[119] was originally dedicated to Saint *Demetrius*, a not-so-subtle echo of the name of the very goddess whose sanctuary this had been, a goddess of special import in Julian's cosmology, and of lingering concern, still, to many Eleusinians today.[120]

Thus, not only do the major city sites and sanctuaries survive; in certain settings, they actually *prosper*. The most important religious sites of the ancient Greek world, according to the combined testimony of Pausanias and Julian, were maintained as Christian sanctuaries in the massive building campaigns of the early fifth century. In the *countryside,* by contrast, many of these same emperors suggested that temples and sanctuaries be torn down, quietly and without fanfare, in 399 CE.[121] It seems as if "paganism" took a very long time to die in the *pagus* from which it took its name, since sacrifice and nocturnal initiation rites are *repeatedly* condemned well *after* the formal closure of the sanctuaries in 395 CE.[122] As late as 423 CE, the Code refers to yet another prohibition of paganism across the board, sponsored by Honorius and Theodosius this time, "although We now believe there are [no pagans left]."[123] Clearly, in the countryside at least, there were. And in the cities, there were still large temples ornamenting the urban landscape, still sumptuously decorated with statues and painting, so long as pagans did not try to worship in them. In other cases, the buildings remained, entirely stripped of their icons and images. Many of these structures would be transformed into churches in the ensuing centuries.

So, in a curious way, Julian's attempts to force these issues had the ironic and opposite effect of those he intended. Forcing the issue with the Sasanian Persians led to a substantial Roman military defeat,[124] and forced Julian's Christian successor, Jovian, to make a treaty on embarrassing and unfavorable terms.[125] Forcing the issue in the schools by creating a sort of religious test for educators had the ironic end result of *enabling* the Christian establishment to make the decisive distinction between Hellenism as a cultural and a religious category that would eventually help to turn pagan temples into museums and Hellenic culture into one of the significant elements of that majestic Christian-Hellenic synthesis we call Byzantine. Julian ironically *confirmed* Christianity's place at the Byzantine banquet, and it is to Byzantium's own ambivalent relationship to religious and Hellenic images that we turn in the next chapter.

CHAPTER FIVE

Icons and Incarnation
HELLENISM BECOMES A HERESY

Standing, then, in the very center of the Hill of Ares, Paul said, "Men of Athens, you seem to me most religious (deisidaimonesterous) in everything. For as I wandered about your city and observed your objects of worship (ta sebasmata), I even discovered an altar (bômon) inscribed, 'To an unknown god' (Agnôstôi Theôi). This god you worship as unknown is the selfsame god I proclaim before you today. The God who made the world and everything in it, this God is lord of heaven and earth. He does not live in temples made by human hands (cheiropoiêtois naois), nor can he be served by human hands (oude hypo cheirôn anthrôpinôn therapeuetai) as though He had needs. He Himself gives life and breath and everything, to everyone."

—Acts of the Apostles 17:22–25

The sanctuary (hieron) of Athena Chalinitos is right by their theater and houses a naked statue (xoanon gymnon) of Herakles which they claim as the work (technên) of Daídalos. All of the works made by Daídalos, odd (atopôtera) though they are to the eye, nonetheless have something inspired (entheon) about them.

—Pausanias, *Greek Walkabout*, II.4.5

Our forefathers set up statues and altars and the care for eternal flame—and all other such things—as symbols of the presence of the gods (symbola tês parousias tôn theôn). Not that we believe them to be gods, but rather we serve (therapeusômen) the gods through them. Since we are embodied (ontas en sômati), we worship the gods in a bodily (sômatikôs) way, even though they are bodiless (asômati). . . .

Gazing upon the statues (agalmata) of the gods, then, let us not believe that they are stones (lithous) and wood (xyla), nor that they are gods (theous) in their own right. . . . The man who loves the emperor (philobasileus) takes joy in the emperor's image (eikona). The man who loves his child (philopais) delights in the child's image, just as the loving child (philopatôr) delights in the father's. So too, the man who loves God (philotheos) delights in the statues (agalmata) and images (eikonas) of the gods, feeling both reverence and awe before the gods who gaze back upon him from the unseen world (ex aphanous).

Julian, *Letter to a Priest* 293a–294d

PRELIMINARIES

Much has been made of the historic papacy of John Paul II, whose clear and unwavering commitment to more traditional Catholic values, as well as to the ecclesiastical offices of the formal Church hierarchy, has been married nonetheless to an equally dramatic globalism, one whose mission has been characterized by specific papal attention to regions—from Mexico and Guatemala and Brazil, to Israel and the Palestinian Mandate, to Russia and his Polish homeland—not nearly so evident in recent years. Many have attributed this newfound spirit of cosmopolitanism to the fact that this is the first *non-Italian* Pope the College of Cardinals has elected since the death of Adrian VI of Utrecht in 1523. There is a politics behind all of this, naturally, and the modern papacy has effectively detached itself from its own tormented political history—just one feudal fiefdom, among countless others on the Italian peninsula, so it seemed—in this century, with Mussolini's ironic assistance. As the demographics of world Catholicism continue to change, it would seem to be a matter of time only before a Latin American cardinal is elected to this highest office.

But there is another kind of politics attached to the papacy—what we might call a cultural politics—one far older than the Slavo-European struggles with which most of the world was forced to grapple during the Cold War era. A cursory glance at *the names* of the earliest popes recognized by ecclesiastical tradition tells an interesting story. Five of the first 13[1] of them were "Greeks" who hailed from the Pausanian Greek mainland—with names like Evaristus (99–105 CE), Telesphorus (125–136 CE), Iginus (136–140 CE), Anicetus (155–166 CE, who may have been from Syria), and Eleutherus (175–189 CE). Even some Italian bishops had Greek names—like Anacletus of Rome (78–90 CE), Alexander of Rome (105–115 CE), and Soter of Campania (166–175 CE).[2] Even the first pope, so-called—whose given name was Simon, but who had been nicknamed "the Rock" by his Lord (the Aramaic word is *Cephas*)—would have this *Aramaic* nickname translated into the *Greek* gospels as *Petros*. And it is from this that we get the Italian name of Pietro, and the English name of Peter. Names, as I have said repeatedly in this book, are important details to mark, and still more important details to ponder.[3]

Five, or else eight, of the first 13 popes were "Greeks," depending on how one understands the meaning of this complicated term. There were 13 popes who hailed from "Greece" in the church's first four centuries. There has not been a "Greek" pope since the fifteenth century, and the controversial Avignon papacy of Alexander V of Crete, who died in 1410 CE (Crete was still a *Venetian* holding, thereby making Alexander a vaguely "Italian" figure himself). How, then, did this *Latin* church detach itself from its own inescapable and originary *Greekness?*

This is a question that the comparative study of the scriptural monotheisms may help to answer, by carving one essential factor into higher relief. It also serves to reinforce the complexity of "Greek" identity in the so-called Byzantine period. The best way of entering into these deep and rather muddy waters is to get at them, once again, through the names. The contemporary name for a "Jew" derives from the Hebrew term *yehudai*—literally a "Judahite," and thus originally the designation for one of the 12 tribes of Israel. The manner in which this originally tribal designation became the name for a global religion involves us in a complex matrix in which history, regionalism, conquest, and dispersion all play a role. What we know is that the Hebrew scriptures themselves highlight the issue already in the second century BCE, when a member of the Judean diaspora named Mordecai, living in the Persian city of Susa (his great-grandfather, Kish, had been taken off in the Babylonian Exile of 586 BCE), is identified as *both* a Judahite *and* a Benjaminite. He was thus a member of the tribe of Benjamin who was also called a "Jew" in something like our modern sense (perhaps) of the term.[4] What we are witnessing here is a recognizable dance between tribal and collective identity, between the local and the global, a contest that was, as it normally is, a very long time in resolving. Judah-ism at some point was no longer a tribal designation, but rather the name for the entire movement.

We witness much the same thing in the early period of Islamic expansion and self-definition, beginning in the seventh and eighth centuries CE. The tension between the Arab and the Muslim identity runs deep in Islamicate politics, and has presented an episodic and ongoing dilemma throughout most subsequent Muslim history.[5] The dilemma is framed by the name, "Arab," which may or may not be perceived as compatible with participation in a multicultural, and multiethnic, not to say multireligious, empire. The twinned, and only partially compatible, modern phenomena of Arab nationalism and trans-Muslim identity are best read within the framework of these long-standing political developments and ethno-religious concerns.

Our question, then, is the following: what is the cognate *Christian* category? Was there a core ethnic identity that had to be redefined, renegotiated, and ultimately domesticated, under the larger umbrella of Christian convictions? My suggestion is that the answer to this important question is "Yes," and that the identity in question was "Greek." Negotiating between the Greek and Christian identity is one significant form this dilemma took, although there were doubtless others. Certainly articulating the relative compatibility or incompatibility of the Christian identity and its core practices within the ambient Greek culture of the eastern Mediterranean was one of the primary preoccupations of the first several generations of Christian proselytes[6] and apologists.[7] And *detaching* Christianity from the assumption of its essential and overarching "Greekness" was one major accomplishment of the Latin-speaking churches. This fundamental tension—between west and east, between Latin and Greek—had a long and especially tumultuous history, which culminated in the "Great Schism" between the eastern and western churches in 1054 CE, followed by the sack of Constantinople by Frankish, German, and Venetian troops involved in the Fourth Crusade in 1204 CE.

But *how* did the Latin church detach itself from its own inescapable Greekness? I want to begin to attempt an answer to that question in an unusual way, by making a statement that we have been trained to think of as improbable: The Roman Empire did not "fall" until 1453 CE. This simple claim flies in the face of what we have been taught to think of as Rome's "decline and fall."[8] It also flies in the face of what most North Americans learned in whatever version of a "western civilization" course they took, or were required to take, in college. While it is the case that the Italian peninsula was invaded, and its capitol was sacked, several times in the fifth century CE— by Goths under Alaric in 410 CE, then again by Huns under Attila in 452 CE, and finally by Vandals under Gaiseric (or Genseric) in 457 CE[9]—and while the western provinces of the Empire succumbed to various pressures of "barbarian" invasion and conquest, the eastern half of the Empire in these same centuries was remarkably stable. In fact, the Italian peninsula was destined to become a battleground between Goths and Byzantines, both of whom arguably saw themselves as "Roman" at the time. It was not until the rise and expansion of Arabist Islam in the mid-600s CE that the eastern half of the Roman Empire faced anything resembling the disruptions the western provinces had seen. The rhetoric of the "fall" of the Roman Empire at some time around 476 CE thus recreates the problem we met in the term "Greco-Roman." It joins terms that are not fully equatable, and severs terms that better belong together. It contributes to an inherited sense that Greek and Roman were happily and seamlessly the same thing, whereas pagan antiquity and late antique Christianity were two entirely different things. In some ways, this latter position was Julian's, one-sided and marginal though it proved ultimately to be.[10] These terms invite us to forget the enormously volatile and complex set of cultural negotiations that take us, *very* gradually, from paganism to Christianity throughout the Roman world in the fourth and fifth centuries of the Common Era.

This confusion also makes it difficult for us to look at two of the premier cities in the Late Antique world: Rome and Constantinople. In Rome's case, we have inherited a subtle sense that *pagan* Rome was one thing, whereas *Christian* Rome was something altogether different. And we have inherited a vast confusion about how to comprehend Constantinople at all. Today, this is perhaps symbolized most clearly by the fact that the Roman Forum and Colosseum, powerful symbols of Roman antiquity, stand all on one side of the River Tiber, while the Vatican lies at some august remove, on the other. But this is a hard distinction to maintain in the city for long. For that same Vatican stands immediately adjacent to the Mausoleum of the emperor Hadrian (d. 138 CE), an enormous structure that would eventually serve as Papal headquarters (the Castel Sant'Angelo) when the Papacy moved out of the Lateran palace to Avignon in 1309, then returned in 1377. So, too, with the Colosseum, that remarkable pagan fixture commemorated by the Church (and eventually by the contemporary Hollywood film industry) as the arena in which many (how many we will surely never know[11]) martyrs met their end in faithfulness to a challenging and difficult "way." The Colosseum was restored, ironically enough, under the aegis of several popes in the nineteenth century (Pius VII [1800–1823], Leo XII [1823–1829], Gregory XVI [1831–1846], and Pius IX [1846–1878]), and large marble placards affixed to the ancient walls broadcast the fact. The layers of ancient, and medieval, and modern history are hopelessly jumbled—or, rather, they are beautifully mingled—in such cities as these.

If that is true of Rome, and of Athens, then how much more true is it of Constantinople, the Emperor Constantine's city, established as capitol of the eastern half of a far-flung Mediterranean Empire in 330 CE. The complex marriage—happy or unhappy, as you will—of pagan and Christian things was a part of what made the fabulous cultural fluorescence we call "Byzantine"[12] possible. They themselves simply called it "Roman" (*Romaios*); it would never have occurred to them to call it anything else. But "westerners" have never known quite how to stitch the phenomenon of Byzantium into the quilt we are trained to call "western civilization." The common strategy since the nineteenth century has been either to ignore it altogether, as we have been taught to ignore Islam, or else to write off Byzantine civilization as somehow "frozen" and inconsequential.[13]

Yet Byzantium was neither frozen, nor inconsequential, nor short-lived. The very fact of the existence of the Byzantine Empire announces an astonishing fact to us: There was a self-styled "Roman" Empire, thriving and in place almost continuously until May of 1453 CE, when the capitol city of Constantinople finally succumbed to an overwhelming assault by the Ottoman Turks under the new Sultan, Mehmet II. The problem with the Byzantines—which is also to say, the problem of fitting "them" into "our" story—is that they were both Christian and Greek. Given the tried-and-true Romantic distinction between "the ancients and the moderns"—which is to say, between pagan Greeks and Christianized Romans—we do not know *how* to think about a culture which claims its roots in both. But this was precisely the cultural achievement of Byzantium. It saw itself as ancient *and* modern; it was *both* Christian *and* Greek. And this Byzantine mentality lies probably closer to the heart of Roman and Mediterranean affairs than we are normally inclined to realize.

HELLENISM AS HERESY

I say this in this way because such "both-and" reasoning, along with the complex cultural negotiations it entails, lie at the very heart of the Christian story. If Europe and the Americas continue to insist on their own lingering Christianness, then this continues to be a piece of the story of western civilization, too. To encounter Paul's rhetoric, or Luke's, is to be made aware of the fact that their thought-world was neatly divided in two. The names for the two worlds in which they lived were "Jewish" and "Greek." And while Paul's rhetoric occasionally seems to suggest that such terms (to the degree that they name national or cultural identities) no longer matter,[14] it would be closer to the truth of the New Testament to say that the people who began to call themselves by a *new* name, *Christiannoi*,[15] were endeavoring to explain how it was that they could be *both* Jewish *and* Greek. Whenever debate on these matters arises, these are the terms available to them to describe themselves and their world.

I am suggesting that for "Christians" in the late first and early second century CE, "Jew" (*Ioudaios*) and "Greek" (*Hellēn*) were, if not quite neutral, then certainly and solely descriptive categories. Judaism (*Ioudaïsmos*) and Hellenism (*Hellēnismos*) were the cultural forces that were then assembled into a new, and highly creative, but also highly volatile mix. The remarkable thing about these names is the manner in which their meanings change, the way they ceased eventually to be neutral or descriptive at all. If Judaism and Hellenism are the cultural building blocks out of which Christianity was assembled in the first three centuries CE, then they had become *heresies* by the seventh and eighth. This is an old story. Once you believe that you have successfully made something new, then the challenge before you is to explain how this new thing is *un*like the older things out of which it emerged. If Christianity was built out of Judaism and Hellenism, then it became a matter of the first importance to explain how it was *not* Jewish or Hellenic anymore. Once easy way out of the impasse was to write off the former terms as "heresies."

Still, the student of Christian theology will rightly object at this point. Judaism is not a Christian heresy *per se*. The theological relationship between these two cultures and communities of faith is different, and far more complex, than that. And the same ought to be true of Hellenism, in principle, although far less attention has been paid to that problem in the modern period.

While this may be the case doctrinally today,[16] it was not always so. There were powerful claims to the contrary that animated Christian rhetoric and the emerging Christian self-definition in the Byzantine period. A highly influential example may be found in the writings of John of Damascus (c. 675–749 CE), whose *Font of Wisdom* (*Pēgē Gnōseōs*, perhaps better translated as the *Spring of Knowledge*)[17] was to have a decisive influence on later Christian thought, especially in the more encyclopedically inclined Middle Ages. John's popularity was enormous in the medieval world— Thomas Aquinas refers to him with special appreciation[18]—and he was formally recognized by Pope Leo XIII as a Doctor of the Church in 1890.[19] The *Font of Wisdom* is trinitarian in its structure[20] (as was the entirety of John's thought), dealing first with Philosophy (*Dialektika*), then with Heresy (*Peri Haireseôn*), and finally with the Orthodox Faith (*Ekdosis Akríbês tês Orthodoxou Písteôs*). It is the oft-neglected second section, "On Heresies," which is so astonishing, from the point of view I am developing in this book.[21]

John begins by throwing down the theological gauntlet: "The mothers and the prototype (*mêteres kaì prôtotypon*)[22] of all heresies are four in number: Barbarism, Scythianism, Hellenism, and Judaism. Out of these four arose all the others."[23] This should seem an odd list. Hellenism and Judaism are listed not only as heresies, but actually as arch-heresies, the very mother and prototype of every subsequent, specifically Christian, kind of folly. In fairness, it should be noted that, like Pausanias before him, John is attempting to make an *historical* argument. He is hanging the Epiphanian framework of heresy that he has inherited on the historical narrative we meet in the first 11 chapters of Genesis. So: "Barbarism" is the font of all unrighteousness that takes us from Adam to Noah; "Scythianism" prevailed from the times of Noah to the building of the Tower at Babel; "Hellenism" arose in the age of Abraham's great-grandfather, Sarug; and "Judaism" emerged in the times of Abraham himself, symbolized by the twinned developments of circumcision and covenant.

The problems with Barbarism and Scythianism are quickly established. Barbarians are, each one of them, a law unto themselves. And Scythians moved into the lands of Europe (*to tês Europês klíma*). John tells us no more about Barbarism, and he does not even bother to tell us specifically *what* the heresy of the Scythians entailed, only that they brought it with them to "Europe." By contrast, John tells us a great deal about Hellenism and Judaism, identifying nine separate heretics under the umbrella-concept of Hellenism (Pythagoreans [or Peripatetics], Platonists, Stoics, Epicureans, Samaritans, Gorthenes, Sebyaeans, Essenes, and Dosthenes) and seven under the umbrella of Judaism (Scribes, Pharisees, Sadduccees, Hemerobaptists, Ossenes, Nasaraeans, and Herodians). There then follows a list of some 83 more heresies, the last two of which will prove to be of some special interest to us.

Now what in the world does the "heresy of Hellenism" entail? The answer will not surprise us, after our walk through the material we have visited in the last two chapters, and given the vast interest in temples and cult-statues we met in Pausanias's and Julian's writings. For Hellenism, according to John of Damascus, "grew out of idolatry" (*enarxamenos tês eidôlolatreías*), in an age "much given to superstition (*deisidaimonían*)," when the races (*genê*) of men began to live in cities (*epi to malista politikôteron*) and first began to make gods (*etheopoion*)—which is to say, to fashion idols (*eidôlôn*) in their own likenesses. John goes on to catalogue the comparative technologies of such idolatry—from paint, to ceramic, to stone, to metal, and wood. Egyptians and Babylonians and Phrygians and Phoenicians all engaged in "this kind of religion" (*tautês tês thrêskeías*), with its statue-making and its mysteries (*agalmatopoiïais te kaì mystêríois*). But it was the Greeks (*Hellênes*), in the age of Cecrops, who perfected it.[24]

This is a critical point, for several reasons. On the one hand, we see how "Greek" and "Hellenization" have become nearly synonymous with "idolatry" in the language of mature Christian theology. On the other, the passage places us in a better position to understand the nature of John's theological innovation more clearly. The last two heresies he discusses highlight the circularity of his entire argument. The last heresy John discusses is that of those he calls *Aposchistai,* or *Doxarioi.* These are essentially latter-day Christian "barbarians," who recognize no law but their own, refusing to acknowledge the power of any holy image (*septên eíkona*). The penultimate heresy John discusses is that of the *Christianokatêgoroi,* or Iconoclasts. They, too, refuse to venerate icons, and accuse Christians who do of worshiping them as gods, *kathaper Hellênes,* "just like Greeks."[25]

So the last two heresies in John's impressive catalogue are nothing more than Christian recapitulations of the first: Barbarism and Hellenism. And crucial to John's purposes is the larger explanation of how Christianity is *not* Hellenism—which is to say, how a Christian *icon* is not the same thing as a Greek *idol*. Small wonder that John of Damascus is better known to subsequent history as the first stalwart defender of the Christian icons. Let us turn to the nature, and to the shortcomings, of his defense.

ICONS AND ICONOCLASM

Two recent developments have contributed to our ability to address these iconic questions with renewed sensitivity and insight. One is the newfound interest in "material culture" within comparative religious studies to which I have referred repeatedly, a materialism that recommends attending both to the practices and the material accoutrements that form such a large part of religiosity, and that have become such a major preoccupation in this book. The point here is the comparative one of recognizing that there is indeed more to "religion" than sacred texts and theology. The second development is more concrete. Impressive caches of heretofore unknown Christian icons were discovered in the late 1950s, then published episodically in the following two decades. These comprised collections in excess of 200 icons from the monastery of St. Catherine's on Mount Sinai, as well as several other, somewhat smaller and loosely related discoveries of imported Byzantine icons and Roman replicas, in Rome, at roughly the same time. So we just so happen to have an enormous body of new icons to evaluate, "thus putting the study of icons on a firm basis for the first time."[26]

Icons were a primarily Greco-Byzantine phenomenon. And, as we have seen, the Christian world, like the later Roman Empire, was a bipolar one, divided in two from the very beginning. The loss of three of the five Christian patriarchates to Muslim expansion,[27] leaving only Rome and Constantinople in Christian control, simply made more dramatic what was already a long-standing cultural fact: the vast cultural divide between east and west. These rather different churches developed different ecclesiastical cultures, with quite distinct church traditions. The eastern churches used leavened bread at the Eucharist, while the Latin churches insisted on the use of unleavened bread (called *azymes*), in commemoration of the Passover Jesus had been celebrating. Eastern priests could marry, whereas western priests could not.[28] Some of the defining Christian creeds—especially those defining the nature of Christ's Incarnation (the Nicene Creed of 325 CE), and the mystery of the Trinity (the Chalcedonian Creed of 451 CE)—had initially been written in Greek, then translated into Latin. Debates about allegedly improper theology imported into these Latin translations, especially that of the Chalcedonian Creed, frequently recurred.[29] The monastic tradition took a radically different form in the deserts of Egypt than it did in the wooded forests of Ireland and France.[30] Finally, in the east, a Byzantine tradition of devotional painting evolved that had no direct parallel in the west. These were the "holy icons,"[31] possessing a surprisingly attenuated canon of forms,[32] limited in the main to the depiction of Christ, of Mary (apparently always depicted with the infant Christ at first, and thus always marked as mother, but then later rendered in her own right[33]), of angels, and of a fairly small but expanding circle of saints.

One should not make too much of this fairly restrictive canon of images. Archaic and Classical Greek art, which has occupied our attention in the previous three chapters, also worked within a surprisingly attenuated canon. The abundance of *kouroi* (free-standing nude male figures) and *korai* (free-standing clothed female figures) from the Archaic period speak to this point: The artists' goal was to render the expected image well, *not* to innovate, and *not* to celebrate his or her own creativity. Even in the Classical period this continued to hold true: There is a mature iconography attached to each god or goddess, so that we know—at a glance, in most cases—who they are. The angled head of a goddess, as well as what she wears, the serene equipose of a wounded warrior, the body of an athlete or a beautiful youth . . . they always look the same. And where a dramatic innovation *does* occasionally intrude—for instance, the renowned Artemis with the hundred breasts, at Ephesus[34]—then this, too, becomes simply another canonical form, endlessly reworked. Innovation, that is to say, was never the premier aesthetic value in antiquity. It is entirely plausible that this modern (and eminently Romantic) concern for artistic innovation and creativity chiefly characterizes what Hans Belting refers to as "the era of Art."

To return, then, to the Byzantine icon. These images were venerated in the east, were at times even believed to possess enormous saving power. In 726 CE, a controversy erupted between the eastern and western churches—or, more precisely, and still more decisively, between the secular and ecclesial authorities throughout the Roman empire[35]—over the religious validity of these icons.[36] The disagreement was severe enough to serve as a premonition of the more formal schism between these churches that came to pass finally and decisively in 1054 CE. It was a battle that had taken many forms. It seems as if the "cult of the icons,"[37] had very nearly supplanted the cult of the saints and their relics in some parts of the eastern empire. It was the very ascendancy and popularity of these icons, then, which may have fueled the forces of reaction.

Added to this was the continued challenge and influence of Islam on the Byzantines. At the turn of the eighth century, the Muslim Empire that fronted the Byzantine frontier had entered a more aggressively aniconic phase, itself, even deleting the image of the Caliph from its own coinage. In 721 CE, Caliph Yazid I went so far as also to impose a ban on images in *Christian* churches within his empire.[38] In short, Islam had become an inescapable and permanent piece of the intellectual furniture of the Byzantine world. And Muslim concern over images and their practical place in worship became a significant and burning theological question. The Arabs put Constantinople on notice quite early, laying siege to it as early as 674 CE, a siege that lasted, off and on, for four years. They returned in 717 CE, but were again violently repelled. No doubt the force and vitality of this worthy adversary-culture made a lasting impression on the emperor who withstood this second siege—namely, Leo III.

The forces of Christian iconoclasm were rallied, in any case, by Leo III (717–741 CE)—called "the Isaurian," and himself a native of Muslim Syria—and they were further advanced by his son and successor, Constantine V (741–775 CE). The debate pitted the so-called Iconodules (*eikôn* + *doulos,* "one who serves the icons") against the so-called Iconoclasts (also called Iconomachs, *eikôn* + *machos,* "one who battles with the icons"). But why *battle* with icons? In this case, at least superficially, because the icons *seemed* to be such a clear violation of the First and Second Commandments— on the most rigorist and totalizing reading of the relevant passages in Exodus and Deuteronomy.[39]

This debate was resolved in the way most ecclesial arguments in those early centuries were resolved—through the calling of an "ecumenical council" (modeled on the paradigmatic one depicted in Acts 15:1–29) to debate the question. This was the Seventh (and, as things turned out, the last[40]) Ecumenical Council, held in Nicaea (as the First Council of 325 CE had been), well to the east of Constantinople, in 786–787 CE. At this Council, the position of the Iconodules eventually triumphed, and the place of the holy icons within Christian worship was relatively assured[41]—at least until the Protestant Reformation raised some of these same iconoclastic questions again.

But how in the world could you *defend* a practice that seemed[42] so clearly to violate the First and Second Commandments? Even the most adamant and convicted Iconodule was forced to begin on scriptural and legal grounds, admitting to the problematic character of the use of representative images in monotheistic worship. This is how John of Damascus, one of the first contributors to the controversy, begins his own "apology" on behalf of icon-veneration—namely, with an analysis of the *Christian* implications of these commandments.

The so-called Iconoclast Controversy, a veritable "civil war waged over the icon,"[43] spanned several generations, and the two premier documents—position-papers really, drafted in the white heat of controversy, and the very real threat of the destruction of precious devotional artifacts—which have survived from the controversy lay out the Orthodox position on icons quite nicely. But there were important differences between them, as we will see, the most significant of which concerns the lingering religious status of "being Greek."

The earlier of the two was drafted by John of Damascus, during the reign of Leo III, composed while John was in residence at the Palestinian monastery of St. Sabbas. It is important to take note of this location. John himself was born in Damascus (his given name was Yanah ibn Mansur ibn Sargum), and he succeeded his father as the chief Christian representative (*logothetê*) to the Caliph, which post he resigned in 716 CE to make the move to Sabbas. John was thus writing far from the eye of the storm of iconoclastic controversy in the imperial capital of Constantinople. He was in the Holy Land, as well as in the Islamic orbit, and thus was freer to compose his treatises in the relative anonymity provided by the Muslim caliphs in Damascus and later by desert monasticism. John did not live in the Byzantine Empire. "Greek" culture was something altogether foreign to him. The iconoclastic orders of a Byzantine emperor no longer touched John's churches in the same way as they might have done 50 years before. Islam was on the rise, and Byzantium on the wane, in the early years of Leo's reign.

The same may not be said of the second generation pamphleteer for the Iconodules, Theodore of Studion (also known as Theodore the Studite, 759–826 CE),[44] a Constantinopolitan monk who assembled his far more reasoned and coherent ruminations about the icons in the very thick of things, inside the imperial capital of Leo V, in the "second wave" of imperially sanctioned iconoclasm. Theodore's residence in the imperial capital was the complicated result of a complicated life lived in complicated times, amply illustrating his dilemma, and ours. Theodore was first installed in the monastery of Sakkoudion, in Bithynia, in roughly 780 CE, and became its leader in 794 CE. He moved to Constantinople with a number of the monks in his charge four years later, due to sustained Arab raiding in Bithynia, and he installed himself in the then-failing monastery of St. John.

This monastery of St. John the Baptist is the oldest surviving Christian sanctuary in the modern city of Istanbul. The church was built on the southwestern fringe of the extended Theodosian city near the expanded circuit of city walls raised in 463 CE, under the auspices of the Roman patrician, Studius, who lent his name to the monastery that grew up around the church. In its heyday, the Studion housed 1,000 monks, but it succumbed to iconoclastic pressures in 754 CE, when Leo's son, Constantius, closed its doors. They were reopened in 787 CE, after the first victory of the Iconodules, and Theodore was installed as *hêgoumenos,* or abbot, in 798 or 799 CE. It was Theodore who made the Studion the premier religious center of the Byzantine world. In addition to being a fierce defender of the icons, Theodore was also a vocal critic of the morals at the imperial court. Already in 796 CE, while still in Bithynia, he had vocally opposed what he considered to be the adulterous marriage of Constantine VI, and was exiled to Thessaloniki for three years for his trouble. Theodore was exiled no fewer than four times in his career—in 796 CE, in 809 CE, and again in 815 CE, after which he was recalled sporadically to the capital until his death in exile on the largest of the so-called Prince's Isles in the Sea of Marmara in 826 CE. He was buried in the monastery there, until his remains were restored to the Studion at the end of the Iconoclast Controversy, on January 26, 844 CE.[45]

Now, these differences in location are significant, but at first sight somewhat perplexing. John's treatises seem to be far more polemical, less tightly reasoned, even inconsistent at times on matters of the very iconic terminology he is out to defend.[46] In saying this, I am once again contradicting the received wisdom of later Christian tradition. John, after all, not Theodore, is recognized as one of the foundational "doctors of the Church." On the matters at issue in *this* controversy, however, Theodore is clearly the more reasoned, and ironically the more "orthodox," voice.

John calls his work "apologetic" (*apologêtikos*), despite the fact that *his* churches are not directly subject to Byzantine attack, and he explicitly addresses his treatises "To Those Who Attack the Holy Icons" (*Pros Tous Diaballontas Tas Hagias Eikonas*).[47] Theodore, too, addresses himself "Against the Iconoclasts" (*Kata Eikônomachôn*),[48] but he does so with a much more sophisticated spiritual and philosophical lexicon. John may be tripped up on several important errors, he occasionally misreads scripture, and he can contradict his own previous claims. This Theodore rarely, if ever, does.

Granted, Theodore clearly has John's popular and widely circulating polemics, as well as two generations of subsequent thinking, on which to draw. But it is more than this. He also—and this is crucial, in my judgment—has a subtly different agenda. He was a Greek in a way that John was not; he was a Greek in much the same way that Pausanias was a Greek (and, presumably, in a way that a late Roman emperor, or a Damascene theologian, was not). Theodore "was more concerned with the veneration than with the image."[49] That is to say, where John is attempting to articulate a "Christian philosophy of the image," Theodore wishes to articulate the appropriate manner in which such images may be *venerated*. It is partly a distinction between theoretical and practical concerns. In any case, I will be dealing more substantially with Theodore's treatises that with John's. It would never have occurred to Theodore to call Hellenism a heresy, after all.

ICONS AND INCARNATION

Theodore basically articulated five distinct reasons—recurring in all three essays, and developing one sustained argument—to legitimate the veneration of holy icons in Christian worship. First, and perhaps foremost, Theodore makes the expected distinction between the "new law" and "the old," drawing a careful distinction between what Christians traditionally refer to as "the Old Testament and the Gospel." This distinction would become crucial to medieval summarians like Aquinas, and would be asked to bear even greater weight by Protestant Fundamentalists and Evangelicals in the United States in the twentieth century.[50] Theodore is arguing that God has worked in human history through various "dispensations," and that God's rules are essentially different in each historical period:

> When and to whom (*pote kai tísi*) were these words [Exodus 20:4] spoken? Before the age of grace (*pro charitos*), and to those who "were confined under the Law" (*toís hypo nomon phrouroumenoís*).[51]

And again:

> [W]hatever the Law (*ho nomos*) says, it says to those who live within the Law (*toís en tôi nomôi*). The ancient commandments should not be imposed on those who live within grace (*toís en charíti*). If they were, we would keep the Sabbath, and be circumcised, and many other things which are forbidden to us. These things are shadow-writing only (*skiagraphía monon*). For the Law is a shadow (*skían*), and not a true image (*eíkona*) of things.[52]

Theodore is making the rather obvious point here that Christians are no longer Jewish exactly, and that they are no longer obliged to live under the Mosaic Law. Circumcision and the Sabbath were the two issues with which most Christians in this period made that distinction clear. They also mark the site where John of Damascus drew this line, and Theodore concurs. "These things were imposed as laws (*nenomothetêto*) upon the Jews on account of their tendency to idolatry (*eidôlolatreían*)," John says. "But as for us . . ."[53] well, Christians are allegedly free of all that now. What neither John nor Theodore say very clearly is how difficult it is to explain *which* commandments a Christian must still follow, and which ones he or she may be permitted to ignore. That has been one of the more enduring questions in Christian theology, as well as in the ongoing definition of the Christian cultural identity.

Second, Theodore distinguished quite carefully—more carefully than John did—between an icon and an idol. Theodore freely admits that idolatry is a sin. But an icon, he insists, is not an idol. And his reasons for so saying are directly relevant to our present purposes.

> What person with any sense (*noun echôn*) does not understand the difference between an idol (*eidôlou*) and an icon (*eíkonos*)? That the one is darkness (*skotos*), and the other light (*phôs*)? That the one is deceptive (*planon*), the other infallible (*aplanes*)? That the one belongs to polytheism (*polytheías*), whereas the other is the clearest evidence of the divine economy?[54]

This crucial distinction—between polytheistic practices (which are "idolatrous" almost by definition) and the true worship of the Orthodox Christian (namely, the veneration of icons)[55]—inclines Theodore to make a related point, concerning the nature of the materials being used in Christian, as opposed to polytheistic, worship.

> The mind does not remain within the materials (*enapomenoí*), because it does not trust in them: that is the deception (*planê*) of the idolaters. Through the materials, rather, the mind ascends toward the prototypes (*prôtotypa*): this is the faith of the orthodox.[56]

Theodore is making an essentially Platonic point here,[57] by claiming that certain beautiful physical materials can in fact bring the mind to reflect upon higher things. Thus, the icons have become one of the unique instruments of the church in this importantly God-directed spiritual work.

Third, and related to this last distinction, Theodore manages a technical distinction between worship (*latreía*) and veneration (*proskynêsis*), and here again we find no such clear distinction in John's treatises:[58]

> Worship (*hê latreutikê*) is unique, and belongs to God alone; but other kinds belong to other things. Kings and rulers are venerated (*proskynountaí*) by us all, masters by their servants, fathers by their children. But not as gods. Although veneration has the same outward form, it varies in intention (*dianêseôs*). For they are only human beings. . . . Therefore, if one recognizes the diversity of the forms of veneration (*proskynêseôs*), when the prototypes are venerated through their representations, then we have given veneration properly so-called in the proper way to God alone. Analogous types of veneration are given to those others who are depicted: to the Theotokos as Theotokos[59] and to the saints as saints.[60]

The icons *would be* a temptation to idolatry, Theodore suggests, *if* they were worshipped as themselves divine. But no one does this. The icons are *venerated,* not worshipped, as windows into heaven, in the preferred metaphor of Orthodoxy. The triune God is the sole source of authentic Christian worship. We *venerate* Mary, the saints, and their icons in His name.[61]

Fourth, and here he remains very close to his Damascene forebear, Theodore appeals to the central importance of non-scriptural church traditions, which have equal validity to anything the scripture mandates. John of Damascus already referred to the "unwritten" (*agraphoís*) as well as to the "lettered" (*grammasí*) traditions of the Church,[62] and in one place he was so bold as to suggest that the icons themselves are actually "books for the illiterate" (*bíblous tôn agrammatôn*).[63] This same curious image of marrying the "written and unwritten" (*engraphôs ê agraphôs*) also appears pointedly in the Nicene Council's Decree. But what sorts of "traditions" do John and Theodore have in mind here? Certainly the doctrine of the Incarnation, and the doctrine of the Trinity—arguably the two most decisive of all Christian doctrines— are not really biblical, at all. They were defined by the fathers of the church at the First and Fourth Ecumenical Councils, in 325 CE and 451 CE, respectively. These creeds attempted to put certain matters of essential Christian belief into a more philosophical Greek idiom.

> There are many unwritten teachings (*ou gegraptaí lexesín*) which have equal force (*isodynameí*) with the written teachings, as proclaimed by the holy fathers. It is not the divinely inspired Scripture, but rather the later fathers, who have made clear that the Son is consubstantial (*homoousíos*) with the Father, and that the Holy Spirit is God, and that

the Lord's mother is *theotokos,* and other doctrines which are too numerous to list. If these doctrines are not confessed, then our true worship *(hê alêthinê latreía)* is denied.[64]

Obviously, Theodore is suggesting that the veneration of icons is another such divinely inspired, and patristically warranted, ecclesiastical tradition. Christ himself did not speak of the Trinity, and he did not himself venerate icons. But that does not mean that later Christians cannot do so, in the name of long-established church tradition.

It is Theodore's fifth assertion that is the real heart of his argument, however, and the real argument-stopper. He turns, as theologians in these centuries seemed *always* to turn, to the idea of the Incarnation.

> There are many forms of circumscription *(perígraphês)*: containment, quantity, quality, position, space, time, shapes, bodies—all of which are denied in the case of God, for the divine has none of these things. But Christ Incarnate *(epanthrôpêsas)* is revealed within these parameters. For he who is uncontainable was contained in the Virgin's womb; He who is measureless became three cubits tall; He who has no quality was formed in a certain quality; He who has no position stood, sat, and lay down; He who is timeless became twelve years old by increasing in age; He who is formless appeared in human form; He who is bodiless, when He had become *(gegonôs)* a body, said to his disciples, "Take, eat, this is my body." Therefore the same one is both circumscribed and uncircumscribable, the latter in His divinity and the former in his humanity—even if the impious iconoclasts do not wish it so.[65]

We are engaged here in a profound meditation on the philosophical implications of making the outrageous assertion that an infinite God "became" finite and incarnate. Christ did not worship icons, in all likelihood, for the simple reason *that Christ was an icon.*[66] The Orthodox argument traced out here is that God appeared in human form—*as a sort of icon, himself*—and that this world-historical event has baptized the human form, and made it an acceptable tool in religious worship, perhaps for the first time.

The Incarnation, arguably the most *un*Jewish (but eminently Hellenic) of all emerging Christian ideas,[67] is the very thing that allows Christians to do freely what Greeks had long been doing improperly, and what Jews had been forbidden from doing. This has to do with depicting the divine visually . . . and, in the Greek case— as had been so since the time of Iphitos's Olympic revival—with doing so *in human form.* Christ Himself has made icons and human iconography legitimate, according to Theodore's understanding of the Byzantine marriage of Hellenism and Christianity. God has baptized the human form, by adapting it to His own iconographic and salvific purposes. The Incarnation has "deified the flesh" *(tên sarka etheôse),* as John puts it.[68] Thus the icons serve as a kind of ecclesial landmark, metaphorical stelae, memorials erected in honor of this vast, world-historical event.

ICONS AND DIVINE DRAMA

Now, there were many twists and turns in the Christian road after this decisive decision to support the Iconodules was made at the Seventh Ecumenical Council and thereafter. Many western church leaders simply refused to accept the Council's decision. Charlemagne himself—no great friend of the icons, *or* of the eastern half of the empire—commissioned a repudiation of the Nicene Council's position, the *Libri Carolini,* and then called a synod of strictly western bishops in Frankfurt in 793 CE, which practically repudiated the Council's decision, by saying that images could be hung in churches but could not be involved in practical worship (or veneration— the distinction seemed semantic in the west) in any way.[69] Charlemagne attacked Byzantine forces in northern Italy in the same decade (788–798 CE), then had himself crowned (Holy) Roman Emperor by the Pope in Rome in 800 CE.[70] Clearly, this fundamental east-west split in the empire had political, as well as theological, resonance.

The *theological* resonance of this debate over religious icons can still be heard as a muted, but distinct, echo in the Protestant Reformation.[71] It seems far from accidental that the Reformers in England took to statues with hammers, and sanded the faces off of the frescoes that decorated the walls of most medieval churches.[72] There is, rather, a kind of sense and even rigor in this Protestant antipathy to the image. Protestantism, which commonly presented itself as the "re-Hebraizing" of the Christian faith, occasionally turned iconoclastic with a vengeance[73]: All in the name of a monotheistic ethical rigorism; all in the name of the First and Second Commandments.

In this period, as well as others, what seems to have worried monotheistic believers was not the fact of religious images *per se,* but, rather, something else, something that was attached to and associated with these images. Sometimes it was the pagan-seeming uses to that they were put. Oftentimes the issue was their three-dimensionality, and hence perhaps their greater corporeality; these statues really looked like people. Christian churches had paintings long before they had statues. Religious statues seemed to have consistently more problematic than paintings, even and especially in the Middle Ages in Europe, when they were gaining in popularity,[74] and quite probably before then. The image on the cover of this book makes the point plainly. Sometimes, it was the attribution of magical or healing power to these images that became a problem. And often it was the fact that these images became objects of pilgrimage, as well as of veneration, thereby changing the very religious geography of the worlds into which they had been introduced. Iconoclastic activity would be consistently justified by an overzealous "aniconic" rhetoric, but such rhetoric almost always overreaches itself and becomes theologically untenable: there simply is no *not* having "images."[75] So it is that periods of image-desecration, in the name of scriptural monotheism at least,[76] tend to be fairly brief.

Clearly, there is a great deal at stake in the institutional trouble taken over these religious images. But there seems to be another aspect of this debate that we have not yet addressed. To get at it properly, we must return to the Platonic doctrine of *anamnêsis,* or "recollection," an idea already utilized by John of Damascus to powerful rhetorical effect. For Plato, the doctrine implied a theory of metempsychosis, the belief that knowledge of a certain sort was actually the transcendental and reincarnated soul's halting inclination to recall forms and images it had once seen, but has now forgotten. In John's view, icons are "imitations" of such "images," but they are also "memorials" (*mnêmai*),[77] memorials erected to commemorate the paradoxical victory of the Christian Cross.

The Greek term for a painting is the same as the word for writing, *graphê.* Pausanias and Julian both toyed with this idea repeatedly in their meditations on ancient texts and monuments. Postmodern theorists, given their own hyperliterate preoccupations, revel in such ancient ironies as well.[78] But the paradox is especially Platonic[79]—deriving more specifically from his winsome discussion in the *Phaedrus,* which also represents his most sustained meditation on memory and its relationship to writing.[80] Books are frustrating, Socrates suggests, because no matter how many times we put a question to them, they return the same answer. The irony of this situation is heightened by a further irony: Most people believe writing to be an aid to memory, and thus an aid to genuine understanding, rather than a hindrance. Socrates demurs, and makes a crucial Platonic distinction in so doing. Writing, he suggests, is very good at *reminding* (*hypomnêsis*), but not very good at *remembering* (*mnêmes*).[81] Writing of a certain sort—a checkbook is perhaps the clearest contemporary example—can assist in reminding us of things we would never otherwise remember. That is what Plato calls *hypomnêsis.* But writing cannot help us to remember what we most desperately need to keep present in our minds. This is what Plato refers to as *mnêmes,* the selfsame word that John applies to the holy icons. Access to this *other* form of truth is active, not passive; so the truth, for Plato, as for John and Theodore, is *performative* in the fullest sense.

One senses that the Christian worry over religious icons—and, still more, over religious statues—is grounded in a similar set of concerns. The worry is that one's commitment to, and devotion to, such material artifacts will be passive, the belief that simply by coming into contact with such a powerful image, however pious and well-intentioned, a sick soul will *automatically* be healed. Such a concept of *therapeia*—the real buzzword in Plato's discussion of piety as we saw in the second chapter, and of special concern to Paul when he was in Athens, as we saw at the outset of this one—is supernatural but not orthodox, precisely because of its passivity.

By contrast, the Eucharist is presented to the Church almost as *an alternative to* icons,[82] as one of its most active performative gestures. The Mass is a *drama,* involving what is arguably the central enactment of the Christian faith, a drama in which the believer is called to participate, ever and again. Attitudes toward the mechanics of the Eucharist—what was changed, at what time, and in what way—as well as attitudes to the practice of the theater—what was played, at what time, and in what way—changed at roughly the same time, in the era of the Protestant Reformation (and its Roman responses). I want to turn, in the next chapter, to the latter of these debates, as one way to gain a better purchase on the former.

CHAPTER SIX

"A Mingle-Mangle of Heathenisme"
RENAISSANCE THEATER, RENEGADE THEATER

O what a rogue and peasant slave am I!
Is it not monstrous that this player here,
But in a fiction, in a dream of passion,
Could force his soul to his own conceit
That from her working all the visage wann'd,
Tears in his eyes, distraction in 's aspect,
A broken voice, and his whole function suiting
With forms to his conceit? and all for nothing!
For Hecuba?
What's Hecuba to him or he to Hecuba,
That he should weep for her? What would he do
Had he the motive and the cue for passion
That I have? He would drown the stage with tears,
And cleave the general ear with horrid speech,
Make mad the guilty and appal the free,
Confound the ignorant, and amaze indeed
The very faculties of eyes and ears.

—*Hamlet*, II, ii.553–569

RECAPITULATION

I have elected to begin this chapter without the "preliminaries." This may seem odd, given that the chapter is loosely devoted to the idea of drama, a modern English term which derives from the ancient Greek *drômenos*—that religious ritual form that we met so prominently in Pausanias's *Greek Walkabout*, the same thing that inspired Julian to attempt his own peculiar kind of pagan revival, the same one that concerned the early Church Fathers to such a degree that they opted to liturgize and domesticate it, rather than to ban drama outright. Long before the rise of the novel, *drama* was presumed to be the premier narrative art form. And we should recall that this book began with an acknowledgment of the power, even when it is a *distorting* power,

of narrative as a form of philosophical or religious argument. In lieu of another preliminary narrative of my own, then, I wanted to provide a sort of recapitulation here
of the path we have traversed thus far, now that we are past the figural halfway point.

In the first two chapters, I posed the titular question of this book—"Was Greek
thought religious?"—and tried to walk through some of the reasons why I believe
that question to be unanswerable. "Religion" is an extremely unstable category, resisting and even refusing simple dictionary definition.[1] "Greek" is an equally unstable term, the Greeks seeming, at times, to be little more than the sum total of what
others have said they were, "from Rome to Romanticism." So it is that *Greek* religion
must seem a still more unstable term, to the degree that it has an in-built tendency
toward innovation and change, symbolized by the fundamental trope we met in
Chapter Two—that of sons who supplant their fathers. How can we ever hope to
speak intelligently about Greek thought, Greek culture, or Greek religion, if what
the Greeks seem to do best is to change?

Perhaps we cannot. But what we *can* reasonably hope to do, and even to do quite well,
is to identify the *ways* in which the meaning of what it was to be a "Greek" changed, religiously speaking, through time. This is an historical account that is not intended to be
a narrative, exactly, in part because it is so very discontinuous and disjunctive. Unlike a
good story, this one moves in awkward stops and starts—like an excavation, and very
much like a human life. As we saw in Chapter Three, what it meant to be a "Greek" was
a question uniquely in play in the imperial Roman period. "The Greeks" (whoever they
were, and Pausanias clearly was one) were forced to renegotiate their relationship to the
Italian peninsula, to the Roman empire, and to an occupying Roman army of singular
destructiveness. Pausanias is a fascinating example of one strategic possibility available
to such "Greeks": he attempted to make "Greek" a *religious* category, by remapping the
Greek mainland and by identifying it as a supremely *religious* landscape. And this marks
the decisive move from which the rest of my book follows.[2]

Once it had been established that "being Greek" was indeed a subtly religious
designation, then the battle lines had already been implicitly drawn. For when the
religious landscape of the eastern Mediterranean was altered so decisively by Christianity in the fourth and fifth centuries CE, then the Greek identity could not fail to
be rendered problematic in an entirely new way. The emperor Julian clearly insisted
that "Greek" was a religious designation, *and* that it was still "orthodox," given his vision of what the late antique Roman empire should look like. Those Christians who
wished to maintain their allegiance *both* to Christianity *and* to Greek letters were
forced to make a crucial distinction: that between Hellenic religion and Greek culture. One might be *culturally* Greek without being so *religiously* (it was only in this latter sense that "Greek" might be equated with "pagan"). A later figure such as John of
Damascus, however, seemed to agree with Julian, ironically enough. "Greek," for
John (and presumably for many Christians before him), was a fundamentally religious tag, and thus an especially complex one. "Hellenism"—however undefined and
undefinable it may be (and in this it is similar to another important Christian construction called "Judaism")—had become a heresy. Hellenism, as we saw in the previous chapter, was actually claimed by John as the mother of all heresy—one of them,
at any rate—the very mother who would assist her renegade sons in their plot to supplant the father. What I want to underline here is the ironic agreement between a
pagan emperor like Julian and a Christian theologian like John. Both were arguing

that "Greek" was a determinately religious category; they were both building on Pausanias's dramatic innovation. They disagree only over the status of Hellenism—as iconodoulic or idolatrous, as orthodox or heretical, as traditional or retrograde.

And now the nature of the oscillation of the problem I have posed begins to come into clearer focus. Since Hellenism itself is a pendular notion, a phenomenon in perpetual motion and a term that was endlessly redescribed throughout antiquity, then we cannot hope to describe it statically. But describe it we can, *as* a concept in motion—very much like "religion" itself. We can discuss Greek identity in ways that admit "Greek" into our lexicon as a category that has always been open to redescription, ever since the Romans came east. Was Greek thought religious, then? The answer depends in large measure on whom you ask, and when you ask them, and in what context you pose the question.

I have tried, since first turning to Pausanias's *Greek Walkabout,* to keep my attention focused fairly closely on the material culture and on the cultural practices of "the Greeks," rather than on theology in the abstract. Even the previous chapter, my most extensive foray into those internal debates that helped to constitute the community of Christians called theologians, attended to icons and images, rather than on conceptual abstractions like the creation of the world out of nothingness, or the hypostatic union within the divine Trinity. I am not convinced that those "religious wars" which divided the imperial capital in the fourth century were matters of abstract philosophical concern, except to unusual minds such as Julian's, and to an unusual class of trained professionals called rhetoricians and theologians. These were the selfsame professionals whose credentials Julian wished to monitor with such care. But most persons' religious identity in these same centuries was less a bookish and theoretical one than it was a question of culture, embodied in a set of fundamental (and for the most part, everyday) cultural practices. They argued about the Altar of Victory in the Senate House, and the rites celebrated at Eleusis, and the contest conducted at Olympia, far more emphatically, and in far greater numbers, than they were to argue about the relation of the Father to the Son.[3]

"Greek religion" involved art and architecture, sacrifice and pilgrimage, athletic festivals and oracles and initiation, the practice of prayer, the performance of burial and of ritual commemoration. In this chapter, and in this chapter alone, I may seem to be straying from my overarching interest in sanctuaries and statues, as I turn to another definitively Greek art form, one that served as another important kind of Greek religious representation: the theater. It was to be in another, considerably later, period of religious wars—when "Protestant" sons sought to undo the perceived excesses of their Roman fathers—that the theater became the premier social institution that served to crystallize a seemingly never-ending debate about "religion," and the vast difference between its various defenders, in much the same way that Olympia and Eleusis and Delphi once had been. What we see in the sixteenth and seventeenth century debate about the theater in Renaissance England is yet another ironic chapter in a story that should be recognizable by now: the story of Greek cultural appropriation, the history of a variety of attempts to answer the question of whether Greek culture was indelibly religious or not. In this period of ecclesial "reformation," then, we find ourselves once again, like Pausanias, coursing over a war-torn landscape, an intellectual and cultural terrain that ought to begin to seem somewhat more familiar to us.

FROM RENAISSANCE TO REFORMATION

It has long been a canon of Art History that certain art-forms virtually "belong" to certain cultures. We speak of *French* painting, of *Italian* opera, of *German* symphonics, of *American* photography and film. Invoke the "Elizabethans," and our attention quite naturally turns to *drama*. Many of us, in our more romantic moments at any rate, seem content to believe that the English have always been in love with the theater, that the British are to plays what the Russians are to poetry. We seem to *want* to believe that once these people had heard honey-tongued Will Shakespeare's (1564–1616) verbal pacing, whether in poetry or in prose, then they were hooked. It is one of history's little ironies (not so little at all, as things turn out) that William Shakespeare departed this life with little fanfare, and that we know little more about him than we know, say, about the Archaic Greek poet, Sappho.[4] Yet—and here is another important similarity to the Greek case—within a generation of Shakespeare's death, there arose a veritable cottage industry built on the concoction of literary biographies, the genre of so-called Lives of Shakespeare.[5] Every person of letters in modern English quite suddenly felt compelled to have something to say about a man who was fast gaining a reputation as *the* Bard.[6] Yet he had not been this in his own lifetime. Why not?

There are many answers to such a bedeviled question, of course. For starters, retrospect lends itself to romance in a way that contemporaneity does not. In his own day, William Shakespeare was no doubt seen as a man who wrote some good plays, some bad plays, some indifferent poems, as well as a host of other memorable and not-so-memorable things. After his death, Shakespeare gradually became what he has since been for most in the English-speaking world, at least since the Romantic era: namely, the Bard (singular) of the modern English language (also singular[7]), the unsurpassed creator of *Hamlet* (1600), *Othello* (1604), *Macbeth* (1605), and *King Lear* (1606)[8]—not to mention *Julius Caesar* (1599), *Romeo and Juliet* (1595), as well as a handful of stunning sonnets and occasional long poems. More recently, *The Tempest* (1611) has been added to this Shakespearean "canon within the canon," recognized as a singular piece of poetic reflection on the *ars poetica* itself.[9] Shakespeare, in short, is a crucial piece, if not *the* crucial piece, in the house of his national literature—ironically enough, in North America every bit as much as in England.[10] Shakespeare is now perceived to be *every* English-speaker's birthright, no longer merely a "national" treasure.

But it was not always so. One reason for this (to us) astonishing fact is that William Shakespeare opted to test his mettle in what was probably the most controversial and unforgiving venue of his day: the living stage. Worse still, he acted in as well as scripted his own plays;[11] this was something of a rarity among the writerly set.[12] Actors had an especially troubled reputation in those days, worse even than that of playwrights and poets, and often enough deserved. The stage itself was seen, by some at any rate, as a potentially problematic public institution ("Machiavellian" it would be termed, in Marlowe's case). The death of Christopher Marlowe (1564–1593) in mysterious circumstances in a tavern (whether in a quarrel over the "reckynyngge," or over a question of "bought kisses" seems hardly to matter now)[13] seemed an apt judgment on the dissolute livelihood he had chosen for himself. Marlowe becomes a premonition of the late Romantic image of the inevitable excesses of the true poet, where the brightest stars inevitably burn out first.

In addition to all of this, there is another factor that accounts for Shakespeare's, and the theater's, mixed reception in sunny old England, and that is religion. This will be a piece of what is by now an old story—involving religion on the one hand, and the (pagan) Greeks on the other. Long before "drama" was perceived to be an especially "Elizabethan" invention, after all, it had been a "Greek" one.[14] And the theater's very Greekness rendered it problematic for some people, nowhere more so than under the influence of a new brand of renegade Christian religiosity called "Reformation." One can scarcely overemphasize the forces that these reform-minded movements within northern Europe unleashed upon the face of European politics for fully a century or more. And we should pause here, briefly, to remind ourselves of some of the more obvious dates, and place names, in this calendar of ecclesial reformation.

After skirmishes which broke out in 1517, Martin Luther's (1483–1546) formal break with the Roman church was achieved in three major tracts, all published in 1520: *To the Christian Princes of the German Nation,* a call to the leaders of various Germanic kingdoms to take up the cause of Church reform independently; *The Babylonian Captivity of the Church,* by which he intended a reference to the bondage of Christians to a church that withheld the chalice at communion, and manufactured sacraments, of which the only ones Luther recognized were baptism and eucharist; and *On the Freedom of the Christian,* the clarion call of his ultimate theological conviction, proclaiming that the Christian is saved "by faith alone," and never by "works."[15] On this pamphleteers' edifice, as well the political wedge that Luther's excommunication in the following year created, the so-called Reformation movement was built.

As these events unfolded in various German fiefdoms, events both theological and political took a more volatile turn in the Swiss cantons. Ulrich Zwingli (1484–1531) took up the Lutheran mantle and attempted to impose it on Switzerland. He was ultimately killed in battle (he served as the standard-bearer) against several holdout Catholic cantons in 1531. The Lutheran confession of faith had been formalized (largely through the painstaking work of Philipp Melanchthon (1497–1560), who managed to make a sort of system out of what had been very *un*systematic Christian pamphleteering) as the Confession of Augsburg in the previous year. Then in 1534, John Calvin (1509–1564) was forced to flee France, and two years later he published his massive *Institutes of the Christian Religion,*[16] which was to have such an enormous influence on Reformist developments in western Germany, France, the Low Countries and Scotland. In 1539, he established his version of a Christian state in Geneva, and exported his theocratic rebellion from there. After fully 15 years of turmoil on the Continent, the Peace of Augsburg in 1555 sought to establish "tolerance" of both Lutheranism and Catholicism (but not Calvinism) in the German regions, on the now-outmoded principle of *cuius regio eius religio* ("whosoever territory it is, let it be his religion"). This naive attempt at religious rapprochement failed, and then the real wars began.[17]

France was in a state of virtual civil war, one that positioned French Huguenots against Roman Catholics until the Edict of Nantes in 1598 finally declared the truce of institutional tolerance. The St. Bartholomew's Day Massacre in 1572 was but the most dramatic episode in this exhausting 30-year disturbance. In the Germanic regions, their Thirty Years' War came later (1618–1648), but it was even bloodier and more disturbing, if ultimately indeterminate.

Admittedly, the way in which I have just mapped this conflict is a very modern way of doing so. It relies on a relatively modern map of, and a modern sense of,

Europe, of Europeanness, and of the countries that comprise the two. Then, as now, it appears that one region called "France" and another called "Germany" were vying for the right of self-definition on the continent. Yet neither France nor Germany was a nation-state in any very precise way at the time.[18] As is customarily the case with empires, the borders between them were quite fluid, and these border zones often became the premier battlegrounds. But the *real* action at the time was ironically located elsewhere, in two other "countries" that had (and have) always been somewhat peripheral to Europe and the emerging European consciousness. I am thinking of England and Spain. If England may be thought of as the first modern nation-state,[19] then it is harder to know what to call Spain at this time. Perhaps she may be viewed as the first transnational corporation.

Spain was clearly the dominant power of the day; some have argued that its empire was one of the most overwhelmingly powerful Europe, if not the world, had yet seen.[20] Charles I of Spain (also known as Emperor Charles V [1500–1558], who reigned 1519–1556) has become notorious for the way he advanced the imperial cause in the New World, but he was no less aggressive in pursuing Spanish interests on the Continent. He laid claims to north Italy, and captured Francis I in Pavia in 1525. He overran the Netherlands in 1526. He laid siege to, and subsequently occupied, Rome itself in 1527. Three years later, the Republic of Florence met a similar fate, more permanently so.[21] His empire, while quite hostile to the principate of Rome, nonetheless positioned itself as the great defender of Catholic interests in Europe.

In response, England under Queen Elizabeth (1533–1603, whose reign spanned much of this same period, 1558–1603) positioned itself as the great enemy of Spain—and, thus, almost by default, as the premier defender of the Protestant cause. The repulse of the famed Spanish Armada in 1588 was followed up by ever-more aggressive English meddling in the occupied Netherlands and in the New World colonies.[22] It was a war of religion; it was also a contest between rival empires on the periphery of continental Europe.

The curious course of Reformation in England was the doing of the Queen's father, of course. Yet Henry VIII (1491–1547, who reigned 1509–1547) was, at best, a lukewarm reformer. A man of profoundly Catholic sensibilities himself, Henry had been an outspoken critic of Lutheran attitudes from the start, when he penned his *Assertio Septem Sacramentorum* in 1521, earning a papal epithet as "Defender of the Faith." But then, alas, Henry fell in love—with Anne Boleyn, eventual mother to Elizabeth. The problem, of course, was that Henry was already married—to Catherine of Aragon, who just so happened to be Charles's aunt. When Henry sued for a papal annulment in 1527, Rome had just been occupied by the forces of Charles V, and Pope Clement VII was holed up in the Castel Sant'Angelo, where he would remain until the following year. He was thus powerless to intervene, even had he wished to do so. And so Henry began his political—*not* theological—maneuverings, moves that served to establish the eventual independence of the English Church. In 1533, his marriage was annulled. He married Anne five days later, and was summarily excommunicated by the Pope. In 1534, there followed the "Acts for the Submission of Clergy," and Sir Thomas More was famously executed in the following year for his refusal to accept them. In 1536, the English monasteries were dissolved, and in 1538, in another seemingly Reform-minded gesture, English Bibles were installed in English churches. Yet the fathers of this Reform were not to have heirs; Henry remained Catholic in his broader religious sensibilities, especially in his attention to the power of religious practice. He seems to have been a "practicing," rather than a "believing," Christian, and in significant ways this makes him a Catholic, even if not quite a Roman one. It was only the ulterior practice of his politics that seemed antipapal and anticlerical. So it was left to his daughter to make of England a more Protestant-minded nation.

Even the name "Protestant" (which was coined at the Diet of Speyer in 1529) was intended to name the curious "third way" of English Reformation. Suspicious of Catholics in Rome and Calvinists in Scotland, the English Protestant was equally suspicious of both the medieval-seeming Eucharistic and Purgatorial theology of the Catholics,[23] as well as the extreme biblicism (not to mention the moral unctuousness) of the Puritans in their own midst. Pamphlets flew fast and furious, printed on the newly invented printing press, as these various battles were joined. And it was to be under the influence of this vocal Puritan minority in England that the battle over poets and playwrights took center stage.[24]

This, ironically enough, was Shakespeare's world. Why, one might wonder, had he ever bothered with it?

AN APOLOGY FOR ACTORS

The future of the theater was in doubt often enough in those years. When Elizabeth, a great friend and supporter of the stage and its players, fell ill in 1602, many feared that the London stage scene would die with her. During the long agon of religio-cultural reformation, one essential question for the Puritans—always a minority in England, but a highly influential one—concerned the aesthetic purpose, and equally the moral influence, of the theater. So intense was the controversy leading up to the eventual closing of the theaters in 1642 (a closure that lasted until their "Restoration" in 1660), that another aspiring young poet and playwright named Thomas Heywood (c. 1573–1641) saw his way clear to draw up a pamphlet in defense, not only of the dramatic stage, but actually of the actors themselves. Like Shakespeare, Heywood was an actor as well as a playwright. The two may even have collaborated in some early "play-patching," specifically on a play entitled, of all things, *Sir Thomas More*.

Heywood himself had an interesting dramatic career, one emblematic of many of the issues I have raised in this chapter and in this book.[25] He was born one of no fewer than 11 children to the Revd. Robert Heywood in 1573 or 1574. Solidly middle class, Heywood was a direct contemporary of Ben Jonson (1572–1637), and only a decade junior to the likes of Shakespeare and Marlowe. He was well-educated, having enrolled at Emmanuel College, Cambridge in 1591, but his studies were cut short by the death of his father two years later. Forced back on his own resources and his burgeoning talents as a wordsmith, Heywood found work both as an actor and as a "play-patcher." In 1596, he signed a four-year contract, obliging him to write exclusively for the Admiral's Men. Finally freed of an exclusive obligation to this company in 1600, Heywood became a shareholder in the Earl of Worcester's players. They quickly became a fixture at the Red Bull, London, and Heywood's prolific pen was presumably one significant cause lying behind their commercial success. He was cranking out plays in as short as one month's time—among these, one of his real masterpieces was *A Woman Killed With Kindness* (1606/7), along with a larger body of indifferent and more forgettable work. Plague had caused the theaters to be closed in 1593, and again in 1603; then, when plague returned in 1607–1608, the theaters were shut down for an entire season. Heywood used this stage hiatus to turn his talents to several outstanding prose pursuits: publishing translations of Sallust; adaptations of more contemporary narrative poems; occasional pieces of his own; and one long poem, *Troia Brittanica, or, Great Britain's Troy*—all of these written in 1608–1609. It is likely that Heywood began *An Apology for Actors* in this same plague-induced interlude, although he sat on the manuscript for several years, until its eventual publication in 1612.

Now, the idea of such an *Apology* was not a novel one. Offering Socratic-seeming "apologies" on behalf of poetry in general, and dramatic poetry in particular, had become a cottage industry of its own in the Elizabethan period, much as composing *Lives of Shakespeare* would be for the next generation. A survey of the authors of such apologies is one significant point of entry into the mature world of Elizabethan poetry: Thomas Lodge (c. 1558–1625),[26] William Gager (fl. 1580–1619),[27] Sir John Harington (1560–1612),[28] Robert Greene (c. 1558–1592),[29] Thomas Nashe (1567–1601),[30] Alberico Gentili (1552–1608),[31] and Sir Philip Sidney (1554–1586)[32] all composed something in this vein. But Heywood's *Apology* seems to have been penned in anticipation of coming trouble, rather than as a response to some current event. Eventually published in 1612, the *Apology* prompted an anonymous Puritan who refers to himself only as "I. G." to offer up *A Refutation of the Apology for Actors* three years later, one in which he made his own religious and moral objections to the theater abundantly clear. (Puritanism, of course, was characterized in large measure by this deliberate conflation of the religious and the moral.) These two texts seem to have been laced together already in the seventeenth century, and thus they have come down to us, reprinted once again in the mid-twentieth century.[33]

There are many fascinating dimensions to this highly illustrative example of an early modern "culture war," but I want to focus on several aspects of the debate that have received less attention. This debate, as we shall see, has something to do with the theater's inherent "Greekness." For the theater had belonged to Perikles and Sophocles, long before it came into the possession of Elizabeth and Shakespeare. To be sure, there were a number of fairly standard complaints leveled against the practice of the theater—among the most interesting are the extensive discussions of the moral valence of "playing" persons other than your true self,[34] as well as the specifically scriptural abomination[35] of men "playing" at being women on the stage. This latter charge seems, at times, to have been motivated by the desire to turn cross-dressing into a curious, and quite literal, "Papist habit." Yet there is another aspect to this debate that speaks more directly to my interests in this book. There are several aspects of Heywood's *Apology* that seem to underline his own creativity, and thus the singular contribution he apparently made to this decades-long debate.[36] They are worthy of our closer attention.

Heywood and his refuters alike organized their treatises in a tripartite (or trinitarian) scheme—much as John and Theodore, and a host of Christian pamphleteers before them, had done.[37] Heywood begins by venturing a weirdly utilitarian argument: namely, that the theater (in the guise of its poets and its impersonators, alike) has been good for the English language. He made much of this fact, because he apparently believed that the English language needed all the help it could get:

> [O]ur *English* tongue, which hath ben the most harsh, vneuen, and broken language of
> the world, part *Dutch,* part *Irish, Saxon, Scotch, Welsh,* and indeed a gallimaffry of many, but

perfect in none, is now by this secondary meanes of playing, continually refined, euery writer striuing in himselfe to adde a new florish vnto it; so that in processe, from the most rude and vnpolisht tongue, it is growne to a most perfect and composed language, and many excellent workes, and elaborate Poems writ in the same, that many Nations grow inamored of our tongue (before despised.) Neither Saphicke, Ionicke, Iambicke, Phaleuticke, Adonicke, Gliconicke, Hexamiter, Tetramitrer, Pentamiter, Asclepiadicke, Choriambicke, nor any other measured verse vsed amongst the *Greekes, Latins, Italians, French, Dutch,* or *Spanish* writers, but may be exprest in *English,* be it in blanke verse, or meeter, in Distichon, or Hexastichon, or in what forme or feet, or what number you can desire. Thus you see to what excellency our refined *English* is brought, that in these daies we are ashamed of that *Euphony* & eloquence which within these 60 yeares, the best tongues in the land were proud to pronounce.[38]

I. G.'s answer to this rather grandiose poetic claim is quick, sharp, and to the point. Religious and English nationalism are married here in a manner that anticipates much of what we will see in the guise of the Romantic nationalism that will preoccupy us in the following two chapters.[39] I.G. first expresses his outrage at Heywood's insult to the mother tongue, but moves quickly on to his real linguistic point.[40] It is a not-so-subtly-masked *theological* point, which is what we should expect it to be.

Secondly, hee sheweth (and to the disgrace of his mother tongue) that our English was the rudest language in the world, a Gallymafry of Dutch, French, Irish, Saxon, Scotch, and Welsh, but by Play-Poets it hath beene refined. But doth he not forget, that whiles they adde Greeke, Lattine, and Italian, they make a great mingle-mangle. Nay, before the Conquest by Bastard *William* that the French came in, our English tongue was most perfect, able to expresse any Hebruisme, which is the tryall of perfection in Languages, and now it will very hardly expound a Greeke Lecture. For after that the French had once corrupted it, it was but of late yeares that it could recouer a common Dialect againe.[41]

It is a humorous as well as a fascinating argument. The reference to "Bastard *William,*" and to what the French have done to the English tongue, seems to reverse quite nicely the claims many *French* persons make today about the encroaching Anglicisms on *their* less-and-less pure mother tongue.[42] Even in the realm of language, children are forever undoing the work, and unsettling the houses, in which their parents have lived.[43] Mother- and father-tongues are supplanted by their poetic sons, in turn. But it is the way that I. G. *makes* this important counter argument that especially fascinates.

The Puritan claims that originary English, the primordial language of the isle—and this, despite Heywood's clear contention to the contrary—was a "most perfect" language. I. G.'s definition of linguistic "perfection" tells us a great deal, I suspect, about his barely hidden theological investments. English prior to the Conquest of 1066, according to I. G. at any rate, was "able to expresse any Hebruisme." And that, he insists, "is the tryall of perfection in Languages." He goes on to add, with what can only be a rhetorical sneer, that in his own day, the English language is hardly fit to "expound a Greeke Lecture." Once upon a time, then, the English language had been up to the vast challenge of "speaking Hebrew." Nowadays, given the latter-day Babel of languages on the island, the English language can just barely manage to "speak Greek."[44]

It was a Renaissance innovation that added Greek to the family of theological languages. After the sudden influx of Greek teachers and Orthodox theologians into northern Italy—first at the Council of Florence in 1438, then again after the fall of Constantinople in 1453—Christian Platonism and Christian Classicism became a fashionable new presence in the universities. And the Greek language—both that of the New Testament, as well as the rich tradition of patristic literature—became a major new resource for theologians and Humanists, alike (they were often the same people).[45] Christians in the West had long been dealing with Hebrew and Latin, especially and often exclusively Latin. So Greek, ironically enough, was a latecomer. The Puritans, then, were reacting against these very Humanist innovations and theological hobby-horses.

Ben Jonson utilized this rhetorical trope to great effect in his enormously popular play, *The Alchemist* (1610). Here is a brief snippet from an exchange between Ananias, Jonson's spokesperson for "the Hebraic" (or Puritan), and a man named Subtle, no doubt intended as a symbolic representative of the hyper-subtlety of "Greeks" (Humanist and otherwise), the very people of whom we have been taught to be suspicious, at least since the Roman period.

> An: I understand no heathen language, truly.
> Su: Heathen, you Knipperdoling? Is *Ars sacra,*
>   Or *chrysopoeia,* or *spagyrica*
>   Of the pamphysic, or panarchic knowledge,
>   A heathen language?
> An: Heathen Greek, I take it.
> Su: How? Heathen Greek?
> An: All's heathen, but the Hebrew.[46]

What is the problem with Greek, exactly? Ananias and I. G. answer with one voice: Viewed from their perspective, the Greek is by definition "pagan." We have met this claim many times now, and in many guises: "All's heathen, but the Hebrew."

Now, that is precisely I. G.'s argument *against* the theater. It is enough, he believes, to identify the dramatic stage as the invention of "oversubtle Greeks" to condemn it. Plays, he informs us,

> were first instituted amongst the fabulous Heathen Greekes (the peruerters of all Diuine knowledge) in honour of their Diuell-Gods.

Only too happy to join Greek things and Roman things with the very hyphen I have called into question, this Puritan anti-dramatist insists that the selfsame point holds for the Roman plays (especially Seneca's) that were so popular in the Elizabethan period:

> [T]heir first induction into *Rome* was by the commandement of these Diuell-Gods. For which cause it selfe, as thinges the Diuell most delighted in, all professing the name of Christians should detest.[47]

We are meeting an historical narrative of sorts here, one that is also a quasi-historical theological argument. The Greeks are Chapter One in this oft-told Puritan tale. The Romans are Chapter Two. It is only at the alleged *end* of the Roman chapter (assuming that this chapter ever "ended," as it almost surely did not) that the Christian chapter begins—and takes us in a fairly straight line to the present theological crisis.

But [Heywood, to whom I. G. consistently refers as "M. *Actor*"] must now needs con-
fesse that when Christianitie began publikely to flourish, then Paganisme dayly more
and more was abolished, and at the last vtterly extinct in Christendome: till of late
yeeres first Papisticall Fryers and Iesuits raised it vp a-fresh.[48]

Now we begin to see the true nature and scope of the Puritan problem. And we
begin to see, I think, why the theater became the locus for those debates that so rid-
dled English society in these troubled years. First came the Greeks. Then came the
Romans, who were, for all intents and purposes, Greeks in imperial dress—which is
to say, "heathenishe" and "pagan." Then at last, in the fullness of time, Christianity
arrived at Rome, and ultimately triumphed there, creating what we now know as
"Christendome" in its wake. And yet, paradoxically, it was also in Italy, latter-day
Italy, that certain such devilish troubles reappear—"Papisticall" troubles, all, troubles
that threatened to reinject paganism into the very heart of Christian belief and practice. So there is an unmistakable insight in Nietzsche's famous diagnosis: namely,
that the Reformation was northern Europe's answer to the Mediterranean and to its
Renaissance.[49] Its answer, Nietzsche insists, was an emphatic and totalizing No.

That is very much how I. G. frames the problem here. He is quick, even eager, to
combine "Greeke" and "Lattine" and "Italian" into one ironic "mingle-mangle." I.
G.'s hidden agenda is to subvert Christian classicism—which he sees as just another
brand of neopaganism—whether it be that of the Italian Renaissance, of Roman
Catholicism, or that brand of English Humanism that partially characterized the age
of Elizabeth. He is worried about *paganism,* pure and simple, in all of its forms. This
paganism is a remarkably *un*historical problem for him, and yet an eminently *Greek*
one at the same time. The forces of "the Diuell" are an ever-present threat, after all,
remarkably similar in his own and in every age. The tactics of evil do not change;
they do not need to change, given the constancy of human appetites.

From the Greeks, to the Romans, to Christendom, to Renaissance, to Reformation: We are reminded once again of the prominent chapters in the story of "western civilization" that I have underlined, and called into question, repeatedly in this
book. The selfsame era that witnessed the creation of a national identity,[50] and the
concept of a national literature,[51] provides us with the essential contours and chapter headings of "the story of the west" as well. Renaissance and Reformation, coupled with the new globalism that characterized the great age of European
discovery—all three of these things coexisted uneasily in the seventeenth century, in
certain especially interesting and prematurely modern places, like England.

AN APOLOGY FOR GREEKS

That story has been told many times.[52] It is a drama that takes us to "ancient Greece"
in the first act. And it is a story that will eventually conclude with the recreation of
Greece as a modern nation-state, as we will see in the next chapter . . . and a "European" nation, at that. At its heart, however, this is a story about the new-old fascination with Greek culture, and the concomitant worry about Greek religion, which
has run such a cyclic course through "European" history since Charlemagne.

It is also a story of the reintegration of the Hellenic—the so-called Classical tradition in the plastic arts, in literature, and in philosophy—into the culture of northern

Europe. It is the story of the renewed engagement with Classical thought in Spain, when the Muslim school of Baghdad Peripatetics brought translations of Aristotle— and a hodge-podge of other philosophical and medical writings, but *no* drama—with them to the Iberian peninsula in the twelfth century.[53] It is the story of the rise of Scholasticism within the medieval universities of Europe in the thirteenth century— linking places as distant as Bologna and Paris—a development that rendered the Thomistic synthesis of Aristotle and Augustine, the Greek and the Christian, possible and comprehensible, however controversial it may have been in its own day.[54] (Thomas, after all, knew no Greek.) And it is the story of the northern Italian fascination with everything Greek—especially with Plato, and the poets, and the sculptors—largely inspired by the great Byzantine "brain drain" that followed in the wake of the final Ottoman conquest of Byzantium in 1453.[55] The Italian Renaissance simply places the capstone on a series of nominally late "European" intellectual developments. What they all share is their commitment to the Classical inheritance, their programmatic attempt to find a place for Greek learning and the arts in a broader Christian environment. It was an elaborate attempt to teach Christians to speak Greek, again. In this, they had the work of earlier Christian intellectuals like Gregory of Nazianzus, Gregory of Nyssa, and even Theodore of Studion, on which to draw. And it was precisely to these attempts that certain purists, especially the biblicist representatives of the Reformation, said No.[56]

Viewed this way, their problem *is* a curiously ahistorical one, the sort of thing that makes Nietzsche's theory of the eternal return of the same begin to seem almost plausible. For this was not a uniquely English problem; it was a significantly Jewish problem of long standing. And this is presumably another reason for I. G.'s injection of "Hebruisme" into his argument. For Hellenistic Jews never did make up their mind about how to view either the Greeks or their culture. To put a finer point on it, Jews were never of one mind about the cultural value or the religious status of Hellenism. The Maccabean Revolt (166–164 BCE) which is commemorated at the Feast of Hanukkah, makes this point abundantly clear. Here was a "Jewish" revolt against the overwhelming cultural attractiveness of Greek culture, and its inevitable marriage-partner, "paganism." The first victim of the Revolt was not a Greek but, rather, a Hellenized Jew.[57] The two disastrous revolts against the Romans (in 66–70, and again in 132–135 CE) make this point even more plainly. These "revolts" (they may also be read as "civil wars") were always more popular in Judea than they were in the Diaspora. These were homegrown rebellions in which political and religious impulses were joined. That is not a new development, as we have seen amply documented in this chapter.

Infinitely more important for our purposes, however, is the fact that the Judean revolutionaries never spoke with one voice. Nor did they speak in one language. The Roman Tacitus (c. 55–120 CE) and the Judean Josephus (c. 37–100 CE) agree[58] that the revolutionaries probably did themselves in at Jerusalem when the Romans laid siege to the capital in 70 CE. There were three separate rebel armies inside the city, and they fought against one another while the Romans waited outside the walls for the revolutionaries to do their dirtiest work for them. One reason that the revolutionaries never spoke with one voice is that they had become involved in revolution for very different reasons. For some, the revolts were doubtless a matter of nationalism, of a sort, a matter of cleansing the land of its foreign occupiers. It was an attempt to reassert the Davidic model of kingship and the Solomonic ethos of theocratic empire. For others, the issue was religious, more broadly speaking—religious in that strangely cultural and material sense I have been emphasizing in this book. For such persons, the revolts were attempts to cleanse the land of its pagan cultural accretions, and to reassert the primacy of Jewish (Levitical or Deuteronomic, as you will) law. Such an understanding of the revolts has the inevitable air of ahistory about it. *Every* Jewish age has its "pagan" temptations, after all; what the Canaanites had been to their ancestors, the Greeks and Romans were to this Hellenized generation. The response that their Judean religion mandated had never changed in their view: It called for refusal and, wherever possible, it called for destruction.

For others—and I strongly suspect that they were in the majority—the revolts were unpopular developments, for the simple reason that Greek (and then Roman) culture was *not* perceived to be the enemy in quite the same way, say, that Canaanite culture was remembered to have been. The world had become far more complex in the Hellenistic era, as the reporting of I Maccabees itself makes clear. Even a report on this revolt against Greek culture is written in Greek and conceived in largely Greek terms. Alexander the Great is described[59] in almost glowing terms by our Maccabean author, as fully in command of his world, a world that comprised much of the world these authors presumably knew. There was also much in the Greek culture Alexander exported for a committed Jew of that era to applaud—doubly so, since Judaism in those precise generations was undergoing a massive reassessment and redefinition of its own.[60] Judaism was making the fundamental transition, especially in the Diaspora, to its mature status as a primarily urban (and presumably more urbane?) phenomenon. Gone was the old Exodus narrative of a religion, and a people, at home only in the wilderness. After the Hellenistic era, Jews are defined in large measure by the great Mediterranean cities in which so many of them lived: Alexandria, Susa, Babylon, Jerusalem of course, Ephesus, Smyrna, even Thessalonika and Athens and Corinth. Christians would later come to be associated with many of these same cities.

Moreover, Judaism in the Diaspora had already made its peace with one central aspect of Greek culture: its language. The Hebrew scriptures were themselves translated into Greek, in Alexandria in the third century BCE, in an extraordinary edition called the Septuagint. Greek influence was evident in the arts as well: Late scriptural redactions, like Job, with its vastly stichomythic design, look for all the world like Greek tragedy; the so-called Song of Solomon participates in the more broadly Mediterranean genre of lyric-erotic poetry; and books like Ecclesiastes and 4 Maccabees evidence a definitive immersion in Stoic and Epicurean philosophy. Greek speculative philosophy was thought by many Jews in this period *not* to be antithetical to divine wisdom. In fact, a Classical (by which they would have understood a primarily rhetorical) education could be of infinite service to any participant in such a *scriptural* tradition, one in which reading and writing and interpretation were perceived as essential. In the plastic arts, too—and this will come as no surprise after our survey of this material in the last chapter—compromises with the Hellenic had been made. Excavations in Judea from the Hellenistic period witness to this perplexing fact: Not only did Jews decorate their synagogues with rich visual images, but they saw fit to decorate them with *Greek* images and themes as well—portraits of the four winds, of the signs of the zodiac, as well as those strange Greek gods, were all prominently displayed in mosaics and frescoes that adorned Jewish houses of worship. I. G.'s protests notwithstanding, "Greeke" was never synonymous with "heathenisme," either in antiquity or in the seventeenth century. That seems to have been a later, and always occasional, Christian prejudice, and it was never, ever a unanimous judgment.

Much has been made in recent years of the essentially Hebraic character of the Protestant Reformation and the self-understanding of its most zealous cultural reformers. We may owe this very distinction—between the Hebraic and the Hellenic—as much to the Reformers as to the Romantics who popularized the notion anew in the nineteenth century.[61] The Reformers took Hebrew names for their children, and knowingly adopted place names from the Hebrew scriptures for the cities they founded in the Old World as well as in the New. Closer to home, the fact that the Reformers in England took immediately to the plastic arts speaks volumes about their own religious self-understanding, and just how Deuteronomic it had become. These Reformers were latter-day iconoclasts, as hostile to statues and icons as some Byzantine zealots had been. In general, they did away with the artistic trappings and religious adornments that they associated with "matters Papisticall."[62] In so doing, they likely contributed to the creation of another idea that would resonate powerfully in the nineteenth century, that of "the artless Jew."[63] Thomas Heywood had asserted, in the first of his three treatises, that

> playing is an ornament to the Citty, which strangers of all Nations, repairing hither, report of in their Countries, beholding them here with some admiration: for what variety of entertainment can there be in any Citty of Christendome more then in *London*?[64]

We seem to have entered a more recognizably "modern" world in which the great capitals of several emerging nation-states in Europe (or "Christendome") compete with one another for the public recognition of their cultural superiority. But clearly, Heywood's point would hardly count as a positive argument to a convicted Puritan of the day. Shows and ornaments are the problem, says I. G., hardly an argument at all. Sensing this, Heywood minimizes the point and moves quickly on.

It is obvious that the Puritans, and some other Reformers as well, presented themselves as defenders of "Hebruisme" (not Judaism) within a religious tradition that had gone badly wrong precisely to the degree that it had gone Greek. "Hebruisme," they reminded their religious fellows, not "Greeke," was the "tryall of perfection in language," as it was in other affairs. To that extent, we are merely agreeing with the accepted wisdom about the culture of European Reformation. Yet there is an important caveat begging to be made here, a large one.

The Jews never spoke with one voice about the Greeks in antiquity. There is no reason to think that "Hebruistes" should have done so any more univocally in a more modern era. What we see in *An Apology for Actors,* as well as in its *Refutation,* is some important evidence for that emphatic double-mindedness that has always characterized Hebraic reflection on the Hellenic. The very same text that speaks so damningly of heathen "Greekes and Lattines" nevertheless continues to build its own arguments on a Classical, as well as a Christian, foundation. That grand paradox lies at the heart of the very religious syntheses that gave rise to Christianity at some point between the second and fourth centuries of the Common Era.

Both Thomas Heywood and I. G. share a commitment to the *authority* of the ancient sources. I. G. goes to great lengths to catch Thomas Heywood out in a variety of Classical blunders. He wishes to demonstrate his command of Greek, even when he is condemning it. Heywood had argued that Herakles witnessed dramatic spectacles (the *drômenos* to which I have referred repeatedly) at the very first Olympic Games held in honor of his father, Zeus.

> In the first of the *Olimpiads*, amongst many other actiue exercises in which *Hercules* euer trimph'd as victor, there was in his nonage presented vnto him by his Tutor in the fashion of a History, acted by the choyse of the nobility of Greece, the worthy and memorable acts of his father *Iupiter*. Which being personated with liuely and well-spirited action, wrought such impression in his noble thoughts, that in meere emulation of his fathers valor (not at the behest of his Stepdame *Iuno*) he perform'd his twelue labours. . . . [65]

I. G. cuts immediately to the heart of Heywood's misreading of Pausanias. There was not one Herakles implicated at Olympia, he notes; there were two, if not more, and it was the mysterious *Cretan* Herakles whom Heywood has confused with the later Greek hero.

> Next doth *M. Actor* deriue his originall of acting *Playes* from the first *Olimpiad*. . . . To prooue this false, be it manifested that there were many *Hercules*. . . . The third was *Hercules of Crete*; a famous Souldier, institutor of the *Olympian* Games. This *Pausanias* calleth *Idaeus*, which is the third amongst the six numbred before by *Tully*. And this was that *Hercules* which triumphed as victor on Mount *Olympus*: the other, liued a whole Generation before his time; to whom the ambitious, and fabulous *Greekes* ascribe the labours of the rest. And therefore, as he ordained not the *Olympian* Games, so neither was he victor of them; for we neuer read of two *Hercules* on the Mount at once: Nor in the first *Olympiad* did he behold his Fathers warlike deeds personated before him. Wherefore this *M. Actors* Originall of *Playes*, is to be held disprooued; and that his *Hercules* by probable coniecture, neuer beheld *Play* at all. And so as the Proposition is ouerthrowne, the Assumption of others that should imitate him, is disanuld; and consequently the Conclusion cleane conuinced: and further yet for vnsoundnesse, to be confounded. [66]

But this is a strangely circuitous refutation. I. G. might simply have said that such Olympic dramas were dedicated to "Diuell Gods" and left the matter at that. That *has been* his argument, elsewhere. Greek culture was pagan culture. Yet the strange, subversive authority of the Greeks is not so easily dispensed with. I. G. feels compelled to claim *ownership* of Olympia, to read it *better* than Thomas Heywood has done, not simply to dismiss it out of hand. It is fascinating to see the lengths to which some Reformers will go in this endeavor, granting nearly as much authority to the Greek and Roman "Classics" as do the theatergoers to whom they addressed their criticisms. It comes as no surprise to see Thomas Heywood invoking Sophocles or Aeschylus; after all, he is a friend of their profession. It is odder to encounter someone like I. G. assembling Classical arguments from Classical authors to *dismantle* popular support for the theater in his own day. The Greeks, as we have seen in every chapter of this book, are not so easily dismissed. They may be appropriated, and recreated in the process, but they are seldom if ever abandoned.

AN APOLOGY FOR MORALISTS

I have been trying to comprehend the logic behind the printing of Heywood's *Apology* and I. G.'s *Refutation* together in the same book. I have been trying to attend to the values these authors share, despite the fact that they diverge so dramatically. They share the Greeks in a way, the whole edifice of Classical literature and myth. They diverge most dramatically over religion. There is a relationship between these two terms, as I have emphasized repeatedly in this book, and this complicates the intellectual landscape considerably. Both of these men were Christian, and both shared a certain vague commitment to the indeterminate authority of some Greek "Classics." They even seem to share a reverence for the shrine at Olympia, which is passing strange in the early seventeenth century. More dramatically still, both men are moralists. The Reformation was, Protestant and Puritan alike, animated primarily by this desire for moral reform. Ethics and morality were increasingly thought to be the very essence of religion. In this regard, too, the Greek tradition of poetic and philosophical speculation was believed to provide important resources to the moral cultivation of a human life, Christian or otherwise.

Thomas Heywood returns to the moral question, which was virtually the whole question for Protestantism, in his defense of the theater. In one of his most original contributions to the debate, Heywood insists that the theater has always had a moral and propaideutic purpose.[67] He insists that the theater teaches English history to people who cannot otherwise read about it. And one crucial part of learning such histories is the training it provides in the concomitant virtues of patriotism and civil obedience.

> [P]layes haue made the ignorant more apprehensiue, taught the vnlearned the knowledge of many famous histories, instructed such as cannot reade in the discouery of all our *English* Chronicles: & what man haue you now of that weake capacity, that cannot discourse of any notable thing recorded euen from *William* the *Conqueror*, nay from the landing of *Brute*, vntill this day, beeing possesst of their true vse, For, or because Playes are writ with this ayme, and carryed with this methode, to teach the subiects obedience to their King, to shew the people the vntimely ends of such as haue moued tumults, commotions, and insurrections, to present the [*sic*] with the flourishing estate of such as liue in obedience, exhorting them to allegiance, dehorting them from all trayterous and fellonious strategems.[68]

Heywood also makes several intriguing anecdotal arguments about persons who, confronted with a crime depicted on the stage, are shamed into the confession of their own transgressions. Here is the most noteworthy of them:

> Another of the like wonder happened at *Amsterdam* in *Holland*, a company of our *English* Comedians (well knowne) trauelling those Countryes . . . [here follows the detailed description of the performance of a jealous murder on stage]. As the Actors handled this, the audience might on a sodaine vnderstand an out-cry, and loud shrike in a remote gallery, and pressing about the place, they might perceiue a woman of great grauity, strangely amazed, who with a distracted & troubled braine oft sighed out these words: Oh my husband, my husband! The play, without further interruption, proceeded; the woman was to her owne house conducted, without any apparent suspition, euery one coniecturing as their fancies led them. In this agony she some dayes languished, and on a time, as certaine of her well-disposed neighbours came to comfort her, one amongst the rest being Church-warden, to him the Sexton posts, to tell him of a strange thing happening to him in the ripping vp of a graue: see here (quoth he) what I haue found, and shewes them a faire skull, with a great nayle pierst quite through the braine-pan, but we cannot coniecture to whom it should belong, nor how

long it hath laine in the earth, the graue being confused, and the flesh consumed. At the report of this accident, the woman, out of the trouble of her afflicted conscience, discouered a former murder. For 12 yeares ago, by driuing that nayle into that skull, being the head of her husband, she had trecherously slaine him. This being publickly confest, she was arraigned, condemned, adiudged, and burned. But I draw my subiect to greater length than I purposed. . . . [69]

This argument, if argument this be, is as strange as I. G.'s Olympic musings. By admitting the absolute priority of *moral* concerns in an institution devoted primarily to *aesthetic* entertainment, Heywood has already given up the very ground he ought to be defending. Poor strategic placement of one's forces loses the battle before a shot has been fired.

What I am suggesting is that the assumptions these authors would never think to question may be the most telling part of their arguments, for our purposes. It would never occur to I. G. to question the authority of the Greeks; it would never occur to Thomas Heywood to question the priority of morals and of moralism. If we want a more knowing defense of the theater on this point, along lines similar to the ones Heywood is attempting to traverse, then we might return with profit to William Shakespeare, a man who—deliberately, it may seem—never weighed in on these controversies at all.

Unless *Hamlet* was intended to be his intervention, as I think it may have been. To be sure, *Hamlet* is many things,[70] and Shakespeare customarily plays on many fronts at once. But I want to emphasize the role of religion in contributing to a richer understanding of Shakespeare, and of this play in particular.[71] I wish to return to the selfsame soliloquy with which I began this chapter. We should recall now that *Hamlet* had been performed just five years prior[72] to Heywood's original penning of the *Apology*.

> —Hum,—. I have heard,
> That guilty creatures sitting at a play
> Have by the very cunning of the scene
> Been struck so to the soul that presently
> They have proclaim'd their malefactions;
> For murther, though it have no tongue, will speak
> With most miraculous organ. I'll have these players
> Play something like the murther of my father
> Before mine uncle. I'll observe his looks,
> I'll tent him to the quick. If 'a do blench,
> I know my course. The spirit that I have seen
> May be a de'il, and the de'il hath power
> T'assume a pleasing shape;—yea, and perhaps
> Out of my weakness and my melancholy
> (As he is very potent with such spirits)
> Abuses me to damn me. I'll have grounds
> More relative than this. The play's the thing
> Wherein I'll catch the conscience of the king.[73]

Hamlet has been scolding himself for his inaction. He scolds himself first with the image of actors, worrying that their feigned grief on stage exceeds his own woe, which is real. And yet this dramatic argument results, ironically enough, in further delay. He cannot make the move to vengeance. It may be, Hamlet reasons, that the ghost he has taken to be his father's is in actual fact a demon—the Devil, after all, "hath power / T'assume a pleasing shape." Hamlet worries that what he has seen in reality (and what we have seen on stage) is actually an illusion. So he will concoct yet another illusion, a stage drama—the well known "play within the play"[74]—which is, in the subtlest irony of all, *a true history*. He will show Claudius his own crime—the real thing, but staged as a play—and he will watch him, waiting on the guilty response that will condemn him.

Now, on its own terms, this plan is fairly flimsy. Hamlet has been pretending to be mad—playing, yet again—and the act may have gotten the better of him. But within the larger religio-cultural setting of this play, the plan begins to make better sense. The play's staging in 1600 might actually help to explain Hamlet's *prima facie* confusion. For *Hamlet* is, of all Shakespeare's plays, the one most steeped in Catholic imagery and Catholic conventions.[75] It is the eminently Catholic-seeming worry about catching Claudius at prayer that motivates yet one more in a seemingly endless series of princely delays. Hamlet does not kill Claudius when he has the chance, but his reasons rely on an entirely medieval cosmology of Heaven, Hell, and Purgatory. When *Hamlet* was staged, the Puritans were already questioning the cultural and moral legitimacy of such "Papisticall" cosmologies, as well as such "Papisticall" practices as penitential or intercessory prayer—*and* the theater. Hamlet's argument in this soliloquy deliberately, and brilliantly, joins the debate, turning the arguments of a Puritan like I. G. on their head.

The Greeks had invented their theater, we were told, to celebrate their "Diuell-Gods." Hamlet—and, along with him, William Shakespeare, who probably *played* the ghost of Hamlet's father in this play, as well as scripted the Ghost's own speeches—turns this argument on its head. The Devil is loose in this world, the *real* world, he notes,[76] and if that is true, then the evidence of our senses is not always to be trusted.[77] Given the vast and impenetrable irony of human evil, and given the complexity of perceiving reality well, it may be in a play, ironically enough, that truth is sometimes best revealed.[78] Plays, as Aristotle had it, express universal truths rather than particular ones. They are this more philosophical and, hence, more fully truthful, than history.[79]

So it is that this play, especially in its "play within," serves notice in a very contemporary cultural and religious conflict—the debate about the moral status and the religious future of the English theater. Shakespeare, not suprisingly, weighs in on the side of the theater's friends. A notoriously unschooled poet with "small Latine and lesse Greeke,"[80] Shakespeare nevertheless strains in this play to make "Greeke" and "Latine" fully consonant with, and equal to, the value of any "Hebruisme." That was his gift, or else the "scandalous heathenisme," of his own mingle-mangled poetry, as you will.

In the next chapter I wish to turn to another prominent English voice, that of a dramatist and a poet who earned his fame almost immediately, and did not need to wait for it. He is George Gordon, Lord Byron (1788–1824), an enormously significant Romantic voice, as well as one of the very finest poets the movement produced. He was interested in poetry, in plays, in religion, and in morality. He seemed not to take any of them with any great seriousness (although I have my doubts about that). But one thing he took far more seriously than the author of *Troílus and Cressida* ever did, and that was an idea of singularly long standing: an idea called "Greece."

CHAPTER SEVEN

Childe Harold's Heyday

LORD BYRON AND THE LEVANT LUNATICS

Happy the nations of the moral North!
  Where all is virtue, and the winter season
Sends sin, without a rag on, shivering forth
  ('T was snow that brought St. Anthony to reason);
Where juries cast up what a wife is worth,
  By laying whate'er sum, in mulct, they please on
The lover, who must pay a handsome price,
Because it is a marketable vice.

—Byron, *Don Juan* I,§64 [1819]

The Isles of Greece, the Isles of Greece!
  Where burning Sappho loved and sung,
Where grew the arts of War and Peace,
  Where Delos rose, and Phoebus sprung!
Eternal summer gilds them yet,
  But all, except their Sun, is set.

—Byron, *Don Juan* III,§86 [1821]

Byron! how sweetly sad thy melody!

—Keats, *"Sonnet to Byron"* [1820/1]

PRELIMINARIES

It began, for me, each day around lunchtime. Perhaps it started before then, but that was when I noticed it. Each day. Every day. I had been living in Athens for well over a year, by then, wondering, however half-wittingly, how long you had to live in a place before you ceased to be a pilgrim and became something else again—a so-journer, perhaps? a resident-alien such as Aristotle had been for long years? I had been living in Greece for so long at that point that it had begun to feel like home, and I had begun to feel very nearly like an adoptive Greek, myself. It *was* home, to me, after all, and I had learned the language by then. Accounting for this mysterious sense of surreptitious adoption has been a large part of the story I am trying to tell in this book.

I was living in a lovely apartment, one of the loveliest physical spaces I've ever had the privilege of calling "home." It had been passed down from one archaeologist to another, remaining within the extended family comprised by the American School of Classical Studies for several decades now, and its *apothêkê* was filled with drafts and sketches, charts and plans, all of the accumulated detritus of the archaeologist's strange trade. I had inherited the home from a good friend who worked on Classical literature, a fellow student who had lived there with his equally charming Russian girlfriend for over a year. We had first come together through an informal collective reading of Mikhail Bulgakov's *The Master and Margerita;* before I knew it, I was living in their home, as they betook themselves of a second year abroad, in Rome this time.

I was nominally roughing out a dissertation, one committed to the strange and long-standing attraction of the idea of tragedy[1]—in Classical Athens primarily, then essentially off and on ever since then. I had happened on a rhythm that worked especially well for me; it allowed me to pursue the semblance of getting real work done, and had the added boon of keeping me on in Greece.

They are largely details, disjointed details, that I remember now, and I am painfully aware as I consider jotting them down that there will be no objective way of accounting for any of this, no way to give the *reader* some sense of what the *writer* felt about what he saw in those years. For the better part of 2500 years, or more—and certainly since Pausanias wrote up *A Greek Walkabout*—pilgrims and travelers have struggled with the same writerly dilemma that especially haunts the modern ethnographer—how to communicate the eerie power, and the special aura,[2] of *place.* Failing that, why bother to write at all? I have never come to any very felicitous answer to these important questions. So I content myself with prosaic stabs into the past's larger, encompassing darkness. This, too, has been one of this book's major preoccupations.

A large red, slightly dented, coffee pot. It came with the apartment. And, oddly enough, that's what I remember best. It was the first sight that greeted me, each and every morning, and it never failed to make me smile. Never mundane, it was one of those everyday objects that always managed to keep its aura. Rising early, at 6:00 AM on the dot, I would boil water for coffee on a small propane cooking stove, then contentedly drink Nescafe throughout the morning—heavy on the sugar, heavier still on the sweet, canned milk. I worked hard, for five hours at a stretch, reading and writing and drinking what seemed to be one continuous, and apparently bottomless, cup of coffee. Then I'd pass by the American School of Classical Studies to log on to what was then the sole, long-suffering computer there, to type up the scattered leaves of what I'd drafted earlier in the day. Armed with a printout of the day's production around noon, I would take the long route back home, passing by a lovely little wine store that had heavy red wines and retsinas from Santorini stored in large oak barrels along the wall. If you'd bring a container, any container, they would fill it, for a dollar or two. The day's work now largely finished, the most difficult deliberation facing me was "red or retsina?" Decision made, I hefted my papers, along with the wine, and headed thirstily home.

A short nap to shake off the morning's clutter of thinking. Then, shortly into the prettiest part of afternoon, I moved outside with a glass of wine—nominally to proof-read the day's copy, more often than not simply to gaze and to ponder. My apartment had happy access to two separate verandas: A small, enclosed porch replete with painted table and two wobbly chairs, invisible to the city behind high stuccoed white walls; and a larger rooftop with one of the clearest and most unobstructed views of the Akropolis available anywhere in the city. When I opted for this latter venue, as I normally did, I was also subtly broadcasting my intention to pay closer attention to the wine than to the word. And so, seated at last, mulling over my glass, smoking dis-tractedly, there came a diurnal vision of which I've never yet made full sense. In this book, I am grappling still with a problem that first posed itself there. As I sat smok-ing, sipping, and sorting, positively delighting in each and every sun-bleached day, I observed a seemingly endless caravan of Japanese tour buses making the long, tortu-ous climb to the Areopagus, at which point they disgorged their impressive cargoes of flashbulb-popping, video-toting visitors for their final, halting assaults on Athena's rocky summit. Ironic it seemed, in the extreme, these curious video montages of a building that had not moved in two and a half millennia—save for one ill-fated day when Venetian troops under Count Morosoni (the self-styled "Peloponnesiacus") lobbed a shell in from the Philopappis Hill across the way, detonating the Turks' pow-der magazine and shattering one entire side of the temple, in the early evening of September 26, 1687.[3] Venice's intentions I could just barely fathom, or at least so I believed at the time; this curious *Japanese* connection perplexed me, though. What in the world had *they* come for? What had they come to find? Surely not their "own" roots, and surely not some elusive sense of native self.[4]

Then it was, honest self-criticism always being a latecomer to philosophical re-flection, I suppose, that the more proximate question hit me full in the face, cutting a cruel swath through the pleasant haze of midday drinking: What in the world had *I* come here for? Wasn't this place as foreign to me as it was to them? If this were in fact a pilgrimage of sorts, then in whose name had I undertaken it, under what di-vine or human sponsorship, and what would announce itself as the authentic expe-rience, the moment of true arrival? In the intervening years, I have come across several answers to these vexed and vexing questions, some of them appearing from some rather unexpected quarters. This book is one attempt to answer them, and I have relied heavily on Byron's example in questing for an answer.

BYRON AND SHELLEY IN ITALY

It would be hard to overestimate the influence that Lord Byron (1788–1824) seems to have had in his own day—even and especially on the continent. Even Bertrand Russell, no great sympathizer with the vast seas of Romantic impulse, recognized the necessity, if not quite the poetic justice, in devoting *a full chapter* of his history of west-ern thought *to Byron*. "Among those whose importance is greater than it seemed," he grudgingly admits, "Byron deserves a high place."[5] The meteoric rise to international fame of a gifted wordsmith, his dissolute recklessness and the inevitable scandals that followed, the self-imposed exile, the histrionic death in a Grecian thunderstorm at the age of 36. . . . Byron's life seems larger, somehow, than the stage on which it played. Yet there is another factor lying at the very heart of the Byron myth, the thing from which I believe most everything else follows: his twofold "pilgrimage" to Greece.

If he had ever written a line worth leaving, Byron liked to say, then Greek air and Mediterranean light had been the inspiration. Some interesting attention has been paid of late to Byron's two Greek trips,[6] but the precedent for this Mediterranean intrigue was established already in the nineteenth century. Edward John Trelawny (1792–1881) spent a great deal of time with both Percy Bysshe Shelley (1792–1822) and Lord Byron, in Italy, until the former's untimely death came in 1822. Trelawny then enlisted in the Greek cause and traveled there with Byron in 1823. In 1831, he published a rather fanciful and self-serving autobiography, *Adventures of a Younger Son*, but then he turned to his memories of the two poets. Published first in 1858 as *Records of Shelley, Byron and the Author*, the book was reissued 20 years later as *Recollections of Shelley and Byron*.[7]

The premise of the book is interesting enough. Trelawny suggests a *comparative* study of these two supremely Romantic poets,[8] men who shared so much in the way of biographical details, and so little in the way of character. Both were self-styled exiles from England, both came to detest the proprieties of upper class British society, both were unhappily married, according to Trelawny's judgment, both died young. And they were fast friends, a point that, one suspects, Trelawny could not abide, and for which he seems never to have fully forgiven Byron.[9]

Despite these profound biographical convergences, though, Trelawny emphasizes the oppositions in their character: Shelley the avowed atheist, Byron the closeted Christian who could never fully flee his lingering Christian sensibilities;[10] Shelley the voracious reader and obsessive writer, Byron the lackadaisical late-night sketch-artist;[11] Shelley the old man in the body of a boy, Byron the eternal youth housed in the frame, and the fame, of a mature man-of-the-world;[12] Shelley, the long-suffering husband, Byron the divorcee and *cavalier servente*;[13] Byron drinking and joking and laughing, Shelley never.[14] It is, in its own way, an endlessly fascinating account, in large measure because the two main characters are so inherently fascinating. But Trelawny's "record" must be read with caution, for one very simple reason: he loved and admired Shelley immoderately, and he seems ultimately to have despised Byron. His own verdict could not be clearer; it is, in fact, the very first thing he tells us: "No two men could be more similar in all ways, yet I have seldom known two men more unhappy. . . . I have met men similar to Byron, but never to Shelley; he was the ideal of what a poet should be."[15] The careful reader cannot escape the feeling that Trelawny, himself a restless egomaniac, preferred the company of the unassuming Shelley to that wizened student of defective human nature, Lord Byron, a man who, moreover, seems to have seen through Trelawny's self-promotion almost at once.

Trelawny's recollections are most useful to me, then, for the details that come unintentionally and unannounced. What I wish to take away from his intriguing reminiscence are two other details, one final similarity between the two men, and one profound difference. Both Shelley and Byron were positively obsessed with water,[16] especially with the open ocean (although, tragically, Shelley could not swim). And while both men wrote encomiastically about Greece, only one of them actually ever traveled there. That man was Byron, who did so twice.

Byron was also famous, at a time when Shelley was forced to pay for the publication of his own poems.[17] Accounting for that odd-seeming contrast in the reception by their contemporaries requires some careful explanation, and some situating of the poets in their times. Without denying him the mastery of his Muse, Byron's times do account for a large measure of the poet's vast and controversial appeal. In Byron better than in Shelley, we seem to have the ideal poet for an overripe age. A great many of the premier tropes of Romanticism coalesced in Byron's own character, however artistically elaborated and exaggerated they may have been.

First, and perhaps foremost, we meet the newly privileged realm of Art (best thought of with a capital A), thoroughly detached now from the canons of orthodox religious representation. The creative imagination had gained a new prominence among philosophers, aesthetes, and theoreticians. How much the more, then, did these same thinkers revel in the exaggerated skills with which a poet could display his own versatility. Poetry, in this same era, was asserting its preeminence; a literary son supplanting the fatherhood of sculpture and of painting, rulers in a vast aesthetic hierarchy that had arguably held sway since the Renaissance.[18] Byron, then, was an *artist* in precisely these terms, a supremely imaginative, and at times rather self-absorbed, *artist*. Better still, he was a *poet*. And this accounts for some of his appeal, but only some of it. Shelley, after all, was both of these things, and more.

Several other of Byron's more singular attributes added to the fascination. He was an aristocrat by birth (albeit an illegitimate one, and thus a latecomer to his wealth), yet he remained committed to revolutionary politics—in England, in France, in Italy, in the New World colonies, and, most dramatically, in Greece herself. He flirted with the idea of joining Simon Bolivar in his revolution in New Grenada;[19] in fact, when he and Shelley commissioned boats to be built for their entertainment in Italy in the winter of 1821–1822, Byron named his *Bolívar*. Shelley, by contrast, named his skiff *Don Juan,* and died in her later that same summer.[20] Byron ultimately cast his lot with the Greeks in their struggle for independence against the Ottomans (1821–1830), and he died there, at Missolongi, in 1824, two years before the city was ultimately destroyed in a prolonged and especially wretched siege. There was also in Byron a studied and carefully crafted melancholy, a poetic voice that he never entirely abandoned, save in his hilarious master stroke, *Don Juan.* Byron and Byronism were different things, as we will have occasion to say many times.[21] In this crucial capacity of reinvention, as well as in the tone established by this essential self-division, Byron often anticipates Kierkegaard, that other troubled Romantic troubadour and troubling knight of faith.[22] Finally, Byron possesses some of that same intriguing (however ungrounded,[23] in his case) spiritual longing that one associates best with Romanticism. And therein lay the test.[24]

BYRON IN GREECE

Lord Byron took a long trip, composed an epic poem about it, called the trip a "pilgrimage," and that poem made him famous overnight. Byron famously quipped that, upon publication of the first two Cantos in 1812, he "awoke to find [him]self famous."[25] I have already suggested that Byron was the right poet at the right time. And so he surely was. But *Childe Harold's Pilgrimage* was also the right poem for a generation, a poem that knowingly referred to itself as a "pilgrimage."

Byron departed England in July of 1809 with John Cam Hobhouse (1786–1869); while Hobhouse returned within a year of their departure, Byron stayed on for two, and did not return to England until July of 1811. It was, for both men, a somewhat unusual version of the so-called Grand Tour, that finishing touch to a gentleman's education whereupon one was expected to survey the Continent (France, Switzerland, and Germany, at a minimum) and then to get at least a taste of the Mediterranean world,[26] by heading south, and east—toward the sunshine, toward a more budding sensuality, toward second childhood in a way,[27] and toward that exotic-seeming spirituality long associated with "the east."[28]

Edward Said has suggested that such "pilgrimages"—made inevitably to a place called "the east" in those years—played an important role in the creation of what he calls "Orientalism" in the nineteenth century. He is interested in the way that the *European* identity was manufactured through the deliberate positioning of itself *over against* the primarily Ottoman east,[29] as well as over against the vast collection of New World and Indian colonies.[30] But European power-politics were destined to play a still more complex role than Said allows,[31] since Europe in the early nineteenth century was never a singular entity. "Europe" was, in fact, the most hotly contested concept of them all. And the greatest single contest over the idea of Europe, that initiated by Napoleon Bonaparte (1769–1821), significantly altered both the style and the tenor of the English Grand Tour in the first two decades of the nineteenth century, until the Greek War for Independence broke out in 1821. Most British Tourists in the eighteenth century—and here Goethe was ironically a Teutonic pioneer[32]—had wandered across the Channel first, and then across the Continent. For the vast majority of them, *Italy* was the aristocratic pilgrim's goal—a land of abundant sunshine, easy sexuality, a rather pagan-seeming brand of Catholicism, and, increasingly, a land that embodied all of the drama and all of the romance of Classical antiquity. Rome was all romance and ruins, and if the Vatican figured at all in these pilgrims' meanderings, then it did so largely for its new Museum of Pagan Antiquities (created by Clement XIII, who was pope for only a decade, 1758–1769, and whose own funerary monument would be carved by Canova). This relatively newfound fascination with Classical antiquity (in this case genuinely "Greco-Roman") was fast becoming the premier source for that "ungrounded spiritual longing" to which I have alluded before.

But Napoleon's forces had occupied northern Italy for the first time in 1796, well before his Egyptian campaign of 1798–1800, and when war broke out between France and Great Britain in May of 1803, Napoleon issued his infamous decree that made all British subjects between the ages of 16 and 60 nominal prisoners of war. When crowned king of Italy in 1805, Napoleon closed most of that peninsula to the British as well.[33] The British traveler was thus pushed further east in order to touch on some version of those "classical" southern treasures. We are witnessing a well-worn path here, the trajectory of an idea that will take us from Rome to Romanticism: from Italy to Greece, from Rome to Athens, from a piece of Europe to a long-suffering province of the then-Ottoman Empire. From now on, British travelers[34] (as well as the French,[35] but remarkably few Germans until the formation of the German nation-state in 1871[36]) would make their pilgrimages to Greece in ever-increasing numbers. Moreover, a virtual cottage industry of publications about such trips emerged in these same decades;[37] we are witnessing the birth of the genre of the amateur travelogue as well.[38]

Byron's and Hobhouse's trip just so happened to anticipate this trend. And not only this: for the British and the Ottomans had gone to war briefly in 1807, but had signed a peace in January of 1809, making travel to Greece possible for British

Grand Tourists once again. Here, as so often in his later travels, Byron was lucky, as well as plucky. His trip was a decided novelty, something of a first and therefore something of a phenomenon. While British *scholars* had long been subsidized to course over Greek as well as Roman antiquities, and then to publish their sketches and research,[39] a Greek *Tour* was different. The Grand Tour was about *modern* times, as much as it was about antiquity, and therein lies the heart of Harold's different-ness. It is a key part of what made *his* trip a "pilgrimage."

A careful survey of Appendix One makes one thing abundantly clear: *Childe Harold's Pilgrimage* (on which Byron began working on the road with Hobhouse, in Ioannina in November of 1809) *precisely* maps the trip that Byron and Hobhouse actually took. Harold's trip just *is* Byron's; but Byron uses the mythical figure of his Harold to transform this trip into a spiritual event, a veritable pilgrimage of the Ro-mantic soul. And that was the stroke of poetic genius.

The first two Cantos of this pilgrimage poem were published in March of 1812 and caused an immediate sensation. They take us from Portugal to Spain (Canto One), and then flit briefly past Italy on the way to Albania and "Greece" (the quo-tation marks here are intended to remind us that Greece was an idea at the time, not yet a nation-state). So the poem is simply an epic presentation of what was nonethe-less a very personal trip.

What accounts for its enormous and immediate appeal to a wider public? To be sure, the poem has some memorable images, and some especially memorable lines. But it is also often disjointed and dispersive, and it is always episodic, imagistic and non-narrative. It cuts very much against the contemporary taste for travel writing, with some notable and noteworthy exceptions.[40] How, then, did Byron manage it?

Byron very deliberately made a myth of himself, creating what was to be the de-finitive Romantic image of the melancholic and world-weary traveler, coursing over history and semisacred Mediterranean water. As Bertrand Russell puts it, "he was more important as a myth than as he really was."[41] This Byronic myth, that creates the very distance which separates Byron from his Byronism, was in large measure built on the pretense that Harold[42] simply was not like other men. The lion's share of the first two cantos of *Childe Harold's Pilgrimage* is devoted to literary musings at bat-tlefields and Classical ruins of other kinds. But Harold is knowingly cynical about these sorts of things.

> 'T was on a Grecian autumn's gentle eve
> Childe Harold hail'd Leucadia's cape afar;
> A spot he longed to see, nor cared to leave:
> Oft did he mark the scenes of vanish'd war,
> Actium, Lepanto, fatal Trafalgar;
> Mark them unmoved, for he would not delight
> (Born beneath some remote inglorious star)
> In themes of bloody fray, or gallant fight,
> But loathed the bravo's trade, and laughed at martial wight.[43]

Harold is moved by passion, romantic passion, more than by "war and war's alarms."[44] And Byron's actual sojourn, for its part, was true to this Romantic code, banging and crashing as he did from one tortuous involvement to another—especially in the year following Hobhouse's departure, and Byron's long residence in Athens.[45]

This remained true when Byron finally returned to England in 1811. Byron's mother died in the very month of his return. Several months later came the poem, and then immediately on its heels came fame. Two years—and two tumultuous affairs—later, Byron was finally engaged to Annabella Milbanke (after she had curiously put the poet off twice). The two were finally married after some delay in January of 1815, and in December, their daughter, Augusta Ada, was born. Then, with some of the inevitable drama and mystery[46] that necessarily attaches itself to Byron's name, Lady Milbanke returned to her family in January, and the whispering campaign commenced. In April 1816 the couple legally separated. Deadened now by scandal of a less saleable kind, and beset by worrisome debts, Byron departed England in the same month, never to return.

BYRON IN ITALY

And so began a second Byronic Tour, less Grand perhaps, but really no more purposeful. Appendix One once again provides the particulars. Between April and August of 1816, Byron took a more traditional Tour, exploring portions of Belgium and Germany and Holland, then he settled in at Geneva in the company of the Shelleys, also fleeing romantic scandal of their own, and of Claire Clairmont, who would bear Byron's second child, a daughter named Allegra, in January of 1817. In August, John Cam Hobhouse arrived to lend Byron his emotional support, and to travel with him again—to Italy, this time. They settled in Milan first, and finally in Venice, where Byron was destined to remain for several years. This trip inspired a Third and Fourth Canto of *Childe Harold's Pilgrimage* (the poem, along with *Don Juan,* was always unfinished in Byron's mind, always potential inspiration for one more canto), and in 1818 Byron dedicated the entire composition to Hobhouse, his longtime friend and traveling companion. Canto Three is all northern Europe: Waterloo and Napoleon ("a kind/ Of bastard Caesar," as Byron refers to him now[47]), Switzerland and Rousseau. Canto Four is Italy, all Italy, and in it, Byron drops the last lingering pretense of Harold's being a personality separable in any meaningful way from himself.[48]

There are many tropes we will have come to expect by now in these Third and Fourth Cantos. There is Byron's eloquent paean to the creative imagination:

> 'T is to create, and in creating live
> A being more intense that we endow
> With form our fancy, gaining as we give
> The life we image, even as I do now.
> What am I? Nothing: but not so art thou,
> Soul of my thought! with whom I traverse earth
> Invisible but gazing, as I glow
> Mix'd with thy spirit, blended with thy birth,
> And feeling still with thee in my crush'd feelings' dearth.[49]

There are some remarkable musings on the agony of exile, even when and where one desires it:

> Once more upon the waters! yet once more!
> And the waves bound beneath me as a steed

That knows his rider. Welcome to their roar!
Swift be their guidance, wheresoe'er it lead!
Though the strain'd mast should quiver as a reed,
And the rent canvas fluttering strew the gale,
Still must I on. . . . [50]

In addition, the poet now strikes notes far more personal than any we have heard before. He comments on the failure and dissolution of his marriage:

I have not loved the world, nor the world me,—
But let us part fair foes; I do believe,
Though I have found them not, that there may be
Words which are things, hopes which will not deceive,
And virtues which are merciful, nor weave
Snares for the failing; I would also deem
O'er others' griefs that some sincerely grieve;
That two, or one, are almost what they seem,
That goodness is no name, and happiness no dream. [51]

And still more poignantly on the practical loss of his daughter:

Is thy face like thy mother's, my fair child!
ADA! Sole daughter of my house and heart?
When last I saw thy young blue eyes they smiled,
And then we parted,—not, as now we part,
But with a hope.— [52]

There is more than mere autobiography here, although there is a great deal of that in Canto Three. The Fourth Canto of the *Pilgrimage* especially is a long, at times a somewhat tiring, catalogue of great *Italian* poets and sculptors—Canova, Tasso, Alfonso, Boileau, Torquato, Ariosto, just to name a few. [53] Florence is invoked as "the Etrurian Athens." [54] Venice is "Europe's bulwark 'gainst the Ottomite." [55] And Rome is . . . well, Rome is the capital of the Mediterranean world.

In fact, it is *Rome,* not Athens, which seems to mesmerize Byron now, its ruins and antiquities, museums and galleries—in short, the very things that had impressed Hobhouse, not Byron, in Greece. [56] Byron understood the ugly paradox of modern Eurohellenism. [57] The modern European who loved Greece so much that he wished to loot her, to bring her treasures home with him, was a strange friend, indeed. Byron met many such "friends" during his first trip, one of whose stories I will tell in the next chapter. Byron made much of what he considered the shameful pilfering of Greek antiquities by his fellow Scotsman, Lord Elgin, in the original two cantos of the *Pilgrimage,* [58] and he composed a deadly serious satire on this theft while in residence again in Athens in 1811. [59] The poem, like the controversy, caused quite a local stir at the time.

Byron was more interested in Modern Greece than he was in Greek antiquity, in part, because he was always suspicious of Romantic reconstructions of the past. The only real complaint that the original cantos of the *Pilgrimage* received was that the poet painted too nasty a portrait of the past. Byron's answer—and this is the heart and soul of his Romantic anti-romanticism—was that the age of chivalry was none-too-chivalrous. The knights were all unknightly. In any case, Byron appended this point to the Preface of his poem in 1813:

Now, it so happens that the good old times, when "l'amour du bon vieux temps, l'amour antique," flourished, were the most profligate of all possible times. . . . The vows of chivalry were no better kept than any other vows whatsoever; and the songs of the Troubadours were not more decent, and certainly were much less refined, than those of Ovid.[60]

If that was true of the Middle Ages, then it was even more the case with the ancient Greeks. There were Romantics, like Hobhouse and Shelley and Trelawny, who faulted the modern Greeks for looking so little like Classicizing fictions made the past out to be. Never Byron. In the little harbor at Leghorn (from which Shelley would depart on his doomed last voyage in the following year), Trelawny took Shelley on a walking tour of the many foreign ships tied up at the docks—French, American, Spanish, Austrian, Dutch, Danish, Russian, and a bevy of boats from throughout Italy. There was also a Greek bombard in port, and Trelawny knew her captain. "As you have lately written a poem, 'Hellas,' about the modern Greeks," Trelawny opines, would it not be as well to take a look at them amidst all the din of the docks?" Having surveyed the men in the rigging of the *San Spiridione*, Trelawny queries the Poet: "Does this realize your idea of Hellenism, Shelley?" The reply is predictably negative: "No! But it does of Hell!"[61] Nineteenth-century travel writing about Greece is full of such stuff, which makes its absence in Byron's writings all the more telling.

Byron's appreciation for modern Greece and modern Greeks derived from the fact that he was already interested in the Greek independence movement. He pleads eloquently for European support of what he understood must nonetheless be a *native* independence movement. He appeals to ancient monuments, like the ones at Marathon and Delphi, to help ground the originary myths such nationalist movements often require,[62] but he insists on the essential *difference* between ancient stones and modern movements. More particularly, the fact that Europeans support Greek freedom fighters should not serve as justification for the kind of looting of antiquities that had begun in Egypt under Napoleon.[63] We would do well to recall that members of what was called "the Morea Expedition"—French troops landed in support of the Greek independence movement in 1828—turned immediately to an "excavation" of the Temple of Zeus at Olympia almost as soon as the shooting stopped.[64] Byron seems intent on distinguishing as clearly as he can between the Greek antiquity he may or may not have admired—this ambivalence, perhaps more than anything else, is what made him an unusual kind of Romantic—and the contemporary Greek world he had come to love.[65] One cannot, after all, love an idyll—even if his name is Harold, even if her name is Hellas.

While more muted in Rome, Byron never loses hold of this insight entirely, the sense of the gulf that separates antiquities from more contemporary concerns. Even in Rome, several long years after the original Tour, Byron's Pilgrim still maintains the poetic pretense of being unlike other men, in art now, as well as in politics.

> There be more things to greet the heart and eyes
> In Arno's Dome of Art's most princely shrine,
> Where Sculpture with her rainbow sister vies;
> There be more marvels yet—but not for mine;
> For I have been accustom'd to entwine
> My thoughts with Nature rather in the fields
> Than Art in galleries;[66]

Schooled on Nature, rather than on art and artifice, Harold has apparently *achieved* his pilgrim's goal, in this, the fourth and final canto. At least so Byron would have us believe:

> But I forget.—My Pilgrim's shrine is won,
> And he and I must part,—so let it be,—
> His task and mine alike are nearly done;
> Yet once more let us look upon the sea;[67]

We are now II stanzas from the conclusion of the poem, and we have not yet been told why this was called a "pilgrimage" to begin with, nor where its author has been aiming. Several possibilities suggest themselves, here, in the Fourth Canto. Greece has given way to Italy, for starters. Byron seems singularly impressed by Rome—perhaps this was a pilgrimage to the self-styled capital of the Mediterranean world.[68] He is most impressed by the architectural perfection he associates with Hadrian's Pantheon—so perhaps this is a pilgrimage to the paganism of antiquity we met already in Pausanias, represented here in its purest aesthetic expressions.[69] Or it may be that Byron was simply making pilgrimage to the south, and to the east, as so many other Tourists—whom Byron referred to as "Levant Lunatics"[70]—were to do, in increasing numbers in ensuing decades. I have already commented on the curious path that takes us back and forth between Greece and Italy in the nineteenth century. But there is more, and I suspect that the last line I quoted tells the tale. Byron concludes his elegiac pilgrimage with a quieter kind of meditation *on the sea*. The Ocean is where this Pilgrimage, like the poem itself, comes to rest. And it is only now that we realize how much time Byron and Harold *both* have spent at sea. Byron was, in any case, always *enormously* popular among seafarers.[71]

BYRON AT SEA

Joseph Conrad, who along with Herman Melville[72] and Byron, was one of the greatest water-writers in the English language, composed a little-known but deeply personal meditation on his own lifelong immersion in and relation to the sea, at the very end of his writerly career. The book was not published until 1906. Conrad makes any number of interesting observations in this little book, but he makes one that calls Byron immediately to mind. Astonishingly, Conrad tells us that no sailor worth his rum and hardtack loves the sea. What sailors love are *ships*.

> I suspect, leaving aside the protestations and tributes of writers who, one is safe in saying, care for little else in the world than the rhythm of their lines and the cadence of their phrase, the love of the sea, to which some men and nations confess so readily, is a complex sentiment wherein pride enters for much, necessity for not a little, and the love of ships— the untiring servants of our hopes and our self-esteem—for the best and most genuine part. For the hundred who have reviled the sea, beginning with Shakespeare in his line—
>
> More fell than hunger, anguish, or the sea
>
> down to the last obscure sea-dog of the old "model" having but few words and still fewer thoughts, there could not be found, I believe, one sailor who has ever coupled a curse with the good or bad name of a ship.[73]

Sailors, in short, may be all-too-generous in their bestowal of curses on the waters, but on a gunwhale, never. Why? The answer is simple: The sea is dangerous; ships—"the craft[s] which, made by man, [are] one with man"[74]—are our only protection from her (or it, or him).

> The sea—the truth must be confessed—has no generosity. No display of manly qualities—courage, hardiness, endurance, faithfulness—has ever been known to touch its irresponsible consciousness of power. The ocean has the conscienceless temper of a savage autocrat spoiled by much adulation. He cannot brook the slightest appearance of defiance, and has remained the irreconcilable enemy of ships and men ever since the ships and men had the unheard-of audacity to go afloat together in the face of his frown. From that day he has gone on swallowing up fleets and men without his resentment being glutted by the number of victims—by so many wrecked ships and wrecked lives. To-day, as ever, he is ready to beguile and betray, to smash and to drown the incorrigible optimism of men who, backed by the fidelity of ships, are trying to wrest from him the fortune of their house, the dominion of their world, or only a dole of food for their hunger. If not always in the hot mood to smash, he is always stealthily ready for a drowning. The most amazing wonder of the deep is its unfathomable cruelty.[75]

The attentive reader will surely notice that the sea is masculine in this sailor's telling of the matter; it is ships that are feminine, so named and so loved by men. For loved they surely are, almost idolatrously. Why do sailors, then, remain incapable of loving the sea? Because the sea cannot love, himself. The sea, you see, is a terrifying place. Be sure to note that Conrad calls it "unfathomable." Therein lies the tale. The sea is a terrifying basin of deep water, not a matter of sunshine-and-surface at all.

It seems crucially important to recall that Byron and Shelley, unlike Conrad, did not know "modern" ships. By that I mean *metal* ships, for, as Conrad rightly reminds his not-so-seafaring audience, "in his own time a man is always very modern." Conrad makes this observation when he is comparing modern, metal ships to those marvelous wooden craft that had been the only ships ever known to man or woman until the mid-nineteenth century. Mark Twain—very like Joseph Conrad, and very *unlike* Lord Byron—already lives in a different maritime world:

> [Y]our modern ship which is a steam-ship makes her passages on other principles than yielding to the weather and humoring the sea. She receives smashing blows, but she advances; it is a slogging fight, and not a scientific campaign. The machinery, the steel, the fire, the steam have stepped in between the man and the sea. A modern fleet of ships does not so much make use of the sea as exploit a highway. The modern ship is not a sport of the waves. Let us say that each of her voyages is a triumphant progress; and yet it is a question whether it is not a more subtle and more human triumph to be the sport of the waves and yet survive, achieving your end.[76]

In an age innocent of cruise ships and airplanes, dangerous, and boring, and overlong sea-travel was *the* way in which the Grand Tourist got from place to place, places which are still referred to, rather aquacentrically, as "foreign shores." They are perceived as "shores" only from the perspective of a ship, seldom from an airplane, which "sails" above the clouds. There was no jetlag in the nineteenth century. Travel from-here-to-there took months, as it always had done.

Sea-travel in wooden ships, then, was the norm for Byron, for Shelley, and for virtually everyone whom I have discussed in this book. It was so in a manner almost entirely foreign to anyone reading Byron and Shelley today. Still more significant, sea travel in wooden, wind-driven craft was a very, very different enterprise from the cruder slugfest of steam-and-steel so aptly and ambivalently described by Conrad. Modern shipping has turned the sea into a highway, he notes, decisively altering the human relationship to basins and seas that had reigned for millennia. Byron writes on the far side of this divide. His was an age in which shipwrecks were a commonplace, not an anomaly. The idea of wreckage and of ruin captured the popular and poetic imagination of the nineteenth century, the great age of imperial colonial expansion that was driven, as colonialism always was, by boats. Note that this compelling imagery of sea-wreckage did not need a name, then . . . *Monitor, Titanic, Lusitania,* these were ironclads, all. Shipwrecks were a *generic* idea in the nineteenth century.

All of this is relevant to Byron's career. He spent more than one full year of his short life on boats. And yet, Conrad notwithstanding, Byron was not a ship-person. Trelawny makes this point with ill-disguised contempt; the Pilgrim, he sneers, learned only enough about boats to *write* about them.[77] But Conrad gives us a deeper insight into the mind of this poet. If the true sailor loves ships and hates the sea, then the true swimmer loves the sea and remains indifferent to boats. Byron took no care of boats, not even his own. But he, like Harold, loved the sea immoderately.

Byron and the sea, Byron and swimming. These ideas make up what proves to be a large constellation, vaster in its own way than the Byronic pilgrimage undertaken in the first canto of *Childe Harold's Pilgrimage.* In an uncanny, impossible-to-summarize recent book that might best be read as a cultural history of recreational swimming, Charles Sprawson[78] demonstrates how Byron created this myth, too, and, eventually, a European taste to go with it. On his original Tour with Hobhouse, in May of 1810, Byron made a very public point of swimming across the Hellespont,[79] an especially deep waterway that separated one fiction called "Asia" or "the East" from another one called "Europe." Byron referred repeatedly to this swim throughout his life, claiming (in his correspondence, especially)[80] that he was prouder of this than any of his impressive poetic accomplishments. Another curious pilgrimage industry would develop in the wake of this remarkable swim,[81] and the increasing posthumous fame of this remarkable poet, one in which Sprawson himself happily participated. One actually makes pilgrimage now—"to swim where Byron swam"—all across the Mediterranean, from Portugal to Turkey, but especially here, in the Dardanelles.

Why was this swim so dramatic, why was the grip it had on the European imagination so profound? Byron, after all, was an addictive and rather constant swimmer. Trelawny tries to portray him as a poor swimmer well past his prime, but his accounts lack credibility.[82] In Venice, Byron made a very public point of spending six hours at a stretch in the canals. Why, then, is it the Hellespont that we remember? The symbolic cache of this swim is clear enough, especially in European cities poised for war "'gainst th' Ottomite" in Greece and elsewhere.

Yet it was clearly more than this. The Hellespont is an unusually deep water basin that narrows, and shallows, to a fairly tight channel in relatively short space. The enormous volume of water filtering through the decreasing space of the channel creates some pretty treacherous currents. This forces the would-be Hellespontier further out, to make what is a much longer swim over much deeper water. And it is this *depth* that many people, myself included, find especially unnerving about a swim in the open ocean.

Byron never did. His reasons are especially interesting: He lived his life the way he swam, Byron insisted, by thinking only on the surface of things.[83] Swimming the Hellespont was, for this poet, a lazy enough swim (only an hour and ten minutes, in total, though admittedly on his second attempt) over a relatively calm sea surface. The depths here did not trouble him, as they troubled many another Romantic poet, because he simply refused to think on them. Drowning was to become a trope nearly as commonplace as melancholy for most Romantic poets in this generation. Shelley was but one on a surprisingly long list of Romantics—and friends of Byron—who met a watery end.[84]

Later, in Italy, when Byron, Trelawny, and company cremated Shelley's exhumed body (as well as another, that of E. E. Williams, who drowned with him) on a beach in the Gulf of Spezia where it had been recovered, Byron could not handle the inescapable depth of this scene. As Shelley's heart bubbled but refused to burn, and as Trelawny fished it from the furnace, Byron retreated, as he so often did, by stripping down in mid-ceremony and entering the ocean, returning from an especially long swim only when the pyre had consumed itself and his friend.[85] Everything washed clean by the sea. If Harold's trip was indeed a pilgrimage, then it was one aimed at the sea, the *Mediterranean* Sea.[86]

So this "pilgrimage" ends tentatively in 1818 with a vision of an ocean, and "Harold" ends at sea. There is a curious kind of hard-won calm that comes with staying closer to the surface of things:

> Roll on, thou deep and dark blue Ocean—roll!
> Ten thousand fleets sweep over thee in vain;
> Man marks the earth with ruin—his control
> Stops with the shore . . . [87]

And again:

> Time writes no wrinkle on thine azure brow:
> Such as creation's dawn beheld, thou rollest now.[88]

This selfsame sea would prove to be the only lasting love the poet ever knew, and this fictional Childe was ultimately a child of those same waters:

> And I have loved thee, Ocean! and my joy
> Of youthful sports was on thy breast to be
> Borne, like thy bubbles, onward: from a boy
> I wanton'd with thy breakers—they to me
> Were a delight; and if the freshening sea
> Made them a terror—'t was a pleasing fear,
> For I was as it were a child of thee . . . [89]

There were, of course, other Romantic children running wild over this same storied land-and-seascape in these same years. I turn, in the next chapter, to another such young man, one whose path crossed Byron's at a decisive point in his first Tour. His name was Charles Robert Cockerell.

CHAPTER EIGHT

From Greece to Germany, From Aegina to Munich:

CHARLES COCKERELL AND THE DISCOVERY OF THE PEDIMENTAL SCULPTURE FROM THE TEMPLE TO APHAIA

Yes, 't was Minerva's self; but, ah! how changed,
Since o'er the Dardan field in arms she ranged!
Not such as erst, by her divine command,
Her form appear'd from Phidias' plastic hand:
Gone were the terrors of her awful brow,
Her idle aegis bore no Gorgon now;
Her helm was dinted, and the broken lance
Seem'd weak and shaftless e'en to mortal glance;
The olive branch, which still she deigned to clasp,
Shrunk from her touch, and wither'd in her grasp;
And, ah! though still the brightest of the sky,
Celestial tears bedimm'd her large blue eye:
Round the rent casque her owlet circled slow,
And mourn'd his mistress with a shriek of woe!

"Mortal!"—'t was thus she spake—"that blush of shame
Proclaims thee Briton, once a noble name;
First of the mighty, foremost of the free,
Now honour'd less by all, and least by me:
Chief of thy foes shall Pallas still be found.
Seek'st thou the cause of loathing?—look around.
Lo! here, despite of war and wasting fire,
I saw successive tyrannies expire.
'Scaped from the ravage of the Turk and Goth,
Thy country sends a spoiler worse than both.
Survey this vacant, violated fane;
Recount the relics torn that yet remain:
These Cecrops placed, this Pericles adorned,
That Adrian rear'd when drooping science mourn'd.
What more I owe let gratitude attest—
Know, Alaric and Elgin did the rest.

—Byron, *"The Curse of Minerva"* [1811]

Travel to Greece, in the manner of finishing off a university education, was really a creation of the nineteenth century.[1] It was often couched, given the loose-fitting spirituality of the age, as a "pilgrimage." And it was performed, as often as not, by comparative "children"—like Harold, like Byron, and like other children of the age. While hardly student backpackers, there are nonetheless parallels between this flood of British tourism and the flood of contemporary EuroAmerican undergraduates who descend on modern Greece each summer.

There was a very narrow window in which such Romantic pilgrimages occurred, however, one lasting not more than 20 years in all. It began in 1803, when a notorious Napoleonic edict, combined with French successes in northern Italy, effectively closed the Italian peninsula to British traffic, forcing the would-be Grand Tourist further to the east. And it came to an end rather suddenly in 1821, when the Greek revolution against the Ottoman Empire broke out. That war would not conclude until the Conference of London in 1830, and its dramatic endgame: The creation of a fledgling nation-state confined within fairly narrow Peloponnesian borders, replete with a British constitution drafted by Jeremy Bentham[2] and a Bavarian king. By the time travel to the eastern Mediterranean really picked up again, the age of steam had commenced. The train and iron steamship transformed this part of the world and essentially democratized the phenomenon of Mediterranean tourism,[3] just as surely as the displacement of Romanticism by the Victorian ethos would transform British society. These transformations can be overstated and too much made of them; still, it seems clear, from the perspective of Greek travel at least, that the second half of the nineteenth century bears scant resemblance to the first.

It was in the first decade of the nineteenth century that the fledgling "science" of Archaeology was born as well. Here again, what counted as "archaeology" was a very different matter from what went by that name when Heinrich Schliemann (1822–1890)[4] exposed enormous portions of the ancient cities of Troy (1871), Mycenae (1876), and Tiryns (1884). When French troops under Napoleon invaded Egypt in 1798, the force included a veritable army of scientists to accompany the more traditional army of soldiers.[5] Given the mania for Egyptology characterizing the Parisian intellectual scene just then, there was real eagerness to "excavate" the pyramids and other such funerary institutions.[6] Many of these artifacts—granite obelisks, mummies, as well as the famed Rosetta Stone[7]—were to make their way back to France, on the French retreat and their eventual expulsion in late 1800. So it was that the precedent—along with a veritable science of looting—was born. Greece, of course, would be looted throughout the nineteenth century,[8] and most of her most famous works of ancient art were to end up in the great capitals of Europe: The Parthenon marbles went to London in the first decade; the Aphrodite of Melos (Venus de Milo) and the Winged Victory of Samothrace went to Paris in the age of Napoleon; the Pergamene Frieze went to Berlin immediately after the formation of the German nation-state in 1870/1. And, as we shall see in this chapter, through a complex and fascinating combination of bizarre events, the pedimental statues from a lesser-known temple, that of Aphaia on the island of Aegina, went to Munich in the third decade of the nineteenth century.

If my titular question in this book has emphasized Greek "thought," it will nonetheless be clear how much time and attention I have devoted to the *material* culture of Greek religion. And so, in this chapter, my question changes slightly. Was Greek *art* religious? What has not been sufficiently remarked is the way in which ancient Greek *religious* art was detached from its religious context in the nineteenth century, and placed in a decidedly modern context, something called a "museum." Such "houses of the Muses" may not be houses of worship, exactly, but worship of a sort did decidedly take place there.[9] Greek art still functions, however subtly, as *religious* art, if for no other reason than that "Greek" has so consistently denoted something vaguely "religious"—from Rome until Romanticism.

THE ELGIN PRECEDENT

After three months in Turkey, Lord Byron and John Hobhouse departed Constantinople on July 14, 1810. Three days later, they were on the island of Kea, just off the eastern coast of Attica. And here they parted, Hobhouse bound directly back to England, Byron intent upon Athens. After travelling through the Peloponnese, and after paying special attention to Pausanias's Eleia, Byron made it back to Athens on August 19, 1810. He and Hobhouse had lodged the previous year in the home of Procopius Macri (d. 1799), former British Consul in Athens. Procopius's widow, Theodora (née Vrettos) would take in British visitors throughout the first two decades of the nineteenth century, and her home was to become a mandatory stop on the British Tour, after Byron immortalized the youngest Macri daughter, Teresa, in a poem entitled "Maid of Athens" (1810), just prior to his Turkish trip.[10] She would become something (and the objectification here is deliberate) on which every subsequent traveler felt the need to comment: Whether she was as beautiful as Byron had made her out to be; the nature of her character, and her manners; the good fortune of her marriage to a career British diplomat named Black; how well, or how poorly, she had aged.

On returning to Athens in the summer of 1810, Byron felt the need to put some distance between the Macri household and himself, as his casual flirtation with all three daughters—Mariana, Katinka, and Teresa—threatened to become a more serious entanglement. The girls' mother was intent on marrying Teresa off to this handsome (but not yet famous) English Lord. So Byron installed himself in the Capuchin Convent, a famous Athenian landmark built at the foot of the Akropolis in such a way that it actually incorporated the Hellenistic Lysicrates Monument into its outer walls. The convent would become an ever more popular hostelry until the outbreak of the War of Independence, when it was dismantled. Only the Lysicrates Monument remains on the spot today.[11]

Byron spent the winter of 1810–1811 here in Athens and recalled it ever after as one of the happiest times in his life. There just so happened to be a remarkable circle of European expatriates living in Athens at the time—all of them cultured, all of them interested in ancient archaeology and in contemporary art—where a casual circuit of dinners, excursions, and even the occasional ball, kept them thoroughly entertained throughout the cool winter months.

One of the main topics of conversation and controversy that year (the other being the possibilities and prospects of a Greek revolution) concerned the dismantling of the Parthenon, high atop the Akropolis and prominently visible from the

Capuchin Hostelry. The work was nearly finished by then, and would in fact be completed that same winter. It was organized and financed by Thomas Bruce, Seventh Earl of Elgin (1766–1841),[12] an ill-fortuned career diplomat who would lend his name both to this Classical collection ("the Elgin Marbles") as well as to an infamous new French term for pillage (*elginisme*).[13] After service in Brussels and Berlin, Elgin was assigned as British ambassador to the Sublime Porte (as Constantinople was then known) in 1799. When the French suffered their reverses in Egypt in 1800 (repulsed by the Ottomans, whose province it was), and the British star was on the rise, Elgin leveraged this position to acquire a now notorious *firman* that, when loosely interpreted, permitted his men not only to affix scaffolding on the Temple of Athena so as to sketch it, but actually "to take away any piece of stone with old inscriptions or figures."[14] Presumably, the Turks anticipated Elgin's making plaster casts of these pieces; Elgin, however, was hellbent on taking them back to England.

The work commenced in earnest in 1801, employing upward of 400 workmen at times. It was directed by Giovanni Battista Lusieri (d. 1821), a Neapolitan artist who would always be Elgin's man in Greece. Elgin and his wife visited the site in the Spring of 1802, remained in Greece from April until June, then returned to Turkey, where they arrived in the Porte in January of 1803, shortly before Elgin's recall to London. They made their way slowly home—via Athens, Rome, and Paris. And Elgin just so happened to be in Paris on May 23, 1803, when Napoleon's notorious edict made him a nominal prisoner of war. Elgin was detained until 1806, at which point he was released on the promise that he would return if recalled by the Emperor Napoleon.[15] Next, the Turko-British war in 1807 further disrupted Elgin's activities in Athens; it was only in 1809 that work on the dismantling of the Athenian Akropolis recommenced. It was this phase of the work that was coming to a close when Byron returned, fresh from swimming the Hellespont, to Athens.

The debate that was joined at that time has continued unabated to the present day. The points worth emphasizing are few, and predictable enough. The dismantling of the Parthenon was as clear a case of upper-class pillage, animated by an almost bizarre sense of aristocratic privilege, as any. But it was also characteristic of the age. Elgin clearly manipulated his political position in order to gain access to the site in the first place. By contrast, he paid for all of this out of his own pocket, and essentially bankrupted his family in the process. Elgin accepted an insultingly small sum from the British government, despite others' willingness to pay considerably more for the collection, because he considered it a point of national honor that the entire collection remain in London, intact. These treasures would have been looted at some point, by someone, said Elgin's friends; better that they fell into the hands of a country with the resources and the will to care for them properly. These marbles are in a far better state of preservation today, to be sure, than the pieces that stayed behind in Athens. Moreover, to return the Elgin collection now would set a dangerous precedent, one that would surely signal the death-knell of the modern EuroAmerican museum. Still, this collection seems different, somehow; these statues, in particular, have become symbolic of all "the glory that was Greece" in the Classical age. They could also be returned quite easily, since the Greeks have already planned a museum explicitly designed to house them, one that seems destined to stand idle and empty at the foot of the Akropolis. This strange cycle of art-historical charges, pleas, and denials continues to this day.

Similar debates raged already in the winter of 1810–1811. And Lord Byron, as I indicated in the previous chapter, was one of the first to understand the deeper paradoxes implicit in such British philhellenism. (Keats, by contrast, seemed entirely unaware of the problem when he penned his sonnet, "On Seeing the Elgin Marbles" in 1819.) Elgin, to be sure, had proclaimed himself a lover of Greece. But he loved Greece immoderately, was even willing to waste his fortune in coming into possession of a piece of her. This kind of philhellenism fixated on Greek *antiquity,* to the exclusion of more contemporary concerns. It relied on the assumption, one we meet continually in most nineteenth-century travelogues, that there is no connection whatever between modern Greeks and their ancient forebears. Thus might the modern country be justifiably looted, since in so doing they were not perceived to be violating any spiritual or moral obligation owed to the Classical Greeks of yore.

Byron spoke out against Elgin's looting in *Childe Harold's Pilgrimage,*[16] but he also composed a short poem in that same winter, while in residence among the Capuchins and in clear sight of the Akropolis scaffolding. That poem is "The Curse of Minerva,"[17] and in it, Byron envisions a tattered image of Athena returning to earth to protest Elgin's predations. Now a sworn enemy of her former friends, Athena/Minerva lays an elaborate curse on Elgin's head, *and* on the British empire. Personally, Elgin will suffer romantic catastrophe: His children will all be idiots; his wife will leave him for another man (because he does not cut nearly as fine a figure as his statues do); and, in perhaps Byron's cruelest cut to date, Elgin will ironically *end* his life by resembling one of his treasured Greek statues (he contracted a deteriorative disease in Constantinople, probably syphilis, and eventually lost his nose). Politically, the goddess continues, the British empire will lose all of her colonial holdings—in the Baltic, in India, in the New World. George Washington[18] was but the first of Britain's many Neohellenic nemeses.

So far, so good. And yet—irony being the very stuff of life in the strange career of nineteenth-century Hellenism—when Byron finally did depart from Athens for England in April 1811, he did so aboard HMS *Hydra.* Byron himself was carrying draft notes for *Childe Harold's Pilgrimage* as well as the final draft of "The Curse of Minerva" back with him to England. Giovanni Lusieri was also on board. And below decks, presumably unknown to Byron, was the last large consignment of Elgin's ill-gotten loot.[19]

FROM ATHENS TO AEGINA

While Byron made final preparations for his departure, a small caique was seen leaving the Piraeus Harbor. Spotting Byron's boat, the sailors swept up beneath her fantail and began singing one of Byron's favorite tunes, badly out of key. He invited the party of four men aboard, and they shared a final round of port on *Hydra's* fantail before they parted. They had all been a part of the preceding winter's social circle; Byron sailed for England in the morning, whereas the four men left that same evening for Aegina, a small island lying just 12 miles to the south of Athens. They arrived at dawn.

One of the four was Charles Robert Cockerell (1788–1863),[20] a young man of 22 who had made his way to Athens along a path somewhat different from the more privileged route charted out by Byron and Hobhouse. Newly rich, the son of an extremely ambitious and savvy professional architect, Charles R. Cockerell (the third of 11 children) had secured the crucial advantage of a public school education, enrolling in the Westminster School in 1802. He left three years later to take up an architectural apprenticeship with his father. His first Tour, of sorts, to the West Country and Wales—and in his case, such trips were always nominally work-related, intended to give him a taste of various influential architectural styles—came in 1806. After a year in the architectural office of Robert Smirke (1781–1867), Cockerell determined to get to Greece himself. Just six years Cockerell's senior, Smirke was back from a five-year tour of Greece (1800–1805), and had worked extensively on the Akropolis as Elgin's men dismantled its statuary.

Cockerell got to Athens along a rather more circuitous route. His father had arranged him passage, as an unpaid courier bearing government correspondence to the British fleet in Cadiz, Malta, and Constantinople,[21] and it was there that he first met Byron and Hobhouse, when he arrived in the Sublime Porte in May 1810. He had been transported there on something of a curiosity, the government dispatch HMS *Black Joke,* equipped, he writes, with "ten guns, thirty-five men, one sheep, two pigs and fowls."[22] At the ripe old age of 22, Cockerell was rapidly acquiring the taste for travel, so well attested in his journals from the period, *Travels in Southern Europe and the Levant, 1810–1817,* published much later (in 1903) by his son, Samuel Pepys Cockerell. The Cockerell who drafted these notes and reflections was away for seven years in total, and he settled in all of the popular Mediterranean locales we mentioned in the previous chapter: Turkey, Greece, and Italy, most notably. It was Italy that Cockerell desired to see and study the most. Presumably, all architects of the time did. Only the Napoleonic disturbances kept him away. So, when Napoleon abdicated in April 1814, Cockerell, wasting no time, headed straight for Rome several months later. (See Appendix Two for a detailed account of Cockerell's unusually extensive version of the Grand Tour.)

Arguably a lesser light than some of his traveling companions in those years, Cockerell was by all accounts extraordinarily handsome and extremely charming. So, for that matter, was Byron. But unlike Byron, Cockerell made friends easily, and was always a welcome addition to any table or excursion. He formed extremely close attachments in the years he was abroad,[23] most notably to John Foster (c. 1787–1846),[24] a fellow architectural student whom he met in Constantinople shortly after his arrival in June of 1810, within days actually of his first meeting with Byron and Hobhouse. Foster was born and raised in Liverpool, but had moved to London to study architecture with Jacques Wyatt. His Tour lasted until 1814, the same year that he married the daughter of the Russian Consul in Smyrna, whom he met in February of 1812. The second most significant friendship Cockerell formed at the time was with the Baron Carl Haller von Hallerstein (1774–1817),[25] a somewhat older Bavarian architect who had studied at Nuremberg and Berlin, and who just so happened to be in Athens when Cockerell and Foster arrived. Both of these men were with Cockerell, *en route* to Aegina, having been joined by Jakob Linkh (or Link, or Linckh, 1786/8–1841),[26] yet another Bavarian artist.

Haller was the senior member of the party. An architect and amateur archaeologist (there was no other kind in the early nineteenth century, of course), he had obtained leave in order to move to Rome in the Autumn of 1808, and he remained there until June 1810, when he finally crossed over to Greece. There were a number of Teutonic expatriates, mostly Bavarian, living in Rome at the time, since they were not citizens of an empire then at war with Napoleon. Their progress to Italy was still unimpeded, by and large. (The various Teutonic kingdoms had already been defeated, and were under the nominal control of Napoleon, their sometime king—this was an especially vexed and confusing political problem on the Italian peninsula at the time, as we shall see shortly.) Haller, in any case, departed Rome with two other Teutons: Linkh, who was a landscape painter originally from Cannstadt, and Otto Magnus von Stackelberg (1787–1837), originally from Estonia, who abandoned an intended career as a diplomat in order to become a landscape painter and architect. Stackelberg—like Haller, Foster, and Cockerell—would remain in Greece for many years.

Their reasons for traveling to Aegina had everything to do with their common architectural interests, and a common desire for aesthetic self-cultivation. We should recall that these young men were all artists, or at least they aspired to be; their Mediterranean wanderings were thus intended as a time of careful observation, sketching, and apprenticeship to the Classical. They were drawn in this case to what they believed to be the Temple of Panhellenic Zeus, mentioned appreciatively by Pausanias in his description of the only Greek island he provides,[27] as visible from the Athenian Akropolis on a clear day. *Jupiter* Panhellenius is what they called him— which, as we have seen, is an interesting and, for the times, instructive Greco-Romanism. The four intended an imaginative reconstruction of the temple, with elaborate sketches of the extant temple architecture. In order to accomplish this, they first needed to clear the entire foundation of the site. Already on the second day of this "clearing" operation, and no sooner had they begun to sink their shovels in the thin surface soil, they began pulling statues and frieze-work out of the ground. They discovered a warrior's head carved in pure Parian marble on the second day. Larger, more impressive finds followed immediately, most of them in a condition far superior to that of the Parthenon marbles, so long exposed to weather and the elements. This same splendid accident would occur to the group again in the following year, in the Temple of Apollo at Bassae,[28] where they acquired the extensive frieze that is now also housed in the British Museum. It would not be until 1860, after the death of his three colleagues, that Cockerell would finally get around to the publication of his first-hand report of these discoveries. That volume is impressively illustrated with his own sketches, but by then the tide of the Neoclassical had turned in England. In any event, the Aegina group was, and remains, a stunning collection of *both* pedimental groups (and more) from the original temple that we now know, based on epigraphical evidence, to have been dedicated to Aphaia, the patron nymph of the island.

By the time the Aeginetan collection had been completely excavated, cleaned, and reassembled after five weeks of intensive labor (the young men and their assistants lived in tents on the site), Lord Elgin's collection had made its long and disastrous trip home. Some of this Athenian cargo had sunk in 1802, and it required two years for Elgin's personal secretary, William R. Hamilton (1777–1859), to arrange for its recovery, at a personal cost to the ambassador of roughly £5000. After two months of public hearings, a select committee in the House of Commons ultimately vouchsafed Elgin's rights to their acquisition and subsequent sale (on March 25, 1816, by a vote of 82–30), but recommended a purchase price of £35,000. This sum represented less than half the cost that Elgin reported incurring for the marbles' disassembly and transport to London, as well as for the recovery of one shipload from the bottom of the sea.

The select committee endeavored to establish several troublesome points of law and aesthetics: 1) whether Elgin had the rights of ownership to his collection (determining that he saw himself acting on his own authority, rather than the Crown's, the committee finally concluded that he did); 2) an authoritative assessment of the actual value of the entire collection (expert testimony provided estimates ranging from £25,000 to £60,000—thus, the committee's final figure of £35,000 was quite arbitrary); and 3) whether public funds might in fact be used to acquire such a collection for the government (for a number of complex reasons having everything to do with the strange career of Hellenism I am charting out in this book, they decided that they might indeed be so used).[29] Elgin finally accepted the offer, when it became clear that there would not be another; he had the solace of being named as a Trustee of the British Museum, and the ironic knowledge that the collection would always (if notoriously) bear his name. Moreover, he could not imagine the collection's leaving the shores of England, having expended so much personal energy and treasure to get it there in the first place. The relationship between Romantic nationalism, Classical aesthetics, and the competition between modern nations for the status of their Classical collections is another crucial piece of this story. Immediately after Waterloo, many of Napoleon's dubious acquisitions were forcibly removed from Paris and returned to the places from which they had been looted. Art and restitution, then, was on many politicians' minds at just this time.[30]

Cockerell and his friends were determined to learn from Elgin's ongoing travails so as to avoid a similar financial disaster themselves. Moreover, since the group was composed equally of representatives from Great Britain and Bavaria (two members apiece), the group could not agree among themselves on a single home for the collection. After "excavating" the Aegina marbles in April and May 1811, Foster and Linkh transported the marbles secretly to Athens for reconstruction, while Cockerell and Hallerstein remained on the island to secure their *purchase*—for 800 piastres, or roughly £40.[31] In a rented warehouse in Athens, the four men pieced together the entire collection—some 16 pieces, plus fragments, in all—and estimated its value at between £6000 and £8000.

Fearful that their collection would fall into the hands of Turkish officials, the four subsequently packed up the collection on a muletrain and hiked it overland to Porto Germeno (or Livadostro?) on the Corinthian Gulf, and then arranged for its secret shipment to the island of Zante in July 1811.[32] This island, latter-day Zakynthos, was never part of the Ottoman Empire and happened then to be in British control, although the French were quite active in the Ionian islands.[33] (Cockerell, in fact, was subsequently enrolled on the faculty of the fledgling "Ionian Academy" on the island in that same year—as a professor, all things, of Archaeology.[34]) The four friends determined finally to sell the collection in its entirety (that point was non-negotiable[35]) at a public auction, which they scheduled to take place on Zante, on November 1, 1812. Advertisements were included in all the major *Gazettes,* and Mr. Georg Gropius (d. 1845)—a painter from Berlin who had also made his way from Berlin to Rome, and who was now residing semi-permanently in Athens—was appointed as director of the sale in the anticipated absence of the original members of the archaeological party. They were, as I indicated, off to further adventures on the Peloponnese—in Bassae and elsewhere.

Here our story takes a more complicated political turn. Britain and France and the kingdom of Bavaria were engaged throughout these decades in a significant rivalry for the acquisition of Greek antiquities. The Crown Prince Ludwig of Bavaria (1786–1868, reigned 1828–1848), still smarting from the loss of the Elgin collection he had coveted, determined to have this Aeginetan collection at any cost. Elgin, of course, took a significant financial loss rather than countenance the statues' removal from England. Ludwig would later install his son, Otho, as Greece's first king after the Greek "liberation" from the Ottoman Turks and the Conference of London in 1830. At the same time Cockerell's enthusiastic letters— both to Ambassador Elgin's former secretary, and now British Undersecretary of State for Foreign Affairs, William R. Hamilton, (who originally arranged Cock- erell's passage to the Mediterranean) as well as to his parents in London—had un- wittingly led the Crown to believe that the sculptures were theirs for the having. When two British warships, one of them the brig o' war HMS *Paulina,* arrived in Athens on November 29, 1811 to purchase the group for £6000 and then to trans- port them home to England, Cockerell had the unenviable task of explaining to Captain Perceval, not only that the sculptures had been moved to Zante for safe- keeping, but also that they were to be auctioned publicly and did not belong to the Crown. Adding insult to injury, when rumors of an imminent French attack on Zante arrived in Athens, Cockerell pleaded with the fleet to remove the sculptures to British-held Malta for safekeeping (most of Elgin's collection had stopped over here as well). Since the Ionian Academy was linked to sister institutions in Malta, Venice, Milan, Florence, Rome, and Naples, it is not surprising that the Aeginetan collection was moved from Zakynthos to Malta. What *is* remarkable, and sure tes- timony to Cockerell's shining social skills, is that the move was made by the British navy.[36] That arranged, Cockerell headed off for a tour of Crete and (abortively) of Egypt.[37]

The auction was scheduled for the following year, on November 1, 1812. It took place, as originally advertised, on Zante, where Gropius was, and not on Malta, where the sculptures were. This created a bizarre situation in which collectors would be bid- ding on statues they had never seen. The British delegate, Mr. Taylor Combe (1774–1826)—who was then Keeper of Antiquities at the Townley Gallery of the British Museum, and who had arrived earlier at Malta—would not believe that the auction could have been scheduled to take place anywhere other than where the sculp- tures were kept. Suspecting foul play, he refused to leave Malta, and thus missed the auction altogether. Thus did the British miss their opportunity to bid for the collec- tion. Cockerell himself blamed Combe's "idiocy" for the loss, and returned to Zante in 1813 in an attempt to undo the damage—to no avail. Another auction, for the Bassae frieze this time, took place on Zante in May 1814, and was more favorable to British interests. These marbles, as I say, are also in the British Museum in London.

In fact, only one representative, a Bavarian, appeared in Zante on the day of the sale, and while the French government made a written offer of 160,000 francs, it could not be guaranteed in the absence of their representatives. The Bavarian rep- resentative, Dr. Johann(es) Martin von Wagner (1777–1858),[38] is yet another in our growing list of aspiring young artists and Levanto-Mediterranean lunatics. He stud- ied historical painting in Vienna (his "Judgment of Agamemnon," based on Book One of the *Iliad,* resides now in Munich), then moved to Rome in May 1804. When Ludwig took his Tour to Rome in the following year, Wagner was one of the expa- triate German artists with whom the Crown Prince fell in. The two corresponded regularly for the rest of their lives. And when news of the Aeginetan auction reached

the Prince several years later, he drafted a letter (received on July 21, 1812), urging
Wagner to make the trip to Zante as his representative. Wagner attempted to get out
of the trip: He spoke no Greek; he could not locate a good map of the country; and
he was a committed Romanophile to boot. But the Crown Prince was insistent. So
Wagner hired an Italian guide, Pacifico Storani, and the two set off by ship, from
Rome to Naples, on September 8, 1812. (See Appendix Three for a detailed chronology of Wagner's journey to Greece.)

It was a difficult year for travel of this kind. Wagner was only three days outside
of Naples when he was sent back by French soldiers, on foot and without his luggage,
for an additional letter from the French Consul in Naples. Sea-travel was especially
difficult to arrange, with the British blockade complicating matters for all parties.
On September 29, 1812, Wagner was in Otranto, where the French Consul assisted
him in making all of his travel arrangements. Wagner slept that night lulled by the
sounds of a distant cannonade, care of several blockading British warships in the
area. Wagner's Neapolitan captain, Saverio Castagnola, departed at dusk on the following evening, successfully ran the British blockade, and arrived in Corfu on October 2, 1812. Here Wagner was stuck once again, for nearly two weeks this time, trying
to manage a way over to Zante. The dilemma here was that no traveler was permitted to pass directly from a French port of call (Corfu) to a British one (Zante), so
Wagner was required to touch down first on Ottoman soil. After a harrowing further delay of two weeks, one that took him to four different islands and a number of
sites on the Greek mainland, Wagner finally departed from Prevesa without the
proper papers and headed for Santa Maura, from which point he intended to move
on to Zante. By now, he was less than a week away from the advertised date of the
auction, and after several days' further delay due to bad weather, he arrived in Zante
just two days prior to the auction date of November 1st.

Newly arrived and in quarantine, Wagner arranged a meeting with the Bavarian
party from Athens, all of whom had come to Zante to witness the auction (Cockerell was on a trip to Sicily at the time). Haller, Linkh, and Stackelberg arranged for
Wagner to meet with Gropius, the director of the auction, and Wagner was informed that he was the only formal representative to have made it successfully onto
the island. The Bavarians agreed that the sculptural group should be acquired "for
Germany," and that it must in no case go to England, which was far too "inaccessible." That point settled, Wagner learned only now that the sculptures were not on
Zante but, rather, were in storage at Malta.

This placed him in an awkward position. Wagner had virtually limitless credit
available to him in the Crown Prince's name, and he had made careful arrangements
with creditors both in Naples and in Athens. But now he would be required to purchase the collection sight-unseen. His Bavarian friends assured him of their excellence and value, and so he finally purchased the collection as described in the
manifest in the name of his Prince—for 10,000 sequins (I have seen conversion estimates ranging from £4500 to £6000)—but the deal was conditional on his actual
review of the pieces. Given the difficulties of sea travel in a Mediterranean world at
war, the group suggested an overland return to Athens rather than a dangerous sea
crossing to Malta, since some of the finest pieces were being held in Athens for safekeeping by the French Consul in Athens, Louis François Sebastian Fauvel
(1753–1838), another European who had traveled extensively in Turkey and Greece
since 1780, and who had settled semi-permanently in Athens in 1803. Fauvel had

observed Lord Elgin's activities carefully, and was intent on keeping French interests alive in this elaborate game of Greek spoliation. He did so with some notable successes until the outbreak of the Greek War in 1821, at which point he moved to Smyrna (latter-day Izmir), where he remained until his death.

Wagner's itinerary between Zante and Athens mirrors almost stop-for-stop the one that Byron and Hobhouse used four years earlier: Gastuni and Elis, Andravada and Lechaina, Achaia and Patras, Naupaktos and Vostizza, Delphi and Arachova, Chaironea and Livathia, Thebes and Athens. When Wagner arrived in Athens on December 14, 1812, he immediately presented himself to Fauvel since, as a resident in Italy, he was nominally subject to French authorities. Wagner stayed in Athens for three months in all, most of it spent lodged in the Capuchin Monastery. He was delighted with the quality of the Aeginetan pieces in Fauvel's possession, since they exceeded even his own expectant hopes. He and Fauvel got on famously and spent a great deal of time together, but Wagner was extremely put off by Gropius who, he believed, was trying to extract excessive additional funds from his Prince in arranging the marbles' shipment from Malta and Athens to Rome. That matter resolved, with Fauvel's decisive intervention, Wagner departed Athens on March 15, 1813, and arrived back in Rome on August 4. The statues arrived a little more than one year later.

FROM ATHENS TO ROME

Between 1815 and 1818, Wagner oversaw the "restoration" of the Aeginetan collection in Rome. Ludwig had commissioned the famous Danish sculptor, Berthel Thorvaldsen (1770–1844)[39], to "restore" his new collection. Thorvaldsen, who had shown outstanding artistic promise at a very young age, moved to Rome in 1797 to pursue his artistic career. He was to remain there for many years. Famous, among other things, for a marble bust of Lord Byron that he carved in 1831 (housed now in the Thorvaldsen Museum in Copenhagen), Thorvaldsen was considered—along with Antonio Canova (1757–1822)—among the most preeminent sculptors in Italy, if not the world. He and Wagner had met in Rome in 1811, and while Wagner seems not to have liked him personally, the two men collaborated for two years (1816–1818) on the Crown Prince's new acquisitions.

Thorvaldsen was in charge of a kind of "restoration" that, in those Romantic days, involved a great deal more intrusiveness and obfuscation than is artistically acceptable today. (Canova had refused Lord Elgin's request similarly to "restore" the Parthenon collection). Thorvaldsen was required to make a number of decisions about the piecing and placement of various fragments—what heads belonged to what bodies, how the figures were originally arranged in relation to one another, their various bodily poses, and the like. Wagner occasionally offered alternative interpretations, some of which were borne out by subsequent research. Thorvaldsen also carved new body parts to replace pieces missing from the originals. The aesthetic goal was to "complete" (*ergänzen*) the collection, to make it appear whole, and, presumably, more as it did in antiquity. But the design was also implicitly intended to make the gap between past and present disappear. It was an enormous creative undertaking, and there was no real precedent for it.

At the same time, Wagner was commissioned by the Prince to draft an art historical report on the collection. His "Report on the Aeginetan Sculptures in the Possession of

His Royal Highness the Crown Prince of Bavaria"[40] was edited by the noted Romantic philosopher Friedrich W. J. Schelling (1775–1854) and published in 1817, before their "restoration" was complete. The text is itself a remarkable example of early nineteenth-century Classicism. On the one hand, Wagner provides a detailed description of each piece in the collection, no matter how fragmentary, as well as how it appeared prior to Thorvaldsen's "restoration." On the other, Schelling saw fit very nearly to "restore" Wagner's *Report;* his copious critical appendices are often equal in length to, or even longer than, Wagner's original text, and they are every bit as interesting in their own way.[41] It is occasionally unclear whether a critical note belongs to Wagner or to Schelling, and such ambiguities are themselves often quite telling. Here we have a remarkable text that combines profound and insightful commentary on some of the artistic masterpieces of Greek antiquity, sensitively located in their own cultural and historical setting, side-by-side with some of the most off-putting claims of Greek cultural superiority and its *continuity* with—not difference from—more contemporary *European* tastes.

Both Wagner and Schelling illustrate some of the areas of chief interest of the times, matters on which the Aeginetan sculptures had much to say. They both recognize the collection as importantly transitional, sculptural pieces that map out the stylistic transition from the Archaic to the Classical age. Both men freely acknowledge the Greek debt to Egyptian and Near Eastern sculptural antecedents, while also speaking intelligently to the essential differentness of Greek art. The Greeks did not blindly copy what they appropriated; neither, for that matter, did the Romantics. Wagner is especially interested in discussing the surprising discovery of painting on these statues—they were decorated in brilliant reds and blues and greens, and must have looked for all the world like the Catholic religious images one sees in Bavaria and in Rome, he observes. Finally, both men comment at length on the existence of an "Aeginetan school" of sculpture, one well attested in antiquity, especially by Pausanias.[42] In short, this is an *encyclopedic* Report in the very best sense of that term, one that makes scholarly sense of an exciting and important new discovery, locating it helpfully in its own times, as well as in the contemporary world of Classical scholarship. And it *was* timely; Cockerell, be sure to recall, did not publish *his* reports until 1860. By then, virtually all of our protagonists were dead and gone. Writing, as Pausanias knew well, is sometimes the only remedy against loss and general forgetting.

FROM ROME TO MUNICH, AND BEYOND

So great was Ludwig's excitement at having finally acquired a first-rate Classical collection, and the scholarly *Report* to go with it, that he determined to build a neoclassical museum for the express purpose of housing it. This is the Munich Glyptothek,[43] still housing one of the finest collections of Classical and post-Classical art in the world. It was only the second such *public* sculpture gallery in Europe, the Townley Gallery in London being the first. Ludwig's intention was to make Munich the new capital of his father's (Maximilian I, 1756–1825) Bavarian regime:—"Athens on the Isar," they called it—designed to supersede, architecturally speaking, the older capital at Regensburg. He sponsored an architectural competition, soliciting designs for the entire project on the so-called *Königsplatz,* or King's Plaza, well to the northwest of the city center. Carl Haller von Hallerstein submitted one of the unsuccessful plans for this building complex, the commission for which was finally awarded to Franz Karl Leo von Klenze (1784–1864). The ultimate point was that it had to be "Greek."[44]

The plans called for an impressive program of new building on three sides of the *Königsplatz*. To the north side of the Platz would be the *Glyptothek*, designed in the Ionic order and completed in 1830, when the Aeginetan collection was first made available to the public. Across the way to the south, the *Ausstellungsgebäude* was designed in the Corinthian order and was completed in 1845. It has served many purposes over the years, and is now also a museum that houses Ludwig's impressive collection of ancient Greek pottery and smaller finds. To the western entrance of the Platz, a model of the Athenian *Propyläen,* the monumental gateway to the Akropolis, was completed in the Doric order in 1862. But by this time, as I say, virtually all of the main characters in my story had passed away.

Carl Haller remained in Greece as one after another of his friends made their way back to Italy, more specifically to Rome. Having acquired a taste for excavation in Aegina and Phigalia, Haller was excavating in Ampelakia, in northern Greece, when he took ill, and died quite unexpectedly on November 5, 1817 in the Tempe valley, not far from Delphi. He was taken to Athens for burial. Jakob Linkh left Athens in company with Charles Cockerell on January 15, 1815. They made their way slowly through the Peloponnese, then sailed on to southern Italy, Naples, and Rome. He remained in residence in Rome until 1825, then returned to Stuttgart, where he died on April 4, 1841. Otto Stackelberg remained in Greece until 1816, but then he, too, returned to Rome, where he settled for the next twelve years. Before shifting his interests to the study of art and archaeology, Stackelberg had intended to pursue a diplomatic career. He spent the rest of his scholarly life in several of the great capitol cities of Europe, researching and writing extensively about his mingled Classical and Mediterranean interests.[45] He was reunited with Cockerell in Venice in 1816, and then he moved: first to Paris and London (1828–1829), then to Dresden (1833–1835), and finally to St. Petersburg, where he died two years later on March 27, 1837.

John Foster returned to Liverpool after his Grecian sojourn ended in 1814, where he settled back in at home and devoted a long creative life to commissioned projects, even securing several for his friend Cockerell, who refused to solicit creative work on his own behalf. Foster had designed a great many of Liverpool's premier public monuments, most famously, their new Customs House. He retired from public life in 1835, and died ten years later, at his home in Liverpool. Charles Cockerell returned to England in 1817, after fully seven years overseas. He would think of himself, ever after, as "half a Mediterranean."[46] He returned to national acclaim and some limited fame, receiving several important commissions on the basis of his trip and the name it had helped establish for him. Among Cockerell's most notable architectural achievements are: additions to the Harrow School (1818) and Chapel (1838); the renovation of St. Paul's Cathedral (1821–1822); one wing of the University Library, Cambridge (1829–1837); the Ashmolean Museum and Taylorian Institute, Oxford (1839–1845); the Branch Bank of London in Plymouth (1842); a library addition to Queen's College, Oxford (1843); the Fitzwilliam Museum, Cambridge (1845); the Flaxman Gallery, University College, London (1849–1857); St. George's Hall in Liverpool (1851); and the Liverpool Free Library and Museum (1856).[47] As we will recall, Cockerell possessed an artistic temperament and did not work well in competitive settings. It is remarkable how many of his own classicizing concepts would be rejected in favor of Gothic designs; the Classicizing wave had crested by the time Cockerell returned to England and began working seriously. So it was only at the end of a long and distinguished career that he finally arranged for the publication of his Aeginetan and Arkadian sketches, plans, and excavation reports—in 1860, long after the deaths of all of his friends in the field, and just three years prior to his own.

Johann Martin von Wagner returned to Rome after fulfilling his Grecian duties in 1813; he remained there for the rest of his life. Ludwig had a veritable army of artists whom he trusted—Thorvaldsen, Canova, and Haller, among others—all of whom were commissioned to keep an eye open for ancient art worth acquiring. But with Wagner, the King retained a closer, more personal relationship. Wagner arranged for the transport of the restored Aeginetan collection to Munich in 1828, where Thorvaldsen saw to the integration of the ancient art into the modern building. Wagner continued to acquire antiquities on Ludwig's behalf, most of which are now also housed in Munich and Würzburg. In 1827, Ludwig was made the Custodian of the Villa Malta in Rome, a Bavarian holding where Wagner had long been in residence. He remained there for 30 more years, until his death on August 8, 1858.

Work would continue in a disjointed way throughout the nineteenth and twentieth centuries at most of the archaeological sites on Aegina, under primarily German supervision.[48] But it was the *Königsplatz* itself, as well as the Aeginetan collection, which were destined to undergo the greatest transformations in the twentieth century.[49]

The debate over the Thorvaldsen "restoration," of which Cockerell had been quite critical in 1860, was really joined in 1901, when Adolf Fürtwangler discovered the statue-bases[50] for the pedimental groups at Aegina, thereby confirming some of the erring guesses the Dane had made. After World War I, the fledgling National Socialist Party enjoyed some of its earliest support in Munich. It was in Munich that Hitler staged his abortive "Beer Hall *Putsch*" in 1923, and—after a brief imprisonment, and the penning of *Mein Kampf*—it was to Munich that he turned his earliest attentions, when he finally came to power in 1933. Indeed, his early career as Chancellor might best be viewed as a never-ending commute between Munich and Berlin.[51]

Hitler's interest in art and architecture is well attested. He, too, was a frustrated and largely unsuccessful watercolorist. Several of his earliest political commissions would be for the building of new quarters—Party Headquarters, as well as his own personal quarters—*both* in Munich *and* in Berlin. Albert Speer (1905–1981) handled the Berlin project, and Paul Ludwig Troost (1864–1934) handled Munich. The site chosen for the Munich building program was, of all places, the *Königsplatz*. Since the eastern end of the Platz remained open, Troost proposed closing it off with four new buildings. Two smaller structures flanked the entrance onto the Platz. These *Ehrentempeln,* or "temples of the heroes," were squared, open-air *faux*-Doric temples in which the bodies of the "martyrs" of the failed 1923 *Putsch* had been installed. Hitler expressed his wish to be buried here in his will.[52] The two larger buildings were the *Führerbau,* Hitler's regional Chancellory and living quarters, and the *Verwaltungsbau,* Party Headquarters of the NSDAP in Munich. It has not been sufficiently remarked that one curious collection of ancient Greek statuary has served as the magnet that has attracted all of this seemingly bizarre subsequent attention.

Munich was heavily bombed during the Second World War. The Glyptothek itself was badly damaged when a bomb struck it directly in 1944, but the *Ehrentempeln* were amazingly undamaged. They were both dynamited by the Germans themselves in 1947, and in the following year, the two larger structures were converted to other

uses. The *Führerbau* became the *Amerika-Haus,* a sort of North American cultural center, and still later, it housed the reading room of the Bavarian State Library. The *Verwaltungsbau* was used as a sort of clearing-house for the repatriation of international
art that had been systematically looted by the Nazis.[53] Today, the *Führerbau* houses the
Hochschule für Musik, and the *Verwaltungsbau,* among other things, houses the Archaeological Institute of the Munich University system.

Since the Glyptothek needed to be rebuilt virtually from the ground up, and since
its elaborate nineteenth-century interior was already lost, the then-director of the
collection, Dieter Ohly, called for the dismantling, or "derestoration," of the Aeginetan collection. This was accomplished between 1962 and 1966, and in 1972, the
Glyptothek Museum was reopened to the public, with a very different interior design, and a very different group of Aeginetan pediments.

Images have power. And material culture has a funny way of providing the inspiration behind a great deal of spiritual activity, in every age. The nature of this activity changes; the energy, it would seem, does not. In charting out the long, strange
trajectory that takes these 16 statues from Aegina, to Athens, to Corinth, to Patras,
to Zante, to Malta, to Rome, to Munich, we have seen a variety of things that are
representative of the larger points I have been trying to make in this book.

Most of the philhellenes I have been discussing in this chapter were amateurs,
most of them were quite young, most were aspiring artists of one form or another,
and they all operated on the assumption of what must now seem an almost outrageous sense of aristocratic privilege. They loved what they took, took what they
loved. They referred to the systematic looting of one poor province on the outskirts
of the Ottoman Empire as a "science" of sorts, whether one deemed it Art History
or Archaeology. Viewed through the lens of such art history, as well as the phenomenon of the modern "museum culture," we see how much of this "rediscovery" of
Greek things was bound up in a revaluation and a refashioning of the *European* identity. The so-called Great Powers were instrumental in setting Greece's political and
military destiny. They were also responsible for the simultaneous looting and
restoration of countless Greek archaeological sites. As Thorvaldsen's work illustrates
with special poignancy, there is no gain without a commensurate loss. That is the
strange paradox of such Hellenism.

I have devoted two chapters now to the early nineteenth century, because it seems
to me a sort of watershed, an historical turning point in the larger story of Hellenic
appropriation I am attempting to tell. Here, cloaked in the accoutrements of an
emerging new European order, "Hellenism" was being redefined—as a scholarly discipline, as a Romantic idyll, and as a cultural alternative to what was then thought to
be a dying Christian civilization. It is in this sense that Romanticism can still seem so
very current, its language and its worries still alive and well in our own times—and
not only in our museums. I turn in the next, and final, chapter, to what is arguably
Romantic Hellenism's single greatest achievement: the Modern Olympic Revival.

I am interested in the sorts of assumptions that underlay these political developments: the fascination with travel writing, especially in the English language; the
birth of an amateur archaeological elite in England and Germany and France; the
fascination with the Classical ideal in art. These profound cultural developments
help to explain, I think, some of the political tensions and dilemmas that have continued to haunt the Neohellenic consciousness in this century. I turn to that century,
and to some of its most prominent ghosts, in the next chapter.

CHAPTER NINE

The Ethos of Olympism
GREEK RELIGION FOR THE MODERN WORLD

But the delight of mortal men
  flowers,
    then flutters to the ground,
      shaken by a mere
        shift of thought.
Creatures of a day!
What is someone?
    What is no one?
Man: a shadow's dream.
      But when god-given glory comes
a bright light shines upon us and our life is sweet.
Dear mother Aegina, guide this city in the ways of freedom!
Zeus, join with her, with mighty Aiakos,
Peleus, Telamon the brave, and Achilles!

—Pindar, *Eighth Pythian Ode* (446 BCE)

"Somewhere over there," said my guide, "the Trail of Tears
started." I leant towards the crystalline creek. Pines
shaded it. Then I made myself hear the water's

language around the rocks in its clear-running lines
and its small shelving falls with their eddies. "Choctaws,"
"Creeks," "Choctaws," and I thought of the Greek revival

carried past the names of towns with columned porches,
and how Greek it was, the necessary evil
of slavery, in the catalogue of Georgia's

marble past, the Jeffersonian ideal in
plantations with its Hectors and Achilleses,
its foam in the dogwood's spray, past towns named Helen,

Athens, Sparta, Troy.

—Derek Walcott, *Omeros* Book 4, Chapter 35

Late one evening in early August 1996, I found myself seated with several members of the Greek National Olympic Committee as well as, much to my own astonishment, an impressive young woman who was introduced as the expatriated Princess of Greece.[1] We were drinking beer, snacking, and discussing how the Olympics had been going.

Overall, they had been going *very* well for the Greeks: a gold medal won in Yachting; three golds, two silvers, and a bronze in Weightlifting; fifth place in Men's Basketball; sixth place in the Women's High Jump; and so on. Things were going so well, in fact, that the prime minister had commandeered an Olympic Airways 747 and sent it to Atlanta with the express purpose of bringing the triumphant athletes and the entire Greek delegation home in style. It was, they told me later, quite a flight.

I had met these men—and all save the Princess *were* men—on the same Friday as the Games began. I was standing on Peachtree Street, milling about with one half-million others, waiting for the Torch Relay to pass by, and I was trying to make a phone call. Behind me, three men complained that these American phones were impossible to figure out. I turned sympathetically, and offered to assist them; they stared at me as if I were crazy. They had been speaking to one another in Greek, and I unconsciously answered them in the same language. We laughed, trotted off for a drink, and then coffee. They gave me two tickets to the Opening Ceremonies that evening, at which I was seated with the Greek delegation—and so began our whirlwind month together.

Lost in this reverie over how I'd come into this singular good fortune, I failed to register the princess's question, until one of my new friends nudged my knee under the table.

"I'm sorry," I said, slowly returning from happy thought, "What was it you asked me?"

"I was wondering how you are finding the Olympics?" she repeated. "What are your impressions, as an American?"

I made a point of saying, first and foremost, that I'd been rather disappointed when I learned that the Centennial Games were not to be held in Athens but, rather, in Atlanta. That decision was made in 1990, and I just so happened to be living in Athens when the decision was annouced. They all clapped me on the back for saying so, *and* for meaning it, as I did. They referred to me as their adoptive "Greekling," and ordered another pitcher. I smiled, reflecting again on how very well things were going.

"Yes, but Atlanta," pressed the Princess, not to be denied. "What do you think about what they have done *here?* How did you like the Opening Ceremonies, for instance?"

I shared some casual first reflections. But then I made a fatal mistake; I acted like a scholar. Worse still, I philosophized. Despite the long-standing cultural pride in Socrates, Plato, and Aristotle, the native sons who got this "philosophical" enterprise going, modern Greek culture seems more given to pragmatism now, justly suspicious of intellectual abstractions.

I was abstracting. And they were skeptical.

"What struck me the most, I suppose," I added when pressed, "was how *religious* the Ceremonies seemed."

A deafening silence descended on the table. The fresh pitcher arrived. Chairs creaked uneasily under the shifting weight of their occupants. No one said a word.

At first I thought perhaps my Greek was even worse than I knew, and that I'd un-wittingly said something other than what I'd intended to say. But it became clear that they *had* understood what I'd said; they simply did not know how to register a remark like that.

Only later did it dawn on me how this comment might have sounded to my new Greek friends. No doubt they scrolled through the 60-some channels on the Mar-riott televisions; no doubt, they had happened on televangelism, American-style. In all likelihood, then, they feared that I was just one more North American, trying for-ever to turn the talk back to God—and a Protestant God, at that.

By the time I realized the nature of my misstep, the princess had excused herself. The beer remained unpoured. And in no time at all, my friends had all trotted off to other engagements. I was left at the table alone, stuck with the bill I only barely managed to pry loose from a puddle of condensation. "Greekling" no longer.

There had been a serious point in what I was trying to say. But I lacked the cap-tive audience—and the language—I needed to say it properly. Readers, whether they realize it or no, tend to be a far more captive audience. So, the reader of this book now takes the ironic place of a Princess and her court, the ones to whom I'd initially intended to address these impressions.

I believed, and I still do believe, that the Olympic Opening Ceremonies are pro-foundly religious—in conception, and in fact. They are not *Christian* rituals, to be sure—at least not directly—but they are *religious* ones, nonetheless. That was the dis-tinction I failed to make clear to my fairweather Greek friends.

As a sort of first pass at explicating this rather odd Olympic observation, let me turn to what Pierre de Coubertin—the singular founder, or *Renovateur,* of the Modern Olympic Movement—said about what he sold to the world as "Olympism." This was written in 1929, just before construction began on the U.S. Supreme Court building, along with its pediments and friezes. And it recalls a point I have been making repeat-edly in this book: that religion is not the same thing as Christianity; and that Hellenism has served as the functional equivalent of a religion, from Rome to Romanticism.

Here is Coubertin, then, on the spirit of his version of Olympism:

Our over-simple habit of cataloguing things leads us to call paganism the worship of idols; as though every religion, even the most materialist, did not have its spiritual fol-lowers, and as though every religion, even the most mystical, did not have its idolators, if only of the golden calf which today is more powerful and more incense-wreathed than ever. *But there is a paganism—the true form—which humanity will never shake off, and from which—I will risk this seeming blasphemy—it would not be well for it to free itself completely:* and that is the cult of the human being, of the human body, mind and flesh, feeling and will, in-stinct and conscience. Sometimes flesh, feeling and instinct have the upper hand, and sometimes mind, will and conscience, for these are the two despots who strive for pri-macy within us, and whose conflict often rends us cruelly. We have to attain a balance. We reach it, but we cannot hold it. . . .

It was the immortal glory of Hellenism to imagine the codification of the pursuit of balance and to make it into a prescription for social greatness. Here—at Olympia—we are on the ruins of the first capital of eurhythmy, for eurhythmy does not belong to the art-world alone; there is also a eurhythmy of life.

Let us therefore meditate among *the ruins of Olympia, ruins which are still alive,* as is indicated by the ceremony which I recalled just now. And from there we perceive *the alternations between paganism and asceticism which form the warp and woof in history,* a warp and woof neglected by historians because in order to see it one must look beneath the events which cover it, and proceed more in the manner of an archaeologist than a historian.[2]

Building on this essential insight—that certain historical questions are best approached as archaeological ones—the logical next questions are Socratic in nature: What *is* a religion?[3] And, more to the point, what did Coubertin mean by "paganism?"

As a student of comparative religion with a particular interest in Greek things, it has seemed to me that an entirely separate approach might actually be the best way to get at this complex and fascinating question. This book is one result of that thought-experiment. We cannot and should not try to get at questions like "what is a religion?" head on; that was the mistake I made with my Greek friends. Coming at them from the side may be the better part of valor, *and* a more appropriate intellectual strategy.

So I would now like to take a closer look at this enormously popular, and distinctly modern, Neohellenic movement in which the "religious" status of the enterprise was once far clearer than it is now. For a variety of reasons, religions like to hide their origins. That movement, of course, is the modern Olympic movement, which began a little more than 100 years ago.

WHAT THE OLYMPICS ARE NOT

I come to most of this material as an amateur, and there continues to be a real virtue in this status. The International Olympic Committee (IOC) acknowledged only recently (in 1992) that the status of the "amateur" was virtually impossible to translate into meaningful cross-cultural terms[4]—terms that would be *equally* applicable in the former Soviet Union and the United States of America, let's say—and thus we have the "Dream Team" now to enjoy, or by which to be scandalized, as we choose.

Amateurism in the intellectual life, however, has traditionally been a less romantic ideal than its athletic counterpart. Amateur athletics was something we were in the habit of celebrating at the Olympics until quite recently. But *intellectual* amateurism is a bit harder to celebrate. Intellectuals are supposed to be professionals, just as they are supposed to be experts. But as a committed interdisciplinarian, and according to one definition of academic professionalism, I can be neither. What I have learned is that, by immersing ourselves in a variety of Hellenic materials—ancient *and* modern materials—we can learn a great deal more when we compare them.

The *modern* Olympic movement is just over 100 years old, and we ought to remind ourselves of what it really looked like at its inception, especially since we have already, in the relatively short course of one dramatic century, forgotten most of the spiritual and cultural roots of the movement,[5] as well as the origins of a number of Olympic traditions we continue to hold dear. Traditions, as I say, like to hide their origins. That is the perspective, in any case, to which the amateur—who is both an interdisciplinarian and a comparativist—can speak most meaningfully.

Let me begin, then, by saying a word more about what this chapter—and, by implication, the modern Olympics themselves—will *not* be. It will not really be about the idea of amateurism—an idea that has attracted a great deal of attention in the last decade. The myth of the amateur athlete had little currency in antiquity, and it has little currency now in the twentieth century[6]—except in a few lingering sports, such as international soccer. So I will pass over it in relative silence.

This chapter also will not speak to the ideal of world-peace, nor about the brotherhood and sisterhood of all people—at least not directly. To be sure, these are bold
and noble ideals, as worthy of discussion today as they were when a number of Hellenistic and Roman philosophers began doing so, under the aegis of the dawning
idea of a world-city, or *cosmopolis*.[7] These ideas are a large part of what we *think* the
Olympic rituals were designed to celebrate. And so they are.

Still, these ideas have had a peculiar history in this century.[8] Shortly after the resurrection of the Olympic ideal in Athens in 1896, and after four inconsistent[9] modern Games in Paris (1900), St. Louis (1904), London (1908), and Stockholm
(1912), World War I broke out in 1914. Ironically, the 1916 Games had been scheduled to take place in Berlin, but they did not. It was a shattering moment for the
modern Olympic ideal. According to the beliefs of the time (beliefs that are disconfirmed by ancient history, and by most of the archaeological facts[10]), the Greeks had
been able to set aside their petty regionalisms and rivalries in order to celebrate
something larger, something of enduring cultural significance, in quadrennial contests (*agônes*) which were sanctified by a sacred truce[11] that allowed free-passage for
all athletes and spectators to and from the Games.[12]

The classical Olympic ideal—so said the reigning Olympic mythology, at any
rate—was stronger than the forces of war.[13] In the twentieth century, the forces of
war proved to be stronger than that ideal. World War I dealt a deathblow to a variety of pacifist movements in Europe, and presented an extraordinary challenge
to the Liberal Protestant presuppositions on which much of this pacifism had been
built. But the World War also decisively interrupted the sequence of modern
Olympiads. And there was real question, in some quarters, as to whether it was
morally meaningful to pick up where they had left off for the 1920 Olympic
Games.

A rather significant, and really quite moving, decision was made by the fledgling
IOC. First, they decided to forge ahead and hold the Olympic Games. Second, and
far more important, it seems as if these Games were deliberately staged in that part
of Europe that had arguably been most devastated by the Great War—very close to
the killing-fields of Flanders. So the decision was made to hold these Games in
Antwerp in 1920.

This same pattern asserted itself again during and after World War II. In yet another of Modern Olympism's many historical ironies, the last Games *before* this second World War were held in Berlin in 1936. These were the now-notorious Games
presided over by Adolf Hitler, who had come to power in 1933, and immortalized by
Leni Riefenstahl's important aesthetic documentary, *Olympia*.[14] The 1940 Games
were scheduled to take place in Tokyo. They did not. The 1944 Games were can-
celled as well. Again, the question of what to do in the war's aftermath was a pertinent and poignant one. And here again the IOC's answer was telling. The 1948
Games were held in London, a city that also had been singularly ravaged by the war.
It was, in one sense, Antwerp revisited. One wonders if we might hold the Olympic
Games in Sarajevo again one day, to make a similarly potent Olympic statement.
Now-retired IOC President, Juan Antonio Samaranch, suggested such a possibility
at the Opening Ceremonies in Atlanta, committing IOC funds to an athletic re-
building program in the former Yugoslav metropolis.

Thus our modern wars, while temporarily stronger than the so-called Olympic
truce (there is really no modern analogue to the ancient truce, since modern war is

so very unlike its ancient counterpart), have *not* proven to be stronger than the Olympic ideal. We make much of this fact—as well we should.

Let me pause briefly to emphasize what I have been trying to do here at the outset. While attending to certain moral *questions,* I do not want to *moralize* the phenomenon of modern Olympism—either positively or negatively. I do not want to sing the praises of some myth of amateurism that was not ancient and cannot be modern. Nor do I wish to hymn the ideal of world peace and fellowship, since wars and political intrigue plagued the ancient festivals at Olympia throughout antiquity, and since the shattering history of this century is so thoroughly stitched in to the very fabric of the modern Olympic movement.

But if I do not come to praise the modern Olympics, neither do I come to bury them. Too much demythologizing becomes debunking, and I have no wish to debunk either the ancient or the modern Olympic festivals, different as they no doubt are. If I do not want to talk about truces or amateurism, neither do I want to talk about big money and the mass media. I do not even want to talk about the corrosive forces of modern nationalism, and the notorious medal counts at the modern Games. I want to bracket *all* of these important moral questions, because I think all of them are *secondary* questions. Secondary to what?

Secondary, I believe, to religion, as well as to the intellectual environment of the nineteenth century in Europe. I want to place more emphasis on certain intellectual, cultural, and historical developments than is customary in talking about modern Hellenism in general, and the Olympics in particular, in order to make good on my larger thesis: that the modern Olympic revival *was* a pretty clearly religious movement, *and* that it still is. This has been my point about virtually every example of Hellenic appropriation I have examined in this book.

As the Baron Pierre de Coubertin (1863–1937) said time and again, without the extraordinary ritual frame of the Opening and Closing ceremonies (the hardest tickets to come by, by far) the Olympic Games would simply be another set of World Championships . . . and there were already enough of those.[15] The modern Olympics are *not* World Championships, and will never be, at least not in the foreseeable future. That is a fact worth pausing over. They are not World Championships; they are intended to be something else. Defining that "something else" could be the task of a lifetime, I have discovered. I have been calling it "religion," for the purposes of this book.

My thesis, then, about the religiosity of the modern Olympics is part of a larger hunch to which I have turned repeatedly in the book as well—namely, that we in the modern world are still trying to work out questions, and perhaps even some answers, which we have inherited from the nineteenth century. The modern Olympic movement is just one salient entry on what is a surprisingly long list of such things. To make good on that odd-sounding thesis, I need to take up Coubertin's challenge—one which was echoed by another French intellectual in the twentieth century, Michel Foucault—and to begin to think about these matters more as an *archaeologist* might.

THE ARCHAEOLOGY OF THE OLYMPICS

Really to understand the modern Olympic movement, I think, we must take the *image* of archaeology seriously[16]—and by this I am not referring to the British traveler, Richard Chandler (1738–1810), who "discovered" the site of ancient Olympia in 1766,[17] nor to the tentative "excavations" by the French army under Albert Blouet at the Temple of Zeus in 1829,[18] nor to the vast German archaeological activity that began in 1875 under Ernst Curtius, intensified prior to and briefly during the years of Occupation in World War II, and continues unabated to this day.

Rather, I would like to use the image of Archaeology as a *parable* for understanding certain complex cultural formations like the international Olympic movement. In excavations, everything is temporally reversed. The last things come to the surface first. The first thing you find on an archaeological site sits on the last level of human habitation. The last thing you find was the first thing to be deposited on the site. You are traveling through time, in reverse. There is thus no way back, back to antiquity, much less back to the beginning (the word, "archaeology," is a Greek word, implying "the study of origins"), save through every subsequent layer of history and material accumulation.

What we quickly discover in the intellectual excavation we are undertaking here at Olympia is that there is a pronounced historical gap between the cancellation of the ancient Olympic Games in or around 395 CE, when all the major pagan sanctuaries in the ancient world were shut down—for *religious* reasons, as we saw in the fourth chapter[19]— and the "resurrection" of the modern Olympic Games in 1894–1896. Specifically, the archaeological layer of the *nineteenth century* proves to be the most significant, and the largest, single layer in this vast project of intellectual recovery. To understand the modern Olympic movement properly, we will need to pay careful attention to the cultural context of the nineteenth century in Europe. Only *after* we have done that will we be able to understand the modern Olympic movement in any significant detail. And only after we have done that will we be able to go back to the *ancient* Greek festivals in any meaningful and credible way. Unthinking our prior assumptions about the Olympics and the Greeks is the first task in this sort of temporal and theoretical excavation.

Everything is in reverse, jumbled and upside-down. There is no way back to antiquity, save through the thick layers of more recent Hellenic accumulation. And there is no way back to ancient Greece, save through the nineteenth century, when the real excavating, at Olympia and elsewhere, began. That is the fundamental paradox of Neohellenism.

THE NINETEENTH CENTURY

And that has been my primary point throughout this book. What I would like to do here is to underline ten separate but related developments, most of which I have discussed at least peripherally in previous chapters, and all of which, taken together here at the end, may begin to achieve their full significance regarding this large matter of Hellenic appropriation, especially the Romantics'. Here, then, is a parting sketch of certain developments in the nineteenth century in Europe—the intellectual, and political, and cultural developments that contributed to the creation of the kind of Hellenism to which we are still heir today.

One: "Greece" Itself

This was a century that saw a great deal of new interest in old Greek things.[20] The Greeks themselves (with a good bit of European prodding and support, as I have said)[21] successfully overcame 400 years of Ottoman occupation in the War of Independence (1821–1830).[22] A great many young Europeans, many of them university students, got involved in this war. Lord Byron popularized the War for many, of course, as we saw in Chapter Seven, through his own participation; he died in Greece, of a fever, at Missolonghi in 1824.

Greek fraternities—which are a rather unusual and deeply interesting cultural and ritual form we rarely analyze the way an anthropologist would, or should—*seem* to have been formed in some cases as a way to express solidarity with these self-styled Greek "freedom fighters."[23] So it was that the modern nation-state of Greece was born in the third decade of the nineteenth century. Some 60 years later, European and North American athletes would travel to this new-old country, to the newly excavated and refurbished Panathenaic Stadium in Athens, to play their modern Games there. And we will return to do so again, in 2004. Then, as now, such evocative trips to Greece are styled as "pilgrimage."

Two: Archaeology

Archaeology, one on a long list of burgeoning "human sciences," was really born in this same century, as we saw in the previous chapter. The first activity we might call "archaeological" in any meaningful modern sense seems to have taken place during the Napoleonic campaign and occupation in Egypt (1798–1801).[24] A great many ancient granite obelisks and other artifacts, including mummified human remains, made their way back to the great capitals of EuroAmerica after Napoleon's (1769–1821) activities[25]—the two most famous being, of course, Cleopatra's Needles in London and New York.

Then, in the first decade of the nineteenth century, Lord Elgin (1766–1841), a Scot, acquired his notorious *firman* from the Ottoman authorities and looted the Athenian Parthenon of its major pedimental statuary, metopes, and friezework.[26] These pieces are, offensively from the modern Greek perspective, still housed in the British Museum in London. *Most* of the masterworks of ancient Greek sculpture, for that matter, are now housed in the great capitals of EuroAmerica. We should reflect more than we normally do on the moral statement these collections make.[27]

In the *second* decade of the century, as we saw in the previous chapter, a little-known student of architecture named Charles R. Cockerell (1788–1863), along with three young friends, made astonishing discoveries of statuary at the Temple to Aphaia on the island of Aegina just south of Athens (this collection came to be housed, through an extremely confusing set of political circumstances, as we saw, at the Glyptothek Museum in Munich), as well as at the Temple of Apollo at Bassae (whose exceptionally high-quality frieze is now also in the British Museum in London).[28]

Shortly thereafter came the pioneering work of Heinrich Schliemann (1822–1890), who excavated at Troy on the western coast of Asia Minor from the 1870s to the 1890s, as well as at Mycenae and Tiryns on the Greek mainland in the later 1870s, with astonishing discoveries of treasures in all three places. By now, the great age of Greek Archaeology, conducted primarily by the European Great Powers, had begun.

What is important to note is that such investigation was the rather casual, and as yet dramatically *un*scientific, pastime of wealthy European aristocrats (the discipline, in Greece at least, still bears the stamp of this classist Classicism). This biographical observation well fits the Baron Pierre de Coubertin,[29] along with many others in the inner circle of his Olympic revival. That they were digging into the past was clear. But *why*? What I am suggesting is that a newfound sense of *communion* with the past invited a significant new engagement with antiquity—especially Greek antiquity, and especially in the nineteenth century.

Three: Museums

Archaeology, especially when it is a discipline that measures its success in the acquisition of art historical treasure, required *museums* in which to deposit such treasure. The nineteenth century is the great age of the museum treasury, a uniquely European cultural artifact that is still very much with us. To be sure, there had been galleries and private collections before, especially in some of the extraordinary papal villas in Italy. But these were private concerns, and personal holdings, open only to the elite friends of the elites who owned them. The museum, as a decisively *public* institution, really was something new under the sun. This is part of what had justified spending public monies on the Elgin marbles, for instance.

The Louvre, arguably the first modern museum in the world, opened its doors in 1793, but it provided a venue for painting primarily, not ancient sculpture. The Townley Gallery in London was the first fully public gallery devoted exclusively to the collection of sculptural masterworks of Greek and Roman antiquity,[30] and the Glyptothek in Munich was only the third museum on this august list (it officially opened in 1830). By the end of the century, museums had sprung up throughout Europe and North America. A museum, it was now felt—along with an opera house, and perhaps an athletic stadium—was one of the things every European capital was expected to have. Athens, ironically enough, would have the latter long before she acquired the former, since so much of her art had been looted prior to 1830. In any event, the modern Olympic movement takes on a very peculiar shape in a "museum culture"[31] such as our own. These are the quasi-religious, non-sectarian institutions to which all are invited—to commune with the past and to be granted new epiphanies.

Four: The Classics

Classics, too, had become a separate discipline within the university systems of Europe. *Philologie*, as it was called in German,[32] was first made into a "department," thereby defining a coherent and independent course of study, in the late eighteenth century in several German-speaking universities.[33] Friedrich August Wolf (1759–1824)[34] coined the term, and created the discipline, according to his younger contemporaries (Nietzsche among them),[35] and his own intellectual influences were clearly religious in nature—nowhere more clearly than on matters of textual criticism, which he learned from his Protestant colleagues in biblical studies in the previous generation, and then applied to the Homeric poems.

For my purposes, what is significant is that a great many educated social elites made the reading and memorization of Greek and Latin literature, as well as the immersion in ancient art and ancient history, the primary goal of their college years. These would be the same men who made the Grand Tour of what they then were calling "southern Europe," who later became "archaeologists" and "art historians," and finally even "Olympians," later in the century.

Five: Art History

"Art History" was a product of the same passion and the same period. Another German-speaking scholar, Johann Joachim Winckelmann (1717–1768)[36] is credited with the invention of this new body of knowledge, which was also incorporated into a revised university curriculum in the next century. His works, most notably the *History of the Art of Antiquity* (1764) and *Reflections on the Imitation of Greek Painting and Sculpture* (1765), created a discipline, as I say, but they also created a *taste*. It was a taste that partially, but only partially, succeeded in secularizing Greek art—by removing it from its location on temples and reinstalling it in the secular sanctuary called the museum, a site that was designed to foster the singularly Romantic pilgrimages they so often inspired.

These things had been removed from Greece. But Winckelmann, much like Goethe—and even like Nietzsche, fully 100 years later—never went to Greece. He traveled extensively, and even chose to live, in Italy. His canons of classicism were thus derived not from a study of Greek art but, rather, of Roman imitations and copies of Greek originals. Such was the power and the prestige of Greco-Romanism. In fairness to Winckelmann, it should be said that travel to Greece in the late eighteenth century was dangerous. Brigandage was common: Otto Stackelberg was kidnapped and ransomed back to his friends in 1814; Charles Cockerell nearly met the same fate in the previous year. Disease, including plague, was widespread: Carl Haller died in Greece in 1817, as Byron did in 1824, and as Cockerell nearly did on two separate occasions. Moreover, Winckelmann—unlike Goethe and Nietzsche—was endeavoring to travel to Greece, when he was murdered *en route* in 1768.[37]

But my larger point is that Greece was not really thought to be part of "the west," nor of Europe, at the time—not in the way that Italy was. Greece was exotic, Oriental,[38] in much the same way it *still* is for many student backpackers (and for other students, such as myself, who were fortunate enough to live there for a longer period of time). The student backpackers and Levant lunatics of the early nineteenth century—men like Charles Cockerell, and even Lord Byron in his way—were largely from Great Britain and France.[39] The German-speaking world (save for the Bavarians, of course) that was so integral in "rediscovering" and even "reinventing" Greece as a subject of philological and art historical investigation did not really start traveling to Greece until the *end* of the century.[40]

Pierre de Coubertin, for his part, traveled *extensively* in Europe and North America before he ever made it south, and east, to Greece. As Coubertin himself freely admits, Olympia had always been a "dream city" to him. After some 30 years of German excavation there, he notes: "Germany has brought to light what remained of Olympia; why should not France succeed in rebuilding its splendors?"[41] The French, he believed, would help to restore Olympia's ancient *ritual* aura, under the aegis of his modern Olympic movement.

Six: The Philosophy Of History

That Greece was only gradually brought into the European fold has other important implications for these Olympic developments. European philosophers—beginning with Hegel (1770–1831) in the first and second decades of the nineteenth century—began telling the story of something called "the philosophy of history,"[42] a story in which the Greeks were consistently described as "Chapter One" (Egypt and India *were* mentioned, as part of "the Oriental World," but they served only as a sort of preface to the real story, which was a *Greek* story, or rather, a bit disingenuously, a nominally *European* one).

Greece, that is to say, was made Chapter One in the story of *Europe*. "Among the Greeks," Hegel says, with mingled astonishment and delight, "we feel ourselves immediately at home."[43] These complex developments also help to form the cultural and intellectual backdrop to the reestablishment of the modern Olympic Games, *in Athens*, in 1896.[44] Europe, it was believed, was coming home, returning to its own mythic origins. But of course you cannot travel backward in time, anymore than you can make a permanent home in Paradise. Europe, interestingly enough, did not stay in Greece for long,[45] but rather brought the Greeks, and their Games—along with a good bit of their ancient art—back home with them to Europe. I have already said something about that, and will do so again.

Seven: The Idea of Aesthetic Materiality

It was left finally to the philosophers to reflect on the nature of the religious sculpture (which mimicked real bodies, as we have seen), and of the religious architecture (which housed these same bodies), that they were appropriating from the eastern (and southern) Mediterranean. A great many buildings—such as the ones in our own capital—took the interesting form of Classical Greek (when they were not Roman) temples. As I noted in the first chapter, the U.S. Supreme Court, completed in 1935, is one premier example of this aesthetic taste.

It is hardly accidental, then, that "Aesthetics" was another important creation of the nineteenth century. The so-called science of perception was coined by Alexander G. Baumgarten (1714–1762) in his *Reflections on Poetry* (1735),[46] then reified by Immanuel Kant (1724–1804) in his *Critique of Judgment* (1790).[47] It was Friedrich Schiller (1759–1805) who took the Kantian interest in "sublimity" and the deliberately oxymoronic idea of a "disinterested interest," and made it passionate, with his highly influential discussion of the "play-drive" (*Spieltrieb*) as essential to both moral and philosophical development.[48] Hegel's massive *Lectures on Aesthetics*,[49] compiled after his death in 1831, well illustrate the philosophical and cultural obsession with Greek antiquity that underwrote so much of this newfound aesthetic sensibility. From Germany, these bodies of knowledge also migrated to England and France and the New World.

It was in Paris that Pierre de Coubertin ingested these ideas and took them to heart—a heart that is now buried quite instructively, rather far from its body, in a lead box under a marble stele at Olympia. In the words of Coubertin's superb biographer, John J. MacAloon,[50] given the Catholic presuppositions of Coubertin's own background, the decision to divide his body in this way—between Lausanne and Olympia, between Europe and Greece, between Catholicism and paganism—was emblematic of his larger refusal of a strictly Christian death and commemoration. He preferred to remain at ancient Olympia, at least in part.

There were interesting Romantic antecedents to this decision, which was mandated by Coubertin's last will and testament. First, we should return to Italy. We may recall the perfectly bizarre scene recorded by Edward Trelawny that involved the burial of Shelley's corpse on the beach at Spezzia, its subsequent disinterrment, followed then by its dramatic immolation. We also should recall Trelawny's description of fishing Shelley's heart out of the furnace with a bare hand when it would not burn, as well as Byron's disgust with the scene. Trelawny then sealed the heart up in a lead box and presented it to Shelley's widow.[51] The body was achieving new interest, as a material fact; this new interest led to some strange and aberrant funerary practices,[52] as well as contributed to the creation of modern Olympism.

Next, we may turn to Greece. The modern Olympic revival relied heavily on the philanthropy of two enormously wealthy diasporic Greeks: Evangelis Zappas (1800–1865), who made a fortune in Rumanian real estate, and Giorgios Averoff (1818–1899), an Alexandrian Greek famous, among other things, for donating funds for the reconstruction of the ancient Panathenaic Stadium prior to the 1896 Olympic Games, as well as for the construction of the very first modern battleship in the Greek navy.[53]

When Greece achieved her independence in 1830 with some considerable European assistance, and after the treaty was signed in London in 1832, she was also provided with a European king—the Bavarian King Ludwig's son, Otto—who arrived in Athens in 1833. In 1837, Otto I enacted a series of national gatherings, both athletic festivals as well as others that had a more industrial focus. Evangelis Zappas, an Epirote veteran of the Greek War for Independence, wrote to the king in 1856, offering virtually unlimited funds for these athletic contests, as well as for the construction of new buildings for the agricultural and industrial fairs Otto envisioned. Zappas died in 1865, having seen only some initial work done on his beloved Panathenaic Stadium, whereas work had not yet even begun on the exhibition hall that would eventually bear his name—the Zappeion—which is now located in the National Gardens in Athens.

Zappas's will had one rather odd provision. He was to be buried in Rumania. But after four years, his body was to be exhumed and decapitated. The body was then to be reinterred at a school in northwestern Greece (in Epirus, where he was raised), but his head was to be installed in the new "Olympic" building with a plaque bearing the inscription: *enthade keitai ê kephalê Euangelê Zappa,* "Here lies the head of Evangelis Zappas." Somewhat later than originally planned (on October 20, 1888), Zappas's head was duly installed in the now-complete Zappeion.[54]

Coubertin spent considerable time at the Zappeion, during his first visit to Athens in November 1894. He was there to organize the Athenian Olympic Committee, and he wished to make the Zappeion the Committee's headquarters (this pun was unintentional). Surely, then, he had ample time to muse over this curious plaque, and the curious connection between person and place that it so richly symbolized. It is likely that here, at the Zappeion, Coubertin first hatched the plan that would result in his own eventual dismemberment, and the installation of his heart at Olympia. Paying careful attention to the practical facts of human embodiment lay, in any case, at the very heart of his Olympic revival.

Eight: Travel Writing/The Historical Novel

The nineteenth century, especially in the English-speaking world, also saw the birth of two fascinating new literary genres. The modern travel journal is an intriguing genre in its own right, whose relevance to the cultural matters before us cannot be overestimated.[55] The Frenchman, Hippolyte Taine (1828–1893), had written several enormously popular books about his travels in England—*A History of English Literature*

(1869), and *Notes on England* (1871)—attending to the character of the English people and their public institutions. These works had an enormous influence on Coubertin.[56] Alexis de Tocqueville (1805–1859), of course, had provided the same service in analyzing things North American (*Democracy in America*) in 1835. And Coubertin, so observed his friend and American publicist Albert Shaw, had made himself "the De Tocqueville of our day."[57] To be sure, "popular ethnography"[58]—seeing, and smelling, and competing with "others"—is a large part of what the Olympics are allegedly all about. It was in this way, in any case, that they were believed to contribute to global understanding and that alternately noble and naive cause of "universal peace."

Leaving France and turning to England, then, we discover that Alexander William Kinglake's (1809–1891) enormously popular *Eothen*, first published in 1844,[59] was journalistic in the truest sense of the word. It was a deeply *personal* journal. No mere invocation of culture and place (his "place" was pretty exclusively the then-Ottoman Empire), Kinglake's was one of the very first books to place a very distinctive personality, his own, *in* that place—as participant-observer, and as vaguely cynical, less vaguely snobbish imperial observer. Mark Twain would mimic this same style brilliantly, while covering much of the same ground (*and* adding Greece to his itinerary), in *The Innocents Abroad* (1869—this book sold 100,000 copies in two years).[60] Kinglake carefully cultivated this rather stylized image of himself to such a degree that the book was as much about himself as it was about the Ottomans. Person and place were intimately linked, once again, much as they were thought to have been in the ancient Olympian (*epinikian*) poetry of Pindar.[61] By the mid-nineteenth century—and inspired by the poetry of Pindar, the musings of the Byronic tradition, and the archaeological record presented in Pausanias—a virtual cottage-industry of travel journals from Greece had emerged.

So much for *us* travelling *there*. Travelling in the opposite direction, the historical novel[62] was also born in the world of English letters in the early nineteenth century with the work of Sir Walter Scott. In the words of Georg Lukács, the famous Marxist literary critic, with quite astonishing suddenness the taste for fiction "flavoured with the portrayal of historical place"[63] arose right around the time of Napoleon's defeat. Such a taste firmly established itself in the minds of literati and their readership alike. There had been a time when the Holy Family was painted with a fitting Teutonic or North Italian landscape behind it, dressed in all the finery of the painter's own times. But now a *new* taste was emerging—the attempt, however flawed and imperfectly conceived, to render them in their *own* place and in their *own* clothes.

Person and place, again. We are witnessing here, I think, the (re?)emergence of a, tentative perhaps, but more authentically *global* perspective, borne quite possibly of the experience of building an Empire on which the sun allegedly never set.[64] The world is a vast theater, peopled with an impossible array of cultures and human kinds. And our aim *should* be to tell every one of their stories well.

These ideas resonated most strongly with Pierre de Coubertin's ideas concerning *cosmopolitanism* and *internationalism* as the very essence of the modern Olympic revival. These were the things, Coubertin insisted, which made the modern movement most *unlike* its ancient predecessor, a religious festival that had been limited to the Greek-speaking world, and unified by a coherent set of religious beliefs, cultural practices, and myths. "The art of living," Coubertin said,

was at its apogee, and the art of dying followed from it quite naturally; people knew
how to live without fear and to die without regrets for the sake of *a changeless city* and *an
undisputed religion*—something which—alas!—we know no longer.[65]

The modern Olympic movement, Coubertin now realized, would have to derive *its*
unity from some *other* spiritual source. This was his notion of "paganism," perhaps.

Nine: Sociology

The human science of Sociology, especially the sociology of *religion,* claims two men
as its godfathers, a Frenchman and a German: Emile Durkheim (1858–1917); and
Max Weber (1864–1920). Durkheim is the more important figure for our purposes.
He clearly represents the intellectual tradition which was most influential on Pierre
de Coubertin.

Durkheim was, in the words of Robert Bellah,

> a philosopher and a moralist in the great French tradition of moral thought. He was
> even more than that. He was a high priest and theologian of the civil religion of the
> Third Republic and a prophet calling not only modern France but modern Western so-
> ciety generally to mend its ways in the face of a great social and moral crisis.[66]

Durkheim spoke appreciatively of Judaism and Christianity, but he saw both religions as morally exhausted, as outmoded ways of religious life. What rendered them
problematic, in his judgment, was their impoverished *ritual* sensibility. Attracted as
he was to "primitivism,"[67] for its emphatic socialness and its ritual sophistication,
Durkheim's own commitments were to the more modern-sounding ideals of rationality, of science, and most significantly, of the then-dawning concept of "humanity."
He decried the loss of ritual in a mechanized and secularized world (much as Coubertin did), and we have probably all heard that, in his later writings, the idea of "society" does most of the hard work once done by "God." But here, too, Bellah reminds
us of the significance in his language:

> It is not that Durkheim makes an empirical society into an idol. It is that he so elevates,
> purifies, and deepens the word "society" that it can, not unworthily, take the place of
> the great word it supersedes.[68]

Elevation, purification, deepening—these are Coubertin's precise images, whenever
he discusses the modern Olympic Games. What he intended to create was a ritual
form that would be better suited to the religious-and-secular tastes of modernity.
The endless back-and-forth—between the individual competitor, and the various
collectives of audience, and team, and nation—was precisely the dance that Coubertin intended to orchestrate.

Ten: International Public Spectacles

It was in this area most especially that Coubertin was well *ahead* of his time, intellectually speaking. It was not until 1912 that Durkheim would acknowledge the power,
and the need, for what he termed "feasts and ceremonies of the future."

If we find a little difficulty today in imagining what these feasts and ceremonies of the future could consist in, it is because we are going through a stage of transition and moral mediocrity. . . . *In a word, the old gods are growing old or are already dead, and others are not yet born.* . . . But this state of incertitude and confused agitation cannot last for ever. A day will come when our societies will know again those hours of creative effervescence in the course of which new ideas arise and new formulae are found to serve for a while as a guide to humanity. . . . As to the question of what symbols this new faith will express itself with, whether they will resemble those of the past or not, and whether or not they will be more adequate for the reality which they seek to translate, that is something which surpasses the human faculty of foresight. . . . [69]

By the time this idea was published, Coubertin's revival was celebrating its Fifth Olympiad. Less reflective and more pragmatic than Durkheim, perhaps, Coubertin intended to see to it that these "feasts and ceremonies of the future" both did and did not "resemble those of the past." Still better, he intended to make them marry various conflicting aspects of the collective European past.

That said, the impulse for grandiose quadrennial international spectacles was hardly new.[70] In the same spirit that gave us the museum, these festivals were broadly conceived as museums on the move—museums, that is to say, which *traveled.* Coubertin did not invent this taste, but he was uniquely attuned to the power of this new international ritual genre. Coubertin read the signs of his times quite sensitively, and recognized the power of what modern technology, among other things, could achieve.

There had been a native French tradition lying behind such affairs: the salons of Louis XIV, and the Napoleonic exhibitions of 1804 and 1806, for instance. But in 1851, the London Crystal Palace drew over six million visitors to what was intended as a coherent monument to Victorian culture and its own vision of moral and aesthetic "progress."[71] The idea of the unity of humanity, invoked by Prince Albert in his Opening Speech, was also prominently and paradoxically displayed at all such international events. It was a celebration, all at once, of things distinctly British, *and* of the spirit of internationalism. There then followed a series of decennial "Universal Expositions" in France[72]—the first under Louis Napoleon in 1856,[73] another in 1867,[74] and again in 1878 (the first one attended by Pierre de Coubertin, at the ripe age of fifteen).[75] Sixteen million persons had attended that fête. Then, in 1889, somewhere between 24 and 32 million visitors attended the Paris Exposition, fully 1.5 million of them from foreign countries. The marvels of electricity were prominently displayed here,[76] as was the Eiffel Tower, which so transformed the Parisian skyline.[77] Modern technology had at last outdone the Egyptian in obelisk-construction. The same taste that made the museum such a potent cultural artifact made this spectacle of ritualized internationalism a hit as well.

The voracious appetite for global festivals was translated quite easily to the New World. In 1893, both the "World's Columbia Exhibition"[78] and the "Parliament on the World's Religions"[79] met in Chicago,[80] in the so-called "White City" built expressly for the occasion. The dramatic and expansive neoclassicism of the site made a huge impact.[81] On the one hand, the Greek temple was invoked as that architectural form that "belonged to everyone." The Greeks were fast becoming a symbol of ecumenical nonsectarianism that made the ironic first thinkable, and then actual: A Greek temple now served as sacred-*and*-secular "ecumenical space." The U.S. Supreme Court, completed in 1935, is, as I have already indicated, a model of the

Athenian Parthenon, inspired by the success of the Chicago Exhibition and the aesthetic power of the White City. Ironic it is, that this, our constitutional shrine to the alleged separation of church and state is, itself, modeled on a religious temple.[82] But irony is the very stuff of life in the storied career of modern Neohellenisms.

Pierre de Coubertin happened to be in the United States in 1893; he attended both the Exhibition and the Parliament.[83] In the very next year, back in Paris, he organized the Sorbonne Conference at which the modern Olympic revival was formally proclaimed and approved. Yet, ironically enough, the ritual power of these World's Fairs nearly derailed the nascent Olympic movement, as I mentioned.[84] The 1900 Olympic Games were held in Paris, so as to coincide with the Parisian World's Fair. They were completely upstaged by the Fair. So, too, in 1904, when the Games were brought to the United States. They had originally been scheduled for Chicago, but were transplanted at the last moment to St. Louis, where the World's Fair was to be held. Here, again, the Fair far overshadowed the Games. The same problem presented itself in London in 1908. It was not really until 1912, in Stockholm, that the IOC sponsored Games that were truly independent in a ritual sense, worthy of the profound aspirations so many had by this time hung on them.

THE QUESTION OF ROMANTICISM

But why *Olympic* Games? Why *Greek* Games at all? Coubertin insisted that the Olympic "name forced itself upon us; it was not possible to invent another."[85] Why not, we may reasonably ask? The answer has a great deal to do with "Romanticism." To be sure, this is an extraordinarily difficult term, if for no other reason than that so many of the people I would want to consider representatives of a definitively Romantic *style*—Byron, for instance, and Goethe, even Nietzsche in his way—all rejected the term and did not want to be associated with it. What is Romanticism, if some of its purest representatives refused to call themselves by that name? And how does it relate to the name of its nearest cousin, Victorianism? These terms and temporal periods overlap, to be sure, more than we realize. Moreover, "Romantic" as a terminology seemed to mean rather different things to artists, to philosophers, and to poets. Just as it meant quite different things in Germany, in France, in England, and in the United States.[86]

For my present purposes, I believe that we can best think of Romanticism as an intellectual and spiritual recovery (and, as it often was in practice, a recreation) of ancient Greece, and an attempted communion with that vision of antiquity. A great many Romantic poets made careers out of translating Archaic and Classical poetic fragments into modern, Romance languages.[87] The aesthetics of the fragment, much like the idyll of the marble ruin in a wooded glen, became an essential Romantic image.

These same poets fostered the image of the Artist (conceived with a capital A, as I indicated in the previous chapter) as a visionary mystic and a supplier of epiphanies.[88] Coubertin and others would make these same sorts of claims about the modern *Athlete* (perhaps also best conceived with capitalization). He or she presents us with epiphanies, moments of transcendent grace, beauty, and clarity. Here is how Nietzsche, still working as a Classicist, understood this Greek tradition in 1876:

The passion in Mimnermus, the hatred of age.

 The deep melancholy in Pindar; only when a ray of light comes down from above does human life shine.

 That life is to be understood out of suffering—that is the tragic in tragedy.[89]

And here is Pindar, the epinikian poet whom Nietzsche was recalling. First and foremost, for Pindar, comes the bitterness:

> Not for them, as for you,
> a sweet return from Delphi,
> no light laughter
> rising from their mother's lips
> in welcome. No,
> they slink back alleyways,
> shunning enemy eyes
> and nursing pain,
> the bite of defeat.

Then, and only then, is a space opened for the benediction, with which I began this chapter:

> But he who has achieved a new success
> basks in the light,
> soaring from hope to hope.
> His deeds of prowess
> let him pace the air,
> while he conceives
> plans sweeter to him than wealth.
> But the delight of mortal men
> flowers
> then flutters to the ground,
> shaken by a mere
> shift of thought.
>
> Creatures of a day!
> What is someone?
> What is no one?
> Man: a shadow's dream.
> But when god-given glory comes
> a bright light shines upon us and our life is sweet.[90]

Pindar's athletic vision is a somber and ambivalent one. The bite of defeat, and the sting of this most public form of Greek shame, cut deeply. But so, too, does the aspiration toward a kind of athletic immortality. We are both creatures of a day, and the stuff that eternity is made on.

 What I have been trying to suggest in the previous chapters is that the Romantics' Greece was, in many important ways, a fantasy-world that had never really existed. It was an ideal created in the hopes of *reclaiming* such a lost paradise in the degenerate, "modern" present. We have the Romantics to thank, in no small measure, for turning "Modern" into a proper noun, *and* into a tremendous spiritual problem.

Greece, they argued, was a crucial *alternative,* providing as it did an image of lost innocence and lost wholeness. Greece, they believed, provided an escape from "modern times."[91] In a variety of pursuits, like *swimming,*[92] nineteenth-century Romantics attempted to recreate that image of lost innocence, of reintegrated natural humanity, as a means of escaping from the perceived decadence and the spiritual malaise of their own situation. The modern Olympic Games were conceived as an important piece of that Romantic reconstruction.

OLYMPISM AS RELIGION

Which is what makes the modern Olympic movement a *religious* movement, in my judgment, and why I did not have sufficient time to explain my meaning to the Princess. It was the Romantics who helped to make our own rhetoric of "the ancients and the moderns" meaningful. "Antiquity," especially *Greek* (as opposed to Roman)[93] antiquity, was conceived as an antidote to "modern times." That language, and indeed that powerful sense of Hellenic *nostalgía,* is inseparable from the modern Olympic movement and the precious idea of a modern Olympic revival.

The Romantics, many of them in any case, thought that the Christian culture of Europe was dying. The question for them thus became how to breathe new life into dying sacred institutions, or else to dispense with those institutions altogether. Returning to the *Greek* roots of the Christian faith was a trajectory charted out by a great many disaffected Romantics. But, in "going back to Greece," the question of where, and when, you wish to go emerges with special urgency. This is another point I have made many times in this book, and it hinges on an *archaeological* question, a question of historical layers.

Go back to a certain epoch—the third or fourth century of the Common Era, let's say—and we get to a kind of Christianity, *Orthodox* Christianity, which represented the road not taken in Latin-speaking, western Europe. These Greeks were Christians, but Christians of a heretofore unknown sort.[94] Heavily liturgical and ritualistic, like their Catholic cousins, the Orthodox were nonetheless perceived to be less hierarchical and, well, as less *Roman* than their Latin counterparts. They represented an exciting alternative kind of Christianness—a *Greek* kind—as they still seem to be to many searching Protestants today.[95]

Go back further still, and you leave Christianity behind altogether. Many Romantics opted to go there, back to the pagan, *pre-*Christian world whose loss we examined in the fourth chapter—Goethe and Byron tended rather tentatively in that direction, Nietzsche did so far more emphatically—and what they discovered was another sort of "religion" altogether, an alternative kind of spirituality, which might also be the very antidote to a dying Christian worldview they had been seeking. The so-called New Age religions of this generation are not the first to call for a return to paganism as a way to overcome the alleged sickness at the heart of Judeo-Christianity. Many of the Romantics said this nearly 200 years ago. In fact, one of the many fascinating details so carefully orchestrated by Pierre de Coubertin was his decision to hold the first modern Olympic Games on Easter Monday. Through an apt and quite rare calendrical accident, the Eastern and Western Easter fell on the same day that year, March 23, 1896.[96] "It will be early Spring when the celebration takes place," said Ioannis Gennadius, a native Greek philhellene and philanthropist, on the eve of the Games:

the sweetest and loveliest season in a climate always benign, when the very stones of Greece seem to blossom with flowers. It will be Easter-tide, the great festival of the venerable Church of the East, heralding joy and hope to all. It will be the seventy-fifth anniversary of the outbreak of the Sacred Struggle for Independence—a triple inspiring symbolism of resurrection, such as only Greece can supply from the wealth of her poetic traditions.[97]

So there was a kind of narrowly Christian ecumenism—as well as an implicit notion of pagan resurrection, not to mention a spirit of nationalist revival—embedded in the very fabric of these Opening Ceremonies.

One thing was abundantly clear: Pierre de Coubertin envisioned these resurrected Olympic festivals as an alternative model of the spiritual life, of a vital, and an emphatically *embodied*, spiritual life. This is what he called "paganism," in its "true form." "Muscular Christianity" was one of the British buzzwords of the day,[98] the idea being to restore integrity and legitimacy to the human body, which had labored for too long under the uneasy gaze and guilty conscience of what Coubertin called "medievalism."[99] Coubertin reserved kind words for certain creations of the Middle Ages: The new intellectualism that helped to create the Sorbonne in Paris;[100] the grand tournaments and jousts that were a singular form of feudal entertainment *and* a prelude to his Olympic festivals;[101] and most significantly, the cult of *chivalry* which Coubertin deemed so essential to modern Olympism.[102] The Baron spoke unabashedly of the *religio athletae*,[103] although he was never able to say any more clearly than our Constitutional framers could precisely of what that "religion" consisted.[104] So he contented himself by and large with oblique allusions to his "pagan-seeming revival."[105] It was all to be a vast *spirituality* of sport.

Coubertin mentions certain abstract ideas—like our common embodied humanity,[106] and internationalism,[107] and even the idea of Peace, which he concludes, "has become a sort of religion"[108] among us. "Modern athletics, gentlemen, shows two trends to which I would draw your attention," he adds. "It is becoming firstly democratic and secondly international."[109] This comments bears emphasis. It lies at the heart of Coubertin's reformative vision in education, in international politics, as well as in what, for lack of a better term, we might simply call the spiritual life.

Shortly after the conclusion of the first international Olympics, Coubertin penned an important article for the *American Review of Reviews*, the journal he often used to communicate with a North American audience. It was entitled "Does Cosmopolitan Life Lead to International Friendliness?"[110] and it was designed to distance himself from the overly sentimentalizing and naive support that his Olympic reforms had generated. Coubertin understood himself, after all, to be a cultural critic and an *educational* reformer.[111] The short answer to his question, Coubertin suggests, is No. Cosmopolitanism, perhaps more than any other idea, suffers from the inherent dangers of trivialization and irrelevancy. If "cosmopolitan" is what we choose to call the singularly *aristocratic* European experience of living in a hotel in Paris, but having your laundry done in London and traveling for surgery to Munich, then no, "cosmopolitanism" clearly serves no pedagogical or political interest whatsoever. That is the truncated version of "cosmopolitanism" popularized by touristic associations and social elites who spend most of their time abroad shopping for bargains and complaining about the native cuisine. By attending to such trivial matters as diet and dress and only to these things—whether to despise them, or else

vainly to attempt to "go native"—the important cultural transactions that cosmopolitanism can and should make possible are missed. This is what the Grand
Tourist and the student backpacker too often miss. Coubertin achieves a kind of
studied irony here that was unique in his prolific journalistic career. "What connection can possibly exist between the fact that the Americans drink iced water and
eat fried oysters and their methods of government and education?" Coubertin asks
wrily. "Would they be less good Republicans if they ate macaroni?"[112]

By focusing on such cultural incidentals as cuisine and couture, Coubertin insists,
the essential opportunities, the truly *educational* opportunities, are missed. The good
traveler will educate him- or herself before the trip. Such self-education consists primarily of a careful study of social and political institutions, as well as the relevant national literature, not merely the culinary eccentricities. "Cosmopolitanism" is merely
a name, a simple statement of the facts of modern life; *internationalism* should be the
goal of the Olympic and other such modern revivals. And it is that distinction—between crass cosmopolitanism and an authentic spirit of internationalism—that
Coubertin relentlessly drove home in all of his writings.

Modern sport, he insists, has become more democratic and more international.

More democratic: it is easy to lose sight, from the perspective of this country and
our own very different egalitarian assumptions, of how radical Coubertin was in his
own day. Like Byron, he was Liberal in the most scandalous sense of the term; he was
a French aristocrat who meant what he said about the various social "classes," and the
various "races," competing together. His vision of what this might entail one day was
truncated, limited quite naturally by the times in which he lived. Asia and Africa did
not appear on his Olympic map, South America only barely did.[113] These were
"white" games, just as they were European games, and much as they were still aristocratic games. But Coubertin's commitment to the "ambulatory" nature of these
games, just like his commitment to full participatory democracy and the franchise,
was heartfelt. The Olympics have thus become, I believe, ever more fully what he intended them to be.

More international: here is the crux of the matter, the paradox lying at the heart
of Olympism. Coubertin genuinely believed that a collection of young men from
various countries wrestling and running together would emphatically serve the cause
of world peace.[114] Why? What belief could possibly seem more naive than this? Coubertin insisted that the regnant European (and vaguely Christian) beliefs about loving one another were naive in a way that his version of Olympism was not. "Men are
not angels," he noted near the end of his life in 1935, "and I do not believe it would
benefit humanity if the majority of them became angels."[115] His reasons for saying
this are, however, extraordinarily idealistic ones. So he continues:

> To ask the peoples of the world to love one another is merely a form of childishness. To
> ask them to respect one another is not in the least utopian, but in order to respect one
> another it is first necessary to know one another. . . . [This] is the genuine foundation
> for a genuine peace.
>   Having reached the end of my journey, I take advantage of the approach of the
> Games of the XIth Olympiad to offer you my good wishes and my thanks, and at the
> same time to express to you my unshakeable faith in youth and the future![116]

If we cannot learn to love one another, then we may surely learn respect. That is the
essential emotion congruent with a serious internationalism. And it was "Olymp-

ism's" intention to give that idea a ritual form. Where human beings deny the essential place of the *agôn*, the competitive contest, they will have its great, and quite literal, alternative: *ant-agôn-ism*, a Greek word that simply refers to what we have "*instead of* the *agôn*." "In the place of war," Coubertin concludes,

> a state of things has arisen which is built on rivalry [I would call this his Olympic *agonism*], on competition, and which will be productive of happy results for humanity only in so far as that rivalry shall be amicable and that competition shall be legal.[117]

"Internationalism," we now see, encompasses all of this.

Yet Coubertin speaks also of nationalism, of athletes swearing oaths[118] before their respective national flags,[119] as well as before the five-ringed Olympic Flag.[120] He knows that we can no longer swear our oaths to Zeus.[121] World War I and its aftermath has made these claims more difficult for latter-day Olympians to swallow. But Coubertin was insistent—his whole Olympic program required it—that one could indeed promote "patriotism without nationalism."[122]

Which brings us, at long last, back to religion. Echoing Durkheim—not to mention Hölderlin and Nietzsche—the fear was that the old gods were dead or dying . . . and new gods were still waiting to be born. Coubertin, for his part, was not consistently trying to bring such pagan gods back to life. But he *did* want their ritual; he simply could not say precisely what he wanted it for.[123] One thing he did say most eloquently, though, and that is that attending to the complexity of the category of "religion," especially in its Hellenic context, is an important first step.

> First of all I must explain the term "religious," which has here a special significance. The true religion of the athlete of antiquity did not consist in sacrificing solemnly before the altar of Zeus; this was no more than a traditional gesture. It consisted in taking an oath of honour and disinterest, and above all in striving to keep it strictly. A participant in the Games must be in some manner purified by the profession and practice of such virtues. Thus were revealed the moral beauty and the profound scope of physical culture.[124]

Coubertin was surely wrong about the "incidental" nature of the sacrificial hecatomb and the sacred meal in antiquity. He considers them incidental in the same way he considers cuisine incidental for the morally serious cosmopolitan traveler. But religion, as I have said repeatedly in this book, is all about such ritual practices, not only about doctrines or texts or even an "ethical culture." Coubertin does know this. Olympism, the modern form of it at any rate, was conceived as a deliberate and self-conscious resurrection of a certain kind of spirituality, and a certain "ethic"—the ethos of learning how to win graciously and how to lose well—as well as a kind of "physical culture"—which was so essential an aspect of the lingering Romanticism of the European *fin de siècle*.[125]

THE IDEA OF ATHLETIC LIMIT

I have mentioned Friedrich Nietzsche several times in this book, and especially in this chapter; I would like to do so again now, at the end of both. He is, to my mind, an enormously significant figure in charting out these vast Olympian developments. Consider this short list of by no means accidental facts. Nietzsche taught as a professor in the fledgling department of *Philologie* for ten years at the University of Basel, before poor health and professional frustration forced him into early retirement in 1879. He remained interested in the Greeks all of his life, for reasons that were directly related to his lifelong interest in religion, a thoroughly broadened understanding of *non-Christian* religion. He venerated the *competitive* spirit he thought he found there, best of all. While his creative life ended tragically with his collapse in 1889,[126] Nietzsche lived for 11 years more and died in the grandly symbolic year of 1900.

Nietzsche's quarrel with the classics—it was surely one of the important reasons he left the university—was that they were too nostalgic, too nostalgic about the Greeks. He said very consistently that he wanted to *use* the Classics, not to be enslaved by them. He also suggested that the Classical world provides us with an extraordinary range of spiritual and aesthetic models with which to compete and to *surpass,* not an ancient world to *imitate.*

> *Imitation* of antiquity: hasn't the principle finally been refuted?
>   *Escape from reality* to the classics: hasn't the understanding of antiquity already been falsified in this manner?[127]

The moderns, he noted, are not like the ancients, and cannot be again. Using the ancients as a model—as he emphasized, a competitive model to be *surpassed*—the moderns would be rendered capable of creating things of which the ancients could never have dreamed.

> So if we fully understand Greek culture, we see that it's gone for good. Hence the classicist is *the great skeptic* in our cultural and educational circumstances: that's his mission.—Lucky the classicist who, like Wagner and Schopenhauer, has a presentiment of those auspicious strengths in which a new culture is stirring.[128]

And again:

> To *surpass* Greek culture by action—that is the task. But to do that, we must first know it.—There is a learned thoroughness which is only an excuse for not acting. Think how much Goethe understood of the ancient world; certainly less than a classicist, but enough to grapple with it creatively. We *should not* know more of a thing than we can creatively use. Besides, the only means of really *knowing* something is by trying to *do* it. Try living classically—by so doing you immediately get a hundred miles closer to the classics than with all the learning in the world.—Our classicists never show that they *emulate* antiquity in any way—hence, *their* antiquity has no effect on their students.
>   *Curriculum of competition* (Renaissance, Goethe) and *curriculum of desperation!*[129]

Competition, striving, living classically, the whole modern surpassing of antiquity: We should hear an echo of the Socratic trope of sons supplanting their fathers again here. Coubertin said much the same thing about his modern Olympians.

But there is a deeper point to Nietzsche's classicism, a point that is overlooked in too many sophomoric portraits of Nietzsche as the artistic self-creator. Nietzsche knew well that artists, very much like the rest of us, cannot bear too much freedom. When Zarathustra realizes for the first time that all things recur, he nearly faints at the thought.[130] The thought that "God is dead" is placed in the mouth of a madman.[131] Ultimately, there is no doing away with the idea, or the constraint, of God—not so long as we believe in the rules of grammar, rules we simply cannot do without.[132] Art—like language, and very much like critical thought—*requires* constraints, rules, *limitations.* Nietzsche grappled with this truth throughout his life.[133]

A sonnet is beautiful for many reasons—the English Romantic poets wrote many memorable ones—but one of the most significant is due to the way it meets the rules of structure and of meter, and *plays* with them. Byron found a similar challenge, and similar potential for play, in English rhyme.[134] Poetry thus seizes on a limitation, a set of rules, and it asserts a mastery over them. Such *mastery* lies at the heart of the artistic adventure, Nietzsche believed. It lies at the heart of athleticism, too. Says Coubertin:

> What is a sporting result? It is a figure or a fact. You have a maximum height above which you cannot jump, a minimum time below which you cannot sprint a hundred metres. The weight which you lift and the rope which you climb also express in kilos or in metres the value of your effort. If a rock-climber, you are capable of climbing this mountain and not that; if a rider, of mastering this horse but not that other. On all sides you encounter restrictions of a more or less mathematical severity. But you could not see them when you began. Nobody knows his exact limitations in advance. Only one road leads there—training and hard work.[135]

The body imposes certain clear and occasionally quantifiable limits and constraints on us, and athletics asserts a sort of mastery over the body. That is one reason that the Greeks were so much impressed by athleticism. It was, in any case, precisely this "philosophico-religious doctrine"[136] that Coubertin most wished to recover for his "deeply and oddly philosophical spectacle."[137]

CONCLUSIONS

One serious message in my efforts at Olympic archaeology is that the modern games are much more *unlike* their ancient predecessors than they are like them. The nineteenth century looms between the Greek games and our own. Let me use one example to illustrate this point, an example that troubled Pierre de Coubertin a great deal: There were no team sports in antiquity, excepting teams of horses.

The Ancient Olympic festivals provided an arena for *individual* human excellence. And Coubertin, for his part, remained committed to the rather narrow view that the central focus of Olympic attention should remain on the young adult male who was an individual athlete.[138] No women, no children, no teams—we have clearly moved *very* far from his ideals here.[139]

Our modern team sports have three very interesting components, some of which may have existed in antiquity, yet which seem far more pronounced today:

- most of them use elaborate *playing fields,* with a great many complex *lines;*
- a good many of them rely on the *clock,* focussing attention on the passage of *time* (regularized pendulum timekeeping was another northern European invention, precisely datable to the year 1687);[140]
- and most of them have elaborate and complicated *rules.*

Each of these factors—spatial boundaries, temporal boundaries, and rules—are *limits* imposed on the modern athlete. And this closes the circle of this final chapter, returning us to the area of profoundest *continuity* between ancient and modern athleticism.

Athletics—ancient *or* modern athletics—represent a profound meditation on the phenomenon of human limitation, and the ways in which that limitation may be dealt with, played with, extended or surpassed.[141] "Mortals and immortals" was, after all, *the* fundamental taxonomy of ancient Greek religions.[142] Christianity may have blurred this line, but it could not erase it.[143] Instead, certain essential Christian doctrines, like the Incarnation that I discussed in the fifth chapter, actually rely on it and derive their power from its deliberate exploitation. As Athanasius of Alexandria put it, "[God] was made man that we might be made divine."[144] This is the Orthodox doctrine of *theôsis*. It is telling to recall that Pausanias, who was traveling and writing at roughly the same time that Christianity was beginning to make significant inroads in the Greek-speaking world, insisted on a similar connection—the one between Eleusis and Olympia.

> There are many truly wonderful things (*thaumatos axia*) to see and hear in Greece, but there is a unique divinity of disposition (*ek theou phrontidos*) about the Mysteries at Eleusis (*tois Eleusini drômenois*) and the Contest at Olympia (*agôni tôi en Olympiai*).[145]

At Eleusis, the gods suffer their version of the mortal lot, or come as close to this as they can ever get. A mother loses a daughter, grieves almost without limit, and while she is eventually reunited with her, she will always lose her daughter again, cyclically and eternally. The gods at Eleusis taste grief, lose friends, and in their encounter with such emphatic existential limits, come ironically closer to the human condition and to us. At Olympia, by contrast, mortals are granted a brief taste of immortality. As Pindar tells it, a ray of light shines down from above, making human life shine with a divine brightness, however briefly. And so it goes. Mortals and immortals: as different as the moral universes they seem to inhabit, they can be closer than we know. The ritual attempt to map that kind of transcendence is one way we try to express this sacred search.

Thus by exploring how we may be human in a fittingly human way—embodied, mortal, and profoundly limited, but capable of rare and soaring moments of athletic grace and transcendence—we come to the astonished realization that *transcendence,* of a sort, is in fact one of the essential marks of being human in a distinctly human way. And this is what links us so intimately and ironically to certain gods. Transcendence makes no sense apart from some prior notion of limitation. One must, after all, have something to transcend. That aspiration toward transcendence lies at the heart of the religious gesture, and it seemed to animate many of Coubertin's reflections on the *religio athletae*.

There is another serious message in my attempt at Olympic retrieval here. It is the notion that there is a lot more to the modern Olympics than athletics. It is the realization that "religion" is in reality a far broader, and far more fluid, category than most of us realize, most of the time. And it has a deep connection to another equally fluid category: "Hellenism."

We still live within a fascinating set of nineteenth century concerns,[146] even in a world we so boldly (and far too quickly) label "postmodern."[147] We have these concerns mediated to us by the twentieth century, by the haunting memory of two world wars, and by the legacy of institutional genocide. We combat terrorism—even at the Olympic Games—fearing all the while that certain tendencies in the history of EuroAmerican gunpowder imperialism, and an almost paranoid suspicion of centralized government that is built in to our own constitutional process, may have come dramatically home to roost at the modern Olympia. The bombing of Olympic Centennial Park in Atlanta seems to have been a homegrown terrorist act, unlike its tragic Munich counterpart. The 2002 Winter Olympics in Salt Lake City positively *loomed* on our moral horizon, in the light of the tragic events of the last year.

We have never fully made up our minds *how* to feel about the nineteenth century in Europe. Coubertin referred to it, quite aptly, as "a century which was deeply evolutionary but full of illusory achievements."[148] It seems a veritable test case of moral ambivalence to many of us (but then, what century was not?). Words like colonialism, imperialism, slavery, racism, and sexism haunt us, causing us important and grave moral concern. They are an indelible and inescapable part of the nineteenth century. But so, too, are the first halting steps taken toward a greater internationalism, toward more open (if not freer) markets, toward more open philosophical eyes, and even toward the kinds of international festivals like World Fairs, Parliaments on the World's Religions, and the modern Olympic Games, which have become my strange topic in this chapter.

The roots of all these things lie in the rich soil of the nineteenth century—where Hegel, in the first decade, asked of human consciousness if perhaps God weren't dead there, at times,[149] and where Nietzsche insisted so emphatically, in the last decade that, in Christian clothing at least, God was indeed.[150] In the confrontation with this kind of death, a great many reflective people sought ways to resurrect a ghost, while simultaneously reconstituting *alternative* spiritual practices to feed a powerful and as-yet unfulfilled religious yearning.

In a world where a great many people say—despite what knowing pollsters are quick to tell us—that they do *not* consider themselves to be "religious," but *do* think of themselves as very "spiritual," then the modern revival of Olympism functions as a *religio,* indeed. Olympism was conceived as a religious festival in antiquity. The archaeological evidence suggests that the cult of Zeus predates the athletic contests at Olympia by two centuries at least. The Games were apparently shut down by the recently and sporadically Christianized Empire in 395 CE—again, for religious reasons. Modern Olympism was explicitly revived as a *religio,* by Coubertin and the International Committee he founded. It still functions as one, fully one hundred years after its revival.

As is the case with most religions, it is important to know where certain traditions initially came from. There usually are reasons, *symbolic* reasons, lying behind *why* we do what we do, although our traditions have a way of masking this, as often as not. I have tried to sketch some of the reasons behind some of the ritual attached to the modern Olympic movement, in the clear conviction that they, too, constitute a tradition, as worthy of study as any we may have inherited from church, synagogue, mosque, or temple.

In the last week of March 1996, a select group of Atlantans traveled to an *ancient* Greek temple, to ignite a sacred flame in the Altis, the inner sanctuary at Olympia. The ceremony was presided over by seven native Greek priestesses, appointed for this Olympiad alone. They toured Greece briefly for five days, then brought this *sacred* flame back to the United States, where they toured with it once again, touching each of the 48 contiguous states, and then using it to light the centennial flame on

July 19, in the eloquently trembling hands of a former Olympic athlete who had once made a bold public matter of his new religious identity in taking the name we now know him by: Muhammed Ali.[151]

Such a tradition, so rich in Neohellenic symbolism, was created by the German National Olympic Committee for the Berlin Games of 1936.[152] The flame provides the precise image with which Leni Riefenstahl began her famous film. Yet we think of this flame today not as a *Nazi* tradition but as an *Olympic* one. Explaining that sense of ownership, that profoundly Romantic sense of what constitutes a "tradition," as well as the soaring aspirations symbolized in such a gesture, seems to me to lie at the heart of the mystery of Neohellenism and of the modern Olympics, alike.

True to the comparativist spirit, then, I have tried to accomplish two things in this chapter. First, I have tried to *display* what I see when I look at our modern Olympic rituals. I have simply tried to indicate how a scholar trained in the field of comparative religion orders his affairs. Trained this way, one simply sees different things. I have endeavored, then, to describe something of what I have noticed. I notice how "religious" Pierre de Coubertin was, and how prone to ecstatic visions: at Thomas Arnold's grave in Rugby;[153] at the Altis in Olympia quite near to where his heart is buried;[154] at the graves of George Washington,[155] and of his own great-uncle in Paris.[156]

I am also making a somewhat stronger claim. Apart from a heightened sensitivity to the complexity of these only superficially simple categories—"religion" and "Greek"—we will miss important dimensions of the very things we claim we wish to study. We will badly misunderstand the creation of, and the long-standing fascination with, Hellenism itself. This book thus represents one person's attempt to "find religion" in places we do not normally think to notice it. The Olympic spectacle is a profoundly religious spectacle. It attempts to map transcendence. It does so in ritual categories. But it is also an eminently *Greek* event, a deliberate revival of an ancient Greek ritual form. And "Greece," as we have seen, has been perceived to be an especially "religious" category for nearly 2000 years. This is the other essential thing we tend *not* to notice about the Neohellenic, especially in its Romantic clothing.

This, in any event, is what I was *un*able to say to my Greek friends in August of 1996, while the Games were still in full swing—namely, why I thought the Olympic opening ceremonies seemed so "religious," and why that seemed so significant to me at the time. So perhaps this entire book has been Romantic in the purest sense: It is little more than the tentative answer of a sometime-Greekling to the question of a Greek Princess, who asked.

George Gordon, Lord Byron (1788–1824)

A Chronology

This chronology of Byron's life, with special attention paid to his Mediterranean travels, has been compiled with the help of four sources, primarily:

- Stephen Minta, *On a Voiceless Shore: Byron in Greece* (New York: Henry Holt and Company, 1998)
- Charles Sprawson, *Haunts of the Black Masseur: The Swimmer as Hero* (New York: Pantheon, 1994)
- Edward John Trelawny, *Records of Shelley, Byron, and the Author*, with an Introduction by Anne Barton (New York: New York Review of Books, 2000)
- Hugh Tresgakis, *Beyond the Grand Tour: The Levant Lunatics* (London: Ascent Books, 1979)

PRELIMINARIES

January 22, 1788:	George Gordon born in London, the first and only child born to "Mad Jack" and Catherine Gordon. He grows up in Aberdeen, Scotland, solidly middle class.
1790:	His father leaves home for France, in search of fortune, or escape.
1791:	His father dies in France at the age of thirty-five.
1795:	The death of an obscure relative at the siege of Calvi in Corsica makes George Gordon heir apparent to the Byron estate.
1798:	Death of Gordon's great-uncle. George Gordon is installed at the age of ten, as the sixth Baron Byron of Rochdale. He moves to Newstead Abbey in the county of Nottinghamshire, on the edge of Sherwood Forest.
1801:	Byron is enrolled in the Harrow School, a breeding ground for British leaders. He forms several extremely close attachments to fellow students there.
1805:	Byron enrolls at Cambridge University, but is bitterly unhappy there, after the comparative intimacy of Harrow.

July 1809:	Byron departs on his version of the Grand Tour, with John Cam Hobhouse. Their itinerary includes Portugal, Gibraltar, Malta, Sardinia, Greece, Albania and Turkey.
September 19–23,1809:	The two sail from Malta to Greece.
September 26, 1809:	Landfall at Patras.
September 28, 1809:	Prevesa.
October 1, 1809:	Arta.
October 5, 1809:	Arta to Ioannina, Turkish administrative capital of western Greece. William Martin Leake in residence there (Ioannina).
October 11, 1809:	Ioannina to Zitsa.
October 13, 1809:	Zitsa to Libohova.
October 17, 1809:	Libohova to Tepelena.
October 17–23, 1809:	Repeated visits with Ali Pasha, independent Turkish ruler of Albania and western Greece.
October 23–26, 1809:	Tepelena to Ioannina.
October 26-November 3, 1809:	Ioannina. Byron begins work on *Childe Harold's Pilgrimage*. Excursion to Dodona on October 29.
November 4, 1809:	Ioannina to Prevesa.
November 5, 1809:	Abortive trip from Prevesa to Patras. Ship is blown off course to the north and finally lands at Parga.
November 11, 1809:	Return to Prevesa.
November 13, 1809:	Prevesa to Loutraki.
November 14–20 1809:	Loutraki to Missolongi.
November 21–22 1809:	The two stay in Missolongi.
November 23, 1809:	Missolongi to Patras.
December 4, 1809:	Patras to Vostitsa (latter-day Aigion). Byron and Hobhouse spend nine days there.
December 14, 1809:	The two cross the Gulf of Corinth, travelling north by boat.
December 16, 1809:	Delphi.
December 17, 1809:	Delphi to Livadha. Excursion to the battlefield of Chaironea.
December 19–22, 1809:	Livadha to Orchomenos to Mazee to Thebes.
December 23–28, 1809:	Thebes to Skourta to Phyle to Athens.
January-February 1810:	The two stay in Athens in the home of Theodora Makri. The youngest daughter, Teresa, is popularized as the so-called "Maid of Athens." Symbolic excursions to Marathon and Sounion. Debates about Lord Elgin's looting of the Parthenon.
March-June 1810:	Excursion to Turkey: Izmir, Ephesus, the Troad, Constantinople. Byron swims the Hellespont on May 3. Hobhouse returns to England; the two part at Kea.
July 1810-April 1811:	Byron in Athens. Lodging in the Capuchin Monastery. Period of greatest sexual adventurism. Excursions to Peloponnese; return to Vostitsa, Sounion.
April 22, 1811:	Byron departs Athens for Malta on HMS *Hydra*, on board with the very last of Elgin's marbles.
May 1811:	Malta.
June 2, 1811:	Departs Malta for England aboard the frigate *Volage*.
July 14, 1811:	Landfall in England.

August 1, 1811:	Byron's mother dies in London at the age of forty-six.
March 1812:	*Childe Harold's Pilgrimage* published, making Byron famous overnight.
1812:	Byron's romance with Lady Caroline Lamb.
1813:	Byron's romance with his married half-sister, Augusta Leigh.
September 1814:	Byron proposes, for the second time, to Annabella Milbanke.
January 2, 1815:	Lord Byron and Annabella Milbanke are married.
December 10, 1815:	Byron's daughter, Augusta Ada, born.
January 1816:	Annabella leaves Byron and returns to her parents' home.
April 21, 1816:	Byron signs Deed of Separation.
April 23, 1816:	Byron departs London for Dover in the face of advancing financial problems and increasing scandal.
April 25, 1816:	Byron sails from Dover to Ostend, never to return to England.

May 1816:	Bruges, Ghent, Antwerp, Brussels, Cologne, Mannheim, Karlsruhe, Basel, Sécheron.
May 27, 1816:	Byron lodges outside of Geneva. First meeting with Percy Bysshe Shelley, who had just left his wife and eloped with Mary Godwin. Byron's romance with Mary's stepsister, Claire Clairmont.
August 1816:	The Shelleys and Lady Clairmont return to England. Hobhouse arrives; he and Byron set off for the Alps.
October 5, 1816:	Byron and Hobhouse depart for Italy.
October 12, 1816:	Milan.
November 10, 1816:	Venice.
January 1817:	Claire Clairmont gives birth to Allegra, Byron's second daughter
1817–1818:	Venice: sexual adventurism and hints of dissolution.
January 22, 1818:	Byron meets Teresa Gamba, now the Countess Teresa Guiccioli, on her honeymoon in Venice.
April 1819:	Romance with Teresa Guiccioli.
December 1819:	Byron moves into the Guiccioli home, as *cavalier servente*.
July 1820:	Teresa leaves her household and returns to her family, in Ravenna; the Gambas all involved in radical politics.
February 1821:	The Gambas exiled from Ravenna. They move to Bologna, then Florence, then Pisa.
April 1821:	Greek Independence declared; War of Independence begins.
November 1821:	Byron joins the Gambas in Pisa. Reunion with Shelley.
January 1822:	Alexander Mavrocordatos elected President of Greece.
April 20, 1822:	Byron's daughter Allegra dies.
July 1822:	The Gambas exiled from Pisa to Genoa.
July 8, 1822:	Shelley drowns in a shipwreck in the Gulf of Spezzia.
Winter 1822:	Byron's first protracted illness.

March 3, 1823:	London Greek Committee formed; Hobhouse a founding member.
April 5, 1823:	Edward Blaquiere calls on Byron in Genoa on his way to Greece; he enlists Byron's support in the cause.

July 24, 1823:	Byron departs Genoa for Greece aboard *Hercules,* heavily equipped with stores, medical supplies, weapons, and cash.
August 3, 1823:	Byron lands at Cephallonia.
August 10–17, 1823:	Excursion to Ithaka. Byron falls ill upon his return to Cephallonia.
December 1823:	After months of political infighting between Androutsos, Kolokotronis and Mavrocordatos, Byron's casts his lot with Mavrocordatos.
December 30, 1823:	Sails with Mavrocordatos to Zante (Zakynthos).
January 4, 1824:	Byron finally succeeds in entering Missolongi.
February 15, 1824:	Byron suffers a serious convulsive episode (epilepsy?).
Spring 1824:	Byron occupied with training an artillery brigade ("the Byron Brigade"), arming a personal band of Suliotes, and vain attempts to unite the various Greek revolutionary factions.
April 9, 1824:	Byron caught riding in a rainstorm.
April 10, 1824:	Byron ill but still active.
April 14, 1824:	Byron confined to bed.
April 16, 1824:	Byron is bled via incision; some twenty ounces of blood are taken.
April 17, 1824:	Byron is bled three times this day.
April 18, 1824:	Byron's condition deteriorating. He speaks for the last time: "I want to sleep now."
April 19, 1824:	Byron dies at dusk, amidst a terrible thunderstorm.
April 1826:	Final siege and massacre at Missolongi.

CHILDE HAROLD'S PILGRIMAGE: A POETIC OUTLINE (1812) (1816) (1818)

The universe is a kind of a book, one where we've only read the first page, one where we've only seen its countryside (*pays*). I flipped through a good enough number of pages, all of them equally bad (*mauvaise*). This examination was not at all unfruitful for me, though. I hated my native country (*patrie*). All the impertinence of the diverse peoples among whom I have lived has reconciled me with her. If I had no other benefit for my voyages, excepting only that, I would regret neither the costs nor the fatigues.

—*Le Cosmopolite*

First Preface:	the poem is inspired by a real trip
	but it is emphatically not (?) autobiographical
Second Preface:	some complain that the character is "unknightly"
	well, the knights were unknightly.

CANTO ONE: PORTUGAL AND SPAIN

I=invocation of the Muse
II-XIII=dissolute, melancholy, Harold decides on a trip
XIII=Harold's farewell song
XIV-XXVI=Portugal's "ruin'd splendour"
XXXI-end=Spain
    XXXV-LVIII=battles with French
    LIX=Spanish ladies
    LX-LXIV=Spain compared favorably to Greece
    LXVIII-LXX=religion: Protestants, Catholics, Pagans
    LXXXII-LXXXV=first love-song to Inez. Departure
    LXXXIX=Spain, the fading imperium

I-X=meditations on faded glory, special attention to temples
XI-XV=Elgin's looting of the Parthenon
XVI-XXI=return to Harold, aboard ship
XXII=Gibraltar
XXIII-XXVIII=the solitude of sea travel
XXIX="Calypso's Isle"
XXX-XXXIII=Florence, perceived as a woman
XXXIV-XXXV=general advice on women
XXXVIII=Albania
XXXIX-XLI=passes Ithaka (Penelope) and Leucadia (Sappho)
    then Actium-Lepanto-Trafalgar
    but Harold is moved by passion, not by war's exploits
XLII-LXVI=Albania, again
XLVI=there are mountains here, all unknown, but prettier than anything in Attica
LVII-LIX=this is real multi-culturalism
LXVII-LXXII=ship blown off course
    sojourn among the Suliotes
    during the revels, Harold remains at a remove
LXXIII-XCII=Greece
    call for Greek independence
    it must be a native movement
    meditation on ancient monuments (Marathon-Delphi)
XCIII=the ancient stones should remain on native soil
XCV-XCVIII=he suffers the loss of a loved one to death
    and thus he departs yet again. . . .

CANTO THREE: *NORTHERN EUROPE: FRANCE, GERMANY, SWITZERLAND*

"So that this application forces you to think of some other matter; in truth, there is no other remedy than this, and time."

—Letter from the King of Prussia
to d'Alembert (Sept. 7,1776)

I-VII=invocation of his daughter, Ada
    now taking to ship again
    exile from England
    emphasis on *the creative imagination,* which can in fact create new worlds
VIII=this is Harold again, but he's changed now
IX-XVI=he has returned to his own country
    becomes disaffected with people
    finds solace in Nature
    goes into self-exile
XVII-XXXVI=Waterloo
XXXVII-XLV=Napoleon
XLVI-LXI=the Rhine
LII-LV=Harold's longing for his one true love, "bound by stronger ties / Than the church
    links withal"
LXII-CIX=Switzerland

LXII=The Alps
LXIII-LXV=Battlefield of Morat (equated with Marathon)
LXVI-LXVII=Julia and her father
LXVIII-LXXV=Lake Leman
    meditation on aloneness and exile
    "to fly from, need not be to hate, mankind" (LXIX)
LXXVI-LXXXIV=back to Switzerland . . . and Rousseau
LXXXV-XCVIII=meditation on mountains
XCI=Persian high places vs. "columns and idol-dwellings, Goth or Greek"
XCIX-CIV=Clarens
CV-CIX=Lausanne and Ferney
CX=Italy
CXI-CXIV=misanthropic melancholy
CXV-CXVIII=final adieu to his daughter

CANTO FOUR: *ITALY*

The sight of Tuscany, Lombardy, Romagna
The mountains, the land, Italy,
dividing one sea from the other, che la bagna.

—Ariosto, *Satire 3*

Dedication to John Cam Hobhouse:
    Venice and Rome are now to them what Athens and Constantinople used to be
    There's less of Harold in this Canto,
    And when Harold does appear, he is Byron
    Sings the praises of Italy: literature, Canova, politics, spirit of political independence
    Compared favorably to England
I-VII=Venice, historical reflection
VIII-X=regret for England
XI-XIV=Venetian decline
XIV="Europe's bulwark 'gainst the Ottomite"
    mention of Candia and Lepanto
XXV-XXXV=shifts gaze back to Italy, entire
XXXVI-XLI=poets: Dante, Tasso, Alfonso, Boileau, Torquato, Ariosto
XLII-XLIII= viva Italia. . . .
XLIV-XLVI=compared to Greece, now in ruins (as England is soon to be)
XLVIII-LX=Florence, "the Etrurian Athens"
LXII-LXXIV=roaming in the north
LXIII-LXXIV=Italian Alps, not as grand as the Swiss
LXXVIII-LXXXVIII=Rome
LXXXIX-XCVIII=Napoleon, "a kind / Of bastard Caesar"
    and the bloodiness of France
XCIX-CV=Metella's grave
CVI-CIX=incredible meditation on time, transience, and the (inevitable?) collapse of
    culture
CVIII=There is the moral of all human tales;
    'T is but the same rehearsal of the past,
    First Freedom, and then Glory—when that fails,
    Wealth, vice, corruption,—barbarism at last.

And History, with all her volumes vast,
   Hath but *one* page,—
CIX=Admire, exult, despise, laugh, weep,—for here
   There is much matter for all feeling: Man!
   Thou pendulum betwixt a smile and tear,
CX-CXVII=Rome, again
CXVIII-CXXVII=long meditation on Love's sorrows (esp. CXXI)
CXXVIII-CXLV=Coliseum, fatality, gladiators
CXLVI-CLIX=the Pantheon, purer than any other temple
CLX-CLXIII=Vatican galleries
CLXXV-CLXXXIV=final homage to *Ocean*

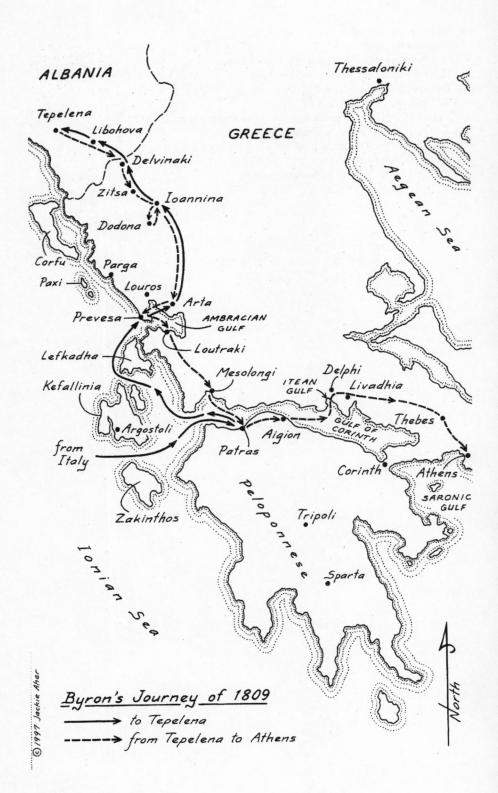

ALBANIA

Tepelena *Libohova* GREECE

Delvinaki

Zitsa

Dodona *Ioannina*

Parga

Corfu

Paxi *Louros*

Prevesa *Arta*

AMBRACIAN
GULF

Lefkadha *Loutraki*

Kefallinia *Mesolongi* *Delphi* *Livadhia*

ITEAN
GULF

Argostoli *Aigion* *Thebes*

GULF OF
CORINTH

from
Italy *Patras* *Athens*

Corinth

SARONIC
GULF

Zakinthos

Peloponnese *Tripoli*

Aegean
Sea

Thessaloniki

Ionian
Sea *Sparta*

North

Byron's Journey of 1809

⟶ to Tepelena

⤍ from Tepelena to Athens

© 1997 Jackie Aher

Charles Robert Cockerell (1788–1863)

GRAND TOUR ITINERARY

A great deal of attention has been paid to Cockerell's activities in Greece and Turkey in recent years. I have drawn primarily on Cockerell's own publications, *Travels in Southern Europe and the Levant, 1810–1817,* ed. Samuel Pepys Cockerell (London: Longmans, Green and Co., 1903), and *The Temples of Jupiter Panhellenius at Aegina and of Apollo Epicurius at Bassae near Phigalia in Arcadia* (London: John Weale, 1860).

The following secondary sources have also been of value:

· C. P. Bracken, *Antiquities Acquired: The Spoliation of Greece* (London: David & Charles, 1975), 106–136;
· Russell Chamberlin, *Loot! The Heritage of Plunder* (London: Thames and Hudson, 1983), 28–37;
· Hugh Tresgakis, *Beyond the Grand Tour: The Levant Lunatics* (London: Ascent Books, 1979), 106–139; and
· David Watkin, *The Life and Work of Charles R. Cockerell* (London: A. Zwemmer Ltd., 1974), 3–37.

April 19, 1810:	Cockerell departs Plymouth, armed with despatches for Sir Robert Adair, British Ambassador to the Sublime Porte. The ship calls at Gibraltar and Malta.
June 6, 1810:	Landfall at Constantinople.
June 7, 1810:	First meeting with Byron and Hobhouse, then in Constantinople.
June 1810:	Cockerell first meets John Foster.
July 14, 1810:	Byron and Hobhouse depart Constantinople. Cockerell presents Hobhouse with new journal as parting gift.
September 9, 1810:	Cockerell and Foster depart for Greece in the company of Sir William Amcotte Ingelby.
September 19, 1810:	Landfall at Salonika.
October 6, 1810:	The two depart by boat for Athens.
October 7, 1810:	Zagora.
October–November 1810:	Tinos, Delos (his first "excavation"), Kea. Ingleby departs at Kea. Cockerell and Foster move on to Athens
Winter 1810/1811:	The grand winter in Athens with Byron, et.al.

April 22, 1811:	Byron departs for England. Cockerell, Foster, Haller and Linckh depart for Aegina. Final port-party on *Hydra* at dusk.
Late May 1811:	Return with statues to Athens.
June/July 1811:	Completion of the assembly of the Aeginetan collection. Gropius, the Austrian consul, appointed as agent.
July 30, 1811:	First batch of marbles moved to Zante. Corinth-Patras-Zante. Auction set for November 1, 1812.
August-September 1811:	Excursion to the Peloponnese. Pyrgos-Olympia-Kalamata-Kardamyli (the Mani).
August 18, 1811:	Departure of Cockerell, Gropius, Haller, Foster and Linckh.
October 1811:	Return to Athens.
November 28, 1811:	Captain Percival arrives on the brig-o-war *Pauline*. Marbles shipped from Zante to Malta.
December 1811-May 1813:	Excursion to Crete, Egypt, Turkey, Malta, Italy, Sicily.
December 1, 1811:	Departure of Cockerell, Lord Guilford, Frederick Douglas, and John Foster for Crete.
December 3, 1811:	Xania.
Mid-December 1811:	Herakleion.
December 24, 1811:	Lord Guilford on Dia.
December 25, 1811:	Party's reunion on Dia.
January 1812:	Siphnos. Guilford abandons trip to Egypt as too dangerous. Chios. Douglas returns to England. Guilford stays on Chios. Cockerell and Foster travel to Smyrna.
February 1812:	Foster falls in love with the daughter of the Russian consul, Mary Maraccini.
April 1812:	Cockerell makes a tour of Anatolia alone. Unexpected reunion with Lord Guilford on Rhodes. Asia Minor, Malta, Italy.
November 1812:	Auction of the Aeginetan Marbles on Zante. The British representative, Taylor Coombe, is on Malta with the statues. Mr. McGill, Gropius's agent on Malta, assures him that the auctioneer will arrive there. On Zante, the French bid 160,000 francs (£ 4000). Johann Martin Wagner bids 10,000 sequins (£ 4500) on behalf of Crown Prince Ludwig, and this reduced price is affixed.
March 1813:	Cockerell on Sicily learns of the auction's results.
May 1813:	Cockerell returns to Athens. Haller and Linckh have been digging at Bassae. Cockerell and Haller move outside of town to Patissia.
August 22, 1813:	Cockerell falls seriously ill.
September 1813:	Cockerell well enough to return to Athens.
September 23, 1813:	Otto von Stackelberg departs Athens for Vienna. Euboea-Khalkis-Xerochori. Hires a *trabakalo*. Kidnapped by Albanian klephts. Finally ransomed by Haller for £500. Stackelberg nursed in Athens until March 1814.
October 29, 1813:	Arrival in Athens of Thomas Smart Hughes and R. Townley Parker.
	They lodge in the famed hostelry of Theodora Makri. They fall in with Cockerell, now recovered, and Haller, who is famous for the Stackelberg affair.
November 29, 1813:	Excursion to Albania with Cockerell, Hughes, Parker, and General Davies, quartermaster general to the Mediterranean forces.
November 29, 1813:	Phyle.

November 30, 1813:	Mount Parnes-Thebes.
December 1–10, 1813:	Livadhia. Hughes taken ill.
Mid-December 1813:	Chaironea-Delphi-Salona-Galaxidi. Reunion with General Davies's gunboat. Cross to Patras-Levkas. General Davies falls ill, dies that Winter on Zante.
December 27, 1813:	Prevesa.
January 6–26, 1814:	Ioannina. Cockerell, Hughes and Parker party are housed with Nicolo. Argyri, Byron's and Hobhouse's host. Cockerell blasted by Athanasios Petrides Psalidas for his "excavations" at a dinner party. Meetings with Ali Pasha until January 14.
January 27, 1814:	Cockerell sets out alone for Athens over the Pindus mountains.
March 1814:	Another major social scene in Athens. John Oliver Hanson arrives from Smyrna with Stephen Maltass (formerly British Consul at Alexandria) and a Mr. Grabau of Hamburg.
	Thomas Burgon and John Foster have also arrived (both had married in the previous weeks).
	Gropius, Haller, Linckh, et al. are still in Athens.
April 1814:	Excursion to Zante. Hanson, Maltass and Grabau arrive April 15. Cockerell, the Burgons, the Fosters, Haller, and Linckh all arrive April 20. Gropius and Masson arrive April 23. Napoleon abdicates.
May 1, 1814:	Auction of the Phigalian Marbles. Purchased by General Sir James Campbell on behalf of the Prince of Wales for approximately $60,000.
May 3, 1814:	Hanson, Grabau and Stackelberg depart on a Greek ship for the Adriatic and home.
July 11,1814:	Cockerell returns to Athens, sick again. Arrival shortly thereafter of John Spencer Stanhope, an old school chum, and Thomas Allason.
Summer 1814:	Excursion to Marathon, Tanagra, Aulis Eretria and Euboea in company with Stanhope and Allason.
Mid-October 1814:	Sick again, Cockerell is taken to Eleusis for a "change of air."
November 1814:	Last trip to Aegina, to correct and revise his drawings of the Temple.
January 15, 1815:	Europe now open to Englishmen again, Cockerell finally departs Athens with Linckh and another companion named Tupper. Final passing sweep through the Peloponnese. South Italy-Naples-Rome. Cockerell stays on in Italy for two years, finding old cronies in Naples, Rome (Canova, Thorvaldsen), and Venice (Stackelberg).
1817:	Cockerell's landfall in England.
October 5, 1817:	Haller dies in the Vale of Tempe.

Johann Martin Wagner (1777–1858)
ITINERARY OF HIS GREEK JOURNEY, 1812–1813

I owe this itinerary to my review of Wagner's Diary of the trip, reprinted in Reinhard Herbig, ed., *Johann Martin von Wagners Beschreibung seiner Reise nach Griechenland (1812–1813)* (Stuttgart: Verlag von W. Kohlhammer, 1938).

I am especially grateful to the Deutsches Archaeologische Institut in Rome, which permitted me access to their collections. I spent a lovely day in July 2000 reading through Wagner's Diary in this delightful setting, little more than two city blocks from where Wagner lived for most of his adult life.

Wagner has been living in Rome since May 31, 1804. He met Crown Prince Ludwig there in 1805, and they become lifelong friends. He met Bertel Thorwaldsen there in 1811.

July 21, 1812:	Receives a letter from Ludwig asking him to make the trip to Greece. He protests that he does not know the language and cannot locate a Greek map (*charte*) anywhere. Ludwig insists, so he hires a multi-talented assistant, Pacifico Storani, and they prepare to set off.
Sept. 8, 1812:	Depart Rome in a *vetturín* to Naples.
Sept. 9,1812:	Spend their second night in Terracina. Pacifico picks up a dog for two days, calls it their "good genius," names it Fundi.
Sept. 11, 1812:	Capua, where they are sent back by French soldiers, on foot and without their luggage, for the required French consulate's note in their papers.
Sept. 12, 1812:	Back in Naples. Wagner stays a week to arrange credit with bankers here and in Greece.
Sept. 19, 1812:	Feast of Saint Januarius. They depart at night.
Sept. 20, 1812:	Pass through Avellino, "not a bad spot in the Apennine hills." Stay at Aviano, much to see the next day.
Sept. 21, 1812:	Ordona.
Sept.22, 1812:	St. Cassiano, plain of Apuleia, Adriatic Sea in sight Wagner wants to leave from Barletta, but cannot find a boat for Corfu, as everyone there fears being seized by the English. Otranto is recommended to him.
Sept. 25, 1812:	They take a *fuhrman* (a kind of small carriage he's only seen on Malta, with glass on three sides, "with room for two, if they're not fat"). Barletta-Andria, passing through Molfutta with Bari on the right.

Sept. 26, 1812:	Midday at Mola. Evening at Monopoli (small seaside town with a rich, red local Apuleian wine).
Sept. 27, 1812:	Midday at Ostuni. Evening at St. Vito.
Sept. 28, 1812:	Coast of Brindisi in view. Cellino by day (awful). Lecce at night, he calls it "another world."
Sept. 29, 1812:	Midday at Garrano. Evening at Otranto, French consul is very helpful, and even arranges his transport. Sounds of cannonade at night, from the English blockade.
Sept. 30, 1812:	Aboard at sun-up on a Neapolitan *sciabeko* (Capt. Saverio Castagnola). They depart with four other boats at dusk, but theirs is best. Wagner immediately seasick, captain on the lookout for British warships all night. They arrive at the island of Fanno (or Fanoo) (now Othoni), a French battery.
Oct. 1, 1812:	Depart midday from Fanno. Arrive at the "Canal von Corfu" at 11:00 PM.

LANDFALL IN GREECE

Oct. 2, 1812:	*Festungs Commandanten*, General Lanzalotte. *Ordinateur General*, Chevalier Thieboult (who receives his papers from Naples). Police Directeur Fouchier (who did all he could). Wagner has permission for travel to Patras, Prevesa and Athens, but not Zante. "Things went as well as I could have hoped, better perhaps than I expected."
Oct. 2–10, 1812:	Stuck in Corfu, seeking passage. Wagner cannot travel directly from French to English territory, so he must touch on the Turkish coast first.
Oct. 10, 1812:	Corfu to Cephallonia.
Oct. 11, 1812:	Unknown island off the Albanian coast.
Oct. 12, 1812:	Departure, forced to return, stay on another vaguely "Turkish" island.
Oct. 13, 1812:	Stuck there due to adverse winds.
Oct. 14, 1812:	Depart in the morning, settle at the harbor of Barga (now Parga), which is both Greek and French.
Oct. 15, 1812:	Depart Barga early. Get as far as Regnossa, then forced back by English corsairs to the harbor of Fanari. Lousy meal onboard ship.
Oct. 16, 1812:	Unsure of the sea passage, they send their baggage ahead with two greeks, Tomassio Tavesi of Patras and Andrea Zornarello of Zephalonia. They stay in a Turk's home, on a full moon; sleep outside by the fire, near the sea.
Oct. 17, 1812:	Come to the old ruins of Nicopolis, established by Augustus after Actium. Pass by Artea Actium and on to Prevesa, where they get food and wine. Wagner searches for the French consul, but finds "a lousy Greek" instead. He puts Wagner up with an old lady across the street from himself.
Oct. 17–26, 1812:	Stuck in Prevesa, looking for a way around the French-English problem. Eventually Wagner just rents a ride to Santa Maura, *without* papers.
Oct. 26, 1812:	Prevesa to Santa Maura at midday. Two English soldiers take him to the *Platzcommandant*, a native-born Italian named

Aratta. He sees "Rome," and the purpose of Wagner's trip, and arranges everything. He learned from Ali Pasha of Ioannina (who heard it in Vienna) that Moscow was to be burned, and the news is especially hard on the British, et.al. Talks for an hour to Aratta, then is taken to General Campbell. Campbell is also cool, chats him up, feeds him, accompanies him to his boat for Zante. They take off, and Wagner falls asleep immediately.

Oct. 27, 1812:   Wakes up still in Santa Maura. The Greek captain had returned, Wagner has a fit, and they leave again at midday. A bad storm comes up at noon; they lay up at Mekanissi for the night. They get drenched, and drink "a kind of salve made of talk mixed with rum."

Oct. 28, 1812:   Passage to Fermecolo, also called Felsen.

Oct. 29, 1812:   Good wind straight to Zante.

Oct. 30, 1812:   Gropius appears. Wagner meets (in quarantine) with Haller, Linckh, Stackelberg, Bronstadt and Luz. Only Gropius is unknown to him; Gropius informs him that he's the only representative to have arrived. They all want the sculptures for Bavaria, for Germany, and not for England, which is too "inaccessible." Only now does he learnt that the statues themselves are on Malta! The group of Bavarians guarantees him good pieces but he's still uncertain. The auction is day after tomorrow. . . .

Nov. 1, 1812:   They do the deal. Wagner buys the statues in the name of HRH Ludwig, the full group as listed in the manifest, conditional on actually seeing them. No point in sailing to Malta, when they can ride to Athens, where Wagner can see the Aeginetan pieces still in possession of the French consul, Fauvel. Wagner stays in Zante for a month, with Gropius, Haller, Linckh ("from Constatt"), Stackelberg ("an artist and friend of the arts"), Bronstadt ("an archaeologist from Denmark") and Luz (a Swabian tutor of the Danish consul at Zante).

Nov. 28, 1812:   With Gropius and his servants, they leave Zante for the coast of Morea.

Nov. 29, 1812:   Peneus River. Wagner goes on foot with Gropius to Gastuni, near ancient Elis. Hangs out there with a medical doctor, waiting for their stuff. Gropius is trying to arrange to marry their daughter. Antrovitti (Andravida) to Legonoo (Lechaina).

Nov. 30, 1812:   Sightseeing day, nightfall at Bali Agaja (Ano or Kato Achaia), by ancient Dyme.

Dec. 1, 1812:   10:00 AM in Patras. First encounter with a group of 20 or 30 Turks. (Has a bath "for 30 para, some 10 or 12 bajucchi in Roman money"). He also considers Turks the civilized ones, hereabouts. Three days in town, Gropius on business. English consul, Mr. Strange. French consul, Ercole Russel. American consul, Mr. Contoquri—financial liaison for the sale.

Dec. 4, 1812:   Depart Patras by boat, with Pacifico, Gropius, etc. No wind. Epakta/Naupaktos to Vostizza (Aegium). Evening at the island of Trifonia.

Dec. 6, 1812:	Giving up on the wind, they land at Scala Von Salona eat lunch, and explore Krissa, where they stay.
Dec. 7, 1812:	Rain in the morning, the *scirocco* is up explore. Krissa again (cyclopean walls, boustrophedon script, designs). Parnassus-Delphi-Castalian Spring-Arachova (spend night). Cisma (where Oedipus killed Laius)-Platanos-Chaironea. Return to Livathia.
Dec. 9–11, 1812:	Livathia (Gropius involved in more *Heyrathsspeculationen*). Wagner just explores and looks at ancient art.
Dec. 12, 1812:	All except Gropius depart. Evening at Thebes, they sleep outside on the mountain.
Dec. 13, 1812:	Explores Thebes at dawn, depart at 8:00 AM or so. Roman aqueducts on the road. Fort of Phyle, border of Boeotia and Attica. First sight of the Akropolis!
Dec. 14, 1812:	Excited, they make an early departure for Athens. Get to the gates at 3:00 PM, but are forced to wait, as 3 Turks have just died of plague (*Pest*) in Thebes. Wagner asks for his consul, who is French, since he lives in Italy which is then under French control. That Consul is Mr. Fauvel; Wagner has a letter of introduction from Consul Rioussel of Patras. Wagner spends a terrible night in a rathole, with a bad breakfast to follow. Waits on Fauvel, explores the city walls, then is moved to nicer quarters by the French.
Dec. 15, 1812:	Fauvel has the best preserved pieces of the Aeginetan collection, and they *exceed* Wagner's expectations. Clearly old-classical, naturalist, the finest art he has seen, etc. 3 or 4 bodies confirm "the heretofore unknown gifts of the Aeginetan school." Wagner confirms the Zante contract, and arranges for payment, through Gropius, to Cockerell, Foster, Linckh and Haller. Now they have to negotiate a contract for the transport from Malta (and Athens) to Rome.
Dec. 15, 1812–March 15, 1813:	Athens. Long drawn-out fight about how to transport, and with whom. Gropius is trying to make money on this end of the deal. Wagner protests to the French consulate, and gets help from Nicola Giograsso. Uses his downtime in Athens to sightsee, lots of touring with Fauvel, whom he likes. Finds the Turks to be more like Germans than anyone else. Lives in the Capuchin Monastery with Father Paulo (near the Lysicrates Monument). Finally departs Athens with Giograsso and Luz.
March 15, 1813:	Departs Athens. Piraeus-Salamis-Megara-Corinth.
March 17–18, 1813:	Corinth.
March 23, 1813:	Crossover to the Gulf of Corinth.
March 25–April 19, 1813:	Patras.
April 21, 1813:	Patras-Zante. Reconfirms contract with Gropius, but this time with witnesses: lawyers, governors, and Friedrich Nord
April 21–May 5, 1813:	Zante. Easter celebration, arrival of an English fleet.
May 5, 1813:	Zante-Patras.
May 5–29, 1813:	Patras. Preparations for trip and transport.
May 29, 1813:	Depart Patras.
June 9, 1813:	Landfall at Ancona.
June 13, 1813:	Lazareth.

June 13–July 10, 1813:	Lazareth (quarantine).
July 25, 1813:	Return to Ancona.
July 30, 1813:	Ancona to Rome.
August 4, 1813:	Arrival in Rome.

The statues will not arrive until 1815 in Rome. Thorvaldsen "restores" this collection, 1816–1818. King Ludwig later makes Wagner Custodian of the Villa Malta, a royal Bavarian holding where he had already been living (Via Porta Pinciana, 21). Wagner continues to acquire art pieces for Ludwig's Glyptothek until his death.

Johannes Martin Wagner dies in Rome on August 8, 1858.

There is a museum named for him in Würzburg today.

Notes

1. The archivist in me cannot resist including this marvelous story here:

   There are many dismal images of the fall [of Rome]. One is the statues from Hadrian's Tomb being thrown down as ammunition against the Goths, until the pieces of them were all mingled with the real corpses and stray limbs and heads below.

   Eleanor Clark, *Rome and a Villa* (Pleasantville, NY: The Akadine Press, 1950, 1999), 124.

2. Nietzsche, *The Will to Power*, ed. Walter Kaufmann, trans. Walter Kaufmann and R. J. Hollingdale (New York, NY: Vintage Books, 1967), §306.

   See also Giorgio Colli und Mazzino Montinari, eds., *Friedrich Nietzsche, Sämtliche Werke: Kritische Studienausgabe in 15 Bänden* (Berlin: Walter de Gruyter, 1967–1977), Vol. XII, 273.

3. Nietzsche, *The Will to Power*, §1042; *Kritische Studienausgabe*, XII, 11:

   To demonstrate the extent to which Greek religion was higher than the Judaeo-Christian. The latter was victorious only because Greek religion had itself degenerated (that is, gone *backward*).

4. I am happy to record a debt of thanks here to Professors Richard M. Carp of the Appalachian State University and Mark Juergensmeyer of the University of California at Santa Barbara, to whom I owe my awareness of these theoretical developments. They introduced me to some of the more difficult intellectual terrain in an NEH Summer Seminar entitled "Beyond the Text: Teaching Religion and Material Culture," for which I was selected as a participant in 1993. They held this seminar, moreover, at the gorgeous campus of the University of Hawai'i at Manoa. I recall the spirited conversations and sense of lively engagement of that seminar with real fondness and gratitude.

   Another seminar participant, Thomas V. Peterson, has edited a special volume of *Historical Reflections/Reflexions Historique* 23.3 (1997), on the topic of "Cultural and Historical Interpretation Through Nontextual Material." Of special note is Peterson's Introduction to the volume (259–267), and Carp's essay, "Perception and Material Culture: Historical and Cross-Cultural Perspectives" (269–300).

5. Anne Carson, *Economy of the Unlost* (Princeton, NJ: Princeton University Press, 1999), viii. This book grew out of Carson's Martin Classical Lectures of 1998.

6. There is an enormous body of literature devoted to these complex relations. I am happy to call attention to the significant reconstruction offered by Alan F. Segal in *Rebecca's Children: Judaism and Christianity in the Roman World* (Cambridge, MA: Harvard University Press, 1986). Segal's work with Jewish-Christian relations nicely parallels my own interest in Greco-Christian ones.

7. G. W. F. Hegel, *Lectures on the Philosophy of History*, trans. J. Sibree (New York, NY: Dover Publications, 1956), 223.

1. For more on this, see Edward Lazarus, *Closed Chambers: The Rise, Fall and Future of the Modern Supreme Court* (New York: Penguin Books, 1999). Now a federal prosecutor in Los Angeles, Lazarus clerked for Justice Harry A. Blackmun in the 1988 court term. He faults Chief Justice Rehnquist's failure of nonpartisan leadership, as well as the overzealous political intriguing of a small cabal of antiliberal clerks, who shoulder increasing responsibilities of an overworked Court, with an irregular schedule and working hours—especially when state executions are imminent. This book tells a gripping, and ultimately highly disturbing, story; I am indebted to Mr. Scott Michelman for putting it into my hands.

2. See Antonin Scalia, *A Matter of Interpretation: Federal Courts and the Law* (Princeton: Princeton University Press, 1997), which offers an elegant essay by Scalia, five responses from a variety of jurists and moral philosophers, and a response from Scalia to his critics. Perhaps most surprising, though, in Scalia's self-presentation is his claim that what he offers is a "*science* of construing legal texts" (3), whereas his opponents engage in "an *art* or a *game*" (7), emphases mine.

3. The multivolume *History of the Supreme Court of the United States,* Gen. Ed. Paul A. Freund (New York: Macmillan, 1981) is an essential resource for these architectural developments. See especially, Julius Goebel, Jr., *Antecedents and Beginnings to 1800,* Volume I, 338ff.

4. See Carl Swisher, *History of the Supreme Court of the United States: The Taney Period, 1836–64,* Volume V, 716ff.

5. See Maxwell Bloomfield, "Architecture of the Supreme Court Building," in Kermit L. Hall, ed., *The Oxford Companion to the U.S. Supreme Court* (New York: Oxford University Press, 1992), 43–46.

6. For reasons that are not entirely clear to me, the placement of the Decalogue in a court of law has proven to be more complicated, from a legal standpoint, than its placement in a public school. In 1980, the U.S. Supreme Court declared the placement of panels displaying the Ten Commandments in the Kentucky public school system to be an unconstitutional "establishment of religion," even where the commandments were explicitly presented as having strictly historical and cultural, rather than religious, value (*Stone v. Graham* 449 US 39 [1980]). Presumably, children are considered more vulnerable than adults in the presence of such images.

    Context, and the historical establishment of such a context, has mattered far more in various courtroom settings. In 1993, a U.S. District Court in Atlanta, Georgia ordered a Cobb County courthouse to remove a panel which depicted the Ten Commandments, alongside of the so-called Great Commandment, as depicted in several of the Christian gospels, from its interior. But the Court stayed this order for four months, in order to allow the county time to consider alternative plans for incorporating that panel into a larger display which would lend it an educational and secular purpose, by juxtaposing it alongside of other, more demonstrably secular images (*Harvey v. Cobb County* 811 F. Supp. 669 [1993]). This decision was affirmed without comment by the Eleventh Circuit Court of Appeals in Atlanta (15 F.3d 1097).

    In 1999, a U.S. District Court in Asheville, North Carolina defended the rights of the Haywood County courthouse to display a significantly abbreviated version of the Ten Commandments on the walls of that courtroom (*Suhre v. Haywood County* 55 F.Supp.2d 384 [1999]). In that case, much was made of the fact that the courthouse in question was entered in the National Registry of Historic Places by the U.S. Department of Interior in 1972, and that these tablets of the Mosaic law were in fact dwarfed by a much larger image of the Goddess of Justice overseeing them. The Commandments also could not be removed without damaging the entire display and the structure of the building itself. Still more was made in this case of the fact that this entire installation was designed in 1932, the same year as the south frieze of the U.S. Supreme Court building. And, in fact, Adolph Weinman's image of Moses holding the Ten Commandments was entered as evidence in that hearing!

Finally, in May 2001, the U.S. Supreme Court narrowly refused to hear a case (*Elkhart v. Books,* 00–1407) regarding a display of the Ten Commandments that was carved in granite and erected on the front lawn of a courthouse in Elkhart, Indiana. A federal appeals court had ordered the removal of the marker.

7. One especially interesting answer to this question comes from Justice Stevens's partial dissent in *County of Allegheny v. American Civil Liberties Union, Greater Pittsburgh Chapter* 492 US 573 (1989) 652–3:

> [A] carving of Moses holding the Ten Commandments, if that is the only adornment on a courtroom wall, conveys an equivocal message, perhaps of respect for Judaism, for religion in general, or for law. The addition of carvings depicting Confucius and Mohammed may honor religion, or particular religions, to an extent that the First Amendment does not tolerate any more than it does "the permanent erection of a large Latin cross on the roof of city hall." Placement of secular figures such as Caesar Augustus, William Blackstone, Napoleon Bonaparte, and John Marshall alongside these three religious leaders, however, signals respect not for great proselytizers but for great lawgivers. It would be absurd to exclude such a fitting message from a courtroom, as it would to exclude religious paintings by Italian Renaissance masters from a public museum.... [T]his careful consideration of context gives due regard to religious and nonreligious members of our society. [notes omitted]

My question is a little different than Justice Stevens's here. Granted that Moses and Muhammad are "religious" figures, and even granting that Blackstone and Bonaparte are entirely "secular" ones, how are we to understand the figure of Solon? This abiding confusion as to the comparative religiosity or secularity of the ancient Greeks is the main topic of this chapter, and of this book.

8. There is a growing body of scholarly work devoted to this still somewhat obscure Archaic figure (in this, he is similar to two other ancient Greek notables, Pythagoras and Hippocrates, both of whom will make an appearance later in this chapter). Solon was born in Athens in roughly 640 BCE, and died there in roughly 560 BCE. As archon of the city in 594 BCE, he mediated the divisive clash between a wealthy elite and a disgruntled rural populace overwhelmed by burdensome debts and repeated denial of access to political redress. A number of poetic passages are attributed to Solon, as are a body of laws, after issuing which he went into voluntary exile in Egypt for a decade, so as not to be forced into seizing power himself. While hardly a democrat in the modern sense of the term, many see in these Solonic reforms the first halting step taken toward the more fully participatory democracy that we associate with Athens in its heyday.

Solon's poetic fragments may be found in Martin L. West, ed., *Iambi et Elegi Graeci Ante Alexandrum Cantati,* 2nd Ed. (New York: Oxford University Press, 1989), Volume II, 119–145. They have been translated into English and are available in Douglas E. Gerber, ed., *Greek Elegiac Poetry,* 2 Vols. (Cambridge, MA: Loeb Classical Library of Harvard University Press, 1999), Volume I, 106–165.

A nice discussion specifically of Solon's laws is available in Eberhard Ruschenbusch, *Solonos Nomoi: Die Fragmente des solonischen Gesetzwerkes mit einer Text- und überlieferungsgeschichte,* in *Historia: Zeitschrift für Alte Geschichte,* Number 9 (Wiesbaden: Franz Steiner Verlag, 1966).

All of our biographical accounts of Solon's career are considerably later, composed after-the-fact. The most famous are: Herodotus, *The Histories,* trans. David Grene

(Chicago: University of Chicago Press, 1988), I, §§29–34 (44–48); Aristotle, *Constitution of Athens and Related Texts,* trans. Kurt von Fritz and Ernst Kapp (New York: Macmillan, 1950, 1974), V–XIV (72–82); Plutarch, *Life of Solon* in *The Rise and Fall of Athens,* trans. Ian Scott-Kilvert (New York: Penguin Books, 1960), 43–76; and Diogenes Laertius, *Lives of Eminent Philosophers,* trans. R. D. Hicks (Cambridge, MA: Loeb Classical Library of Harvard University Press, 1972), I,46–69.

    I have profited especially from two secondary sources that discuss Solon's singular achievements: Werner Jaeger, *Paideia: The Ideals of Greek Culture* (New York: Oxford University Press, 1945), Volume I, 136–149; and Kurt A. Raaflaub, "Political Thought, Civic Responsibility and the Greek Polis," in Johann Arnason and Peter Murphy, eds., *Agon, Logos, Politics: The Greek Achievement and Its Aftermath* (Stuttgart: Franz Steiner Verlag, 2001), 72–117, esp. 89–99.

9. Alasdair MacIntyre, *After Virtue,* 2nd Ed. (South Bend, IN: University of Notre Dame Press, 1981, 1984).

10. Jeffrey Stout has been one of the most intelligent and reasoned of MacIntyre's many critics. See his "Virtue Among the Ruins," *Neue Zeitschrift für systematische Theologie und Religionsphilosophie* 26.3 (1984): 256–273, later revised as the ninth chapter in *Ethics After Babel: The Languages of Morals and Their Discontents,* 2nd Ed. (Princeton: Princeton University Press, 1988, 2001), 191–219. See also "Homeward Bound: MacIntyre on Liberal Society and the History of Ethics," *Journal of Religion* 69.2 (1989): 220–232, and "Commitments and Traditions in the Study of Religious Ethics," *Journal of Religious Ethics* 25.3 (1998): 23–56.

    MacIntyre admits (*After Virtue,* "Postscript," 278) that the historical question of how an Aristotelian tradition of the virtues came to terms with a scriptural tradition of revelation is a complex one, calling for some significant revision of his original narrative. The book, he now admits, is best seen as a work in progress.

11. Alasdair MacIntyre, *Whose Justice? Which Rationality?* (South Bend, IN: University of Notre Dame Press, 1988); and *Three Rival Versions of Moral Enquiry: Encyclopedia, Genealogy and Tradition* (Notre Dame, IN: University of Notre Dame Press, 1990).

12. This is the title of Alasdair MacIntyre, *Against the Self-Images of the Age: Essays on Ideology and Philosophy* (Notre Dame, IN: University of Notre Dame Press, 1971, 1978).

13. "Aristotelianism," he writes, "is *philosophically* the most powerful of premodern modes of moral thought. If a premodern view of morals and politics is to be vindicated against modernity, it will be in *something like* Aristotelian terms or not at all" (*After Virtue,* 118).

14. MacIntyre, *After Virtue,* 208.

15. The most significant texts, which focus on the specific narrative MacIntyre uses (rather than on the related question of narrative's usefulness as moral argument) are: *Tragic Posture and Tragic Vision: Against the Modern Failure of Nerve* (New York: Continuum Press, 1994), 11–25; and *Afterwords: Hellenism, Modernism and the Myth of Decadence* (Albany: State University of New York Press, 1996), 91–123.

16. See my "Of Coins and Carnage: Rhetorical Violence and the Macedonian Question," *Soundings* 77.3/4 (1994): 331–366, where I attempted to frame Greek resistance to the naming of the "Former Yugoslav Republic of Macedonia" as a crucial counter-example to MacIntyre's privileging of narrative argument. *Everyone* in the Balkans has a narrative history, and every one of them seems to involve a story of their respective "greatness."

    The Greater Serbia, the Greater Greece, the Greater Bulgaria, the Greater Albania—all of these aspirations to territorial "greatness" lay claim to the same sad piece of contemporary real estate: namely, "Macedonia." Narrative and historical arguments will resolve these divisive questions as little as they will do so on the West Bank of the Jordan River.

17. MacIntyre, *After Virtue*, 69.

18. Significantly, my work does not relate to another of the twentieth century's most significant Supreme Court rulings, *Brown v. Board of Education of Topeka*, 347 US 483 (1954). It seems significant that an historical narrative, grounded in Greek and Roman antiquity, was *not* a significant part of that decision, which contented itself with constitutional questions and pragmatic judgments about pedagogy and interpretation of the Fourteenth Amendment. Why is it, I wonder, that the Greeks emerge as a significant piece of the western story just when the talk turns to gender, and to sex, and to death?

    For more on the legal reasoning which contributed to the *Brown* decision, see Morton J. Horowitz, *The Warren Court and the Pursuit of Justice* (New York: Farrar, Straus, Giroux, 1998), 3–31.

19. 410 US 113 (1973). For the text of this opinion and subsequent court discussion, I have benefited enormously from Ian Shapiro, ed., *Abortion: The Supreme Court Decisions* (Indianapolis, IN: Hackett Publishing Company, 1995), 46–70.

    For a summary of some of the arguments presented to the Court, accompanied by an audiocassette, see Stephanie Guitton and Peter Irons, eds., *May It Please the Court: Arguments on Abortion* (New York: The New Press, 1995), 23–45.

    For a superb discussion of this case, the legal background, and the political fallout from the decision, see Lazarus, *Closed Chambers*, 329–424.

20. *Griswold v. Connecticut* 381 US 479 (1965).

21. *Eisenstadt v. Baird* 405 US 438 (1972).

22. Shapiro, *Abortion: The Supreme Court Decisions*, 68.

23. For a disturbing discussion of the practice of securing "expert" testimony in support of capital prosecution, see Lazarus, *Closed Chambers*, 150–151. On the other side, see his discussion of the famous Baldus Study, whose statistics suggested that murder cases in which the victim was white were 4.3 times more likely to result in a death sentence than others. This study was dismissed as statistical sociology, a rather "soft" science, 184–191, 194–217. Much hinges on the power that the claim to "science" has in this culture—which is what makes Justice Scalia's claims about the "science" of his own textual approach so telling, and so odd.

24. Seldom has one justice been identified more thoroughly with a majority court decision than Harry A. Blackmun has been associated with *Roe v. Wade*. This is doubly ironic, since Blackmun was *assigned* the task of roughing out a draft of the majority opinion by Chief Justice Burger. Blackmun researched the case in the Mayo Clinic Library throughout the summer of 1972, substantially revised his initial draft to address the concerns of other justices, friend and foe alike (he added the historical excursus at this stage), and ultimately received the very warmest thanks from the six justices who finally concurred with his decision. Only justices Rehnquist and White dissented.

    See Lazarus, *Closed Chambers*, 350–360.

25. Shapiro, *Abortion: The Supreme Court Decisions*, 49.

26. The modern idea that western, EuroAmerican culture has its roots in Greek classical culture is one that we owe to Hegel as much as to anyone. See *The Philosophy of History*, trans. J. Sibree (New York: Dover Publications, 1956), 223–277.

27. Shapiro, *Abortion: The Supreme Court Decisions*, 49–50, notes omitted.

28. It is surely significant that many graduating medical professionals continue to swear this oath—sufficiently emended, to be sure!—for equally unclear reasons and with equally unformulated intention or consensual understanding. There may thus be some real continuity between the ambiguity of this Hippocratic tradition in antiquity and its ambiguous appropriation today. See Robert D. Orr, Norman Pang, Edmund D. Pellegrino, and Mark Siegler, "Use of the Hippocratic Oath: A Review of Twentieth Century Practice and a Content Analysis of Oaths Administered in Medical Schools in the U.S and Canada," *Journal of Clinical Ethics* 8.4 (1997): 377–388.

       Clearly, a great many EuroAmericans continue to turn to the ancient Greeks, but without any very clear sense of why they do so, or to what ultimate purpose.

29. I am indebted to Owsei Temkin's masterful account, *Hippocrates in a World of Pagans and Christians* (Baltimore, MD: Johns Hopkins University Press, 1991), for highlighting the complexity of this name. A large body of writings which span some 600 years (from the fourth century BCE to the first century CE) took the name of Hippocrates and claimed his authorship and authority. So a Hippocratic physician may be anyone who identifies him- or herself with the copious and expanding writings attached to the name of this legendary Greek figure. Temkin's book is crucial for my purposes, given his explicit interest in religious history, his tracing of the clear articulation of a secular realm already in the Hellenistic period, and his insistence on the simultaneous continuity and discontinuity of Christian culture with its Classical antecedents (7, 241–256). His comments on Hippocratic and Christian attitudes to abortion are also quite apt (40–46, 112, 182, 252). Another more recent treatment of the Hippocratic tradition is Jacques Jouanna, *Hippocrates,* trans. M. B. DeBevoise (Baltimore, MD: Johns Hopkins University Press, 1999).

30. For the Greek Hippocratic texts I am using the four-volume edition of W. H. S. Jones, *Hippocrates,* Volume I (Cambridge, MA: Loeb Classical Library of Harvard University Press, 1923, 1984), 298–301. See also Jones's brief discussion at pp. 291–297, where he makes the important point that we lack all the essential information regarding the provenance and date of this oath. We know virtually nothing about who swore this oath, at what time, and under what circumstances. Moreover, the first unambiguous reference to the Oath does not appear until the first century. Was it only for Hippocratic students? Did it delineate obligations that disappeared at "graduation?" When did Hippocrates pen it, and if so, for what purpose?

31. Shapiro, *Abortion: The Supreme Court Decisions,* 50–51.

32. For a wonderful display of this essential point, grounded in the fact that the "Pythagorean" tradition is as vast and as dispersed as the "Hippocratic," see David R. Fideler, ed., *The Pythagorean Sourcebook and Library: An Anthology of Ancient Writings Which Relate to Pythagoras and Pythagorean Philosophy,* trans. Kenneth Sylvan Guthrie (Grand Rapids, MI: Phanes Press, 1987, 1988).

33. We must develop the habit of being more suspicious of such narrative claims, which assert that a cultural age can "end," as simply and unambiguously as a story does.

34. Shapiro, *Abortion: The Supreme Court Cases,* 51.

35. Interestingly, Blackmun never cites an example of this alleged early Christian opposition to abortion. No biblical texts speak directly to the matter of abortion in any way, despite the vast exercise of biblical scholars to make it so speak. But Blackmun might have turned to the so-called *Didache,* "The Teaching of the Twelve Apostles," which offers an interesting set of prohibitions that directly parallel the Hippocratic:

    The second command of this teaching: Do not murder. Do not commit adultery. Do not engage yourself with children (*paidophthorêseis*). Do not go to a prostitute (*porneuseis*). Do not steal. Do not flirt with magic (*mageuseis*). Do not use potions (*pharmakeuseis*). Do not kill a child in abortion (*ou phoneuseis teknon en phthorai*), and do not commit infanticide. (II,1–2)

    For the Greek text of the Didache, I am using Kirsopp Lake's edition, *The Apostolic Fathers* (Cambridge, MA: Loeb Classical Library of Harvard University Press, 1912, 1985), Volume I, 310–313.

36. Blackmun proceeds with further "historical" analysis of the Common Law, English Statutory Law, American Law, as well as several recent positions taken by the American Medical Association, the American Public Health Association, and the American Bar Association.

37. For a superb summary of the relevant literary sources—Greek, Roman, and early Christian—see Patrick Gray, "Abortion, Infanticide and the Social Rhetoric of the *Apocalypse of Peter," Journal of Early Christian Studies* 9:3 (2001): 313–337.
38. 517 US 620 (1996).
39. See Martha Nussbaum and John Finnis, "Is Homosexuality Wrong? A Philosophical Exchange," *The New Republic* (November 15, 1993): 12–13, for the essential stakes in the debate.

    For reflections on the experience of being called as an "expert" witness, as well as disagreement over the fundamental Greek evidence, see John Finnis, "'Shameless Acts' in Colorado: Abuse of Scholarship in Constitutional Cases," *Academic Questions* (Fall 1994): 10–41, and "Law, Morality and 'Sexual Orientation'," *Notre Dame Law Review* 69.5 (1994): 1049–1076.

    See also Martha C. Nussbaum, "Platonic Love and Colorado Law: The Relevance of Ancient Greek Norms to Modern Sexual Controversies," *Virginia Law Review* 80 (1994): 1515–1651, condensed and republished with a response from Richard Posner under the same title in Robert B. Louden and Paul Schollmeier, eds., *The Greeks and Us: Essays in Honor of W. H. Adkins* (Chicago: University of Chicago Press, 1996), 168–223, and then again in *Sex and Social Justice* (New York: Oxford University Press, 1999), 299–331.
40. Professor Nussbaum was a classicist and moral philosopher at Brown University who has now taken up appointments in the University of Chicago's Law, Philosophy, Divinity and Classics programs. The contemporary connection between Law and Religion is an intriguing one, resulting in the creation of interdisciplinary degree programs at several premier institutions, as well as to appointments such as Professor Nussbaum's. This chapter is, of course, attempting to cover that same troubling curricular terrain.
41. Nussbaum, "Platonic Love and Colorado Law," Appendices I-II, 1607–1622.
42. Ibid., pp. 1597–1601; and amended at *The Greeks and Us,* 199–201.
43. Ibid., pp. 1597–1598.
44. Ibid., p. 1598.
45. Ibid., 1599.
46. For a clever, if somewhat too clever, exploitation of this same historical irony, see Stanley Hauerwas, "Why Gays (As A Group) Are Morally Superior to Christians (As A Group)," in *Dispatches From the Front: Theological Engagements With the Secular* (Durham, NC: Duke University Press, 1994), 153–155.
47. She amplifies this point some years later: "I might add that I believe the compassionate imagining of another person's suffering and joy lies at the heart of what is finest in the Christian ethical tradition. In that sense, studying the Greeks might promote Christian virtue" (*Sex and Social Justice,* 328).
48. Nussbaum, "Platonic Love and Colorado Law," 1601. Nussbaum devotes a subsequent book to this topic, arguing there that the empathetic study of literature is essential to the moral health of a society and the lawyers who are established as custodians of its civil disagreements. In that book, she resuscitates Adam Smith's ideas regarding "sympathy" (from *A Theory of Moral Sentiments*) as perhaps the most generative moral emotion. See *Poetic Justice: The Literary Imagination and Public Life* (Boston, MA: Beacon Press, 1995), xvi.
49. The matter of Sappho's erotic/sexual identity is a particularly vexing one, given the extremely fragmentary nature of her literary leavings, as well as what we might best call the "politicization of her name" in contemporary scholarship. I am developing these issues in an as-yet unpublished manuscript entitled "Putting Helen into Hellenism." In so doing, I have found immense insight in Margaret Williamson's *Sappho's Immortal Daughters* (Cambridge, MA: Harvard University Press, 1995), a masterful example of

balanced and creative scholarship. Of similar interest and impressive scholarly range is Ellen Greene, ed., *Reading Sappho: Contemporary Approaches* (Berkeley: University of California Press, 1996).

50. Two oft-cited resources in this ongoing debate are also the starting-points for most subsequent discussion, as Nussbaum admits. Sir Kenneth Dover's *Greek Homosexuality* (Cambridge, MA: Harvard University Press, 1979), used vase paintings, forensic speeches, the rich sexual vocabulary in Attic comedy, and several late antique examples of dream analysis to argue for the surprising (to us) nonchalance with which "the Greeks" apparently discussed male homoeroticism.

   John Boswell's *Christianity, Social Tolerance and Homosexuality: Gay People in Western Europe From the Beginning of the Christian Era to the End of the Fourteenth Century* (Chicago: University of Chicago Press, 1981), advanced argument considerably by emphasizing two things: first, the importance of lexicography, and a frank confession of our uncertainty about the meaning of certain essential Greek terms which lie at the heart of the current controversy; and second, that the first coherent legislative attacks on male homosexuality may be dated no earlier than the late Roman period. Boswell concluded—importantly, in my judgment, despite my reservations about other parts of his project—that Christian theology could not be the real culprit here, but rather that something in the culture of the eastern Mediterranean changed decisively, independent of developments in theology or church politics during these same centuries. Boswell remained uncertain to the end of his life about what such decisive socio-cultural forces might have been.

   Other authors have made equally notable contributions to these ongoing debates about "antique sexual identities" (bracketing, for now, the still more dizzying suggestion that such a notion is, itself, entirely modern and therefore inapplicable in any way to ancient attitudes). Bernadette Brooten turns her attention to the female side of the homoerotic coin in *Love Between Women: Early Christian Responses to Female Homoeroticism* (Chicago: University of Chicago Press, 1996). Brooten makes the important point that, however "tolerant" Greeks or Romans *may* have been regarding carefully prescribed male relationships, female homoeroticism was *always* roundly condemned.

   Mark D. Jordan makes the case that "sodomy" is actually an untranslatable word we owe entirely to medieval Christian theology in *The Invention of Sodomy in Christian Theology* (Chicago: University of Chicago Press, 1997).

   Three other books have been additionally helpful in matters of vocabulary. Jeffrey Henderson's *The Maculate Muse: Obscene Language in Attic Comedy* (New Haven, CT: Yale University Press, 1975), is a rich resource for the more explicit sexual vocabulary in Classical comedy briefly alluded to by Dover; Saul M. Olyan, "'And With a Male You Shall Not Lie the Lying Down of a Woman': On the Meaning and Significance of Leviticus 18:22 and 20:13," *Journal of the History of Sexuality* 5.2 (1994): 179–206, discusses the most unambiguous biblical proscription of male homosexuality in the Hebrew scriptures. Robin Scroggs lays out some of the essential New Testament material (Romans 1:18–32, I Corinthians 6:9–20, and I Timothy 1:8–11) in an attempt to reconstruct late Roman sexual attitudes and their accompanying vocabulary in *The New Testament and Homosexuality: Contextual Background for Contemporary Debate* (Philadelphia, PA: Fortress Press,1983). That book sparked an interesting debate in *The Journal of the American Academy of Religion* in the mid-1990s. See Mark D. Smith, "Ancient Bisexuality and the Interpretation of Romans 1:26–27," JAAR 64.2 (1996): 223–256, as well as "Responses" in JAAR 65.4 (1997): 855–870. Debates about ancient sexual attitudes clearly mark one of the real "growth industries" in the academy, as they have been in the courts.

51. Nussbaum has tightened up and qualified her views since then, admitting that "the equation of the ancient with the modern should not be done in a facile and histori-

cally naive way" (*Sex and Social Justice,* 331). But her fundamental preferences for Stoic attitudes over what she perceives to have been the dominant Christian ones remain unchanged, and rely on an historically overdrawn distinction between pagans and Christians, as I hope to show in greater detail in the third and fourth chapters.

52. 521 US 702 (1997).

53. 521 US 793 (1997).

54. Timothy E. Quill, "Dying With Dignity: A Case of Individualized Decision-Making," *The New England Journal of Medicine* 324.10 (March 7, 1991): 691–694.

   Quill followed up on this essay with a book, *Dying With Dignity: Making Choices and Taking Charge* (New York: W.W. Norton & Company, 1993), a book that he dedicated to his pseudonymous patient, Diane.

55. The cofounders of this society, Ann Wickett and Derek Humphry, contributed to the fray with *The Right to Die: Understanding Euthanasia* (New York: Harper & Row, 1986).

56. *Quill v. Koppell* 870 F. Supp. 78 (1994).

57. *Compassion in Dying v. State of Washington* 79 F.3d 790 (1996).

58. *Lee v. State of Oregon* 891 F. Supp. 1429 (1995).

59. Actually, a District Court in Washington state judged an antisuicide law to be unconstitutional in 1994. A panel of the Court of Appeals for the Ninth Circuit reversed this finding and reinstated the law in 1995. Then the Ninth Circuit reheard the case *en banc* in 1996, and reaffirmed the ban. The U.S. Supreme Court took up the case in 1997, and reversed the decision once again.

60. *Compassion in Dying v. State of Washington* 79 F.3d 790 (1996) 806–810.

61. "Greco-Roman" is a term that, like the term "Judeo-Christian," probably conceals more than it reveals. Classicists have not been nearly vocal enough on this point. And the courts have inherited the culture's blissful unawareness here. Names matter, especially when we are trying to find suppler ways of talking about religion, of all things, in court settings. I will turn to the specific complexity of the term "Greco-Roman" at the beginning of Chapter Three.

62. The Court is actually quoting here, from A. Alvarez, "The Background," in M. Pabst Battin and David J. Mayo, eds., *Suicide: The Philosophical Issues* (New York: St. Martin's Press, 1980).

63. *Compassion in Dying v. State of Washington* 79 F.3d 790 (1996) 808n25. Also mentioned there are Samson, Abimelech, and Achitophel from the Hebrew scriptures, and Judas Iscariot from the New Testament.

64. Keos is especially interesting, since its rocky terrain could not support a large population. Sectagenarians considered it a civic duty to extinguish themselves. See Anne Carson, *Economy of the Unlost: Reading Simonides of Keos with Paul Celan* (Princeton: Princeton University Press, 1999), 80–81.

65. While not without its own occasional polemics and problems, Arthur J. Droge and James D. Tabor's, *A Noble Death: Suicide and Martyrdom Among Christians and Jews in Antiquity* (San Francisco, CA: HarperCollins Publishers, 1992), is an excellent resource for thinking these matters through.

66. As I try to remind myself and my students regularly, Socrates was a man who made a public point of broadcasting the voices he claimed to have heard in his own head.

67. Emile Durkheim, *Suicide: A Study in Sociology* [1897], trans. John A. Spaulding and George Simpson (New York: The Free Press, 1951, 1979).

68. *Compassion in Dying v. State of Washington* 79 F.3d 790 (1996) 807.

69. Massimo Montinari and Giorgio Colli,eds., *Nietzsche: Kritische Studienausgabe, Sämtliche Werke in 15 Bänden* (Berlin: Walter de Gruyter, 1967–1977), XIII, 80.

70. *Compassion in Dying v. State of Washington* 79 F.3d 790 (1996) 807.

71. See Anthony R. Birley, *Hadrian: The Restless Emperor* (New York: Routledge, 1997), 297–300, as well as the dramatic rendering of these events in Marguerite Yourcenar's

extraordinary historical novel, *Memoirs of Hadrian,* trans. Grace Frick and the author (New York: Farrar, Straus & Giroux, 1954), 280–283.

72. Marcus Aurelius, *Meditations,* I,16, II,3, III,3, IV,10, X,21, XII, 14–15, as well as the remarkable concluding metaphor of human life as a form of play-acting: when the director calls one of us from the stage, it is our theatrical duty to depart graciously, since neither the moment of our arrival, nor the moment of our departure is in our own care.

73. See "Suicide," in Moses Hadas, ed., *The Stoic Philosophy of Seneca: Essays and Letters* (New York: W.W. Norton & Company, 1958), 202–207.

74. Here is where the failure to distinguish between suicide and martyrdom is determinative. As early texts such as *The Martyrdom of Polycarp* make abundantly clear, a major concern of the early movement lay in sketching out the key features of *to kata euangelion martyrion,* "a martyrdom conformable to the gospel"—which is to say, a *non*suicidal obedience to the will of God. See the Loeb Classical Library, Kirsopp Lake, ed., *The Apostolic Fathers* (Cambridge, MA: The Loeb Classical Library of Harvard University Press, 1992), Volume II, 311–312.

75. *Compassion in Dying v. State of Washington* 79 F.3d 790 (1996) 808.

76. Ibid.

77. This is one central thesis of my first book, *Tragic Posture and Tragic Vision,* where I track the debate about the alleged compatibility or incompatability of Classical and Christian thought, from Hegel to Nietzsche.

78. Francis M. Cornford's little-known classic, *From Religion to Philosophy: A Study in the Origins of Western Speculation* (Princeton: Princeton University Press, 1912, 1991), makes this point brilliantly, by insisting upon the complex continuity-in-discontinuity between these related modes of Greek spiritual enquiry.

79. This task was significantly advanced by Winifred Fallers Sullivan in a remarkable book, *Paying the Words Extra: Religious Discourse in the Supreme Court of the United States* (Cambridge, MA: Harvard University Press, 1994). Sullivan was a constitutional lawyer who perceived the way lawyers talk about religion to be largely inadequate. She returned to Harvard to pursue a Ph.D. in Religious Studies, precisely to thicken her own descriptive thinking about religious identity and its complex relation to liberal democracy. That book—like this essay, I'm afraid—does a much better job of naming the problem than it does of suggesting coherent and helpful alternatives.

80. I am thinking especially of the work of Robert Bellah, et al., *Habits of the Heart: Individualism and Commitment in American Life* (Berkeley: University of California Press, 1985). For a critique of the larger project of the book, and its affinity with MacIntyre's cultural critique, see Jeffrey Stout, *Ethics After Babel,* 191–219, and my *Afterwords,* 67–89.

81. Chief Justice Rehnquist, who wrote the majority opinion in both cases, made two important points, for our purposes. In *Vacco v. Quill* 521 US 793 (1997) 807 (in which the U.S. Supreme Court reversed an Appeals Court ruling about assisted suicide), much was made of the distinction between active and passive killing, "the distinction between letting a patient die and making that patient die." Removing a person from life support and overdosing a patient are two very different medical practices and that distinction ought to be maintained in the law. This seems an eminently reasonable distinction to me.

But in *Washington v. Glucksberg* 521 US 702 (1997) 705–715, Rehnquist also provides us with an abbreviated historical narrative, as an attempt to show that this distinction is "not simply deduced from abstract concepts of personal autonomy, but [is] instead grounded in the Nation's history and traditions." This historical narrative is presented in a rather spotty way, but here are the salient facts:

England adopts the ecclesiastical prohibition of suicide in 673 CE, at the Council of Hereford.

Henry de Bracton refers to suicide as felonious murder in his thirteenth-century treatise, *On Laws and Customs of England.*

Sir William Blackstone refers to suicide as "self-murder" and condemns "the pretended heroism, but real cowardice, of the Stoic philosophers" in his *Commentaries on the Laws of England* [1765–69].

The common-law condemnation of suicide and assistance in suicide has been the law of every colony and state in U.S. history since then, until the spate of electoral attempts to change such laws in the early 1990s.

Note that the Court contents itself, by and large, with an analysis of Anglo-American attitudes in the past 300 years. It does occasionally delve more deeply into the past. Yet it will go no further than the early Christian period in England, and refuses so much as to address the conceivably different cultural attitudes of Roman England. The Classics have, in this case, been clearly trumped by Christianity!

82. For an analysis of this overarching disagreement, as well as for my own argument that this quarrel has less to do with "the Greeks" and more to do with a nineteenth-century Romantic fiction of who "the Greeks" actually were, see "Why the Greeks?" in Johann P. Arnason and Peter Murphy, eds., *Agon, Logos, Polis: The Greek Achievement and Its Aftermath* (Stuttgart: Franz Steiner Verlag, 2001), 29–55.

83. In fact, the Court recognizes three different kinds of such judicial "scrutiny." The "rational relations test" is one that rarely serves to call a law's legitimacy into question. It addresses itself rather to such commonsense distinctions as those that discriminate among income levels in assessing tax rates. "Intermediate scrutiny" is applied to other distinctions, sometimes defensible, such as those relating to gender. "Strict scrutiny" is applied to distinctions that are inherently suspect, of which race is the prime example. *Romer v. Evans* marks one of the rare instances in which a rational relations test actually resulted in overturning a law. It remains unclear where sexual taxonomies fit on this sliding scale of court review. See Lazarus, *Closed Chambers,* 142, 293–294, 432.

Predictably, Justice Scalia dissented (with Rehnquist and Thomas joining him) proclaiming that "[t]he Court has mistaken a Kulturkampf for a fit of spite.... [It] places the prestige of this institution behind the proposition that opposition to homosexuality is as reprehensible as racial or religious bias" (*Romer v. Evans* 517 US 620 [1996] 636). Note that we require a *history* to see how racial bias came to be seen as reprehensible, and how religious bias has gradually come to be viewed as a far more complex matter, over time.

84. This point is elegantly made by Jeffrey Stout in his somber meditation on MacIntyre's larger project, "Homeward Bound: MacIntyre on Liberal Society and the History of Ethics," 229, as well as in the Postscript to the second edition of *Ethics After Babel,* 341–355.

85. And may be necessarily co-opted by that same process. For a fascinating sketch of the way in which the Southern Baptist Convention has become more state-like and more democratic as it organized itself politically, see Arthur E. Farnsley II, *Southern Baptist Politics: Authority and Power in the Restructuring of an American Denomination* (University Park: Pennsylvania State University Press, 1994).

86. See *Church of Lukumi Babalu Aye v. City of Hialeah* 508 US 520 (1997), where the Afro-Caribbean syncretic traditions of Santería were first granted recognition as legitimate religion, and then their right freely to practice animal sacrifice was defended against legislative prejudice.

87. These terms were popularized by Matthew Arnold in the 1932 essay *Culture and Anarchy,* ed. J. Dover Wilson (New York: Cambridge University Press, 1990), 129–144. For an incisive questioning of this dichotomy and the politics to which it leads, as well as for an historical argument that Protestantism is best read as "Hebraic" in its own self-understanding, I am indebted to Vassilis Lambropoulos, *The Rise of Eurocentrism: Anatomy of Interpretation* (Princeton: Princeton University Press, 1993).

See also my review of this book, "On Being Greek or Jewish in the Modern Moment," *Diaspora* 3.2 (1994): 199–220.

88. See Nomi Maya Stolzenberg, "'He Drew A Circle That Shut Me Out': Assimilation, Indoctrination, and the Paradox of a Liberal Education," *Harvard Law Review* 106 (1994): 582–667.

89. Jacques Derrida, "Force of Law: The 'Mystical Foundation of Authority'," trans. Mary Quaintaince, *Cardozo Law Review* 11 (1990): 920–1045.

CHAPTER TWO

1. Some representative texts of the Cambridge Ritualists are: Francis M. Cornford, *From Philosophy to Religion: A Study in the Origins of Western Speculation* [1912] (Princeton, NJ: Princeton University Press, 1991); and Jane E. Harrison, *Prolegomena to the Study of Greek Religion* [1903] (Princeton, NJ: Princeton University Press, 1991), and *Themis: A Study of the Social Origins of Greek Religion* (London: Merlin Press, 1963).

   Some important texts from the emerging French school are: Jean-Pierre Vernant, *Myth and Society in Ancient Greece,* trans. Janet Lloyd [1974] (Atlantic Highlands, NJ: Humanities Press, 1980); with Pierre Vidal-Naquet, *Tragedy and Myth in Ancient Greece* [1973] trans. Janet Lloyd (Atlantic Highlands, NJ: Humanities Press,1981); Marcel Detienne and Jean-Pierre Vernant, eds., *The Cuisine of Sacrifice Among the Greeks,* trans. Paula Wissig (Chicago: University of Chicago Press, 1989); and Marcel Detienne, *The Masters of Truth in Archaic Greece,* trans. Janet Lloyd (NY: Zone Books, 1999), esp. 104–106, 135–137.

   A superb introduction to the work of the Centre may be found in the introduction Froma I. Zeitlin prepared for Jean-Pierre Vernant's *Mortals and Immortals: Collected Essays* (Princeton, NJ: Princeton University Press, 1991), 3–24, as well as "Forms of Belief and Rationality in Greece," in Johann P. Arnason and Peter Murphy, eds., *Agon, Logos, Polis: The Greek Achievement and Its Aftermath* (Stuttgart: Franz Steiner Verlag, 2001), 118–126.

2. Friedrich Nietzsche, *The Birth of Tragedy* and *The Case of Wagner,* trans. Walter Kaufmann (New York: Vintage Books, 1967); Giorgio Colli and Mazzino Montinari, eds., *Friedrich Nietzsche: Sämtliche Werke, Kritische Studienausgabe in 15 Bänden* (hereafter *KSA*) I, 11–156.

3. Jacob Burkhardt, *The Greeks and Greek Civilization,* trans. Sheila Stern, ed. Oswyn Murray (New York: St. Martin's Press, 1998).

4. Friedrich Nietzsche, *Daybreak: Thoughts on the Prejudices of Morality,* trans. R. J. Hollingdale (New York: Cambridge University Press, 1982), §§42,102; *KSA* III, 50, 90–91.

5. Tracing the route of presumably Near Eastern healing cults into the Archaic world of the Aegean basin is complicated, indeed. Certainly the Asklepius cult was on the rise in Plato's day, though it achieved an even greater prominence in the next generation, and lasted late. Asklepius's two most prominent sanctuaries—in Epidauros, and on the island of Kos—were both renovated in a major way *after* Plato penned these lines. And the cult lasted later than almost any other pagan cult, surviving well into the fifth or sixth centuries CE.

   Some relevant material may be found in: Walter Burkert, *The Orientalizing Revolution: Near Eastern Influences on Greek Culture in the Early Archaic Age* (Cambridge, MA: Harvard University Press, 1992), 75–79; in Carl Kerenyi, *Asklepius: Archetypal Image of the Physician's Existence,* trans. Ralph Manheim (New York: Pantheon, 1959); Theodore Papadakis, *Epidauros: The Sanctuary of Asklepius* (München: Verlag Schnell & Steiner, 1972); and R.A. Tomlinson, *Epidauros* (Austin: University of Texas Press, 1983).

   Additional material may be found in two important doctoral dissertations. A good archaeological survey may be found in Lynn R. LiDonnici, *Tale and Dream: The Text and Compositional History of the Corpus of Epidaurian Miracle Cures* (Philadelphia: University of Pennsylvania Press, 1989), 15–44. Rene Josef Ruttimann makes an important case for not distinguishing too sharply between early Christian and pagan in *Asclepius and Jesus: The Form, Character and Status of the Asclepius Cult in the Second-Century CE and Its Influence on Early Christianity* (Harvard University Dissertation, 1987).

6. The traditional citation for the Platonic corpus follows the so-called Stephanus pagination. Stephanus is a Latinized version of Estienne, the name of a prominent French publisher of classical and biblical texts located in Paris, then later transplanted to Geneva. This Provençal family is first mentioned as a publisher in 1500. The business was established by Henry (1470–1520), who passed it on to his second son, Robert (1503–1559), who in turn passed it on to his son, also Henry by name (1528–1598). It was especially this latter Henry whose bibliophilic excesses ruined the firm in the seventeenth century; it was later inherited by other more distant family relations, Paul (1566–1627) and Antoine (1592–1674).

   Stephanus's early classical texts, dictionaries, and other scholarly resources were of exceptional beauty, and the edition of Plato's collected works was especially prized. The pages of the Platonic texts (published in Geneva in 1578) were printed in two columns, with the Greek text and Latin translation (by Jean de Serres) running in parallel. The columns were divided into five sections by Stephanus, labeled a to e, and printed between the columns. Most classical texts, whether in Greek or in translation, include some reference to these Stephanus page numbers, and I follow this standard practice here. All Platonic references will be cited parenthetically in this chapter.

   See also Anthony Grafton, *The Footnote: A Curious History* (Cambridge, MA: Harvard University Press, 1997), 221.

7. Nietzsche, *Twilight of the Idols,* "The Problem of Socrates," §12; *KSA* VI,73.

8. This image was traditionally assigned to Simonides (556–467 BCE), one of whose fragments proclaims: *ho logos tôn pragmatôn eikôn estin,* "the word is the image of things." Simonides is the subject—if not actually the victim—of some strange deconstructive handling by the philosophers, most notably by Protagoras and Socrates both, at *Protagoras* 339a–349a.

   For a lyrical meditation on the poetic legacy of Simonides, see Anne Carson, *Economy of the Unlost: Reading Simonides of Keos with Paul Celan* (Princeton, NJ: Princeton University Press, 1999), and Detienne, *Masters of Truth in Archaic Greece,* 107–111.

9. This was to become a point of some real importance in the nineteenth century, as we will see in the last three chapters. Since I will devote significant time and attention to Lord Byron in this book, let me use his comments as exemplary. In the 1823 Preface to Cantos VI, VII, and VIII of *Don Juan,* he says:

   The hackneyed and lavished title of Blasphemer . . . should be welcomed by all who recollect on *whom* it was originally bestowed. Socrates and Jesus Christ were put to death publicly as *blasphemers,* and so have been and may be many who dare oppose the most notorious abuses of the name of God and the mind of man. But persecution is not refutation, nor even triumph . . . and that very suffering for conscience's sake will make more proselytes to deism than the example of heterodox Prelates to Christianity, suicide statesmen to oppression, or overpensioned homicides to the impious alliance which insults the world with the name of "Holy." (Leslie A. Marchand, ed., *Don Juan by Lord Byron* [Boston, MA: Houghton Mifflin Company, 1958], 199).

   This equation of the course of the career of Socrates with that of Christ—so odd-seeming if we consider it historically—was to become a commonplace after Hegel popularized the idea. See his *Lectures on the History of Philosophy,* trans. E. S. Haldane (Lincoln: University of Nebraska Press, 1995), I, 425–448.

10. A phrase I take from Leo Strauss's discussion of this dialogue, and a preliminary account of the common-sense view of piety, "On the *Euthyphron,*" in *The Rebirth of Classical*

Political Realism: An Introduction to the Thought of Leo Strauss, ed. Thomas L. Pangle (Chicago: University of Chicago Press, 1989), 187–206, esp.188.

11. The irony of this last point is not to be missed. As we will see, one of the charges leveled against Socrates is precisely that of introducing new gods into the city. It is in the very nature of an elastic and fluid polytheism to facilitate such introductions—such as the introduction of the Thracian moon goddess, Bendis, here—especially in port cities such as the Piraeus of Athens, or later, the Roman port of Ostia, which became a thriving center for Mithraism.

    We still need a full-length study of the dramatic settings, or narrative frames, in Plato's dialogues and their deliberate relation to the topics they address.

12. In a still more delicate irony, *Plato* seemed especially interested in the practice of pilgrimage, even where he was uncertain as to its efficacy or ultimate purpose. Even in *The Laws,* where Socrates is absent, three old men (from Athens, Sparta, and Crete) are introduced to us in the middle of a long pilgrimage, from Knossos to the Cave of Zeus on Mount Ida in Crete (*Laws* 625b). In a telling image, this exhaustive book begins and ends in the middle. Thus, while it *is* depicted as a religious pilgrimage, the pilgrimage depicts a journey in which the pilgrims never really get anywhere.

13. For more on the relation of these two premier civic institutions, see Stephen L. Glass, "The Greek Gymnasium: Some Problems," in Wendy J. Raschke, ed., *The Archaeology of the Olympics: The Olympics and Other Festivals in Antiquity* (Madison: University of Wisconsin Press, 1988), 155–173.

14. For an intelligent discussion of the social institutions in which Greek love was often housed, see Claude Calame, *The Poetics of Ancient Greece,* trans. Janet Lloyd (Princeton, NJ: Princeton University Press, 1999), 91–109, 153–174.

15. A task I initiated in *Symposia: Plato, the Erotic and Moral Value* (Albany: State University of New York Press, 1999).

16. Alasdair MacIntyre, *After Virtue,* 2nd Ed. (South Bend, IN: University of Notre Dame Press, 1984), 51–78.

17. MacIntyre, *After Virtue,* 121–130.

18. For a highly critical analysis of this feature of Socratism, one which attends specifically to his erotic persona, see Martha C. Nussbaum, *The Fragility of Goodness: Luck and Ethics in Greek Tragedy and Philosophy* (New York: Cambridge University Press, 1986), 165–199.

    For my attempt to defend Socrates against these criticisms, see *Symposia,* 57–69.

19. I am summarizing material I develop in much greater detail in *Symposia,* 83–89.

20. I am using the rough chronology of the Platonic corpus laid out by Alexander Nehamas in *The Art of Living: Socratic Reflections from Plato to Foucault* (Berkeley: University of California Press, 1998), 196n33.

21. Ruprecht, *Symposia,* xiii.

22. Anne Carson, *Eros the Bittersweet: An Essay* (Princeton, NJ: Princeton University Press, 1986), 152–153.

    See also *Phaedrus* 244a –245c, 249d.

23. Nietzsche grudgingly admits that "Socrates was also a fabulous *erotic*" (*KSA,* VI, 71), although it is unclear whether he intended this as a compliment.

    If anything, this same point is made even more explicit in the post-Platonic literature about Socrates. These are dialogues written in the Platonic style, boasting Socrates as their main character, composed in the several centuries after Plato's death. Some of these were included in the first critical editions and commentaries on the works of Plato, compiled in Alexandria in the first century BCE. Most notable about them is the thing on which they all agree: namely, Socrates's status as *erôtikos.*

    So, in the *Theages,* we hear the most astonishing claim yet made on Socrates' philosophic and erotic behalf: he is "better skilled than any person who has ever lived" in "one little subject, *ta erôtika*" (*Theages* 128b). We also have an entire dialogue called

"The Lovers" (*Erastaí*), which is explicitly labeled as a dialogue "on ethics" (*éthikos*). Finally, there are *two* dialogues which bear the name of *Alcíbiades*. The second, and shorter, of the two is a rather crude attempt at Platonic imitation. But even this one concludes with a predictable Socratic wish to "win out as the victor (*kallínikos*) over all his other lovers (*erastôn*)" (*Alcíbiades II* 151 c).

24. The classic formulation of this idea is Sir Kenneth Dover's *Greek Homosexuality* (Cambridge, MA: Harvard University Press, 1979). Much energy has been devoted in the past twenty years to developing, nuancing, and in some cases altogether abandoning, the "pederastic paradigm" he outlined there. I surveyed some of this material in the last chapter, and I believe that Plato also designs to question it himself.

   For a particularly hostile account which nonetheless attends very intelligently to class concerns, see T.K. Hubbard, "Popular Perceptions of Elite Homosexuality in Classical Athens," *Arion, Third Series* 6.1 (1998): 48−78. For a still more thoroughgoing criticism of recent scholarship, with a helpful reminder of all that we do *not* know, see Bruce S. Thornton, *Eros: The Myth of Ancient Greek Sexuality* (New York: HarperCollins Publishers, 1997). James Davidson makes the helpful observation (in *Courtesans and Fishcakes: The Consuming Passions of Classical Athens* [New York: St. Martins Press, 1997], xix−xx) that precious little North American scholarship has been devoted of late to *heterosexual* attitudes in Greek antiquity, despite the overwhelming preponderance of such material. Recent work in Greek (Andreas Ledakis's) and Italian (Claude Calame's) to which I have already referred, are notable exceptions to this trend.

25. Ruprecht, *Symposia,* 56−57.

26. See Alasdair MacIntyre, *Whose Justice? Which Rationality?* (Notre Dame, IN: University of Notre Dame Press, 1988), 360−361, for an important discussion of the project of "modern" philosophy, beginning with Descartes, as the attempt to secure a necessary and noncontingent starting point for critical thought.

27. The confusion is heightened when we recall that Socrates customarily identifies more with the maternal line, claiming to act as a midwife, like his mother (*Theaetetus* 210c-d, and see also *Symposium* 206c−210a), not as a stonecutter, like his father. The place of the mother in a world where sons and fathers vie for control is a vexing one. And it is curious that mothers and fathers should be invoked together by Euthyphro (at *Euthyphro* 5e). I am indebted to Leo Strauss's "On the *Euthyphron*," 193, which first brought this point to my attention.

28. Alexander Nehamas marks this moment as the paradigmatic example of *Platonic,* rather than Socratic, irony. We are invited as readers to feel superior to Euthyphro, given his only superficial commitments and his pretense to a wisdom he clearly does not have. But as we soon as we close the book on this dialogue, and return to our own worldly concerns, we have become precisely what Euthyphro is. See *The Art of Living,* 41.

29. This way of selectively re-telling traditional stories was a famous talent in which Pindar (c. 518−c. 440 BCE) excelled in many of his epinikian odes. The paradigmatic example comes in the First Olympian Ode, where he refuses to believe that Tantalos would have killed his own child, to make a meal of him for the gods.

> It is proper for men that we speak well
> of the gods. The blame is less.
> Son of Tantalos, I will tell your story differently
> than they did of old . . . (I, 35−37)

Pindar claims that Poseidon, enamored of the boy, stole him away from the banquet hall. Given Pelops's sudden disappearance, a rumor of his father's crimes was created to explain it.

For the Greek text of Pindar's Odes, I am using the Loeb Classical edition of William H. Race, *Pindar: Olympian Odes, Pythian Odes* (Cambridge, MA: Harvard University Press, 1997), 50–51.

30. Our main sources for these Daidalic traditions are all Roman, and thus quite late—a point of some importance in the next chapter.

    Far the longest and most detailed account appears in Diodorus of Sicily's (fl. 60–30 BCE) *Library of History (Bibliothêkês Istorikês)* IV.76.1–79.7.

    In addition to this extensive account of Daidalos's various travels—from Athens, to Crete, to Sicily—Ovid's (43 BCE–c. 17 CE) poetic representation of the deadly flight of Icarus appears at *Metamorphoses* VIII.183–216.

    Finally, Pausanias (fl. 150 CE), who is the main subject of the next chapter, presents a nice summary of these same Daidalic traditions in his *Greek Walkabout* I.26.4.

    For a stunning modern treatment, written by a contemporary sculptor and painter, see Michael Ayrton, *The Testament of Daedalus* (London: Robin Clark, 1962).

    A marvelous travelogue, dedicated to Sicily rather than to Crete, and which presents itself as a quest for the cultural and historical figure behind the myth, is Vincent Cronin, *The Golden Honeycomb: A Sicilian Quest* (London: HarperCollins, 1954, 1980).

31. The bibliography on Crete and Cretan myth is enormous and expanding. For an interesting, if dated, essay on Cretan myth and Cretan archaeology, see George E. Mylonas, "Crete in the Dawn of History," *The N. W. Missouri State Teachers College Studies* (1946): 81–103. For a more recent, but equally Romantic account, see Yannis Sakellarakis, *Digging for the Past,* trans. David Turner (Athens: Ammos Publications, 1996).

    For the discovery of the so-called Minoan civilization, heretofore unknown and unsuspected, see Sir Arthur Evans, "Minoan Civilization at the Palace of Knossos," in Brian M. Fagan, ed., *Eyewitness to Discovery: First-Person Accounts of More Than Fifty of the World's Greatest Discoveries* (New York: Oxford University Press, 1996), 186–196. A gorgeous memoir concerning the British monuments built by Sir Arthur Evans to oversee excavation of the palace complex at Knossos prior to the World Wars is Dilys Powell, *The Villa Ariadne* (New York: The Akadine Press, 1973). And for a perfectly stunning tour of the psychodynamics of Cretan myth, see Ruth Padel, "Labyrinth of Desire: Cretan Myth in Us," *Arion, Third Series* 4.2 (1996): 76–87.

    For a nice survey of primarily North American excavation in Crete, see James D. Muhly and Evangelika Sikla, eds., *Crete 2000: One Hundred Years of American Archaeological Work on Crete* (Athens: The American School of Classical Studies, 2000).

    Finally, for a specifically Platonic connection to Crete, see Glenn R. Morrow, *Plato's Cretan City: A Historical Interpretation of the Laws* (Princeton, NJ: Princeton University Press, 1960).

32. See the stunning review of this Daidalian material in Sarah P. Morris, *Daidalos and the Origins of Greek Art* (Princeton, NJ: Princeton University Press, 1992), 36–59.

33. I am much indebted to Barry S. Strauss, *Fathers and Sons in Athens: Ideology and Society in the Era of the Peloponnesian War* (Princeton, NJ: Princeton University Press, 1993), although I differ slightly with his understanding of Socrates's trial at pp. 199–211. Strauss suggests that a "generation gap" emerged in Athens during the Peloponnesian War, especially under the brash leadership of Alcibiades, who hatched the idea of the Sicilian invasion in 415 BCE. When that campaign failed so spectacularly, the older generation reasserted itself and combated any further influence of political youth. Strauss places Socratic philosophy precisely here, in this strange nexus pitting fathers against sons, and while Plato clearly does so as well, he adds an erotic dimension to it that subtly but decisively changes the political and moral landscape.

34. As I indicated in my Preliminary remarks, this confusion between belief and practice is necessary to make this last charge stick.

35. Simonides achieved a reputation for miserliness in antiquity, and was thought to be the first poet who took money for his creations. Socrates makes similar charges against teachers who take money for their teaching, those whom he calls "Sophists." See Carson, *Economy of the Unlost*, 15–44.

36. See James Davidson, *Courtesans and Fishcakes: The Consuming Passions of Classical Athens*, 109–136. See also Andreas Ledakis, *O Erotas Stên Archaia Ellada*, Vol. 3, *Porneia*, and Vol. 4, *Oi Etaíres* (Athens: Ekdoseis Kastaniôtê, 1998, 1999).

   Interestingly, the one kind of prostitution Athens did *not* permit was cultic. See Calame, *The Poetics of Eros in Ancient Greece*, 113.

37. Nehamas, *The Art of Living*, 1–15.

38. The most telling example is also the most poorly understood. Plato is commonly viewed as a philosopher who distinguished radically between the body and the soul, consistently privileging the latter. And yet Socrates could not be clearer in his own conviction that these two elements are joined, that we are "embodied souls" (*Statesman* 261b, 288e), if we are anything at all. This has a powerful erotic implication, of course, if constancy in human relationships is a virtue. For the body will inevitably change. A youth cannot remain forever young. Shall the love change, then, as the lover's body does?

   See Ruprecht, *Symposia*, 79–83.

39. This aspect of the Socratic strategy was emphasized by Gregory Vlastos, in *Socrates: Ironist and Moral Philosopher* (Ithaca, NY: Cornell University Press, 1991). See also Alexander Nehamas, *Virtues of Authenticity: Essays on Plato and Socrates* (Princeton, NJ: Princeton University Press, 1999), 83–107.

40. Even calling the Greeks our "fathers" is rendered ironic and complex by the fact that Plato himself marked the eternal childlikeness of Greek culture in comparison to other, older cultures like the Egyptian (*Tímaios* 21e–23d). Similarly, Hegel would popularize the Romantic idea to which we are all still heir—namely, that the Greeks are the childhood, or at most the early adolescence, of Europe. See his *The Philosophy of History*, trans. J. Sibree (New York: Dover Publications, 1956), 106, 223–224.

CHAPTER THREE

1. *Meteorologíka* 352b2.

   Traditional citation of the Aristotelian corpus derives from the edition of *Aristotelis Opera* (Berolini: apud Reimarum, 1831–1836) edited by Immanuel Bekker in Berlin (and reprinted by Walter de Gruyter, 1960–1987). This four-volume work prints the Greek text in two columns (labeled a and b in citation) each of which run to as many as forty column-lines per page. I will use this traditional Aristotelian citation throughout this book.

   This passage from the *Meteorologíka* is an especially interesting one, since it refers to the time of Deucalion's flood, a matter to which we shall return in Pausanias's account later. Aristotle makes reference to a people on the western coast of the Greek mainland who were first called *Selloí*, then *Graíkoi*, but now are known as *Hellênes*. These *Graíkoi* seem to be the post-flood inhabitants of the region around Dodona and the Acheloös River.

   It is just conceivable that these western peoples, with their singular name, would have been among the first to be encountered by Romans when they came in contact with Greek colonists in the seventh century BCE. But it is more likely that Romans of a later era did what most conquerors do—namely, to select a new name, or else to focus on an oddball local variant, as the name for conquered peoples and their territories.

See the entry for "Graecia" in William Smith, ed., *A Dictionary of Greek and Roman Geography* (London: John Murray, 1878), Volume I, 1010–1018.

2. Still later, it became an administrative province called Achaea, which referred to a sizeable portion of the mainland, the *southern* mainland, known also as the "Peloponnese." This rendering of the entire peninsula as "Pelops's island," is something worth considering further, given the prominence that Pelops enjoyed at Olympia in Pausanias's day.

3. Arnaldo Momigliano will go further, arguing that Greeks studiously avoided the study of, or the participation in, any foreign cultures. See "The Fault of the Greeks," in *Essays in Ancient and Modern Historiography* (Middletown, CT: Wesleyan University Press, 1977), 9–23.

4. See the fine discussion, with helpful bibliography, in A. N. Sherwin-White, *Racial Prejudice in Imperial Rome* (New York: Cambridge University Press, 1967), 62–101, as well as a presentation of the archaeological evidence in Susan E. Alcock, *Graecia Capta: The Landscapes of Roman Greece* (New York: Cambridge University Press, 1993).

5. For more on Nietzsche's Hellenism, see my *Tragic Posture and Tragic Vision: Against the Modern Failure of Nerve* (New York: Continuum Press, 1994), 128–180; *Afterwords: Hellenism, Modernism and the Myth of Decadence* (Albany: State University of New York Press, 1996), 23–63; and *Symposia: Plato, the Erotic and Moral Value* (Albany: State University of New York Press, 1999), 1–20.

See also William Arrowsmith's Introduction to the early unpublished essay, "We Classicists," in Arrowsmith, ed., *Nietzsche: Unmodern Observations* (New Haven, CT: Yale University Press, 1990), 307–320.

6. Two marvelous English versions of Pausanias exist. The first is the now-classic six-volume edition by Sir James Frazer, *Pausanias Description of Greece* (London: Macmillan, 1898). As the date indicates, Frazer's work, combining his anthropological *and* ethnographic *and* classical interests, is an encyclopedic compendium of nineteenth-century Classicism. I will return to that issue later in this chapter, and again in the next.

The second English version of Pausanias, a two-volume edition by Peter Levi, *Pausanias: Guide to Greece*, rev. ed. (New York: Penguin Books, 1979), is an equally representative sampling of twentieth century attitudes and tastes, foregrounding the "scientific" advances, primarily archaeological and topographical, in our understanding of the ancient world. Amazingly, Volume Two of Levi's version, with which I will principally be dealing here, is now out of print.

For the Greek text of Pausanias's *Guide*, I am using that of the Loeb Classical Library in 5 Volumes, W.H.S. Jones, ed., *Pausanias: Description of Greece* (Cambridge, MA: Harvard University Press, 1918, 1992). As was my practice with Plato in the previous chapter, I will include all citations from Pausanias's *A Greek Walkabout* parenthetically in the text.

7. For more on this term, see O. A. W. Dilke, *Greek and Roman Maps* (Ithaca, NY: Cornell University Press, 1985), 23–24, 112–144; James Romm, *The Edges of the Earth in Ancient Thought* (Princeton, NJ: Princeton University Press, 1992), 3–8, 26–31; and Christian Habicht, *Pausanias' Guide to Ancient Greece* (Berkeley: University of California Press, 1985), 1–6.

Of related interest is Denis Cosgrove, *Apollo's Eye: A Cartographic Genealogy of the Earth in the Western Imagination* (Baltimore, MD: Johns Hopkins University Press, 2001).

8. Since my analysis in this chapter and in the following one makes so much of material culture as evidence for religiosity in the ancient world, a survey of the archaeological record is warranted here.

Olympia was excavated briefly by the French in 1829, and has been excavated periodically by the Germans since 1874 (1875–1881, 1936–1941, 1952 -). Delphi was excavated by the French and Germans in collaboration (1838–1861), and has been excavated exclusively by the French since 1892. Eleusis has been a thriving Greek excavation throughout much of the twentieth century. Each of these sites has generated an enormous bibliography, much of it available only in the language of the excavators. I provide a summary of the essential materials here:

Olympia:

German archaeologists have been excavating at Olympia since 1875, as I say. The most important figures in that work have been: Arthur Furtwängler (1875–1881), William Dörpfeld (in the 1920s), Emil Kunze (1937–1942), and Alfred Mallwitz (from the late 1960s into the early 1990s). The Deutsches Archaeologisches Institut has published a series entitled *Olympische Forschungen* (Berlin: Walter de Gruyter) since 1944, and has produced nearly thirty volumes to date. More recent work at Olympia has been summarized by Alfred Mallwitz, in *Olympia und Seine Bauten* (Darmstadt: Wissenschaftliche Buchgesellschaft, 1972), as well as in "Cult and Competition Locations at Olympia," in Wendy E. Raschke, ed., *The Archaeology of the Olympics: The Olympics and Other Festivals of Antiquity* (Madison: University of Wisconsin Press, 1988), 79–109.

The earlier work of E. Norman Gardiner, *Olympia: Its History and Remains* (Oxford: The Clarendon Press, 1925) is badly out of date, but several good modern guides are available in English, notably: Bernard Ashmole and Nicolaos Yalouris, *Olympia: The Sculpture of the Temple of Zeus* (London: Phaidon Press, 1967); Athanasia and Nicolaos Yalouris, *Olympia: The Museum and the Sanctuary* (Athens: Ekdotike Athenon, S.A., 1998); and Spyros Photinos, *Olympia: Complete Guide,* trans. Tina McGeorge and Colin MacDonald (Athens: Olympic Publications, 1989).

Delphi:

L'Ecole Francaise d'Athenes has published a lovely series entitled *Fouilles de Delphes* (Paris: E. de Boccard) since 1927, and has produced some 40 volumes to date. An impressive body of work on specific features of the complex also exists, most of it in French: Pierre de la Coste-Messaliere, *Delphes* (Paris: Editions du Chêne, 1943) and *Les Trésors de Delphes* (Paris: Editions du Chêne, 1950); J. Pouilloux et G. Roux, *Enigmes à Delphes* (Paris: Editions E. de Boccard, 1963); George Roux, *L'Amphictionie, Delphes et le Temple d'Apollo du IVe Siècle* (Paris: Diffusion de Boccard, 1979); Jean Francois Bommalier, *Guide de Delphes: Le Site* (Vol. I) and *Le Musée* (Vol. II) (Paris: Editions de Boccard, 1991); and Anne Jacqueman, *Offrandes Monumentales à Delphes* (Paris: De Boccard, 1999).

Several excellent summaries and guides are also available in English. In addition to Peter Hoyle's *Delphi* (London: Cassell, 1967), several guides have been made available by the Greek Ministry of Archaeology, notably: Sonia di Neuhoff, *Delphi* (Athens: Apollo Editions, 1971); Alan Walker, *Delphi* (Athens: Lycabettus Press, 1977); and Petros G. Themelis, *Delphi: The Archaeological Site and the Museum* (Athens: Ekdotike Athenon, S.A., 1980).

Eleusis:

Greek archaeologists have been excavating at Eleusis since the 1880s, and the names of her directors comprise a virtual roll-call of the previous generation in Greek archaeology: Demetrios Philios (1882–1890); Andreas Skias (1894–1907); Konstantinios Kourouniotes (with Anastasios Orbados and John Travlos, 1917–1945). Their proceedings were published rather unsystematically in a variety of Greek publications, most notably *Praktika* (1882–1890, 1892–1898, 1902, 1918–1920, 1935–1937), *Archaies Ephêmeres* (1886–1890, 1892, 1894–1899, 1901, 1912), and *Deltion* (1930–1935). Kourouniotes also published *Eleusiniaka* (Athêna: Estia, 1932) in two volumes, at the conclusion of his tenure at the site. An important German publication of the same period is Ferdinand Noack, *Eleusis: Die Baugeschichte Entwicklung des Heiligtumes* (Berlin: Walter de Gruyter & Co., 1927).

Far and away the most significant figure at Eleusis, however, was the late George E. Mylonas, who took control of the excavation in 1945, and who wrote extensively about Eleusis both in Greek and in English. Nice summaries of his work are available in *The Hymn to Demeter and the Sanctuary of Eleusis* (St. Louis: Washington University Studies No.13, 1942), and *Eleusis and the Eleusinian Mysteries* (Princeton: Princeton University Press, 1961). Mylonas also provides a helpful summary of ancient Christian writings about the Mysteries celebrated at Eleusis, and demonstrates compellingly why they are not to be trusted, in *Martyriai Christianôn Syngrapheôn dia ta Mysteria tês Eleusinas* (Athêna: 1959), with an English summary at 61–62. In addition, Mylonas published *Proistorikê Eleusis* (Athêna: Estia, 1932), and a three-volume study on the western cemetary, *To Dydikon Nekrotapheion tês Eleusinas* (Athêna: Archaiologikê Etairea, 1975). Other significant Greek studies include: Vas. Vl. Sphyroera and Polly Alexopoulou-Baba, *Istôria tês Eleusinas: Apo tên Archaiotêta mechri Sêmera* (Dêmos Eleusinas, 1985); Demosthenes G. Ziro, *H Kyria Eisodos tou Ierou tês Eleusinas* (Athêna: Archaia Etairea, 1991); Konstantinas Kokkou-Vyridê, *Eleusis: Proimes Myres Thysiôn sto Telestêrio tês Eleusinas* (Athêna: Archaia Etairea, 1999).

Finally, a good English guide to the site is Kalliope Prera-Alexandris, *Eleusis* (Athens: Ministry of Culture, 1991).

9. A telling indication of what Pausanias is after comes in a parenthetic reference to the city of Lepreus in Eleia:

> The so-called Lepreans told me that there was once a temple (*naon*) of Zeus Leukaios as well as the grave (*taphon*) of Lykourgos, son of Aleus, and another of Kaukon in their city. . . . But I saw no memorial (*mnêma*) there myself and no sanctuary (*hieron*) except one for Demeter. Yet this was built of unbaked brick (*plinthou*), and did not even have a statue (*agalma*). (V.5.5–6)

Pausanias, then, seems interested almost exclusively in monumental *architecture*, primarily in marble or local stone, as well as in *statues* rendered in an impressive variety of media, from wood, to marble, to bronze, to ivory and gold.

10. See my "The Ethos of Olympism: The Religious Meaning of the Modern Olympic Movement," *Soundings* 81.1/2 (1998): 292–295, material that is developed and expanded in the ninth chapter.

11. See Frazer, *Pausanias' Description of Greece,* II, 502–514.

   For an account of the myth and some excellent critical commentary, see Helene P. Foley, ed. and trans., *The Homeric Hymn to Demeter: Translation, Commentary and Interpretive Essays* (Princeton: Princeton University Press, 1994).

12. As Patricia Cox Miller notes, Pausanias pays more particular attention to dreams and divination at the Asklepius sanctuaries in Epidauros and elsewhere. See *Dreams in Late Antiquity: Studies in the Imagination of a Culture* (Princeton: Princeton University Press, 1994), 33, 109–117.

13. Habicht, *Pausanias' Guide to Ancient Greece,* 156.

14. For more on Erechtheus and his comparatively late incorporation into the cult of Athena, see Walter Burkert, *Greek Religion,* trans. John Raffan (Cambridge, MA: Harvard University Press, 1985), 49–50.

15. Karim W. Arafat notices that Pausanias rarely deals with Roman dedications or inscriptions in his analysis of these sites at all. See *Pausanias' Greece: Ancient Artists and Roman Rulers* (New York: Cambridge University Press, 1996), 211–213.

16. David Konstan pointed me toward an especially funny example—although significantly, it appears in Book VI, which I do not think could have been organized any better than the sanctuary itself was, when Pausanias visited it. Here is the offending passage:

On the right of the temple of Hera is the statue of a wrestler, Symmachus the
son of Aeschylus. He was an Elean by birth. Beside him is Neolaidas, son of
Proxenus, from Pheneus in Arcadia, who won a victory in the boys' boxing-
match. Next comes Archedamus, son of Xenius, another Elean by birth, who
like Symmachus overthrew wrestlers in the contest for boys. The statues of
the athletes mentioned above were made by Alypus of Sicyon, pupil of
Naucydes of Argos. The inscription on Cleogenes the son of Silenus declares
that he was a native, and that he won a prize with a riding-horse from his
own private stable. Hard by Cleogenes are set up Deinolochus, son of
Pyrrhus, and Troilus, son of Alcinous. These also were both Eleans by birth,
though their victories were not the same. Troilus, at the time that he was umpire, succeeded in winning victories in the chariot-races, one for a chariot
drawn by foals. The date of his victories was the hundred and second Festival. After this the Eleans passed a law that in future no umpire was to compete in chariot-races. The statue of Troilus was made by Lysipppus. The
mother of Deinolochus had a dream, in which she thought that the son she
clasped in her bosom had a crown on his head. For this reason Deinolochus
was trained to compete in the games and outran the boys. The artist was
Cleon of Sicyon.

Konstan adds an important point: if one simply reads such accounts aloud, slowly,
then they take on a far more pleasing conversational tone. Their details also become
far easier to process.

17. See Gregory Nagy, *The Best of the Achaeans: Concepts of the Hero in Archaic Greek Poetry,* 2nd
ed. (Baltimore, MD: Johns Hopkins University Press, 1999), Chapter 6, esp. 116, for
some telling comments regarding the conflict between the hero's locality, and the uni-
versalism of premier Panhellenic sites such as Delphi and Olympia. See also Burkert,
Greek Religion, 190–215.

18. Calasso, *The Marriage of Cadmus and Harmony,* 169.

19. The traditional (re)founding date of the quadrennial Games at Olympia was 776 BCE.
Delphi added her own contests, the Pythian Games, in 586 BCE. Then Isthmia (581
BCE) and Nemea (570 BCE) rapidly followed suit, creating the formal, Classical system in which there would presumably have been a Panhellenic contest held somewhere each and every year.

See Joseph Fontenrose, "The Cult of Apollo and the Games at Delphi," in Raschke,
ed., *The Archaeology of the Olympics,* 121–140, esp.124, and Walter Burkert, *Greek Religion,*
105–106.

Strangely enough, Pausanias assumes that the Isthmian games already existed when
Herakles and Iphitos revived a version of the Olympic contests (V.2.1–2). This would
seem to imply that the Olympics were not the first such athletic festivals in antiquity.

20. Catherine Morgan, *Athletes and Oracles: The Transformation of Olympia and Delphi in the Eighth
Century BC* (New York: Cambridge University Press, 1990), 1–25, 191–194.

21. This seems to have been a point of some note to Pausanias, as it doubtless was to others in Pausanias's day. Pythagoras, for instance, was renowned throughout antiquity
for refusing meat sacrifices of all kinds, as Philostratus relates in his *Life of Apollonius of
Tyana,* F. C. Corybeane, ed., in the Loeb Classical Library (Cambridge, MA: Harvard
University Press, 1917, 1989), 2–9.

For an excellent collection discussing the various politics associated with meat-
eating and animal sacrifice in antiquity, see Marcel Detienne and Jean-Pierre Vernant, *The Cuisine of Sacrifice Among the Ancient Greeks,* trans. Paula Wissig (Chicago: University of Chicago Press, 1989).

A quite remarkable and pathbreaking contemporary treatment of these and related issues is Carol J. Adams, *The Sexual Politics of Meat: A Feminist-Vegetarian Critical Theory* (New York: Continuum Press, 1990).

22. See Alfred Mallwitz, "Cult and Competition Locations at Olympia," in Raschke, ed., *The Archaeology of the Olympics,* 102–103.

23. Xenophon, *Hellenika* VII.4.28, and Mallwitz, "Cult and Competition Location at Olympia," 94.

24. Pausanias relates an especially strange story to emphasize this point (V.2.1–2). When Herakles marched against King Augeas of Elis, who failed to pay him for his famous labor in the stables, he was unable to accomplish anything of significance. Augeas, it seems, had powerful allies, all of them at the peak of their strength and confidence. So Herakles ambushed and killed two of them, the sons of Aktor, who were on their way to compete in the Isthmian Games, and thus were under the nominal protection of the Corinthian truce. Herakles was living in Tiryns when the crime was later discovered, and Elis demanded that Argos remand him to their justice, but the Argives refused to comply. Even in his day, Pausanias notes, Elean athletes do not compete in the Isthmian (or Nemean?) Games for this reason.

25. For an analysis of Pausanias's complex attitudes—toward Mummius specifically, and toward Rome more generally—see Arafat, *Pausanias' Greece,* 89–97.

26. Pausanias specifically mentions the fact that Mummius dedicated twenty-one gilded shields at the Temple of Zeus in Olympia, as a way to commemorate his savaging of Corinth (V.10.5). Tellingly, he calls this "offering" an *anathêma,* and says nothing more about it.

27. Pausanias tells us that this refounding took place 217 years previously, thus indicating that he wrote the Eleian material in 174 CE, during the reign of Marcus Aurelius. The only internal allusion that may be dated later than this one is to Roman victories over Germans and Sarmatians in the summer of 175 CE (VIII.43.6).

For a helpful account of the formal strategy of colonizing and settling military veterans in conquered territories, and the importance of coherent land surveys in so doing, see Brian Campbell, "Shaping the Rural Environment: Surveyors in Ancient Rome," *Journal of Roman Studies* 86 (1996): 74–99, esp. 94–98.

For the specific history at Corinth, see David Gilman Romano, "A Tale of Two Cities: Roman Colonies at Corinth," in Elisabeth Fentress, ed., *Romanization and the City: Creation, Transformations, and Failures,* Journal of Roman Archaeology Supplementary Series, No. 38 (2000): 83–104.

28. Calasso, *The Marriage of Cadmus and Harmony,* 93. I quoted this passage in the beginning of the previous chapter.

29. For more on the lore surrounding these mysterious northern peoples, see Romm, *The Edges of the Earth in Ancient Thought,* 60–67.

30. This is not to deny the indebtedness of Archaic and Classical Greek athletic innovations to their forebears. But, as in most other areas, the Greeks decisively changed whatever they appropriated. See Labib Boutros, *Phoenician Sport: Its Influence on the Origin of the Olympic Games* (Amsterdam: J. C. Gieben, Publishers, 1981), as well as Colin Renfrew, "The Minoan-Mycenaean Origins of the Panhellenic Games," and Jaan Puhvel, "Hittite Athletics as Prefigurations of Ancient Greek Games," in Raschke, ed., *The Archaeology of the Olympics,* 13–31.

31. This term raises yet another transnational dilemma for us. *Agôn* has a resonance in Greek somewhat at odds with the common English rendering of "game." The German *Spiele* and French *Jeux* probably capture the performative and theatrical elements of the Olympics better. I suspect that "Olympic play" is an ideal translation of the Greek idea, but it sounds so odd to the English ear that I have settled on the inadequate compromise of "contest."

For more on this problem, see Christopher Lasch, *The Culture of Narcissism: American Life in an Age of Diminishing Expectations* (New York: W. W. Norton & Company, Inc., 1979), 181–219.

32. Nagy, *The Best of the Achaeans,* 114ff.

33. Pausanias clearly assumes that political control of the region and custodial leadership at the sanctuary are entirely separable things. This distinction was formalized at a later date, in the years after Iphitos's Olympic revival, whereby the Eleans appointed two citizens who were chosen by lot to preside together (literally, they "do the Olympics," *poiêsthai ta Olympia*). In 400 BCE, nine Greek Judgers (*Hellênodikai*) were established as the formal Olympic leadership. In 396 BCE, a tenth was added. In 368 BCE, their number was increased to 12, but in 348 BCE, it returned to ten. This essentially *religious,* as opposed to *political,* structure in Eleia survived into Pausanias's own times (V.9.4–6).

34. A play on the language of Exodus 1:8.

35. Habicht, *Pausanias' Guide to Ancient Greece,* 17–19.

36. This point is well made by David Konstan in "The Joys of Pausanias," Susan E. Alcock, John F. Cherry and John Elsner, eds., *Pausanias: Travel and Memory in Roman Greece* (New York: Oxford University Press, 2001), 57–60.

Roberto Calasso relies especially on Pausanias for his own storyteller's art, especially when he turns to the vast topic of Olympia. See *The Marriage of Cadmus and Harmony,* 169–193.

37. For a nice overview of the literary culture of the period, see G. Bowersock, *Greek Sophists in the Roman Empire* (New York: Oxford University Press, 1969), as well as Ian Rutherford, *Canons of Style in the Antonine Age* (New York: Oxford University Press, 1998).

38. There is an enormous bibliography attached to this emperor and this moment in imperial history. Much of the modern fascination derives, curiously enough, from an historical novel written by Marguerite Yourcenar, *Memoirs of Hadrian,* trans. Grace Frick and the author (New York: Farrar, Straus, Giroux, 1954). The novel has had an enormous influence on my own scholarly practice, as I try to show in "Clio and Melpomene: In Defense of the Historical Novel," *Historical Researches* 23.3 (1997): 389–418.

In a more traditional vein, see Stewart Perowne, *Hadrian* (London: Hodder and Stoughton, 1960), 96–129; and Anthony R. Birley, *Hadrian: The Restless Emperor* (New York: Routledge, 1997), 58–65, 151–188, 259–278. For Hadrian's classicizing transformation of the imperial city, see Mary T. Boatwright, *Hadrian and the City of Rome* (Princeton: University of Princeton Press, 1987) and Dietrich Willers, *Hadrians Panhellenisches Programm: Archäologisches Beitrage zur Neugestaltung Athens durch Hadrian* (Basel: 1990).

39. See William L. MacDonald and Julian A. Pinto, *Hadrian's Villa and Its Legacy* (New Haven, CT: Yale University Press, 1995).

40. I am pleased to note that Simon Swain nonetheless devotes a chapter to Pausanias in his *Hellenism and Empire: Language, Classicism and Power in the Greek World, AD 50–250* (New York: Oxford University Press, 1996), 330–356, paying special attention to the complexity of his political attitudes *vis à vis* Rome and Roman power. For more on Pausanias's specific brand of "archaism," see Arafat, *Pausanias' Greece,* 24–27.

41. A powerful contemporary critique of the "encyclopedic" mentality has been made by Alasdair MacIntyre, in *Three Rival Versions of Moral Enquiry: Encyclopedia, Genealogy, Tradition* (Notre Dame, IN: University of Notre Dame Press, 1990), 9–31, 170–195. At its core, as I indicated in Chapter One, MacIntyre's quarrel with what he refers to as "encyclopedic " knowledge is the way in which such knowledge is ahistorical, failing to locate social practices in the societies and the cultures that give them both credibility

and coherence. Such a charge cannot really be leveled against Pausanias's Greek encyclopedia, which *is* legitimately historical, albeit in a nonmodern way. Pausanias, I am
arguing, attempts to represent a legitimate way of knowing the world when knowledge of *historical origins* is unavailable.

    I am indebted to Michael Maas for helping me to see this point in this way.

42. This style should be called the "second" (*deuteran*) Sophistic, rather than the "new"
    (*nean*) one, since it is itself so very ancient (*archaia*), as Philostratus tells us at the out-
    set of his *Lives of the Sophists,* 481.

    For the Greek text of Philostratus, I am using the Loeb Classical edition by Wilbur
    C. Wright (Cambridge, MA: Harvard University Press, 1952, 1989), 6–7.

43. While lying outside the scope of my present purposes, it seems important to add that
    the Christian Apologetic tradition, with its curious love-hate relationship to Classi-
    cal culture, also participates in this same aesthetic. For an initial pass at their specific
    interests in sculpture (and thus, correlatively, in idolatry), see my "Athenagoras the
    Christian, Pausanias the Travel-Guide, and a Mysterious Corinthian Girl," *Harvard*
    Theological Review 85.1 (1992): 35–49.

    Finally, I cannot avoid mention of Publius Aelius Aristides (117–c. 182 CE), a *precise*
    contemporary of Pausanias, who also hailed from coastal Asia Minor. While an analy-
    sis of Aelius's strange *ouevre* lies outide my present purposes, his *Roman Encomium,*
    which if sincerely intended, is fawning to the point of nauseation, may also be read as
    having a more subversive purpose. Greeks in Pausanias's and Aelius's day knew how
    important the institutional and financial support of philhellenic emperors like
    Hadrian had been to the eastern provinces; they also knew how devastating Roman
    impatience with Greek revolution could be, and the smoking ruins of Corinth are
    clearly much on Pausanias's mind. Encomia aside, Greeks writing about Rome in this
    period display a two-sided anxiety, a concern that Roman friendship will prove more
    lasting than it often was in practice.

    For a nicely nuanced presentation of Pausanias's ambivalent and complex attitudes
    toward Rome, see Arafat, *Pausanias' Greece,* esp. 202–215.

44. This place was famous in antiquity as the realm of Tantalus, Niobe, and Pelops
    (V.13.7), the latter of whom will play a major role in Pausanias's account of Olympia.

    See Habicht, *Pausanias' Guide to Ancient Greece,* 13–16.

45. Two other possibilities suggest themselves. On the one hand, according to later Greek
    and Roman myth, Sardinia was where Daedalus finally settled, then later died or dis-
    appeared. Daedalus, as we have seen, was a major preoccupation for both Plato and
    Pausanias.

    On the other hand, it may simply be the case that the process of Romanization was
    truncated, logistically and culturally, on Sardinia, much as many Hellenes doubtless
    hoped it would be in Greece proper. Sardinians and Greeks, on this view, might be
    read as "brothers in the same distress," to borrow a phrase from Simone Weil. See
    Stephen L. Dyson, "The Limited Nature of Roman Urbanism in Sardinia," in Fen-
    tress, ed., *Romanization and the City,* 189–196.

46. Pliny refers famously (Book VIII, Letter #24) to "the province of Achaia, . . . the
    pure and genuine Greece, where civilization and literature, and agriculture, too, are
    believed to have originated."

47. It is a source of endless delight to me, each and every summer, to see these same re-
    gional place names persisting in the modern bus station in Athens.

48. See E. L. Bowie, "Greeks and Their Past in the Second Sophistic," *Past & Present* 46
    (1970): 3–41.

49. See Pierre Lévêque and Pierre Vidal-Naquet, *Cleisthenes the Athenian: An Essay on the Rep-*
    resentation of Space and Time in Greek Political Thought from the Sixth Century to the Death of Plato,
    trans. David Ames Curtis (Atlantic Highlands, NJ: Humanities Press, 1996), 80ff,

for an analysis of the way in which political interests in local place combined with
then-emerging cartographic interests of the Aegean Greeks.

50. See Alcock, *Graecia Capta*, 174–175; as well as John Elsner, "Pausanias: A Greek Pilgrim
in the Roman World," *Past and Present* 135 (1992): 3–29.

Elsner is particularly apt: he suggests that, in Pausanias, we have one of the very earliest literary examples of religious and ethnic identity merging in a highly self-conscious way. Pausanias, he suggests, is negotiating his own *Greek* identity in a somewhat
foreign, and potentially hostile, *Roman* world. What I wish to add to that crucial insight is the point that joins these two terms: that for Pausanias, "being Greek" has
come to have a decidedly *religious* value.

51. Habicht, *Pausanias' Guide to Ancient Greece,* 11–12, 17–19, 141.

52. The nature of Pausanias's piety—like Socrates's—is not always clear. Echoing a similar trope in Herodotus, he tells us that he feels "bound (*anankê*) to record the Greek
traditions (*ta hypo Hellênôn legomena*), but not bound (*anankê*) to believe them all"
(VI.3.8; see also II.17.4). Later, however—once again in the region of Arkadia, which
clearly made a major impression on his religious sensibilities—Pausanias develops a
more nuanced view of the matter:

When I began to catalogue these Greek stories (*toutois Hellênôn tois logois*) I took
them for nonsense (*euêthias enemon pleon*), but when I got as far as Arkadia I
took a more thoughtful view of them. Those among the Greeks (*Hellênôn*)
who were considered wise (*sophous*) a long time ago spoke in riddles (*ainig-
matôn*) and did not speak straight out (*ouk ek tou eutheos legein tous logous*). Thus
the legends about Kronos now seem to me to be one kind of Greek wisdom
(*sophian Hellênôn*). When it comes to the divine (*to theion*), then, I shall make
use of received tradition. (VIII.8.3–4)

53. We meet another, stranger version of this tale at Corinth. Pausanias begins by referring to Zeus's assault on Aegina, the daughter of Asopus. The father is required to give
a gift to the king of the city—namely, a spring on the Akrocorinth—which inspires
Sisyphus to turn informant, and thus to inform Asopus that Zeus was the culprit. For
this, Sisyphus is punished eternally by Zeus (*hotôi pista,* "if anyone can believe it," he
adds, [II.5.1]). Some say that this spring and the one in Peirene are part of the same
waterway, and while Pausanias is ambivalent about this story, it does remind him of
similar stories he has heard about the Nile. The people at Delos insist that the waters
of the Inopus actually come to them from the Nile (*ek tou Neílou*), whose waters in turn
come from the Euphrates, which disappears into a marsh (*es helos aphanizesthai*) and
then reemerges beyond Ethiopia to become a part of the Nile itself (*authis anionta hyper
Aithiopias Neílon ginesthai,* [II.2.3]).

This presents the extraordinary possibility of a single body of nonoceanic water that
links Greece to both Egypt and Asia. Such interest in the miraculous course of rivers
was a major preoccupation of the ancient geographers, a tradition Pausanias knows
well. See Romm, *The Edges of the Earth in Ancient Thought,* 121–171, esp. 149–156.

54. He goes on the describe the strange phenomenon of dead fishes which sink in this
river, and live ones which float, as well as the general aversion of all living things to its
waters. Elsewhere Pausanias compares Eleian flax and linen favorably to that of the
Hebrews (*Hebraíôn*) (V.5.2).

55. See Frazer, *Pausanias' Description of Greece,* II, 80–81. While he mentions Hadrian as
having *lived* in his own day, Pausanias seems to have composed his *Walkabout* well after
the Emperor's death in 138 CE. An allusion to Hadrian's favorite, Antinous
(VIII.9.7), suggests that Pausanias *could* have lain eyes on the boy, but did not. An
emerging scholarly consensus thus assigns Pausanias a birth date at sometime around
115 CE.

56. For a fascinating analysis of the model of imperial pilgrimage—notably to "Greece" and "the east"—as articulated by Hadrian especially, as well as for the impact it had on later pilgrimage in the Christian era, see Kenneth G. Holum, "Hadrian and St. Helena: Imperial Travel and the Origins of Christian Holy Land Pilgrimage," in Robert Ousterhout, ed., *The Blessings of Pilgrimage* (Urbana: University of Illinois Press, 1990), 66–81.

57. Athanasia and Nicolaos Yalouris, *Olympia: The Museum and the Sanctuary*, 154–157.

58. See also Frazer, *Pausanias' Description of Greece*, III, 595–599.

59. For more on Pausanias's complex relationship to his conception of the past, see Arafat, *Pausanias' Greece*, 43–79.

60. We should hear an echo of the *Euthyphro* here, where the gods are committed to newness (*neôtera*), or nothing.

61. See Frazer, *Pausanias' Description of Greece*, IV, 352–354.

62. Levi, ed., *Pausanias: Guide to Greece*, Volume I, 3.

63. See Frazer, *Pausanias' Description of Greece*, IV, 188–190, as well as the positively luminous modern meditation on this ancient, more enchanted world and worldview, in Calasso's *The Marriage of Cadmus and Harmony*, 349–351, 385–387, which has had such an enduring influence on my reading of Pausanias.

64. Calasso, *The Marriage of Cadmus and Harmony*, 10.

65. Mallwitz, "Cult and Competition Locations at Olympia," in Raschke, ed., *The Archaeology of the Olympics*, 87.

66. Mallwitz, "Cult and Competition Locations at Olympia," in Raschke, ed., *The Archaeology of the Olympics*, 79–81, 99.

67. Calasso, *The Marriage of Cadmus and Harmony*, 9.

68. See the excellent presentation of this point in Tomuko Masuzawa, *In Search of Dreamtime: The Quest for the Origin of Religion* (Chicago: University of Chicago Press, 1993).

69. Daniel Fallon, *The German University: A Heroic Ideal in Conflict with the Modern World* (Colorado Associated University Press, 1980).

For more on the specifically religious and theological dimension of this reorganization, see Richard Crouter, "Hegel and Schleiermacher: A Many-Sided Debate," *Journal of the American Academy of Religion* 48 (1979): 19–43, and Hans Frei, *Types of Christian Theology* (New Haven, CT: Yale University Press, 1992), 95–132.

70. I am thinking of the course of lectures which were posthumously edited and published by his son as *Lectures on the Philosophy of History*, trans. J. Sibree (New York: Dover Publications, 1956).

71. For a critique of such intellectual periodizations, see *Afterwords*, 3–10, 23, 69, 164–169.

72. James Ussher (1581–1656) Bishop of Armagh and Primate of Ireland, formally dated the creation of the world to October 23, 4004 BCE, in his highly influential *Annals of the Old and New Testaments with the Synchronisms of Heathen Story to the Destruction of Hierusalem by the Romans* (London: Tyler & Crook, 1658). He went on to say:

Nor truly is it strange that Heathens, altogether ignorant of holy writ, should thus despair, of ever attaining the knowledge of the World's *Rise* . . . (A-3)

73. As Erich Auerbach famously observed, "The Bible's claim to truth is not only more urgent than Homer's, it is tyrranical—it excludes all other claims." See *Mimesis: The Representation of Reality in Western Literature*, trans. Willard R. Trask (Princeton: Princeton University Press, 1945), 14.

For a fascinating critique of Auerbach's decision (itself heir to fully a century of prior scholarship) to compare Hebrew and Greek narrative strategies, see Vassilis Lambropoulos, *The Rise of Eurocentrism: Anatomy of Interpretation* (Princeton: Princeton University Press, 1993) 3–16, 24–41.

1. Orosius, *Historiae adversus paganos*, Prologue 9. For an English version of Orosius, see Paulus Orosius, *The Seven Books of History Against the Pagans*, translated by Roy J. Deferrari (Washington, DC: Catholic University of America Press, 1964).

   According to Orosius's own account, he was commissioned for this project by Augustine. In completing it, he used Augustine's charter metaphor of the "city of God" to add a polemical edge to the religious status of the countryside:

   > You bade me speak out in opposition to the empty perversity of those who, alien to the City of God, are called "pagans" (*pagani*) from the crossroads and villages of country places, or "heathen" (*gentiles*) because of their knowledge of earthly things (*terrena*).

   For more on changing conceptions of the city in late antiquity, see Robert T. Marcuse, ed., *Aspects of Graeco-Roman Urbanism: Essays on the Classical City* (Oxford: BAR International Series, 1983), and John Rich, ed., *The City in Late Antiquity* (New York: Routledge, 1992). For an intriguing *economic* analysis of the troubled relationship between Rome, as *the* city, and the countryside on which it depended for food and raw materials, see Neville Morley, *Metropolis and Hinterland: The City of Rome and the Italian Economy, 200 BC-AD 200* (New York: Cambridge University Press, 1996).

2. For more on the disciplinary assumptions of anthropology as grounded in some of the same premises which underwrote Victorian empire-building, see Clifford Geertz, *Works and Lives: The Anthropologist as Author* (Palo Alto, CA: Stanford University Press, 1988), 1–24.

   The "encyclopedic" assumptions of such Victorian anthropology have been criticized by Alasdair MacIntyre in *Three Rival Versions of Moral Enquiry: Encyclopedia, Genealogy, Tradition* (Notre Dame, IN: University of Notre Dame Press, 1990), 178–186, as I noted in the previous chapter. But a more sophisticated critical reading of Frazer's project may be found in Ludwig Wittgenstein, *Remarks on Frazer's Golden Bough*, edited by Rush Rhees and translated by A. C. Miles (Atlantic Highlands, NJ: Humanities Press, 1979).

   For a nice introduction to the way in which the emerging discipline of anthropology intersected with, and contributed to the creation of, the comparative study of religion, see Daniel L. Pals, *Seven Theories of Religion* (New York: Oxford University Press, 1996), with pages 16–53 specifically devoted to Tylor's and Frazer's work.

   For an elegant attempt to move beyond such culturally imperialist categories, and thus to write ethnography from the "inside" as well as from the "outside," see Karen McCarthy Brown, *Mama Lola: A Vodou Priestess in Brooklyn* (Berkeley: University of California Press, 1987), 1–20.

3. I have already devoted a book to this topic. See *Afterwords: Hellenism, Modernism and the Myth of Decadence* (Albany: State University of New York Press, 1996).

   There is a Christian precedent to such reasoning, in which antiquity can serve as a proof of legitimacy. See Arthur J. Droge, *Homer or Moses? Early Christian Interpretations of the History of Culture* (Tübingen: J.C.B. Mohr Verlag, 1989), esp. 168–193.

4. Several prominent names are associated with the comparatively recent explosion of scholarly interest in this period, most notably, Glen W. Bowersock, Peter Brown, and Averil Cameron. For a representative sampling of the recent scholarship in this area, and its astonishing range of interests, see:

   G. W. Bowersock, *Hellenism in Late Antiquity* (New York: Cambridge University Press, 1990);

Peter Brown, *The Body and Society: Men, Women and Sexual Renunciation in Early Christianity* (Berkeley: University of California Press, 1991),

——. *The Cult of the Saints: Its Rise and Function in Latin Christianity* (Chicago: University of Chicago Press, 1981),

——. *The Making of Late Antiquity* (Cambridge, MA: Harvard University Press, 1978),

——. *Power and Persuasion in Late Antiquity: Towards a Christian Empire* (Madison: Wisconsin University Press, 1992), and

——. *Society and the Holy in Late Antiquity* (London: Faber and Faber, 1982);

G. W. Bowersock, Peter Brown and Oleg Grabar, eds., *Late Antiquity: A Guide to the Postclassical World* (Cambridge, MA: Harvard University Press, 1999);

Averil Cameron, *Christianity and the Rhetoric of Empire: The Development of Christian Discourse* (Berkeley: University of California Press, 1991),

——. *The Later Roman Empire: AD 284–430* (Cambridge, MA: Harvard University Press, 1993), esp. 85–98 on "The Reign of Julian."

——. *The Mediterranean World in Late Antiquity, 395–600* (New York: Routledge, 1993).

Two other extremely helpful collections are Michael Maas, ed., *Readings in Late Antiquity: A Sourcebook* (New York: Routledge, 2000), and Richard Miles, ed., *Constructing Identities in Late Antiquity* (New York: Routledge, 1999).

5. Polymnia Athanassiadi suggests conceiving of "late antiquity" as the era which takes us "from Augustus to Muhammed," that is, through some six hundred years of Mediterranean history in the Common Era, the epoch in which Christianity emerges as the dominant religion of the empire, but which is itself sandwiched between two other equally coherent world religions: imperial paganism, on the one hand; and Islam, on the other.

 In this she is expanding on the prior suggestion of Peter Brown in his *The World of Late Antiquity From Marcus Aurelius to Muhammed* (London: Thames and Hudson, 1971).

6. A point made decisively by Arnaldo Momigliano in *The Conflict Between Paganism and Christianity in the Fourth Century* (New York: Oxford University Press, 1963).

7. I place this term in quotation marks because debate rages over how Constantine understood the faith to which he had "converted," and the obligations which such a "conversion" laid upon him. What is clear is that he did not understand "conversion" to Christianity in particularly *exclusive* terms, which is to say, as incompatible with the material culture of traditional Roman religion and the panoply of contemporary cults. That would become a *later* Christian preoccupation.

 For a presentation of this conversion as both genuine and heartfelt, see Timothy D. Barnes, *Constantine and Eusebius* (Cambridge, MA: Harvard University Press, 1981), 42–43, 74–76, 269–275. For a particularly nuanced view somewhat closer to my own, see H. A. Drake, *Constantine and the Bishops: The Politics of Intolerance* (Baltimore, MD: Johns Hopkins University Press, 2000), 187–191, 307–308, 393–394.

8. Or so it has been alleged; I will have far more to say about that claim at the end of this chapter.

9. The primary ancient sources for Julian's reign and his attempt to repaganize the Empire, are several. First and foremost, Julian himself left an impressive body of letters, imperial decrees, hymns, satirical essays, and polemical pamphlets, all of which were written in Greek. *The Works of the Emperor Julian* are available in three volumes in the Loeb Classical Library, edited by Wilmer Cave Wright (Cambridge, MA: Harvard University Press, 1923, 1996).

 Julian's close contemporary and Antiochene friend, Libanius (314–391 CE; he was one of John Chrysostom's teachers in Antioch), also dedicated a large body of oratory to Julian's name and subsequent reputation, as well as an even larger body of autobiographical writings and epistolary orations, all available in four Loeb volumes, edited by A. F. Norman (Cambridge, MA: Harvard University Press, 1969, 1992).

Two other Late Antique historians supplement our knowledge of Julian's troubled reign. Ammianus Marcellinus's (c. 330–395 CE) *Histories*, composed in Latin, covers the reigns of Constantius II, Julian, Jovian, Valentinian and Valens, and is quite favorably disposed to Julian, with whom the author had served both in Gaul and in the east. This *History* is available in three Loeb volumes, edited by John C. Rolfe (Cambridge, MA: Harvard University Press, 1935, 1965). Ammianus has been the recipient of considerable scholarly attention ever since Erich Auerbach's discussion of his rhetorical style in *Mimesis: The Representation of Reality in Western Literature*, trans. Willard R. Trask (Princeton: Princeton University Press, 1954), 50–76. See also Arnaldo Momigliano, "The Lonely Historian Ammianus Marcellinus," in *Essays on Ancient and Modern Historiography* (Middletown, CT: Wesleyan University Press, 1977), 127–140.

Finally, Zosimus of Constantinople's *New History*, composed in six books in Greek, and completed at some point after 498 CE and prior to 518 CE (translated by Ronald Ridley [Canberra: Australian Association for Byzantine Studies, 1982]), is interesting for the way it develops an *anti*-Christian reading of imperial developments after Julian's brief reign. Zosimus provides an important counterpoint to the reports of such overtly Christian polemicists as Gregory of Nazianzus (329–389 CE) and John Chrysostom (c. 347–407 CE), as well as to the emerging tradition of Christian historiography embodied by such figures as Socrates of Constantinople (c. 380–450 CE, composer of a *Church History* in seven books), Sozomen of Bethelia (near Gaza, early fifth century CE, composer of a *Church History* in nine books), Philostorgius of Cappadocia (c. 368–c. 439 CE, an Arian church historian of whom little else is known), Rufinus of Aquileia (c. 345–410 CE), Theodoret of Cyrus (near Antioch, c. 393–458 CE), and Eunapius of Sardis (whose hugely influential *Church History* is now lost). Socrates's and Sozomen's *Histories* are available in English, translated by A. C. Zenos and Chester D. Hartranft in *Nicene and Post-Nicene Fathers, Second Series* (Peabody, MA: Hendrickson Publishers, 1994) Volume II. Theodoret's *Ecclesiastical History* is translated by the Rev. Blomfield Jackson in Volume III: 33–159.

I also rely on two modern biographies of Julian. G. W. Bowersock's *Julian the Apostate* (Cambridge, MA: Harvard University Press, 1978) presents an excellent historical summary of the man and his reign. Polymnia Athanassiadi's *Julian: An Intellectual Biography* (New York: Routledge, 1992, a reprint of her 1981 *Julian and Hellenism*) really deals less with Julian's career than with his lifelong endeavor to re-think the nature of "Hellenism" and his imperial responsibilities in its service. For this precise reason, hers has been a particularly provocative resource for much of my own thinking in this chapter.

10. See Athanassiadi, *Julian: An Intellectual Biography*, 24–27, and Bowersock, *Julian the Apostate*, 55–65.

11. A case in point is his *First Encomium to the Emperor Constantius*, where Julian manages to pay special attention to the emperor's subjugation of Celts and Gauls, "nations (*ethnê*) which seemed invincible (*dysantagônista*) in the past" (34c). This piece was probably penned in 355 CE, when Julian was preparing to set off to Gaul himself. So he praises the emperor, but also anticipates his own future successes in the same region. Julian returns to this issue in his *Second Encomium to the Emperor Constantius*, penned when he was well established in Gaul and had already secured the Rhinish frontier (56b). See *The Complete Works of the Emperor Julian*, I, 88–89 and 148–149.

Both of these encomia should be compared to what Julian says in his *Letter to the Council and People of Athens*, drafted in Illyricum in 361 CE, when he was actually on the march *against* Constantius. In this letter, he defends his actions by citing the murderous record of political assassination engaged in by the Emperor. This letter is available in *The Complete Works of the Emperor Julian* II, 242–291.

See also Libanius, *Epitaph for Julian*, Oration 18.8–20.

12. Constantine's father had children by two women: Helena, who was Constantine's mother, and Theodora, who gave birth to Julian's father, Julius Constantius. Moreover, Julian was married to Helena, the daughter of Constantine, linking him to the dynasty both by blood and by marriage.

13. These events are movingly summarized in his *Letter to the Council and People of Athens* 270c–273c, in *The Complete Works of the Emperor Julian* II, 248–255.

14. An event that Julian attributes to divine ordination in his *Letter to the Council and People of Athens* 284c–d, in *The Complete Works of the Emperor Julian* II, 282–283.

15. Libanius suggests (in *On Avenging Julian,* Oration 24.17–21)—given the fact that Julian alone was killed in this skirmish, and given that even his personal cohort escaped entirely unharmed—that the emperor was the victim of an assassination by his own people, presumably a Christian soldier who was upset by his pagan reforms. Libanius urges the new emperor, Theodosius, to investigate the matter and to punish the guilty parties. But, of course, Theodosius ultimately cast his lot decisively with the Christians.

16. Libanius, *Lament for Julian,* Oration 18.303, in *Libanius: Selected Works* I, 482–483.

17. By contrast, the far more damaging criticisms of Christianity penned by Celsus (fl. 175 CE) in his *Alêthês Logos* (best translated as *The True Doctrine,* perhaps) and by Porphyry (234–c. 305 CE) in *On Statues, The Philosophy of Oracles* and *Against the Christians,* all survive only in fragments, most of which derive from later Christian refutations of them. That Julian survives to speak in his own quixotic voice may be due to the fact that his efforts failed so dramatically. Later Christians clearly did not consider Julian a threat in the same way, and his strident polemics often ultimately worked *against* the very cases he was trying to make. Still, even here, not all of Julian's *Against the Galileans* survives.

18. I am thinking, of course, of the *Meditations,* a stunning depiction of the somber and duty-bound credo of Roman Stoicism in late antiquity. *Marcus Aurelius' Meditations* is available in a Loeb volume, ed. C. R. Haines (Cambridge, MA: Harvard University Press, 1953).

    Marcus was a major figure in Julian's roll-call of imperial honor, as we shall see later.

19. See Athanassiadi, *Julian: An Intellectual Biography,* 216–219.

20. See especially *The Order of Things: An Archaeology of the Human Sciences* (New York: Random House, 1966, 1970), 344–387. Later, Foucault would refer to this work as "genealogy," recognizing Nietzsche as the grandfather of this genealogical approach to critical thought.

    See his "Nietzsche, Genealogy, History," in Paul Rabinow, ed., *The Foucault Reader* (New York: Pantheon, 1984), 76–100.

21. One excellent example of an ancient historian with such modern sensibilities is Arnaldo Momigliano. See his "A Piedmontese View of the History of Ideas" and "Historicism Revisited," in *Essays in Ancient and Modern Historiography,* 1–7, 365–373.

22. Nietzsche was arguably the first to undertake such a project, and significantly, he did not complete it. Most of the notes for his decisive essay, "We Classicists," were drafted in 1875–1876, and may be found in William Arrowsmith, ed., *Nietzsche: Unmodern Observations* (New Haven, CT: Yale University Press, 1990), 321–387.

    For a summary discussion of this essay, see my "Nietzsche's Vision, Nietzsche's Greece," *Soundings* 73.1 (1990) 61–84.

    Of course, such a multidiscipline as "Classics" is now may be endlessly subdivided: into ancient archaeology, art, history, and literature. And each of these subdisciplines has developed in very different ways in different countries. For a fine example of a far more specific historical study, devoted to just such a national subfield, see Stephen L. Dyson, *Ancient Marbles to American Shores: Classical Archaeology in the United States* (Philadelphia, PA: University of Pennsylvania Press, 1998), esp. Chapter Four on "The Function of the Museum Tradition" (122–157), which will become a major preoccupation of my own in Chapter Eight.

23. The beginnings of this crucial intellectual detachment—of religion from theology—may best be located in the reorganization of the curriculum at the University of Berlin in 1809. For a general overview of Humboldt's educational reforms, see Daniel Fallon, *The German University: A Heroic Ideal in Conflict with the Modern World* (Colorado Associated University Press, 1980).

    For more on the implicit theological stakes of such a curricular reformulation, see Hans Frei, *Types of Christian Theology* (New Haven, CT: Yale University Press, 1992), 95–132. One of the "creators" both of the new notion of history *and* of the new mode of "comparing" religions was Hegel, and his influence was determinative. See Peter C. Hodgson, ed., *Hegel: Lectures on the Philosophy of Religion* (Berkeley: University of California Press, 1984) in two volumes. For some of the theological implications of this new approach, see Richard Crouter, "Hegel and Schleiermacher at Berlin: A Many-Sided Debate," *Journal of the American Academy of Religion* 48.1 (1980): 19–43.

24. Several excellent examples are Walter Capps, *Religious Studies: The Making of a Discipline* (Minneapolis, MN: Fortress Press, 1995), and Jon R. Stone, ed., *The Craft of Religious Studies* (New York: St. Martin's Press, 1998). Daniel L. Pals offers a helpful summary of the "evolution" of the "scientific" perception of the field from the early nineteenth to the late twentieth century in *Seven Theories of Religion.*

    A more complex treatment is Talal Asad's *Genealogies of Religion: Disciplines and Regimes of Power in Christianity and Islam* (Baltimore, MD: Johns Hopkins University Press, 1993). What seems at first blush to be a history of Religious Studies is actually a history of *anthropology,* the premier human science that dedicated itself to making sense of the evolution of the modern world, and that helped to create the category of "religion" as most subsequent scholars were to understand it. I find especially helpful Asad's suspicion of the usefulness of "belief" as a concept separable from religious practice (27–54), as well as his intriguing suggestion as to the complexity of medieval Christian relations to paganism (37n14).

25. A Protestant atheist is thus still a Protestant. For a discussion of this radical perspectivism, see H. Richard Niebuhr, *The Meaning of Revelation* (New York: Macmillan, 1941), 1–27. By this same logic, Christians were pagan atheists, much as Julian insisted in many of his polemics that they were.

26. For an attempt to cast a wider net in the anthropological study of religion, see the classic statement of Clifford Geertz, "Religion as a Cultural System," as well as the definitive display of his approach in "Deep Play: Notes on the Balinese Cockfight," in *The Interpretation of Cultures: Selected Essays* (New York: Basic Books, 1973), 87–125, 412–453.

    A more emphatically moral critique of this scripture-and-sermon model of religion, with its radically decontextualized way of thinking about religious practices, has been made by Alasdair MacIntyre and Stanley Hauerwas. Both men emphasize Roman Catholic, rather than Protestant, traditions, and both men put a premium on the concept of social practices rather than on doctrinal beliefs. Hauerwas, in particular, has emphasized the twinned modern practices of medicine and care for the mentally handicapped as a way to *display* his understanding of the nature of specifically Christian virtue.

    For the decisive definition of a "practice," see MacIntyre, *After Virtue,* 2nd ed. (South Bend, IN: University of Notre Dame Press, 1984), 187–188. For MacIntyre's first deliberate nod to the tradition of Catholic moral theology, see *Whose Justice? Which Rationality?* (Notre Dame, IN: University of Notre Dame Press, 1988), 1–11, 146–208.

    Hauerwas's Christian critique of biblicism appears in: *A Community of Character: Toward a Constructive Christian Social Ethic* (South Bend, IN: University of Notre Dame Press, 1981), 53–71; and *Unleashing the Scripture: Freeing the Bible from Captivity to America* (Nashville, TN: Abingdon Press, 1993). Some of his wide-ranging discussion of Christian practices, with special attention paid to medical care, are: *Christian Existence Today: Essays on Church, World and Living in Between* (New York: Baker Books, 1988, 1995), 25–97; *Dispatches From the Front: Theological Engagements with the Secular* (Durham, NC: Duke University Press, 1994), 1–17, 177–186; *Naming the Silences: God, Medicine, and the Problem of Suffering* (Grand Rapids, MI: William B. Eerdmans Publishing Company, 1990); and *Truthfulness and Tragedy: Further Investigations in Christian Ethics* (South Bend, IN: University of Notre Dame Press, 1977), 15–39, 147–202. The best summary of his complex positions is still *The Peaceable Kingdom* (South Bend, IN: University of Notre Dame Press, 1983).

For my critique of MacIntyre's and Hauerwas's narrative constructions, see *Afterwords*, 91–161.

A superb defense of this practical narrative approach to the Christian self-understanding is William C. Placher, *Unapologetic Theology: A Christian Voice in a Pluralistic Conversation* (Louisville, KY: Westminster/John Knox Press, 1989).

27. Compare the religious material in Clyde Pharr, ed., *The Theodosian Code and Novels and the Sirmondian Constitutions* (Princeton: Princeton University Press, 1952), 440–476, to the later Justinian material available in Maas, ed., *Readings in Late Antiquity,* 166–191.

28. Although a telling example is evident in Letter No. 8, which Julian addressed to the philosopher Maximus immediately upon taking up the imperium in 361 CE:

> We serve (*thrêskeuomen*) the gods out in the open, and the entire army which is returning with me is composed of god-fearing men (*theosebes*). We sacrifice oxen publicly. We have offered the gods countless hecatombs in thanksgiving. The gods call upon me to purify their rites (*ta panta hagneuein eis dynamin*) and I happily obey them. (*The Complete Works of the Emperor Julian* III, 24–25).

It is telling how this passage was translated originally in 1923:

> I *worship* the gods openly, and the whole mass of troops who are returning with me *worship* the gods. . . . The gods command me to restore their *worship* in its utmost purity, and I obey them . . . [emphasis mine]

This emphasis on worshipful *belief,* rather than on ritual *practice,* is one of the themes to which I return throughout this book. Julian is a crucial transitional figure, in this as in other things.

29. Our primary source for this is L. Cassius Dio (c. 164–230 CE), a Greek senator who penned an exhaustive, eighty-book *Roman History,* available in twelve Loeb volumes, edited by Earnest Cary (Cambridge, MA: Harvard University Press, 1968). This three-day triumph devoted one day each to Augustus's victories over the Gauls and Germans, over Mark Antony at the Battle of Actium, and over the Ptolemies of Egypt. This third, Egyptian triumph featured, among other peculiarities, an effigy of the dead Cleopatra paraded into the Forum on a couch. Dio's description of "the Altar of Victory" follows immediately upon his description of this third triumph:

> After finishing with [the festival], Caesar dedicated the temple to Athena called the *Chalchidikon,* as well as the Curia Julia (*to Bouleuterion to Ioulieion*), which he had built in honor of his father. He set up a statue of Victory (*Nikê*) which is still there now, in order to symbolize that he owed his rule to her. It had belonged to the people of Tarentum, from whence it was taken to Rome, set up in the Senate House (*en te tôi synedriôi*), and decked out with Egyptian spoils (*Aigyptiois laphyrois ekosmêthê*). (LI.22.1–2).

30. See Letter No. 50 to Nilus, surnamed Dionysius, composed in Antioch in the Winter of 362/3 CE, in *The Complete Works of the Emperor Julian* III, 164–165 (this letter also contains a possible reference to the Altar of Victory, at 160–161).

31. This letter is available in *Prefect and Emperor: The Relationes of Symmachus* AD 384, trans. and ed. R. H. Barrow (Oxford: Clarendon Press, 1973), 30–47. Let one especially poignant passage suffice to represent Symmachus's position in the *Plea:*

    And so we ask for peace for the gods of our fathers, for the gods of our native land. *It is reasonable that whatever each of us worships is really to be considered one and the same.* We gaze up at the same stars, the sky covers us all, the same universe compasses us. What does it matter what practical system we adopt in our search for truth? Not by one avenue only can we arrive at so tremendous a secret. [emphasis mine]

    Julian's polemics against Christianity will be fueled by some of this same suspicion of its radically revelatory and theologically particular character, as well as Julian's own convictions about natural piety.
    In *Against the Galileans,* he declares: "The knowledge of God comes, not from teaching (*didakton*), but from nature (*physei*)" (52b). The text of *Against the Galileans,* or as much of it as survives, may be found in *The Works of the Emperor Julian* III, 318–427.
32. The text of this letter may be found in *Saint Ambrose: Letters,* translated by Sister Mary Melchior Beyenka (Washington, DC: Catholic University Press of America, 1954), 37–51. His position, too, is well summarized in the following passage:

    Ponder well, I beg you, and examine the sect of the pagans. They sound weighty and grand; they support what is incapable of being true; *they talk of God, but they adore a statue.* . . . So great a secret, it is said, cannot be reached by one road. We know on God's word what you do not know. And what you know by conjecture we have discovered from the very wisdom and truth of God. Your ways do not agree with ours. You ask peace for your gods from the emperors; we ask peace for our emperors from Christ. *You adore the work of your hands; we consider it wrong to think that anything which can be made is God. God does not wish to be worshipped in stones. Even your philosophers have ridiculed such ideas.* [emphasis mine]

33. These developments are helpfully analyzed in Stephen Williams and Gerard Friell, *Theodosius: Emperor at Bay* (New Haven, CT: Yale University Press, 1994), 119–140.
34. See Bowersock, *Julian the Apostate,* 1–11, for an excellent overview of the ancient sources.
    Julian, like Hadrian, has also been the inspiration for several modern pieces of historical fiction, most notably Gore Vidal's *Julian: A Novel* (Boston, MA: Little, Brown, 1964), and several well-known poems by Constantine Cavafy: "Julian Seeing Contempt" (on the failure of his attempted reforms), "Julian in Nicomedia" (on the necessity of pretending to a Christianity he did not practice), and the unpublished "Julian at the Mysteries" (a fictional account of his momentary loss of pagan faith), in *C.P. Cavafy: Collected Poems,* trans. Edmund Keeley and Philip Sherrard (Princeton: Princeton University Press, 1992), 124, 127, 181–182. For the Greek text of Cavafy's poems, I am using Kavaphês, *Apanta Poiêtika* (Athens: Hypsilon Biblia, 1983) 140, 143, 245–246.
    See R. Browning, *The Emperor Julian* (London: Weidenfeld and Nicolson, 1975) for a helpful survey of this and other material.
35. Already in his *First Encomium to the Emperor Constantius,* Julian refers to "the city on the Bosporus, named after the whole family of the Constantii," in *The Complete Works of the Emperor Julian* I, 14–15.
36. Especially significant to his own intellectual formation was the work of the Syrian Neo-Platonist, Iamblichus, "that truly honorable and divine man, who ranks third after Pythagoras and Plato." This comment appears in Letter #2 to Priscus, composed in 358/9 CE in Gaul, in *The Complete Works of the Emperor Julian* III, 4–5.
37. Athanassiadi, *Julian: An Intellectual Biography,* 46.

38. As Libanius tells it in his *Epitaph for Julian* (Oration 18.21), "He collected all manner of wisdom and displayed it—the poets, the rhetoricians, the whole race of philosophers—much of it in the Greek tongue and not a little in the other."

    See *Libanius: Selected Works* I, 292–293.

39. See the germane discussion, with significant attention to Alexander, in E. L. Bowie, "Greeks and Their Past in the Second Sophistic," *Past & Present* 46 (1970): 3–41.

40. *Symposium at the Saturnalia* 316c, in *The Complete Works of the Emperor Julian* II, 368–369.

41. This loaded phrase has a dual reference. Caesar has referred disparagingly to the force of a mere 10,000 Greeks which Alexander and his father defeated at Chaironea in 338 BCE. But Xenophon's *Anabasis* is a moving account of just how resourceful, as well as how effective and dangerous, a force of 10,000 inspired and well-led Greeks can be.

42. *Symposium at the Saturnalia* 324a, in *The Complete Works of the Emperor Julian* II, 384–385.

43. *The Complete Works of the Emperor Julian* I, 418–419.

44. This point is echoed by Libanius in his *Lament for Julian* (Oration 17.1), in which he quotes Homer to the effect that the grief over Julian's unexpected death is "a matter not just for the Achaeans, but for the entire earth where the laws of Rome are in place. The grief may be greater in that part of the world where the Greeks live (*hên Hellênes oíkousin*), because they are more aware of the evil which has befallen them."

    See *Libanius: Selected Works* I, 252–253.

45. His *Letter to the Council and People of Athens* is a fascinating mixture of self-justification for seizing power, and nostalgic reverie for this much-favored city. Julian courts the Athenians' favor with special passion, and for singularly spiritual reasons. The would-be emperor concludes that, while it is no great thing to find certain individuals who care for justice, in Athens "the entire city and the entire citizenry are passionate devotees (*erastas*) of justice in both word and deed" (269b). It is intriguing, in light of the erotic philosophy of Socrates that we examined in the second chapter, that Julian still describes the Athenians in this way.

    See *The Works of the Emperor Julian* II, 244–245.

46. One interesting clue comes in Julian's *Letter on Behalf of the Citizens of Argos* (Letter No. 28, composed in 362 CE at Constantinople), where he notes how the cycle of Panhellenic contests have developed in his own day. Whereas Elis hosts the Olympic Games once every four years, and Delphi hosts the Pythian Games, Corinth hosts games biannually at Isthmia, and Argos hosts games biannually at Nemea. Argos, moreover, has recently added still more athletic festivals to their calendar, ones dedicated to Hera, among others. This results in making Nemea an *annual* festival ground. It is entirely possible that these changes indicate the changing status of various Greek cities, as well as the changing center-of-gravity on the Greek mainland in the late Roman period. We are moving away from more peripheral western sites, like Olympia and Delphi, concentrating on more central Roman loci, running along the isthmian corridor that links Athens-to-Corinth-to-Argos.

    See *The Complete Works of the Emperor Julian* III, 88–89.

47. Julian, *Against the Galileans*, 99c–106d, 184b–190c, 218b–224d, 235b ff. This text is available in the Loeb edition of *The Works of the Emperor Julian* III, 313–427. For a nice summary of this polemic, see Athanassiadi, *Julian: An Intellectual Biography*, 162–167.

    This text only exists in extensive fragments, most of them excerpts from later Christian authors, as well as quotations from the Septuagint and New Testament. Julian himself tells us that he wishes to make three related points, points that are curiously contradictory in practical terms. On the one hand, the emperor wishes to argue for the superiority of the natural theology of paganism over a religion of scriptural revelation such as the Hebraic. This is of a piece with the larger thrust of the treatise, one that asserts the complete cultural and aesthetic superiority of Hellenism over Hebraic culture. Then, on the other hand, in a final and somewhat forced attempt to secure common ground against the Christians, Julian asserts common cause between Hebrews and Hellenes (and thus against their common enemy, the sect of the "Galileans"), insisting that Greeks and Jews are more similar than dissimilar—if, that is, one can overlook the mandate of monotheism, and the jealousy of the Hebrew God (306b, 354b–c)!

Most likely compiled in the winter of 362 CE in Antioch, while he was clearly pre-occupied with other matters, this is neither the clearest nor the most cogent of Julian's writings, though it possesses enormous historical interest.

48. See *Against the Galileans* 198b–d, for Julian's telling admission that the oracle at Delphi has indeed fallen silent in his own day. His intriguing explanation of this is that the gods have provided *new* cults to replace the *old* ones, most notably the now-prominent cult of Asklepius, and Herakles, and Hermes Trismegistus (176a–c, 200a–b, 235b–c). Here once again, upstart sons have supplanted their spiritual fathers.

By contrast, Libanius seems to suggest, in his *Address to the Antiochenes on the Emperor's Anger* (Oration 16.12), that Delphic oracles are still available.

49. Athanassiadi, *Julian: An Intellectual Biography*, 170.

50. "Hellenism (*ho Hellênismos*) is not yet done as we wish," Julian complains, "on account of those who are doing it. For the worship (*lampra*) of the gods is great indeed, greater than our prayers and hopes allowed."

This comment comes in Letter No. 22 to Arsacius, High Priest of Galatia, composed in the summer of 362 CE (*The Complete Works of the Emperor Julian* III, 66–67).

51. See his *Hymn to the Mother of the Gods* 159a, where Julian insists that it was the decisive adoption of this cult by the Athenians that led to a more coherent cult formation at Eleusis.

This Hymn is available in the Loeb edition of *The Works of the Emperor Julian*, Volume I, 442–503. It is a very difficult text to read, much less to summarize, intended as it is to be an esoteric summary of the true meaning of Near Eastern myth. Let one of his own summary statements (166a–b) suffice as illustration:

> Who, then, is the Mother of the Gods? She is the source (*pêgê*) of both the intellectual (*noerôn*) and the creative (*dêmiourgikôn*) gods, themselves rulers of the visible (*emphaneis*) gods. She is both the mother and the consort of mighty Zeus, a divine being who came into being (*hypostasa*) alongside of and together with the great creator (*tôi megalôi dêmiourgôi*). She is mistress (*kyria*) of all life, the cause (*aitia*) of all creation who effortlessly perfects all created things. She gives birth without pain (*pathous*), creating all things (*ta onta*) with the father. She is a motherless virgin, enthroned with Zeus, and indeed the Mother of all Gods. (*The Complete Works of the Emperor Julian* I,462–463).

This juxtaposition of classical philosophical terminology and classical mythic images is characteristic of Julian's brand of Neo-Platonism. Of special interest to me is the significant overlap between this statement and the then-emerging Christian vocabulary of Incarnation and Trinity. One wonders if this cult of the divine mother was not the most prominent cultural element that Mediterranean Christianity ultimately borrowed from the ambient Hellenic environment.

52. Olympia appears rarely in Julian's writings. It is mentioned twice in his *Second Encomium to the Emperor Constantius* (78c, 83c), and he makes much of the fact that the Cynic philosopher, Diogenes, made a *pilgrimage* to Olympia—for what Julian concludes must have been subtly *religious* reasons.

See also Julian's *Oration to Herakleios the Cynic* (212a –213a, 238a–239c), in *The Works of the Emperor Julian* II, 90–93, 156–161.

53. Mithras appears as a sort of new Apollo in the cosmology Julian constructs in his *Hymn to the King Helios*. For an interesting analysis of the Hymn's Mithraic resonances, see Athanassiadi, *Julian: An Intellectual Biography*, 52–88.

WAS GREEK THOUGHT RELIGIOUS?

For more on the spread of the cult and the ritual practices of Mithraism in the imperial period, see R. L. Gordon, *Image and Value in the Greco-Roman World: Studies in Mithraism and Religious Art* (Aldershot: Variorum, 1986), and David Ulamsey, *The Origins of the Mithraic Mysteries: Cosmology and Salvation in the Ancient World* (New York: Oxford University Press, 1989).

A classic work of the previous generation was Frank Cumont, *The Mysteries of Mithra*, 2nd ed. [1902], trans. Thomas J. McCormack (New York: Dover Publications, 1956), but this approach—based on the fundamental conflict between Christianity and Mithraism for the soul of the Empire—has lost its former ideological grip.

Perhaps the most dramatic *material* evidence of the continuities-*and*-discontinuities between Mithraism and early Christianity exists at the Church of San Clemente in Rome, located just to the southeast of the Colisseum. Here we have a remarkably early Christian basilica built directly over an enormous second-to-third century Mithraeum. See Federico Guidobaldi and Paul Lawlor, *The Basilica and the Archaeological Area of San Clemente in Rome* (Rome, 1990).

54. At *Hymn to King Helios* 153b, and *Against the Galileans,* 200a–b. See also Athanassiadi, *Julian: An Intellectual Biography,* 167–168.

It bears noting that Asklepius was famously invoked by Socrates on his deathbed (*Phaedo* 118b), as I mentioned in Chapter Two (Endnote #5). And it is worth noting that Julian refers to medical science (*tên iatrikên epistêmên*) as divine in origin, in his "Decree Concerning Doctors" (Letter No. 31, composed May 12, 362 in Constantinople), in *The Complete Works of the Emperor Julian* III, 106–109.

55. Julian, *Hymn to the Mother of the Gods* 166a–167a, in *The Complete Works of the Emperor Julian* I, 464–467.

56. See his *Hymn to King Helios,* 130b–131a, where Julian identifies himself as the true King's follower (*opados*). Given his interest in natural, rather than revealed, theology, Julian makes much of his natural affinity, even as a child, for sun and sunlight.

This Hymn is available in the Loeb edition of *The Works of the Emperor Julian,* Volume I, 353–435. Its tripartite mystical cosmology is extremely complicated and often difficult to comprehend. Given the widespread philosophical interest in monism, Julian seems to assert that the One (also the Good) presides over the realm of the noetic gods (*noêtoi theoi*). Between this world of forms and the temporal realm of sense-perception, however, exists a third realm where the intellectual gods (*noeroi theoi*) preside, and where Helios is king (133b-c). The Hymn is rich in the rhetoric of mediation, ultimately using an important Aristotelian term (*mesotês*) to describe the way King Helios establishes an essential link between eternal forms and temporal bodies. Whether the logical conclusion of this cosmology is monotheistic or no remains unclear to me (135d–136a).

57. I have come to believe that this *must* have been a refusal on Pausanias's part, not something of which he remained unaware. As a man who had traveled extensively through the Jordan River valley and in Egypt, and as a religious writer who spent as long in the Corinthia in the late second century as Pausanias did, I find it implausible that he remained entirely ignorant of this admittedly new, but rapidly expanding, renegade spiritual movement. Perhaps the important question to ask is what Christianity looked like in the mid-second century, and what it called itself to an interested outsider, rather than whether Pausanias knew of the phenomenon at all or not.

For more on the common strategies of pagan and Christian historians—that of ignoring one another—see Arnaldo Momigliano, "Pagan and Christian Historiography," in *Essays in Ancient and Modern Historiography,* 107–126, esp. 119.

58. "He was like a shipwright who fits out a big ship with a new rudder after she has lost the old one," Libanius notes, "except that Julian restored our original saviors (*sôtêras*) to us." *Lament for Julian* (Oration 18.129), in *Libanius: Selected Works* I, 362–363.

59. Sozomen, *Ecclesiastical History* 5.18 [Jacques Paul Migne, ed. *Patrologiae Cursus Completus: Series Graeca* (Paris: Bibliothecae Universali, 1857–1866) 67: 1269–1272]; Socrates, *Ecclesiastical History* III.16.1 [Migne, ed., *Patrologiae: Graeca* 67: 417–424]; Theodoret, *Ecclesiastical History* 3.4 [Migne, ed., *Patrologiae: Graeca* 82: 1095–1096]; and Ammianus Marcellinus, *History* XXII.10.7 and XXV.4.20.

The Edict is described as one of the centerpieces of imperial policy by Athanassiadi, *Julian: An Intellectual Biography*, 1–12, and Bowersock, *Julian the Apostate*, 79–93.

60. Pharr, ed., *The Theodosian Code*, 388, No. 5.

61. This document (Letter No. 36) may be found in *The Works of the Emperor Julian*, Volume III, 116–123. I will include specific numerical references from this letter parenthetically in the text.

62. And Julian *was* an emphatic and uncompromising moralist, a fact which ultimately did much to work against his popularity. See Bowersock, *Julian the Apostate*, 66–93.

63. There is a possible play on words here, as there are many in Julian's writings: Is he contrasting the honest (*chrêstos*) man to the Christ-like (*Christos*) one, perhaps?

64. Note that every author on this list, here as elsewhere, is Greek and not Latin.

65. We might translate this term as "crazy" in this context, since Julian concludes his address by confessing that he thinks Christians are insane, and that one does not attempt to argue with insanity, one merely reins it in (424a). It is, in any case, a term Julian uses quite often in his polemics.

66. There is another play on words here, since Julian literally offers them a "heresy," that is, a choice to *opt out* of Christianity.

Note also Julian's reference to "the so-called heretics" (*tôn legomenôn hairetikôn*) in Letter No. 41 to the city of Bostra (dated August 362, and composed in Antioch), *The Complete Works of the Emperor Julian* III, 128–129.

67. For a superb modern criticism of this administrative assumption, see Jeffrey Stout, "Commitments and Traditions in the Study of Religious Ethics," *Journal of Religious Ethics*, 25th Anniversary Supplement, 25.3 (1998): 23–56, esp. 34–35.

68. This letter (No. 19) may be found in the Loeb edition of *The Works of the Emperor Julian* Volume III, 48–55.

69. See the relevant comments in his *Letter to the Council and People of Athens* 277b–c.

70. In fact, there is also a dedicatory statue for Achilles in the same unrooved courtyard. It seemed an odd juxtaposition to Julian at the time, this joining of the images of mortal enemies, yet there were still guides (*periêgêteis*) who could tell the story of how this came to be. Such sites, that is to say, continue to look much as they had in Pausanias's day—replete with local guides and groundskeepers—which proves to be Julian's point in relating this story.

71. Athanassiadi, *Julian: An Intellectual Biography*, 107–111.

72. The note is sounded most elaborately in his satirical *The Beard-Hater* 339c–d. More on this curious document below.

73. Later in this letter, Julian relates how Pegasius took him on a tour of the entire site, opening up the Temple of Athena and showing him all of the cult statues in a state of near-perfect preservation. Julian notices that Pegasius neither hissed nor crossed himself when he opened the temple doors:

For these two things are the height of their theology (*akra theologia*): to hiss at demons, and to make the sign (*skiagraphein*) of the cross on their foreheads.

74. Athanassiadi, *Julian: An Intellectual Biography*, 147.

See also the *Hymn to King Helios* 139b, where Julian insists that "the noetic world is entirely one (*hen*), pre-existent (*proüparchon*) and eternal (*aei*). See *The Complete Works of the Emperor Julian* I, 378–379.

75. Of lesser note than his other satires, this *Symposium at the Saturnalia* is one of the more important works in Julian's corpus. The poetic pretense, as I have indicated, involves a divinely hosted symposium in heaven, one to which all the Roman emperors are invited. Only the virtuous or martially accomplished are admitted however; after Herakles insists on extending an invitation to Alexander as well, a contest is organized to establish who was the greatest of all such rulers. Of the three most obvious contenders—Alexander, Julius Caesar, and Constantine—the first is too hot-tempered, the second is almost impious in his egoism, and the third is obviously outmatched. The garland is awarded finally to Marcus Aurelius (312a, 328c–d, 333c–335c), whose status as a (Greek!) philosopher, and not merely ruler or conqueror, earns him the crown—a telling indication of Julian's own aspirations and imperial self-understanding at the time.

76. Literally entitled *The Beard-Hater,* this text is harder to summarize since it tends to be rambling and repetitive. The beard is Julian's self-appointed symbol of several things: his philosophical commitments, his martial hardiness, and his full manhood. The city of Antioch—pleasure-seeking, effeminate, and given over to excessive and indiscriminate passions—hates its bearded resident emperor for all of these reasons. Perhaps the most telling barb Julian launches concerns the city's eponymous founder, the Syrian Antiochus:

    They say that excessive luxury (*habrotêtos*) and softness (*tryphês*) caused him to fall in love (*erônta*) all the time, and to be loved passionately (*erômenon*) just as often, until finally his own passion (*erôta*) caused him to fall in love (*erasthênai*) with his own step-mother. (347b)

    As was Antiochus of old, so the city of Antioch is today. See *The Complete Works of the Emperor Julian* II,446–447.

77. Athanassiadi, *Julian: An Intellectual Biography,* 185–189.

78. Athanassiadi, *Julian: An Intellectual Biography,* 154.

79. See Letter No. 22 to Arsacius, High Priest of Galatia, composed in Spring 362 CE, in *The Complete Works of the Emperor Julian* III,66–73, as well as the fragmentary *Letter to a Priest,* in *The Complete Works of the Emperor Julian* II, 296–339.

80. This is the major preoccupation of *The Beard-Hater,* especially at 339a–d, 346d, 354b, 356d–357a, 359d.

81. Bowersock, *Julian the Apostate,* 85–88, and Athanassiadi, *Julian: An Intellectual Biography,* 185ff.

82. See the excellent collection of essays edited by Mary Beard and John North, *Pagan Priests: Religion and Power in the Ancient World* (London: Duckworth, 1990).

83. Athanassiadi, *Julian: An Intellectual Biography,* 136.

84. Ammianus Marcellinus, *History* XXII.10.7:

    But this one thing was inhumane (*inclemens*), and ought to be buried in eternal silence—namely, that he forbade teachers of rhetoric and literature (*rhetorices et grammaticos*) to work if they practiced the Christian religion (*ritus Christiani cultores*).

    For the Latin text, see the Loeb edition of Ammianus's *History* II, 256–257.

85. Julian's sacrifices, it would seem, were meat sacrifices, while the common round of ritual sacrifices that Pausanias described at Olympia was largely vegetarian. This is a significant *practical* detail, since blood is always an inconvenient, and often quite disturbing, ritual fact.

    See Bernard M. W. Knox, *The Oldest Dead White European Males* (New York: W. W. Norton & Company, 1993), 32–35.

    For a curious discussion of Julian's own dietary restrictions, see his *Hymn to the Mother of the Gods,* in *The Complete Works of the Emperor Julian* 173d–178a.

86. Bowersock, *Julian the Apostate,* 106; cf. also Libanius, *Lament for Julian* (Oration 18.164), and Ammianus Marcellinus, *History,* XXII.12.1.

87. See Libanius's *Julianic Orations,* in *Libanius: Selected Works* II, 252–487.

88. This point, much disputed in the ancient literature, is resolved by Bowersock, *Julian the Apostate,* 116–118.

89. This work was advanced significantly by another former companion of Julian's from the Athenian period, Gregory of Nazianzus. See his *Orations* 4 and 5, entitled "Against Julian" (*Kata Ioulianou*) and available in Migne, ed., *Patrologiae: Graeca* 35: 531–720, as well as the elegant summary of Gregory's mature position in Werner Jaegar, *Early Christianity and Greek Paideia* (Cambridge, MA: Harvard University Press, 1961), 72–85.

   Jaegar also worked extensively with another of Gregory's Cappadocian colleagues, Gregory of Nyssa. See Werner Jaeger, Hermann Langerbeck, and Henrik Dörrie, eds., *Gregorii Nysseni Opera* (Leiden: E. J. Brill, 1972) in ten volumes.

90. Pharr, ed., *The Theodosian Code,* 472, Nos. 4,5.

91. Pharr, ed., *The Theodosian Code,* 467, No. 6.

92. Pharr, ed., *The Theodosian Code,* 467, Nos. 1,5.

93. One of the more curious interventions of the Emperor Julian in the religious affairs of the Empire was his attempt to sponsor the rebuilding of the Temple at Jerusalem, an ill-augured attempt which also failed dramatically.

   See Bowersock, *Julian the Apostate,* 88–90, 120–122, as well as Julian's "Letter to the Community of Jews" (Letter 51) in the Loeb edition of *The Complete Works of the Emperor Julian* III, 176–181.

94. Pharr, ed., *The Theodosian Code,* 467–471.

95. Pharr, ed., *The Theodosian Code,* 472, No. 1.

96. Pharr, ed., *The Theodosian Code,* 472, No. 2.

97. See Julian's "Edict on Funerals," dated February 363 CE, in *The Complete Works of the Emperor Julian* III, 190–197.

98. Pharr, ed., *The Theodosian Code,* 472, No. 5.

99. Pharr, ed., *The Theodosian Code,* 473, Nos. 9,10.

100. Pharr, ed., *The Theodosian Code,* 473–474, No. 12.

101. Pharr, ed., *The Theodosian Code,* 472, No. 3.

102. This comment needs to be qualified. Roman law is what modern legal scholars would call "common law," a vast corpus of jurisprudence decided on a case-by-case basis, out of which generalizable principles may or may not be discernible. Given this jurisprudential pragmatism, it is possible that the emperor has not "changed his mind" at all, so much as he has been confronted with a different set of issues, in a very different case, in a very different part of the world.

   For more on the difference between "constitutional" and "common" law, and some of its political ramifications, see Antonin Scalia, *A Matter of Interpretation: Federal Courts and the Law* (Princeton: Princeton University Press, 1997), 3–14, with subsequent commentary.

103. This is believed to refer to a temple at Edessa in the region of Osrhoene.

104. Pharr, ed., *The Theodosian Code,* 473, No. 8, emphasis mine; see also Ammianus Marcellinus, *History* XIV.3.3.

105. See the instructive example in Maas, ed., *Readings In Late Antiquity: A Sourcebook,* 183.

106. Pharr, ed., *The Theodosian Code,* 474, No. 13.

107. As I stated earlier, Julian refers to the fact that the four panhellenic sanctuaries are still celebrating their contests—"the greatest and most resplendent *agônes* in all of Greece"—as late as 362 CE, when he composes his *Letter on Behalf of the Citizens of Argos* (408a–b), while residing in Constantinople.

108. Pharr, ed., *The Theodosian Code,* 474, No. 14.

109. Pharr, ed., *The Theodosian Code,* 474, No. 15.

110. Of special concern to Julian during his final winter in Antioch was the temple of Apollo, located in the grove of Daphne outside of the city. The body of St. Babylas, bishop of Antioch, had been buried in this grove shortly after the Christian population of the city destroyed the temple *and erected a Christian altar in its place.* Julian removed the

remains of the saint and restored the temple of Apollo to the site, but some of the citizens of Antioch burned this new temple on the evening of October 22, 362.

See Julian, *The Beard-Hater* 361b–364b; and Libanius, *Monody on the Temple of Apollo at Daphne* (Oration 60), which was composed in November 362 CE, and has been preserved in fragments in John Chrysostom, *Discourse on Blessed Babylas and Demonstration Against the Greeks that Christ is God,* trans. Margaret A. Schation (Washington, DC: Catholic University of America Press, 1985), 75–152.

See also Libanius's *To the Emperor Theodosius, About the Temples,* in *Libanius: Selected Works* II, 92–151, in which the old division of urban center versus countryside continues to be a prime concern.

111. I am indebted to the singular three-volume work of Anastasios K. Orlandou, *H Xylostegos Palaiochristianikê Basilikê* (Athens: Archaiologikês Etaireias, 1952–1956) for much of my summary here. The report on the basilica at Epidauros, with floor plan, may be found at I, 50–51.

112. See Giorgios Sôtêriou, *Archaiai Palaiochristianikai Basilikai tês Ellados,* printed in *Archaiologikê Ephêmeris* (1929) 161–248, esp. 164–165.

113. Orlandou, *H Xylostegos Palaiochristiankikê Basilikê,* I, 144–146, II, 510–516, 525–526; Sôtêriou, *Ai Palaiochristianikai Basilikai tês Ellados,* 171–173; Alfred Mallwitz and Wolfgang Schiering, *Der Werkstatt des Phedias in Olympia, Olympische Forschung* No.5 (Berlin: Verlag Walter de Gruyter, 1964), 16–47.

114. Edward Schwartz, ed., *Acta Conciliorum Oecumenicorum* (Berlin: Walter de Gruyter, 1935), Tom. 2, Vol. 3, Par. 2, p.139.

115. Described by Pausanias, *Greek Walkabout* X.8.6–9.

116. J. Laurent, "Delphes Chrétien," *Bulletin de Correspondance Hellénique* 23 (1899) 206–279, esp. 208–209, 232–233, and the summary at 269–279.

See also Jean Janorray, *Le Gymnase, Fouilles de Delphes* No. 2 (Paris: E. de Boccard, 1953), esp. Plates I and XXX.

117. C. W. J. Eliot, "Lord Byron, Early Travelers, and the Monastery at Delphi," *American Journal of Archaeology* (1967): 283–291, with plates.

118. Sôtêriou, *Ai Palaiochristianikai Basilikai tês Ellados,* 183–184; Vas. Vl. Sphyrera, *Istôria tês Eleusinas: Apo tê Byzantinê Periodo mechri Sêmera* (Ekdosê Dêmou Eleusinas, 1985) *"oi aiônes tês siôpês"* ("the era of silence"), 11–19.

119. Laurent, "Delphes Chrétien," 208–209.

120. See George E. Mylonas, *Eleusis and the Eleusinian Mysteries* (Princeton: Princeton University Press, 1961), 8–9, 287–316.

121. Pharr, ed., *The Theodosian Code,* 474–475, No. 16.

122. Pharr, ed., *The Theodosian Code,* 475–476, Nos. 19,20,21,25.

123. Pharr, ed., *The Theodosian Code,* 476, No. 22.

124. This defeat exacerbated what were already substantial Roman fears of Sasanian Persia by the third century CE. See A. D. Lee, *Information and Frontiers: Roman Foreign Relations in Late Antiquity* (New York: Cambridge University Press, 1993), 15–25, 49–66.

125. Bowersock, *Julian the Apostate,* 118.

CHAPTER FIVE

1. Tradition has it that the first 13 bishops of Rome, whether martyred or no, are all interred together beneath the Altar of the Confession in St. Peter's basilica in Rome, thus lending an ecclesial logic to my dealing with this group *as* a group.

2. See the remarkable resource on ancient nomenclature available in Heikki Solin, *Die Griechischen Personennamen in Rom: Ein Namenbuch,* in 3 Bänden (Berlin: Walter de Gruyter, 1982).

3. A similar sensitivity animates the brilliant essay by Gillian Clark, "Translate into Greek: Porphyry of Tyre on the New Barbarians," in Richard Miles, ed., *Constructing Identities in Late Antiquity* (New York: Routledge, 1999), esp. 112–115.

4. Esther 2:5–6.

5. The premier resource for this material is still Marshall G. S. Hodgson's three-volume *The Venture of Islam: Conscience and History in a World Civilization* (Chicago: University of Chicago Press, 1961, 1974) Volume I, 103–145, 318–326.

   For more on the tension between Arab and Muslim identity, see Bruce B. Lawrence, *Defenders of God: The Fundamentalist Revolt Against the Modern Age* (New York: Harper-Collins, 1989), 87–89, and *Shattering the Myth: Islam Beyond Violence* (Princeton: Princeton University Press, 1998), 3–105.

   Finally, T. E. Lawrence's discussion of Muslim Arabism, with its careful attention to linguistic concerns, is still very much to the point. See *The Seven Pillars of Wisdom: A Triumph* (New York: Doubleday Anchor Books, 1926, 1935), 33–45.

6. See the decisive debate, and its only partial resolution, at the Council of Jerusalem, depicted in Acts 15:1–29, and then narrated with some interesting (and largely self-interested) differences by Paul in Galatians 2:1–14.

   For more discussion of this material, see William F. Albright and David N. Freedman, gen. eds., *The Anchor Bible: The Acts of the Apostles,* volume ed., Joseph A. Fitzmeyer, S.J. (Garden City, NY: Doubleday & Company, 1998) Volume 31A, 538–569.

7. It became a virtual Apologetic pretense, and a generic convention, for Christian apologists to address themselves either "To the Greeks," or else "Against the Greeks." We have numerous examples of this genre of Christian self-definition from Clement of Alexandria (fl. 96 CE), Justin Martyr of Nablus (c. 100–165 CE), and Athenagoras (of Corinth? late second century CE), as well as more extreme versions from Tatian of Assyria (fl. 160 CE) and Tertullian of Carthage (c. 160–220 CE). In that literature, the debate over iconic representation—statues primarily, which were allegedly worshiped as if they were gods—occupies a prominent place, as it continues to do in the comparatively later work of John Chrysostom in Antioch and Constantinople (c. 347–407 CE), whose 21 famous homilies "On the Statues" were delivered in March/April 387 CE.

   These are available in Philip Schaff, ed., *Nicene and Post-Nicene Fathers: Second Series,* Vol. IX (Peabody, MA: Hendrickson Publishers,Inc., 1994), 317–489. See also his *Demonstration to the Greeks that Christ is God (Pros Hellēnas Apodeixis hoti Theos Estin ho Christos),* trans. Paul W. Harkins in *Saint John Chrysostom: Apologist* (Washington, DC: The Catholic University Press of America, 1983), 155–262.

   For a brief look at this essential apologetic trope, and the Christian debate within the Hellenism of which it was a part, see my "Athenagoras the Christian, Pausanias the Travel-Guide, and a Mysterious Corinthian Girl," *Harvard Theological Review* 85.1 (1992): 35–49.

8. We owe this phrase to Edward Gibbon, *The History of the Decline and Fall of the Roman Empire,* in five volumes with notes by Revd. H. H. Milman [1776] (Philadelphia: Porter & Coates, 1880).

   Ironically, Gibbon knew this to be a comparatively late event, concluding his project with a description of the "fall" of Constantinople (V, 410–450) and attention to late medieval papal politics. But see his telling comments on the "decadence" of urban Roman society (I, 249–250 and III, 258–259).

9. For an excellent representation of the range of responses, Christian as well as pagan, to these various sacks of Rome, see Michael Maas, ed., *Readings in Late Antiquity: A Sourcebook* (New York: Routledge, 2000), 26–33.

10. One way to say this would be that Julian failed to recall that sons inevitably supplant their fathers, and that time moves in only one direction. He condemned Christians

for supplanitng their fathers in the faith, and attempted quite unsuccessfully to resurrect the failed faith of those same Roman fathers.

11. For a critique of the Hollywood version of Christian martyrdom, still evident in too much contemporary theology, see my "The Virtue of Courage: On the Penultimacy of the Political," *Soundings* 83.2 (2000): 635–668.

   Also see the fascinating comments by Gibbon, *The History of the Decline and Fall of the Roman Empire,* I, 659–662.

12. The two figures, and subsequent dynasties, most commonly invoked when discussing the Byzantine flourescence are the emperors Justinian (527–565 CE) and Heraclius (610–641 CE).

13. Paradigmatic of this approach is once again Edward Gibbon, who dispenses of the Byzantine Empire with one incredible sentence:

   The majesty of Rome was faintly represented by the princes of Constantinople, the feeble and imaginary successors of Augustus. Yet they continued to reign over the East, from the Danube to the Nile and Tigris; the Gothic and Vandal kingdoms of Italy and Africa were subverted by the arms of Justinian; and the history of the *Greek* emperors may still afford a long series of instructive lessons, and interesting revolutions. (III, 362–363)

   This attitude of dismissive interest in Byzantium has had a long subsequent history. Note the far more recent, and therefore all the more amazing, reference to the fascinating but in the last resort stagnant and suffocating history of Byzantium and its strange, frozen civilization, where Diocletian's empire dressed in Christian vestments continued immobile for another thousand years.

   Dom Gregory Dix, *The Shape of the Liturgy* (New York: The Seabury Press, 1983), 383. One hardly knows what to make of such blanket dismissals of the entire Greek world.

14. Galatians 3:28, 6:15; Colossians 3:11.

15. A name apparently coined in the city of Antioch. See *Acts of the Apostles* 11:26.

16. Even this claim is problematic. In the Decrees of the Fourth Ecumenical Council at Chalcedon in 451 CE, reference is made to those who wish to turn to knowledge of the truth (*eis epignôsin tês alêtheias*) and away from Hellenism (*ex Hellênismou*), from Judaism (*ex Ioudaismou*), and from all manner of heresy (*ex haireseôs hoiasdêpotoun*). That *is* a doctrinal statement.

17. The Greek (and Latin) text is available in Jacques Paul Migne, ed., *Patrologiae Graeca: Cursus Completus* (Paris: Bibliothecae Cleri Universae, 1864) 94: 522–1228.

   An English translation of the *Font* is available in *Saint John of Damascus: Writings,* trans. Frederic H. Chase, Jr. (Washington, DC: Catholic University Press of America, 1958).

18. Aquinas's dependence on the work of Augustine and the man he refers to as "the Damascene" (and whose *Font of Wisdom* would have been available to him in a recent Latin version compiled by Burgundius in 1153 CE) is perhaps clearest in his discussion of Providence and Free Will.

   See Thomas Gilby, ed., *Saint Thomas Aquinas: Summa Theologiae,* Volume 5, *God's Will and Providence* (New York: McGraw-Hill Book Company, 1967).

19. The *Doctores Ecclesiae* are the most influential, and widely regarded, theologians recognized by the Latin church. Originally four in number—Ambrose of Milan (c. 339–397 CE), Augustine of Hippo (354–430 CE), Jerome of Aquileia and Bethlehem (c. 342–420 CE), and Pope Gregory the Great (c. 540–604 CE)—their number exceeds 20 today.

20. This was a point of great mystical importance to Epiphanius of Cyprus (see subsequent note) in "On the Mysteries of Numbers" (*Peri tôn Arithmôn Mystêriôn*), in Migne, ed., *Patrologiae Graeca* 43: 507–518.

21. It is also apparently the least original aspect of John's thought, and therefore representative of a much broader Christian self-presentation in these same centuries. Trac-

ing one hundred and three heresies in all, John adapted his discussion of the first eighty from a much longer work by Epiphanius of Cyprus (c. 315–403 CE), whose *Panarion* (or *Refutation of All Heresies, Kata Haireseôn Ogdoêkanta*) was a highly significant and vastly influential Christian text.

It is available in Migne, ed., *Patrologiae Graeca* (1863), 41: 173–1200 and 42: 9–774.

22. For some reason, these terms are translated into both Latin and English as "parents and archetypes."

23. John of Damascus, "On Heresies," III; J-P Migne, ed., *Patrologiae Graeca* 94: 677.

24. John of Damascus, "On Heresies," III–112; J-P Migne, ed., *Patrologiae Graeca* 94: 680.

25. John of Damascus, "On Heresies," 160–161; J-P Migne, ed., *Patrologiae Graeca* 94: 773–777.

26. Hans Belting, *Likeness and Presence: A History of the Image Before the Era of Art*, trans. Edmund Jephcott (Chicago: University of Chicago Press, 1994), 23–29. Belting's book, despite his repeated—and methodologically unnecessary—slighting of "theology," has been an invaluable resource for my own thinking about these matters.

What is needed now is a more coherent conversation *between* students of material culture and students of theology. I hope to provide the resources for beginning such a conversation in this volume and in this chapter.

For an eloquent plea in this same direction, see Margaret R. Miles, "Becoming Answerable for What We See," *Journal of the American Academy of Religion* 68.3 (2000): 471–485.

27. Antioch and Jerusalem both fell to the Arab advance in 638 CE, and Alexandria followed suit finally in 646 CE.

28. An eminently readable introduction to this material is Timothy Ware's *The Orthodox Church* (New York: Penguin Books, 1964). For this period of gradual Christian detachment—of the eastern world from the western—see pp. 60–81.

29. For the debate about the *filioque* especially, see Ware, *The Orthodox Church*, 56–60.

Basically, the problem was as follows. The original Greek Creed ratified the Trinity in the following terms: the Son has "proceeded from the Father" (*gennêthenta ek tou patros*), and He was the only person so begotten (*monogenê*). The point is that Christ, as the second person in the divine Trinity, was "begotten" rather than "created" (*gennêthenta ou poiêthenta*). Now, in the Latin translation of this Creed, appearing as early as 589 CE, the Holy Spirit was said to have "proceeded from the Father *and from the Son* (*filioque*)." Most eastern theologians felt that this suggested a subordination of the Holy Spirit to the other two persons of the Trinity, and they rejected the *filioque* on these grounds.

30. Ware, *The Orthodox Church*, 45–50. For a luminous description of these various western monasticisms, viewed through the eyes of one whose spiritual eyesight was trained in the east, see Patrick Leigh-Fermor, *A Time to Keep Silence* [1957] (Pleasantville, NY: A Common Reader Reprint, 1997).

For a more thoroughgoing account of the profound cultural and political differences, east and west, see Marilyn Dunn, *The Emergence of Monasticism: From the Desert Fathers to the Early Middle Ages* (New York: Oxford University Press, 2000). I am indebted to my good friend, Theodosios Nikolaïdis of the Ionian University at Corfu, for this reference.

31. See Gordana Babic, *Icons*, trans. Angus McGeoch (Munich: I. P. Verlagsgesellschaft, 1998); Constantine Cavarnos, *Guide to Byzantine Iconography*, Vol. I (Boston, MA: Holy Transfiguration Monastery, 1993); Gennadios Limouris, *Icons: Windows on Eternity, Theology and Spirituality in Colour* (Geneva: World Council of Churches Publications, 1990); and David and Tamara Talbot Rice, *Icons and Their History* (Woodstock, NY: The Overlook Press, 1974).

32. In saying this, I do not mean to parrot the inherited wisdom about Byzantine art—especially the icons—namely, that it represents a "frozen" aesthetic tradition that did not develop significantly for fully a millennium. For a far more nuanced analysis of

Byzantine iconography and its developments, see Patrick Leigh-Fermor, *Mani: Travels in the Southern Peloponnese* (London: John Murray, 1958), 223–229.

33. Belting, *Likeness and Presence,* 63–77, 124–126, 320–348.

34. See the telling cultural sketch available at Acts 19:23–20:1.

35. Belting, *Likeness and Presence,* 109.

36. Ware, *The Orthodox Church,* 38–43; and Belting, *Likeness and Presence,* 144–163.

37. I think of this in opposition to "the cult of the imperial image," the statues that had been a major Christian preoccupation in previous generations. For some surprisingly early evidence of Christian iconoclasm in *that* context, see Carlo Carletti, "L'Ipogeo Anonimo Della Via Paisello Sulla Salaria Vetus," *Revista Di Archeologia Cristiana* 1971: 99–117.

38. Belting, *Likeness and Presence,* 138–139.

39. Ibid., 42,144. For a superb discussion of the "comprehensive" versus "restrictive" interpretations of Jewish law—the former implying some form of Jewish aniconism, the latter implying that "the Second Commandment theoretically licenses all visual images except one," see Kalman Bland, *The Artless Jew: Medieval and Modern Affirmations and Denials of the Visual* (Princeton: Princeton University Press, 2000), 3–12, 59–60. I am especially pleased to record a happy personal debt to Professor Bland, who walked me through this material with his customary wisdom and good cheer, and who generously read several versions of this chapter.

40. Of course, ecclesiastical leaders continued to hammer out matters of doctrine and ecclesial organization, and thus councils were still assembled, but only these first seven laid claim to real "catholicity." The eighth such council (and the fourth of them to be held in Constantinople) met in 869–870 CE, but its legitimacy was recognized only in the Latin-speaking, western churches. Indeed, record of this Council does not exist in any Byzantine canonical collection. Hereafter, "east was east and west was west" in most all questions ecclesial. The matter of iconic representation in Christian worship, however, continued to be a matter of considerable debate, especially in the western churches. In the spirit of this ongoing iconic investigation, and especially in light of aniconic arguments made by some Protestant reformers, the Council of Trent—in its 25th Session, in December of 1563 CE—proved to have a decisive impact.

    For a survey of the Seventh (and "Eighth") Ecumenical Councils, see Norman P. Tanner, S.J., ed., *Decrees of the Ecumenical Councils* (Washington, DC: Georgetown University Press, 1990) Volume I, 131–186. For the relevant decrees from the Council of Trent, see Volume II, 774–776.

41. Events took a more complicated turn in the eastern Roman Empire, actually. Another bout of imperially sanctioned iconoclasm erupted in Constantinople in 813 CE, and was not resolved for another 30 years. It was in this latter stage of the controversy that Theodore the Studite (more on him below) composed his theological reflections on the icons.

    See Belting, *Likeness and Presence,* 159.

42. I emphasize the appearance of this transgression, since Kalman Bland persuasively argues that it is a creation of the nineteenth century: "I argue that were it not for Kant and Hegel, the denial of Jewish art in its present form would not have been invented" (Bland, *The Artless Jew,* 8; see also 15–16).

43. Belting, *Likeness and Presence,* 144.

44. I am pleased as well to acknowledge a debt to Robert C. Gregg, who first introduced me to Theodore's writings, subtly suggesting that, Aquinas notwithstanding, Theodore may have been the more sophisticated "doctor" of the eastern churches on this question.

45. For much of this information about the city, and Theodore's place within it, I am indebted to that marvelous compendium of urban facts, *The Blue Guide.* See John Freely, *Istanbul,* 4th ed. (New York: W. W. Norton & Company, 1997), 211–213.

See also the fine entries in F.L. Cross, ed., *The Oxford Dictionary of the Christian Church* (New York: Oxford University Press, 1958), 1340, and Alexander P. Kazhdan, ed., *The Oxford Dictionary of Byzantium,* in three volumes (New York: Oxford University Press, 1991) III, 2044–2045.

46. More evidence for this point-of-view is available. The Byzantine emperor, Alexis Comnenus (1081–1118 CE), commissioned a monk named Euthymios Zigabenos to compile a collection of all the theological arguments that might "arm" Christendom against heresy, as well as to provide the intellectual "weapons" with which best to attack it. This collection of 28 compact treatises, *The Dogmatic Armory,* contains an intriguing observation at §21. Euthymios lists his sources for us and, while the Decree of the Seventh Ecumenical Council and the works of "the blessed Theodore of Studion" are foregrounded, the works of John of Damascus are not mentioned.

The Greek text of the *Armory* is available in J.-P. Migne, ed., *Patrologiae Graeca* 130: 1163–1174. I am indebted to Father Thomas J. Steele's unpublished translation and summary of the *Armory,* which he very graciously made available to me.

47. See St. John of Damascus, *On the Divine Images: Three Apologies Against Those Who Attack the Divine Images,* trans. David Anderson (Crestwood, NY: St. Vladimir's Seminary Press, 1997).

The Greek texts of John's three treatises are available in J.-P. Migne, ed., *Patrologia Graeca* 94: 1231–1420.

48. See St. Theodore the Studite, *On the Holy Icons,* trans. Catherine P. Roth (Crestwood, NY: St. Vladimir's Seminary Press, 1981).

The Greek text of Theodore's work is available in J.-P. Migne, ed., *Patrologia Graeca* 99: 328–436.

49. Belting, *Likeness and Presence,* 150.

50. For a nice sketch of this idea, and its roots in Christian apocalypticism, see James Barr, *Fundamentalism* (Philadelphia, PA: The Westminster Press, 1978), 191–198.

See also Bruce B. Lawrence, *Defenders of God: The Fundamentalist Revolt Against the Modern Age,* 2nd ed. (Columbia: University of South Carolina Press, 1995), 153–188; Nancy Tatom Ammermann, *Bible Believers: Fundamentalists in the Modern World* (New Brunswick, NJ: Rutgers University Press, 1987); and George M. Marsden, *Understanding Fundamentalism and Evangelicalism* (Grand Rapids, MI: William Eerdmans Publishing Co., 1991), 39–44, 100–101.

51. Theodore the Studite, *On the Holy Icons* I,§5 (page 24); and Migne, ed., *Patrologia Graeca* 99: 333. My translations occasionally vary slightly from Roth's fine and elegant renderings. Note, too, that Theodore is quoting from Paul's letter to the Galatians here.

52. Theodore, *On the Holy Icons,* II,§36 (page 64); and Migne, ed., *Patrologia Graeca* 99: 376.

53. John of Damascus, *On the Divine Images,* I,§8 (page 18); and Migne, ed., *Patrologiae Graeca* 94: 1237.

54. Theodore the Studite, *On the Holy Icons,* I,§7 (page 27); and Migne, ed., *Patrologia Graeca* 99: 337.

55. Here again, Theodore seems to be re-working a much cruder Johannine dichotomy between "Greeks" and "the Church," *Hellênes* and *Ekklêsia.* The force of this is missed when John's terminology is consistently translated, not as "Greek," but as "pagan."

Surely you object, not to our veneration (*proskynêsin*) of icons (*eikonôn*), but rather to the scandalous practices of god-making Greeks (*theopoiountôn Hellênôn*). And yet this pointless practice of the Greeks (*tên tôn Hellênôn atopon chrêsin*) does not invalidate the pious practice of the Church. . . . The Greeks sacrificed to demons. Israel did so to God, but in the form of fat and blood. The Church offers a bloodless sacrifice (*thysian anaimakton*) to God. The Greeks set up icons (*eikonas*) to demons. And Israel made its icons into gods (*etheopoiêse tas eikonas*). . . . But we have dedicated icons (*eikonas*) to the true God, the incarnate (*sarkôthenti*) God, as well as to the friends and servants of God.

John of Damascus, *On the Divine Images* II,§17 (pages 63–64); and Migne, ed., *Patrologiae Graeca* 94: 1304.

Note that John is once again using a fairly crude contrast—between "Jews" and "Greeks" on the one hand, and "Church" on the other. He is echoing "On Heresies," of course. Yet John makes no distinction between "icons" and "idols" at all. We all use icons, John suggests, but we put them to different uses. None of this will be found in Theodore, who is himself a "Greek." Moreover, Theodore is attempting to develop the practical technical vocabulary so evidently absent in John. He concludes, with the Nicene Council, that the icon (*tên eikona*) of Christ, or of Mary, or of a saint, is completely different than the wooden images of ancient Greek divinities (*tois xoanois*) that are in fact "satanic idols" (*satanikôn eidôlôn*).

See Tanner, ed., *Decrees of the Ecumenical Councils*, I: 134.

56. Theodore the Studite, *On the Holy Icons*, I,§13 (page 34); and Migne, ed., *Patrologia Graeca* 99: 344.

57. See *Symposium* 210a–211d, as well as my attempt at a rehabilitation of this Platonic perspective in *Symposia: Plato, the Erotic and Moral Value* (Albany: State University of New York Press, 1999).

John also seems to be playing with Platonic, or else Neoplatonic, imagery when he refers to the "mnemonic" value of true icons. I will return to this idea at the conclusion of this chapter. See *On the Divine Images* I,§13;II,§§10–11 (pp. 21, 57–59). For more on this mnemonic theology, see Belting, *Likeness and Presence*, 9–14.

58. This may seem to be overstated, since, by his third apologetic oration, John has landed on the semantic distinction which works best for him. There are many kinds of *proskynêsis*, John suggests, only one of which—authentic *latreia*—belongs to God. But there are other kinds of submission (*hypoptôsis*) which function in the Church's economy of worship: awe and yearning (*thauma kai pothon*), thanksgiving (*eucharistôs*), need (*endeian*), hope (*elpida*), repentance (*metanoia*), and confession (*exomologêseôs*).

See John of Damascus, *On the Divine Images*, III,§§27–32; and Migne, ed., *Patrologiae Graeca* 94: 1348–1349.

One of the stories that John, and others, clearly have in mind is Alexander the Great's adoption of what was perceived to be a *Persian* practice of *proskynêsis*, that is, the bowing down before one's king. Alexander's insistence on this practice very nearly caused a revolt by his own Macedonian troops. Iconodoulic theologians often cite the veneration one offers to the image of the emperor as an example of the sort of thing involved here. Julian made much the same point in his *Letter to a Priest*.

But notice the trouble John gets into earlier, when he suggests that "I venerate (*proskynô*) one God, one Godhead. But I worship (*latreuô*) a Trinity of persons."

John of Damascus, *On the Divine Images* I,§4 (page 15); and Migne, ed., *Patrologiae Graeca* 94: 1236.

John gets it more nearly correct at I,§14, but in no case are these Orthodox creedal formulations.

59. *Theotokos* is a technical Greek term for "God-bearer," and was established as a doctrinally sound name for Mary, "the mother of God," at the Third Ecumenical Council of Ephesus in 431. There had been some question as to whether Mary was best thought of as the mother of Christ in *human* form (and thus *anthropotokos*), or actually as the bearer of the Incarnate God, and thus more appropriately called *theotokos*. The latter position triumphed at Ephesus.

See Belting, *Likeness and Presence*, 32–36.

60. Theodore the Studite, *On the Holy Icons*, I,§19 (page 38); and Migne, ed., *Patrologia Graeca* 99: 348.

61. This, Theodore's precise language, echoes the language adopted by the Council in 787 CE. They concluded that

we . . . render [the icons] honorable veneration (*timêtikên proskynêsin*] by kissing them and by witnessing to our veneration, not the true worship (*alêthinên latreian*) which, according to our faith, is proper only to the one divine nature. . . .

For the full text of the Council's decision, see Tanner, ed., *Decrees of the Ecumenical Councils,* I: 133–137.

62. John of Damascus, *On the Divine Images,* I,§23; II,§16; and Migne, ed., *Patrologiae Graeca,* 94: 1256, 1301.

63. John of Damascus, *On the Divine Images,* II,§10; and Migne, ed., *Patrologiae Graeca,* 94: 1293. It is worth noting that the Nicene Council seemed to *equate* the bowing and kissing before crosses, before the relics of the saints, *and before the holy books of the Gospel,* with the selfsame "veneration" that takes place in relation to the holy icons. Clearly, then, as material artifacts, such icons are very much "like" the holy books.

64. Theodore the Studite, *On the Holy Icons* II,§7 (pp. 46–47); and Migne, ed., *Patrologia Graeca* 99: 356. As always, John of Damascus is more polemical, more abrupt, and thus perhaps also more memorable:

Where then will you find, either in the Old Testament (*en têi Palaiai*) or in the Gospel (*en tôi Evangeliôi*), the name of the Trinity (*Triados*), or the term "consubstantial" (*homoousion*), or "the one nature of the Godhead" (*mian physin theotêtos tranôs*), or even the "three persons" (*treis hypostaseis*) of God? What about the "single personhood of Christ" (*mian hypostasin tou Christou*), or his "dual natures" (*dyo physeis*)? And yet, even still, the Holy Fathers have identified all of these things, implicitly and in words of equal authority (*ek tôn isodynamousôn lexeôn*), resident in the scripture. We have received them, and we anathematize those who don't.

See John of Damascus, *On the Divine Images,* III,§11 (page 71); and Migne, ed., *Patrologiae Graeca* 94: 1333.

65. Theodore the Studite, *On the Holy Icons* III,§13 (p. 82); and Migne, ed., *Patrologia Graeca* 99: 396.

66. Here, as ever, John's rhetoric is more dramatic and astonishing. It is the astonishment of the Incarnation that drives his entire argument, in fact. There are countless kinds of icons, John reminds us. Among them, amazingly enough, are: the Son, the Holy Spirit, and even human beings! "The Son is the natural icon (*physikê eikôn*) of the Father," he says . . . "and the Holy Spirit is the icon (*eikôn*) of the Son."
    John of Damascus, *On the Divine Images,* III,§18 (pp. 74–75); and Migne, ed., *Patrologiae Graeca* 94: 1340. And once again:

Who first made an icon? It was God Himself Who first begat the only-begotten Son, His Word, the living icon (*eikona*) of Himself, a natural (*physikên*) icon, with a character precisely similar to His own eternity. And then He made the human being as His own icon and likeness (*kata eikona autou kai kath' homoiosin*).

John of Damascus, *On the Divine Images,* III,§26 (p. 80); and Migne, ed., *Patrologiae Graeca* 94: 1345. Now this is truly astonishing news: the Son is an icon of the Father; the Holy Spirit is an icon of the Son; human beings are themselves a sort of iconic representation of . . . what? the Father? the Son? the Trinity? We may applaud John's Christological enthusiasm here—and it has scriptural warrant, since the Septuagint's rendering of Genesis 1:26–27 uses an identical phrase—but these flights of rhetorical enthusiasm are ever absent from Theodore's more sober reasoning. The stakes in his case, one senses, are simply too high for this sort of thing.

67. See Bland, *The Artless Jew,* 144.

68. John of Damascus, *On the Divine Images,* I,§21 (p. 29); and Migne, ed., *Patrologiae Graeca* 94: 1253.

69. Belting, *Likeness and Presence,* 154, 533–535. See also Richard Haugh, *Photius and the Carolingians: The Trinitarian Controversy* (Belmont, MA: Nordland Publishing Company, 1975), 45–53.

70. For a nice sketch of these events from the Byzantine perspective, see C. M. Woodhouse, *Modern Greece: A Short History,* 4th ed. (London: Faber and Faber, 1986), 50–52.

71. But see the important caution about overestimating the aniconic (rather than iconoclastic) impulses in Protestantism offered by Bland, *The Artless Jew,* 66–70.

    See also Belting, *Likeness and Presence,* 458–490, whose important thesis suggests that Protestant iconoclasm actually helped to create the modern concept of art, whereby *the cult of the artwork* supplanted the church's long-standing cult of the holy image, or icon. This is another version of the Christian competition with Hellenism that we met in the previous chapter.

    Finally, see Camille, *The Gothic Idol: Ideology and Image-Making in Medieval Art* (New York: Cambridge University Press, 1989), 338–351, for an intriguing "dialectical" sketch of the negations and transformations that take us from Renaissance, to Reformation, to Modernism, and beyond.

72. For a compelling reconstruction of the surprisingly vital late medieval church in England, as well as a look at the *material* dimension of the Reformation there, see Eamon Duffy, *The Stripping of the Altars: Traditional Religion in England, c.1400–1580* (New Haven, CT: Yale University Press, 1992).

    It is customary to "read" the Reformation as a partial repositioning and a partial rejection of (north Italian) Renaissance humanism and its methods of visual representation. For an intriguing, if quirky, glimpse of some of the visual material that would have been most troubling to some Christians, see Leo Steinberg, *The Sexuality of Christ in Renaissance Art and in Modern Oblivion,* 2nd ed. (Chicago: University of Chicago Press, 1983, 1996). This book does a very fine job of attending to the fleshiness, the often penile fleshiness, of Renaissance depictions of the Christ-child, as well as the bodily scandal represented by his passion and death.

    For an alternative reading of this same material, see Caroline Walker Bynum, *Holy Feast and Holy Fast: The Religious Significance of Food to Medieval Women* (Berkeley: University of California Press, 1987), 307n3, as well as *Fragmentation and Redemption: Essays on Gender and the Human Body in Medieval Religion* (New York: Columbia University Press, 1992), 79–117. Finally, see Steinberg's reply to Bynum in *The Sexuality of Christ,* 364–389.

73. For more on the culture of Protestant "Hebraizing," see Vassilis Lambropoulos, *The Rise of Eurocentrism,* 24–41, 86–87, as well as my review of the book, "On Being Jewish or Greek in the Modern Moment," *Diaspora* 3.2 (1994): 199–220.

74. Michael Camille goes so far as to argue that idolatry "was synonymous with the worship of three-dimensional images during the Middle Ages," in *The Gothic Idol,* 18. He adds that this became virtually a canon of art-historical criticism by the eighteenth century, that is to say, in the era of Winckelmann and what Hans Belting calls the Era of Art.

75. This is Bland's important conclusion, *The Artless Jew,* 152–153.

76. For a nice sketch of some more contemporary iconoclastic desecration of *artwork,* which is not "religiously" inspired in quite the same way, see David Friedberg, *Iconoclasts and Their Motives* (Montclair, NJ: Abner Schram, 1985).

77. I have been much instructed by Alex J. Sider, "'Bright Mysteries': Image, Likeness and the Ethics of Memory," *Scottish Journal of Theology* (2001). Alex is a good friend, who demonstrated this by reading several drafts of this essay with keen insights and suggestions for improvement each time.

78. The paradigmatic example is Jacques Derrida, "Plato's Pharmacy," in *Disseminations,* trans. Barbara Johnson (Chicago: University of Chicago Press, 1981), 63–171.

79. It is perhaps relevant to note that Julian made Plato the chief rival to Adam and Moses and Jesus in *Against the Galileans*. He privileges Platonic vision over Mosaic hearing:

> It may appear more clearly this way who is better and worthier to speak of God—Plato, who venerated the images (*eidôlois*), or the one of whom it is written that God spoke with him, mouth to mouth.(49b)

He privileges Platonic naming over the Adamic:

> Plato gives names to these gods who are visible—whether sun or moon, stars or heavens—but these are all images (*eikones*) of the invisible.(65b)

And he privileges the Platonic account of creation over the Christian:

> The common creator of both realms is the one who made the heavens and the earth and the seas and the stars, the one who begat their archetypes in the realm of intellect.(65c)

Clearly, in every case, it is Plato's sensitivity to images, icons, and forms that accounts for his superiority.

80. See my *Symposia,* 127–140.
81. Plato, *Phaedrus* 275a.
82. For a superb discussion of the formulation of Eucharistic doctrine in northern Europe from roughly 900–1200 CE, see Bynum, *Holy Feast and Holy Fast,* 48–69.

CHAPTER SIX

1. This is fast becoming a truism in the field of Comparative Religious Studies. And one of its most elegant and influential spokespersons has been Jonathan Z. Smith. In the introduction to *Imagining Religion: From Babylon to Jonestown* (Chicago: University of Chicago Press, 1982), he notes:

> If we have understood the archaeological and textual record correctly, man has had his entire history in which to imagine deities and modes of interaction with them. But man, more precisely western man, has had only the last few centuries in which to imagine religion. It is this act of second order, reflective imagination which must be the central preoccupation of any student of religion. . . . *[T]here is no data for religion.* Religion is solely the creation of the scholar's study. It is created for the scholar's analytic purposes by his imaginative acts of comparison and generalization. Religion has no independent existence apart from the academy. For this reason, the student of religion, and most particularly the historian of religion, must be relentlessly self-conscious. Indeed, this self-consciousness constitutes his primary expertise, his foremost object of study.(xi, note omitted)

Smith's primary material in that collection has to do with ancient Jewish materials and some modern, largely apocalyptic ones. A later text devoted to late pagan and early Christian rhetoric and practice is of more direct relevance to my project. That book is *Drudgery Divine: On the Comparison of Early Christianities and the Religions of Late Antiquity* (Chicago: University of Chicago Press, 1990), especially the discussion "On Comparison" (36–53), in which the rivalry between Catholic and Protestant sensibilities appears in some fascinating ways.

2. It is surely important to note that, in refashioning *Greek* identity as a *religious* identity, Pausanias pays especially close attention to monuments and to statues, what we are now trained to understand as "material culture." Virtually an entire Book of his *Greek*

Walkabout (Book VI, the second of the two devoted to "Eleia") is devoted to statuary, and to the kinds of stories such statues are designed to commemorate.

3. I am aware that this is not the common way of characterizing this period. Gregory of Nyssa, referred to as the very "father of fathers" in his own day, makes a justly famous observation about the contested Christian culture of the late fourth century in Asia Minor, shortly prior to the alleged "resolution" of the Christological and Trinitarian debates at the Fourth Ecumenical Council of Chalcedon in 451 CE. Writing in the full heat of controversy, Gregory observes:

> The whole city is full of it, the squares, the marketplaces, the cross-roads, the alleyways; old-clothes men, money-changers, food-sellers: they are all busy arguing. If you ask someone for change, he philosophizes about the Begotten and the Unbegotten; if you enquire about the price of a loaf, you are told by way of reply that the Father is greater and the Son inferior; if you ask "Is my bath ready?" the attendant answers that the Son was made out of nothing.

As quoted in C. M. Woodhouse, *Modern Greece: A Short History* 4th ed. (London: Faber and Faber, 1986), 27.

All I wish to emphasize in this fascinating and justly famous description is that a theologian has made it. Whether the baker and money-changer, or the slave, would have described their religious culture in the same way remains an open question. But I have my doubts.

4. For a nice summary of some of the literary traditions which attached themselves to Sappho's name, see David A. Campbell, ed., *Sappho and Alcaeus,* which is Volume I in the five-volume Loeb edition of *Greek Lyric* (Cambridge, MA: Harvard University Press, 1982), 2–51.

5. For a wonderful survey of this vast literature, see Samuel Schoenbaum, *Shakespeare's Lives,* 2nd ed. (New York: Oxford University Press, 1991).

6. See the superb collection of such sayings in A. N. Eastman and G. B. Harrison, eds., *Shakespeare's Critics: From Jonson to Auden* (Ann Arbor, MI: University of Michigan Press, 1964).

7. For a superb discussion of "what . . . it signif[ies] to speak of a World Literature in English," when the English language is itself a diasporic, colonial phenomenon, and thus not at all singular, see Rita Raley, "On Global English and the Transmutation of Postcolonial Studies into 'Literature in English'," *Diaspora* 8.1 (1999): 51–80.

8. Representative of this viewpoint is the work of the noted (and, in his own terms, really superb) British Hegelian, A. C. Bradley, *Shakespearean Tragedy: Lectures on Hamlet, Othello, King Lear, Macbeth* (London: Macmillan and Company, 1903).

9. For a wonderful attempt to stitch together certain essential biographical texts, like Shakespeare's Last Will and Testament with this, presumably his latest play, see Nikos Kazantzakis, *England* (New York: Simon and Shuster, 1965), 231–274.

See also the fascinating notes on the composition of a 1991 film version of the play in Peter Greenaway, *Prospero's Books* (London: Chatto & Windus, 1991).

It is of special interest to me that, during the years in which Lawrence Durrell was holed up on Corfu (1935–1938), he undertook his first serious study of *Hamlet,* one that led him to identify the resolution of the problems that play posed in *The Tempest.* See Durrell's *Prospero's Cell: A Guide to the Landscape and the Manners of the Island of Corcyra* (New York: Marlowe and Company, 1945, 1996), xviii–xix. I will return to this matter at chapter's end.

10. See the fascinating observations to this effect in Alexis de Tocqueville, *Democracy in America* [1835, 1840], trans. Henry Reeve, and rev. Francis Bowen (New York: Vintage Books, 1945) Volume II, Book 1, Chapter 13:

> The literary genius of Great Britain still darts its rays into the recesses of the New World. There is hardly a pioneer's hut that does not contain a few odd

volumes of Shakespeare. I remember that I read the feudal drama of *Henry V*
for the first time in a log cabin. (58)

11. John Southworth, *Shakespeare the Player: A Life in the Theatre* (Gloustershire: Sutton Press,
2000).

12. Frederick S. Boas makes this observation in his *Thomas Heywood* (London: Williams &
Norgate, 1950):

> The leading Elizabethan dramatists may from one point of view be divided
> into two groups. There are those whose only connection with the professional
> stage was as playwrights. Amongst these were Kyd and Marlowe, Beaumont
> and Fletcher, Middleton and Massinger, Webster and Ford, Tourneur and
> Shirley. Another group combined the roles of actor and playwright. It is
> headed by Shakespeare and included Jonson (in his earlier days), William
> Rowley, Nathan Field, Richard Brome and Thomas Heywood. (11)

13. Although matter this matter surely does. Charles Nicholl, in his *The Reckoning: The Murder of Christopher Marlowe* (Orlando, FL: Harcourt Brace & Company, 1992) brilliantly
establishes the falsity of, as well as the motive behind the creation of, this long-standing historical myth. Nicholl's alternative thesis—that Marlowe was murdered by secret government agents—presents what is, in his own words, "not a pretty view of the
Golden Age of Elizabeth, and . . . not a pretty view of Christopher Marlowe either"
(265). Nicholl's argument highlights the extraordinary tension, an emphatically *religious* tension, of the times. His thesis, briefly, is as follows:

   Marlowe had been taken on as a spy already when he was a student at Corpus
Christi College, Cambridge, between 1585 and 1587. His purpose there was to pose as
a Catholic sympathizer, in order to root out students who were "intent on going to
Rheims," where an expatriate Catholic seminary had been formed (another newly
formed college, Emmanuel, had been established as a Puritan stronghold at Cambridge in 1584, and our own Thomas Heywood likely was enrolled there).

   Marlowe seems to have been in secret government employ again in the Winter of
1591/1592, working this time for Sir Robert Cecil, First Earl of Salisbury (1563–1612),
in a relatively new sphere of operations: the Low Countries, where English forces had
bogged down in an interminable campaign against a Spanish-led Catholic army. Marlowe was arrested in Flissingen, as a counterfeiter "with intent to go to the enemy."
Nicholl argues that he was again posing as a double agent, but was accidentally found
out before he could complete his mission. He was returned to England, then subsequently released without comment. In 1593, he was again posing as a Catholic sympathizer, this time preparing to go "unto the K of Scots," the man who would be James
I. This last accusation, rendered by Thomas Kyd (1558–1594) under torture, was not
fleshed out before Marlowe's murder.

   According to Nicholl's thesis, Marlowe was being used as a pawn in the much larger
court intrigue that pitched Robert Devereux, Second Earl of Essex (1566–1601)
against Sir Walter Ralegh (1552–1618). Robert Dudley, Earl of Leicester (c.
1532–1588, Elizabeth's darling and court favorite) had died, and Sir Francis Walsing-
ham (c. 1530–1590, the prime organizer of Elizabeth's secret police force) died two
years later. Both Essex and Ralegh, then, were jockeying for position in the new court.
By 1592, Essex' star was ascendant, and Ralegh was imprisoned for the first time. And
so we come to the strange Spring of 1593.

   In late March, the Parliament debated two important policies: the nature and extent of religious freedom and toleration; and the continued granting of privileges to
the increasingly unpopular foreign traders resident in London. Both issues had a decidedly religious valence. And Ralegh took unpopular positions on both fronts. He

spoke in support of religious freedom (leaving himself open to the easy charge of
"atheism"), and he spoke against the traders, especially the Dutch.

In April and May 1593, a series of libelous pamphlets were posted around Lon-
don, condemning and even threatening these foreign residents. On April 22, the
Privy Council began to investigate them. On May 5, the most disturbing of them
all, the so-called Dutch Church Libel, was affixed to the Dutch Church in London.
It made several less-than-oblique references to several phrases from several of
Marlowe's plays.

In response, on May 11 or 12, Marlowe's friend and former roommate, Thomas Kyd,
was arrested. Among the personal papers that were seized (or planted) at the time
was one proposing the Unitarian/Arian heresy. Under torture (Kyd would die the following year), Kyd claimed that the paper belonged to Marlowe, and accused him of
"violence" and "atheism" as well. On May 18, a warrant was issued for Marlowe's arrest. On May 20, he was brought before the Privy Council, yet against all expectation,
he was summarily released and ordered to report to them daily. In the interim, further accusations of his "atheism" surfaced, all of them implicating Ralegh and his immediate social circle. First comes the "Remembrances" of one Richard Cholmeley,
and then, on May 27, comes a notorious "Note" penned by a Richard Baines. This was
thought to be the most damaging account thus far of the unorthodox behavior of this
circle of subtle friends. Yet still the plot to discredit Marlowe and Ralegh stalled. Marlowe had backers in high places, Sir Robert Cecil chief among them. He was still "in
play," and therefore still a threat.

Three days later, a secret meeting was called at Deptford Strand, some three miles
outside of London. The Earl of Essex's men—Nicholas Skeres and Ingram Frizer, as
well as another secret serviceman, Richard Poley (freshly returned from the Low Countries)—convened with Marlowe in secret, not in a bar. They talked for fully eight hours.

At the end of that meeting, Marlowe was dead, killed by a stab wound in the right
eye socket. The story issued at the inquest is scarcely credible; it speaks of Frizer's
being attacked somehow with his own weapon, immobilized by the two men sitting
to either side of him, yet managing to disarm, and then kill, Christopher Marlowe.
Still, the case was dismissed in the following week, written off as a simple act of self-
defense. And so the myth of the dissolute poet was born.

Ralegh was investigated belatedly on the same charges of "atheism" in March of the
following year. In 1603, he was implicated in a plot against King James I, and imprisoned again; he was executed 15 years later, in 1618. The Earl of Essex did not last so
long; he was beheaded on Tower Hill in 1601. Skeres disappeared in prison some years
hence, Poley was put out to pasture in 1601, and Frizer died "a well-to-do Kentish
yeoman" in 1627. Nicholl concludes:

Marlowe did not die by mischance, and he was not killed in self-defense. He
had become an impediment to the political ambitions of the Earl of Essex, as
these were perceived and furthered by secret operators like Cholmeley and
Baines, and behind them probably Thomas Phelippes. They had tried to
frame him; to get him imprisoned and tortured; to use him as their "instrument" against Ralegh. They had tried all this and failed. He had proved elusive, a danger, a potential projector against them. His mouth—if it could not
be made to say what they wanted it to say—must be "stopped." To the plausible Skeres is entrusted this delicate task: to try once more to persuade Marlowe to turn evidence against Ralegh, and failing that, to silence him for good.
I do not think the purpose of the meeting was murder. This is not because I
underestimate the ruthlessness of the Essex faction . . . but because if murder
had been intended all along, it could have been better accomplished more

anonymously. Rather, Marlowe's death was a *decision*. It was a point the day reached, by a process of dwindling options. (*The Reckoning,* 327–328)

I elucidate this thesis at length not only because I find it so intriguing and so plausibly reconstructed. I do so because it foregrounds the same essential issue I wish to discuss: namely, the abiding connection between the Elizabethan theater and the religio-political strife of the times, to which I turn below.

14. Or, in Shakespeare's day, *Roman* instead. For a nice discussion of the prominence and influence of Seneca on the Elizabethan stage, see T. S. Eliot, *Essays on Elizabethan Drama* (New York: Harcourt, Brace and World, 1960), 3–55.

15. See Jaroslav Pelikan and Helmut T. Lehmann, gen. eds., American Edition, *Luther's Works* (Philadelphia, PA: Fortress Press, 1958–1967), 44: 115–217, 36: 3–126, and 31: 327–377, respectively.

16. John T. McNeill, ed., *Calvin: Institutes of the Christian Religion,* trans. Ford Lewis Battles (Philadelphia, PA: The Westminster Press, 1960) two vols.

17. It is of special interest to note that, at precisely this time, these various Reform movements either turned especially violent, or else they became pacifist. Moreover some figures, such as Luther, seemed better prepared to countenance significant domestic violence by the state, but not foreign wars.

I am indebted to the work of Stanley Hauerwas for helping me to notice these curious connections. See his "Can a Pacifist Think About War?" in *Dispatches From the Front: Theological Engagements with the Secular* (Durham, NC: Duke University Press, 1994), 116–135. Hauerwas owes a debt that he is eager to acknowledge to the work of Mennonite theologian, John Howard Yoder, especially *The Original Revolution: Essays on Christian Pacifism* (Scottdale, PA: Herald Press, 1971), and *The Politics of Jesus* (Grand Rapids, MI: William Eerdmans Publishing Company, 1972).

18. I am indebted to Liah Greenfeld's *Nationalism: Five Roads to Modernity* (Cambridge, MA: Harvard University Press, 1992) for developing this insight, especially to her discussion of the trajectory of these nationalisms in France (89–188) and in Germany (276–395).

19. Which is Greenfeld's view of the matter, in *Nationalism: Five Roads to Modernity,* 28–87.

20. See Walter D. Mignolo, *The Darker Side of the Renaissance: Literacy, Territoriality and Colonization* (Ann Arbor: University of Michigan Press, 1995), 37. This claim, however, does not fully account for the Ottoman Empire in its heyday.

21. For an especially disturbing eyewitness account of the siege and occupation of Rome, see Luigi Guicciardini (1478–1551), *The Sack of Rome,* trans. James H. McGregor (NY: Italica Press, 1993).

For an important discussion of the relatively late suspicion applied to such eyewitness accounts by modern historians, see Anthony Grafton, *The Footnote: A Curious History* (Cambridge, MA: Harvard University Press, 1997), 40–50.

See Mary McCarthy, *The Stones of Florence* (New York: Harcourt Brace & Company, 1963), 192–219.

22. This picture is complicated by the "development (and imperial) gap" between the emerging English nation and the more global Spanish empire. Whereas both succeeded in establishing their colonial projects in the Americas in the 1600s, the Britons were never able to conceive of their relations with the Ottoman Mediterranean world in even vaguely "colonial" terms. Britons met Turks and Moors as equals in North Africa and the eastern Mediterranean. It was later, in the eighteenth and nineteenth centuries, that they applied the colonizing discourse they had developed in the Americas to the world of Islamdom. And that is the conceptual frame through which the characters we will discuss in the next two chapters viewed the Ottoman east, especially its own western colonial outpost, Greece herself.

See Nabil Matar, *Turks, Moors & Englishmen in the Age of Discovery* (New York: Columbia University Press, 1999).

23. For a fascinating sketch of Catholicism in England on the eve of Reformation, see Eamon Duffy, *The Stripping of the Altars: Traditional Religion in England, 1400–1580* (New Haven, CT: Yale University Press, 1992), where he argues that "*the* defining doctrine of late medieval Catholicism was Purgatory" (8, see also 299–378). For Duffy's specific reading of Elizabeth's reign in the light of this thesis, see 565–593.

24. For a fascinating analysis of the reasons lying behind the selection of the theater as the premier cultural battleground, see Jean-Christophe Agnew, *Worlds Apart: The Market and the Theater in Anglo-American Thought, 1550–1750* (New York: Cambridge University Press, 1986). He notes:

> Mercantilism and Puritanism embraced representational strategies aimed at righting a world that money (among other things) appeared to have upended, a world that threatened to become, in effect, a permanent carnival. For this very reason, perhaps, the theater quickly became the terrain on which this struggle to redefine the grounds of exchange relations was most vividly and vigorously joined. Separated, like the market, from its original ritual and hierarchical aegis, the Elizabethan and Jacobean theater furnished a laboratory of representational possibilities for a society perplexed by the cultural consequences of its own liquidity.(54)

25. The definitive biography on Heywood's career is Arthur M. Clarke, *Thomas Heywood: Playwright and Miscellanist* (Oxford: Basil Blackwell, 1931), on which I am dependent for my summary of his life in these paragraphs.

26. *A Reply to Stephen Gosson's Schoole of Abuse in Defense of Poetry Musick and Stage Plays* (1580?), in *The Complete Works of Thomas Lodge* (New York: Russell & Russell, Inc., 1963), Volume I (48 facsimile pages).

27. Gager worked with Alberico Gentili [see Endnote 31] on the *Lectionum et Epistolarum quae ad I us Civile Pertinent* (1583), shortly after Gentili arrived at Oxford. Gager later engaged in a debate with Dr. John Rainolds, a Puritan colleague, about the moral status of the theater in 1591. Rainolds appended relevant correspondence from both Gager and Gentili in his *Th' Overthrow of Stage Plays* (Middleburgh: 1599).

28. His *Apology for Poetry* was appended to his Introduction of Ludovico Ariosto, *Orlando Furioso in English Heroical Verse* (London: 1591).

29. *A Quip for an Upstart Courtier* [1592], in Edwin H. Miller, ed., *Ciceronis Amor: Tullies Love and A Quip for an Upstart Courtier* (Gainesville, FL: Scholars' Facsimiles and Reprints, 1954).

30. *Piers Penniless, His Supplication to the Devil* [1592], Stanley Wells, ed. (London: Edward Arnold, 1964).

31. His *Commentatio ad L[egem] III C[odicis] de prof[essoribus] et med[icis]* (Oxford: 1593) is available in the original Latin and in English translation in J. W. Binns, "Alberico Gentili in Defense of Poetry and Acting," *Studies in the Renaissance* 19 (1972): 224–272.

32. *An Apology for Poetry* [1595], Forrest G. Robinson, ed. (Indianapolis, IN: Bobbs-Merrill Company, Inc., 1970).

33. Richard H. Perkinson, ed., *An Apology for Actors by Thomas Heywood and A Refutation of the Apology for Actors by I. G.* (New York: Scholars' Facsimiles and Reprints, 1941).

34. Agnew, *Worlds Apart*, 101–148.

35. Deuteronomy 22:5.

36. For further discussion of Heywood's contributions, see Agnew, *Worlds Apart*, 133–135; Boas, *Thomas Heywood*, 77–82; Clarke, *Thomas Heywood*, 69–83.
    Finally, see Huston Diehl, *Staging Reform, Reforming the Stage: Protestantism and Popular Theater in Early Modern England* (Ithaca, NY: Cornell University Press, 1997), 71–72.

37. In Heywood's case, the *Apology* moves from an account of the theater's antiquity, through an account of its dignity, and then on to a defense of its modern qualities. In

I. G.'s case, three points begging to be made concern the theater's status as a "Heathenish and Diabolicall institution," its "ancient and moderne indignitie," and the "wonderfull abuse of their impious qualitie." The discussions naturally overlap in most cases, often point-for-point.

38. Perkinson, ed., *An Apology for Actors,* F-3.
39. Greenfeld, *Nationalism: Five Roads to Modernity,* 73.
40. Vague confirmation of I. G.'s view may be found in a noteworthy comment that George Chapman (c. 1559–1634) made in the preface to his famous translation of the *Iliad* in 1611:

> And for our tongue, that still is so empayr'd
> By travailing linguists, I can prove it cleare
> That no tongue hath the Muse's utterance heyr'd
> For verse, and that sweet Musique to the eare
> Strooke out of rime, so naturally as this.
> Our Monosyllables so kindly fall
> And meete, opposde in rime, as they did kisse;
> French and Italian, most immetricall,
> Their many syllables in harsh Collision
> Fall as they brake their necks, their bastard Rimes
> Saluting as they justl'd in transition,
> And set our teeth on edge, nor tunes nor times
> Kept in their falles. And, me thinkes, their long words
> Shew in short verse as in a narrow place
> Two opposites should meet with two-hand swords
> Unwieldily, without or use or grace.
> Thus having rid the rubs and strow'd these flowers
> In our thrice sacred Homer's English way,
> What rests to make him yet more worthy yours?

See Allardyce Nicoll, ed., *Chapman's Homer: The Iliad,* with a new preface by Gary Wills (Princeton: Princeton University Press, 1998) "To the Reader," 11. This had fast become a standard rhetorical trope in the Elizabethan period.

41. Perkinson, ed., *Refutation of the Apology for Actors,* F 2 (page 41).
42. Alexis de Tocqueville makes some trenchant observations about the forces that contribute to such linguistic change. He notes that an influx of Greek and Latin loanwords has had an enormous impact on French and English, alike. The ideology of North American democracy, he adds, promises to alter the career of the English language still more thoroughly (*Democracy in America* II.1.16, pages 68–74). See also related remarks on the demotic institutions of poetry and drama in America (75–89).
43. See the humorous account of such issues in Bill Bryson, *The Mother Tongue: English & How It Got That Way* (New York: William Morrow and Company, Inc., 1990), and *Made in America: An Informal History of the English Language in the United States* (New York: William Morrow and Company, Inc., 1994).
44. This is a partially historical argument for I. G. And this is so because Greek thought, in his judgment, *derives from* the Hebraic:

> Next, doth M. Actor looke back from Italy into Greece, declaring that the Princes and Sages thereof, being those which were the first vnderstanders, trained vp their youthfull Nobilitie to be Actors, debarring the Mechanicks such imployment. In which, is diuers things to be noted & refuted: First, that not all Greece is to be vnderstood, for Sparta is to be exempted as reiecting such abuses. Secondly, how doth he derogate from the glory of the Hebrewes,

when he riportes that the Grecians were the first Vnderstanders, whereas it
is euident by all History, the Grecians receiued their knowledg from the
AEgiptians, and Chaldaeans, and they from the Hebrewes.

(Perkinson, ed., *Refutation of the Apology for Actors,* C 1, [pages 14–15]).
45. For a fascinating survey of this time, these characters (with special attention to Eras-
    mus and Rabelais), and these linguistic concerns, see M. A. Screech, *Laughter at the Foot
    of the Cross* (Boulder, CO: Westview Press, 1999), esp. 152ff.
46. Jonson, *The Alchemist* II,v,12–17.
47. Perkinson, ed., *Refutation of the Apology for Actors,* D 1 (page 23).
48. Ibid., D 4 (page 29).
49. Nietzsche, *On the Genealogy of Morals* I.16. See also *Human, All-Too-Human* §237; *The Gay
    Science* §§35,148,149,358; and *The Antichrist* §§4,10,58,61.
50. For more on this vexing constellation of ideas, see Benedict Anderson, *Imagined Com-
    munities: Reflections on the Origin and Spread of Nationalism* (London: Verso, 1983). For a com-
    parative political survey of five nations' (England, France, Russia, Germany, and the
    United States of America) paths to nationhood, see Greenfeld, *Nationalism: Five Roads
    to Modernity.*
51. This is an insight that I owe to three distinguished scholars of Modern Greek, all of
    whom I first met at the Ohio State University. Three of their books, taken together,
    lay out this terrain very nicely:
       Gregory Jusdanis, *Belated Modernity and Aesthetic Culture: Inventing National Literature*
    (Minneapolis: University of Minnesota Press, 1991);
       Vassilis Lambropoulos, *Literature as National Institution: Studies in the Politics of Modern
    Greek Criticism* (Princeton: Princeton University Press, 1988); and
       Artemis Leontis, *Topographies of Hellenism: Mapping the Homeland* (Ithaca, NY: Cornell
    University Press, 1995).
52. For my first pass at telling it, which also represents the real prolegomena to this book,
    see "Why the Greeks?" in Johann P. Arnason and Peter Murphy, eds., *Agon, Logos, Polis:
    The Greek Achievement and Its Aftermath* (Stuttgart: Franz Steiner Verlag, 2000), 29–55.
53. The debt that European classicism owes to its Muslim intellectual forebears has been
    the topic of much discussion in recent years. Leo Strauss was one of the first scholars
    in the United States to emphasize this point, at least in reference to the history of Pla-
    tonic interpretations.
       For excellent descriptions of this translation project and its eventual exportation,
    see Dimitri Gutas, *Greek Thought, Arabic Culture: The Graeco-Arabic Translation Movement in
    Baghdad and Early 'Abbasid Society (2nd–4th/8th–10th Centuries* (New York: Routledge, 1998);
    Marshall G. S. Hodgson, *The Venture of Islam: Conscience and History in a World Civilization*
    (Chicago: University of Chicago Press, 1961, 1974) I, 285–318, 434–472; and II,
    159–200, 271–275, 293–328; and F. E. Peters, *Aristotle and the Arabs* (New York: New
    York University Press, 1968).
54. Alasdair MacIntyre has recently popularized just this way of understanding the im-
    plications of the Thomist project.
       See *Whose Justice? Which Rationality?* (Notre Dame, IN: University of Notre Dame
    Press, 1988), 164–208, and *Three Rival Versions of Moral Enquiry: Encyclopedia, Genealogy, Tra-
    dition* (Notre Dame, IN: University of Notre Dame Press, 1990), 105–148, as well as
    the important reservations expressed by John Haldane, "MacIntyre's Thomist Re-
    vival: What Next?" in John Horton and Susan Mendus, eds., *After MacIntyre: Critical Per-
    spectives on the Work of Alasdair MacIntyre* (Notre Dame, IN: University of Notre Dame
    Press, 1994), 91–107.
55. One resource for identifying these sources for the Renaissance in Italy is Jacob Burck-
    hardt, *The Civilization of the Renaissance in Italy,* in two vols., trans. S. G. C. Middlemore

(New York: Harper & Row, 1958) I, 204–205. More recent work has identified the long-standing Byzantine links to Venice as one important conduit through which all the rest flowed. Such a reading of the Renaissance places more emphasis on Venice (and Genoa) than it does on Florence, since the Venetians were a real presence in Greece throughout these centuries, almost constantly at war with the Ottomans.

See Donald M. Nicol, *Byzantium and Venice: A Study in Diplomatic and Cultural Relations* (New York: Cambridge University Press, 1988), and *The Last Centuries of Byzantium, 1261–1453* (New York: Cambridge University Press, 1993).

I am especially indebted to Anastasia Papadia-Lala, who shared her important unpublished manuscript with me, entitled "'Europe' in the Venetian-ruled Greek Territories (13th to 18th Centuries): Perceptions and Realities."

56. Even the Counter-Reformation tried to say Yes and No at once. See Eleanor Clark, *Rome and a Villa* (Pleasantville, NY: The Akadine Press, 1950, 1999), 265–275.

57. I Maccabees 2:23–25.

58. Tacitus, *Histories* V,12; and Josephus, *The Jewish War* V,255.

For a nice discussion of the implications of these extraordinary reports, see Pierre Vidal-Naquet, *The Jews: History, Memory and the Present,* trans. David Ames Curtis (New York: Columbia University Press, 1996), 3–19, as well as my review of the book, "Jewish History: One, Two, Three," in *Thesis Eleven* 53 (1998): 114–125.

59. I Maccabees 1:1–5.

This same evaluation is strangely echoed by I.G., when he refutes Heywood's claim that Alexander was inspired to his vast achievements by the desire to imitate the courage he witnessed on the Hellenistic stage. I.G. seems to attribute Alexander's achievements to (the Christian?) God.

So that not the life of *Achilles* acted before him, but the Diuine Vision prickt
him forwards to the performance of his atchiuements.

(Perkinson, ed., *Refutation of the Apology for Actors,* B 2 [page 8]).

60. Much like Late Antiquity, and much like Late Medieval Venice, the Hellenistic Jewish world has come up for a great deal of contemporary scholarly re-examination.

For discussion of the scholarly developments that helped "to make the study of Hellenistic Judaism one of the growth areas of late nineteenth and early twentieth century philology," see Suzanne Marchand and Anthony Grafton, "Martin Bernal and His Critics," *Arion, Third Series* 5.2 (1997): esp. 20–24.

An excellent contemporary survey of recent scholarly developments is Peter Schäfer, *The History of the Jews in Antiquity: The Jews of Palestine from Alexander the Great to the Arab Conquest,* trans. David Chowcat (Luxembourg: Harwood Academic Publishers, 1995).

61. For a particularly trenchant analysis which suggests that the roots of this Romantic trope may actually be found here, in the Reformation, see Vassilis Lambropoulos, *The Rise of Eurocentrism: Anatomy of Intepretation* (Princeton, NJ: Princeton University Press, 1993), 24–41, as well as my review of the book, "On Being Jewish or Greek in the Modern Moment," *Diaspora* 3.2 (1994): 199–220.

62. For more on these developments, see Duffy, *The Stripping of the Altars,* 377–523, with plates.

63. This is my extension of the fascinating thesis I examined in the last chapter, deriving from Kalman Bland's *The Artless Jew: Medieval and Modern Affirmations and Denials of the Visual* (Princeton, NJ: Princeton University Press, 2000).

64. Perkinson, ed., *An Apology for Actors,* F 3.

65. Ibid., B-3.

66. Perkinson, ed., *A Refutation of the Apology for Actors,* B-1 (pages 7–8).

I. G. also scores an important point when he mentions what Heywood failed to mention—namely, that morally serious and reflective "pagans," such as Plato, had already argued for the closing of the theaters in their Grecian heyday (E 3). Heywood's reply would be that *other* reflective pagans, such as Aristotle, devoted entire books to them (B 3).

67. Another novel strategy which Heywood employs is essentially to take the armory of scripture out of the hands of the Puritans, by arguing that, while the Roman world of the first century CE was thick with theaters and thick with plays, no New Testament text speaks a single word against them. (See Boas, *Thomas Heywood,* 79).

68. Perkinson, ed., *An Apology for Actors,* F 3–4.

69. Ibid., G 2–3.

70. Jan Kott insists on the inevitable plenitude and plurality of readings of *Hamlet* in *Shakespeare Our Contemporary,* trans. Boleslaw Taborski (Garden City, NY: Doubleday and Company, Inc., 1966), 57–73, and then offers us a richly nuanced political reading himself. Another such "political" reading is Francis Fergusson's, in *Shakespeare: The Pattern in His Carpet* (New York: Delacorte Press, 1971), 188–197. My own reading emphasizes the connection between such overtly political concerns and the contemporary wars of religion.

71. Assessing the place of "religion," broadly defined, in Shakespeare's stagecraft has become a major scholarly preoccupation. I sense that this is one reason for the explosion of renewed interest in *The Tempest,* which figures prominently in many of these discussions.

See, for example: Gene Fendt, *Is Hamlet a Religious Drama? An Essay on a Question in Kierkegaard* (Milwaukee, MN: Marquette University Press,1999); Thomas Howard, "Christian Patterns in *The Winter's Tale* and *The Tempest,*" in E. Beatrice Batson, ed., *Shakespeare and the Christian Tradition* (Lewiston, NY: Edward Mellen Press, 1994), 163–175; Steven Marx, *Shakespeare and the Bible* (New York: Oxford University Press, 2000); Gerald M. Pinciss, *Forbidden Matter: Religion in the Drama of Shakespeare and His Contemporaries* (Newark: University of Delaware Press, 2000), esp. 58–77 on Thomas Heywood; and cf. D. Douglas Waters, *Christian Settings in Shakespeare's Tragedies* (Rutherford, NJ: Fairleigh Dickinson University Press, 1994), 208–246, which argues that *Hamlet* is ultimately "a secular tragedy, not a religious one."

72. And was made available in a "clean" Quarto only in 1604/5, making it immediately available for Heywood's scholarly perusal. See Louis B. Wright and Virginia A. Lamar, *The Folger Guide to Shakespeare* (New York: Washington Square Press, 1969), 236–237.

73. Shakespeare, *Hamlet* II.ii.593–610.

74. Which actually consists of two plays, one mimed and one spoken. This has been the source of much interpretive confusion.
See *Hamlet* III.iii,138–274.

75. The classic statement of this view is H. Mutschmann and K. Wentersdorf, *Shakespeare and Catholicism* (New York: Sheed and Ward, 1952), 363–365.
By contrast, Velma B. Richmond's *Shakespeare, Catholicism and Romance* (New York: Continuum, 2000) says not a word about *Hamlet,* though her reconstruction of the religious environment in Shakespeare's day (21–96) is quite helpful.

76. See Henry Morris, *Last Things in Shakespeare* (Tallahassee: University Presses of Florida, 1985), 12–75, esp. 21–34, which insists on the *demonic* identity of the Ghost.

77. See Stanley Cavell, "Hamlet's Burden of Proof," in *Disowning Knowledge in Six Plays of Shakespeare* (New York: Cambridge University Press, 1987), 179–191, which, despite its heavy debt to Freud, concludes brilliantly: "Shakespeare's dramas, like Freud's, propose our coming to know what we cannot just now know; like philosophy."

78. And it is only the grand drama of one such play that will prompt that grandest of all Christian moral transactions: judgment and repentance. Whether forgiveness also has a place in this troubling play's moral universe is a complex question requiring more

discussion than we can assemble here. Forgiveness, however, is ultimately the touch which makes *The Tempest* work.

79. Aristotle, *Poetics* 1451 b1–15.
80. This well-known barb actually comes from Ben Jonson's encomium, penned upon the poet's death.

> And though thou hadst small *Latine* and lesse *Greeke,*
> From thence to honour thee, I would not seeke
> For names; but call forth thund'ring *AEschilus,*
> *Euripides,* and *Sophocles* to us. . . .

The fiction to which this swiftly led was that Shakespeare was a "natural genius," schooled on Nature and Nature alone.

For the opposed modern thesis—that Shakespeare was actually quite well-read, in several languages—see G.K. Hunter, "Shakespeare's Reading," in Kenneth Muir and Samuel Schoenbaum, eds., *A New Companion to Shakespeare Studies* (New York: Cambridge University Press, 1971), 55–66, and John Michell, *Who Wrote Shakespeare?* (London: Thames and Hudson, 1996), 23–26.

CHAPTER SEVEN

1. Published now, *Tragic Posture and Tragic Vision: Against the Modern Failure of Nerve* (New York: Continuum Press, 1994).
2. This deliberately recalls Benjamin's dictum, "that which withers in the age of mechanical reproduction is the aura of the work of art" (Hannah Arendt, ed., *Illuminations: Essays and Reflections,* trans. Harry Zohn (New York: Shocken Books, 1968), 221]. In this chapter, I discuss the quest for that lost aura among poets and Greek travelers; in the next chapter I return to that quest as it focused on the plastic arts.
3. One of the two libraries in which I worked in those years, the Gennadius, which is affiliated with the American School across the street, publishes several scholarly monographs each year. For an excellent bilingual account of these events, see Cornelia Hadjiaslani, *Morosoni, the Venetians and the Akropolis* (Athens: Gennadius Publications, 1987).
4. One partial answer to this question might be that no country has ever undertaken a more disciplined and self-conscious project of simultaneous modernization and westernization than Japan did in the latter half of the nineteenth century. So it is that they inherited "the Greeks," as well.

   For a "western" view of "them," which the Japanese very dramatically embraced and internalized after the war, see Ruth Benedict, *The Chrysanthemum and the Sword: Patterns of Japanese Culture* (New York: Houghton Mifflin Company, 1946, 1989).

   For the suggestion that this book is actually, if ironically, about "us" rather than about "them," see Clifford Geertz, "Us/Not Us: Benedict's Travels," in *Works and Lives: The Anthropologist as Author* (Palo Alto, CA: Stanford University Press, 1988), 102–128.

   For an analysis at once more sympathetic to Benedict's judgments *and* to Japanese attempts to account for them without utterly sacrificing their own cultural identity, see Nicolas Bouvier, *The Japanese Chronicles,* trans. Anne Dickerson (San Francisco: Mercury House, 1989, 1992), 73–84.
5. Bertrand Russell, *A History of Western Philosophy* (New York: Simon and Schuster, 1945), 746.

   A more supple explanation of why this is so may be found in Isaiah Berlin's *The Roots of Romanticism* (Princeton: Princeton University Press, 1999), 8, 131–134, in which he locates Romanticism within an overarching rebellion against Enlightenment values, in favor of two eminent and long-lasting principles: "the necessity of the will and the absence of a structure of things."

6. Hugh Tresgakis cleared the ground for all later digging in his *Beyond the Grand Tour: The Levant Lunatics* (London: Ascent Books, 1979), esp. 66–105, on Byron's and Hobhouse's first tour. Tresgakis penned the book primarily in the beloved Gennadius Library in Athens, a library that today still houses an impressive collection of Byron memorabilia.

   A quirkier and more intimate account, one that has the advantage of dealing with both of Byron's trips, is Stephen Minta's *On a Voiceless Shore: Byron in Greece* (New York: Henry Holt and Company, 1998). I have profited enormously from both books in the preparation of this chapter.

7. It has just been reprinted, as Edward J. Trelawny, *Records of Shelley, Byron, and the Author,* with an Introduction by Anne Barton (New York: New York Review of Books, 2000).

8. Eleanor Clark makes an interesting observation about the proverbial linkage of Shelley to Keats:

   The coupling of the names . . . is by now too ingrained to be stopped—as if one should try to separate Sodom and Gomorrha or Scylla and Charybdis; nobody says Shakespeare, Spenser, Milton, Dante *and* anybody, so the meaning must be that it takes two of these, three with Byron, to make a whole poet.

   (*Rome and a Villa* [Pleasantville, NY: The Akadine Press, 1950, 1992], 300).
   Interestingly enough, much as Trelawney *used* Byron to highlight Shelley's greatness, Clark uses Shelley to render Keats still greater. This is a long-standing literary convention through which, so it seems to me, the singularity of Byron's contributions are inevitably short-changed.

9. Trelawny, *Records of Shelley, Byron, and the Author,* 39, *contra* his statements at 209–210 and 248.

10. Ibid., 25–26, 45–46, 61, 70, 85. It is relevant to note that Trelawny refers to Byron consistently as "the Pilgrim," reserving the epithet of "the Poet" for Shelley alone, until he dies.

11. Ibid., 32, 37–38, 49–50, 64–66, 70–72, 94, 100–102.

12. Ibid., 24, 30, 89, 116–118, 231.

13. Ibid., 50–55, 73–76, 80.

14. Ibid., 10, 56–61, 67–68, 83, 87, 144–145, but see 6 and 78–79.

15. Ibid., 10.

16. Ibid., 95.

17. Ibid., 87.

18. Immanuel Kant (1724–1804) and Georg Wilhelm Friedrich Hegel (1770–1831) are the key figures here.

   See Kant, *Critique of Judgment,* trans. Werner S. Pluhar (Indianapolis,IN: Hackett Publishing Company,1987), §§51–53 (pages 189–201), as well as the wonderful abridged summary of Hegel's impressive body of posthumously published *Lectures on Aesthetics* in Henry Paolucci, ed., *Hegel: On the Arts* (New York: Frederick Ungar Publishing Co., 1979), 64–67.

   Finally, see Stephen A. Larrabee, *English Bards and Grecian Marbles: The Relationship Between Sculpture and Poetry Especially in the Romantic Period* (New York: Columbia University Press, 1943), especially pages 149–174 on Byron.

19. Minta, *On a Voiceless Shore,* 194–214.

20. Trelawny, *Records of Shelley, Byron, and the Author,* 99–108.

21. Ibid., 33, 86–87.

22. An analysis of the connection between these ideas—spirituality and sensuality, morality and transgression, Romanticism and Decadence—one that also derives the image

of Byron's "bad boy" from Milton's highly influential portrait of Satan, is Mario Praz's *The Romantic Agony*, 2nd ed., trans. Angus Davidson (New York: Meridian Books, 1950, 1956), esp. 61–81 on Byron. While self-styled as a "controversial" study when first released, the book has since become a standard reference work.

23. The problem of grounding, of finding solid epistemic (not to mention religious) grounds for belief, was a central preoccupation of the Romantic philosophers after Kant. Their story has been well told by Andrew Bowie, *From Romanticism to Critical Theory: The Philosophy of German Literary Theory* (New York: Routledge, 1998).

    See my review of that book, "So You Do Theory, Do You?" in *Philosophy Today* 42.4 (1998): 439–447.

24. It is fascinating and worth noting, given my interests in this book, that "Romantic" was originally coined as a negative term, one which was gradually rehabilitated in the nineteenth century. See Praz, *The Romantic Agony*, 12ff.

25. Ibid., 73.

26. Dr. Johnson's remark, recorded by James Boswell in 1776, is representative of the regnant aristocratic attitude:

    a man who has not been to Italy is always conscious of his inferiority, from his not having seen what is expected a man should see. The grand object of travelling is to see the shores of the Mediterranean. (as quoted in Tresgakis, *Beyond the Grand Tour*, 5).

27. Hegel would observe famously that Greece represented "the cheerful aspect of youthful freshness"; whether that of childhood or of adolescence, it was always that of *youth*.

    See his *Lectures on the Philosophy of History*, trans. J. Sibree (New York: Dover Publications, 1956), 219–220, 223–224.

28. A fascinating prelude to, and anticipation of, these matters are Lady Mary Wortley Montagu's *Turkish Embassy Letters*, Malcolm Jack, ed. (London: Virago Press, 1993).

29. Edward W. Said, *Orientalism* (New York: Vintage Books, 1978), 166–197. Said aptly notes the rise of the "travel book" as a genre created in part by this culture. And yet he fails to notice, astonishingly and consistently throughout the book, that Greece was not a "European" region, either in antiquity *or* in the nineteenth century (see the telling remarks at 11, 20–21, 56–57, 68).

    What remains to be done after Said, it seems to me, is to "orientalize" Said's (and hardly his alone) mainstream conception of "Greece" and "the west."

30. These colonies become the special concern in Said's companion volume, *Culture and Imperialism* (New York: Vintage Books, 1993), although he continues to insist that the binary ethnographic logic of "us versus them" actually "goes back to Greek thought about barbarians" (xxv). That is a silly claim, one that ignores the Greeks' own remarkable ethnographic innovations. The single greatest insight of Said's enormously influential work is one that justifies even such occasional scholarly overreaching, that extraordinary fact which he never lets us forget:

    from 1815 to 1914 European direct colonial dominion expanded from about 35 percent of the earth's surface to about 85 percent of it. Every continent was affected, none more so than Africa and Asia. (Said, *Orientalism*, 41)

31. A point well made by Bruce B. Lawrence in "Enough Said: Trying the Build Cultural Bridges Instead of Shoring Up Ideological Walls" (forthcoming).

32. Like Byron, Goethe picked up, packed up, and hit the road with some suddenness. And, again very like Byron, he was gone for fully two years. See Goethe's *Italian Journey, 1786–1788*, trans. W. H. Auden and Elizabeth Mayer (San Francisco, CA: North Point Press, 1982).

The connections here run deeper still, as Goethe considered Byron among the greatest (and certainly the most *imaginative*) poets of his generation. He recommended that Eckermann study English if only to be able to read Byron's poetry and plays in the original. See Goethe's *Conversations With Eckermann, 1823–1832,* trans. John Oxenford (San Francisco: North Point Press, 1984), 70–72.

33. Tregaskis, *Beyond the Grand Tour,* 7–11, 49.

34. See Helen Angelomatis-Tsougarakis, *The Eve of the Greek Revival: British Travellers' Perceptions of Early Nineteenth Century Greece* (New York: Routledge, 1990).

35. See Olga Augustinos, *French Odysseys: Greece in French Travel Literature from the Renaissance to the Romantic Era* (Baltimore, MD: The Johns Hopkins University Press, 1994).

36. For a superb survey of the phenomenon of Germanic travel to Greece in this same era, see *Das Griechenland-Album des Grafen Carl von Rechberg, 1804–1805* (Zurich: Verlag der Wolfsbergdrucke, 1974). See also Suzanne L. Marchand, *Down From Olympus: Archaeology and Philhellenism in Germany, 1750–1970* (Princeton, NJ: Princeton University Press, 1996), especially 116–151 on German Hellenism, Nietzsche's Classical revolution, and Schliemann's contribution to the exploration of the material culture of Classical antiquity.

    Contrasted with this philhellenism is the strange nationalist mythology fueled by Roman studies (see 156–162, on "Romandom and Germandom").

37. For two very different accounts of these literary trends in English, see Robert Eisner, *Travelers to an Antique Land: The History and Literature of Travel to Greece* (Ann Arbor: University of Michigan Press, 1991), which lays out the historical terrain quite nicely, and Mark Cocker, *Loneliness and Time: The Story of British Travel Writing* (New York: Pantheon Books, 1992), which focuses more on late nineteenth- and twentieth-century materials.

38. There is another way to read this, as less innocent and far more designed. Travel writing has also been read as a crucial instrument in the project of European imperialism. This far more pernicious understanding of the genre attends to the power of writing in creating a reality to suit itself. Writing about the colonial outpost serves to underwrite the self-understanding of the imperial homeland, on this view. An overall superb presentation of this thesis may be found in Mary Louise Pratt, *Imperial Eyes: Travel Writing and Transculturation* (New York: Routledge, 1992), although her mention of the "account of Lord Byron's South Sea expedition of 1824–5" (157) is astonishing, given that Byron *never* sailed the South Seas, and that he *died* in 1824!

    Pratt is less interested ultimately in the southern Mediterranean and India than she is in Central and South America. A more sophisticated presentation of her general viewpoint is thus Walter D. Mignolo's extraordinary *The Darker Side of the Renaissance: Literacy, Territoriality and Colonization* (Ann Arbor: University of Michigan Press, 1995), in which he argues that imperials must colonize three things primarily: language (with written grammars and lexicons); memory (with travelogues and local histories); and space (with maps). His analysis of the colonization of memory through travel writing may be found at pages 125–216.

39. For a nice summary of this material, going all the way back to Spon and Wheler's famous trip of 1675, see David Constantine, *Early Greek Travellers and the Hellenic Ideal* (New York: Cambridge University Press, 1984).

40. Three of the most consistently interesting contemporary voices I have encountered belong to:

    Nicolas Bouvier, whose *The Japanese Chronicles* I have already mentioned, and whose *The Way of the World,* trans. Robyn Marsack (Marlboro, VT: The Marlboro Press, 1985, 1992), provides a positively luminous account of the singular cadences and rhythms of life on the road;

    Patrick Leigh-Fermor, who has dedicated his uncanny literary talents to the Caribbean (*The Travellers Tree: A Journey Through the Caribbean Islands* [London: John Murray, 1950, 1984]), as well as to his native Greece, where he and his wife, Joan, have settled in a lovely home which they built themselves (*Mani: Travels in the Southern Peloponnese* [London: John Murray, 1958] and *Roumeli: Travels in Northern Greece* [London: John Murray, 1966]). Fermor is currently completing a trilogy which recalls a walk he managed from England to Istanbul between 1933 and 1935. See *A Time of Gifts* (New York: Penguin Books, 1977) and *Between the Woods and the Water* (New York: Penguin Books, 1986);

and Lawrence Durrell, who wrote wonderful pieces on various islands, like Corfu (*Prospero's Cell* [New York: Marlowe & Company, 1945]), Rhodes (*Reflections on a Marine Venus* [New York: Penguin Books, 1952]), Cyprus (*Bitter Lemons* [New York: Penguin Books, 1958]), and Sicily (*Sicilian Carousel* [New York: Marlowe & Company, 1976]). Of equal note is the collection of occasional essays compiled by Alan G. Thomas in *Spirit of Place* (New York: Marlowe & Company, 1969), as well as his final book, *Provence* (New York: Arcade Publishing, 1990).

Durrell has the added virtue of placing many of these same insights into his fiction, nowhere better than in *The Dark Labrynth* (New York: Penguin Books, 1962—originally printed in Britain in 1947 as *Cefalu*) in which he sketches a memorable collection of British character types, all of them united in this, their pilgrimage to warmer, Mediterranean climes.

> drifting south into Italy and Greece, gradually emptying [their] ambitions
> one by one into the slow wake of life which, curiously enough, seemed only
> now to be beginning. (56)

When the venue changes from Greece and the Balkans to Italy, then several women's voices take center stage. For me among the finest are Mary McCarthy, *The Stones of Florence* (New York: Harcourt Brace & Company, 1959) and *Venice Observed* (New York: Harcourt Brace & Company, 1956), along with Eleanor Clark, *Rome and a Villa* (New York: The Akadine Press, 1950, 1999) to which I have referred before.

41. Russell, *A History of Western Philosophy*, 752.
42. And thus Byron himself, despite the poet's repeated authorial disclaimers. See, for instance, the original 1812 Preface to *Childe Harold's Pilgrimage* in *The Works of Lord Byron* (London: The Wordsworth Poetry Library, 1994), 174.
43. Byron, *Childe Harold's Pilgrimage*, II, xl.
44. The phrase is William Butler Yeats, from what is thought to be his final poem, "Politics." See *The Collected Poems of W. B. Yeats* (New York: Macmillan Company, 1952), 337.

    By contrast with these early pilgrimaging sentiments, in the last poem Byron ever wrote, the terms have decisively shifted. There is no more comfort for him in romance now, but he wishes to do something of *military* note, in Greece, before he dies. See "On This Day I Complete My Thirty-Sixth Year," in *The Works of Lord Byron*, 110.
45. See Minta, *On a Voiceless Shore*, 77–82, 148–156, for the now nearly inevitable discussion of Byron's (bi)sexuality.

    The defining work on this material is Louis Crompton, *Byron and Greek Love: Homophobia in 19th-Century England* (Berkeley: University of California Press, 1995), esp. 107–157 on the sexual adventurism of Byron's first Greek Tour. What I find really telling here is the way in which "Greek" came to mean something entirely new in the nineteenth century, as "Greek love" gradually became synonymous with (male) homosexuality.

    I regret that Jonathan David Gross's *Byron: The Erotic Liberal* (New York: Rowman & Littlefield Publishers,Inc., 2001) became available too late for me to make use of it.
46. This episode has been largely "demystified" by Benita Eisler in *Byron: Child of Passion, Fool of Fame* (New York: Alfred E. Knopf, 1999), esp. 433–506. But Eisler chronicles her case largely with letters, which even she admits are often self-serving and composed *ex post facto,* as well as with some fairly crude psychoanalysis of Byron, though curiously, of none of the others who surrounded him.

A more impressive defense of Byron in relation to his unhappy wife may be found in Trelawny, *Records of Shelley, Byron, and the Author*, 50–55, which is remarkable, given his general disdain for Byron's character. Apparently, Trelawny's distaste for women and the institution of marriage was stronger still.

47. Byron, *Childe Harold's Pilgrimage* IV, xc.
48. See the new 1818 Preface to Hobhouse:

With regard to the conduct of the last canto, there will be found less of the pilgrim than in any of the preceding, and that little slightly, if at all, separated from the author speaking in his own person. The fact is, that I had become weary of drawing a line which every one seemed determined not to perceive . . . (*The Works of Lord Byron*, 220)

49. Byron, *Childe Harold's Pilgrimage* III, vi.
50. Ibid., ii. See also III, iii–v.
51. Ibid., cxiv.
   See also III, cxi–cxiii, as well as "So We'll Go No More A-Roving," composed at roughly this same time (1817), in *The Works of Lord Byron*, 100.
52. Byron, *Childe Harold's Pilgrimage* III, i. See also III, cxv–cxviii.
53. Byron, *Childe Harold's Pilgrimage* IV, Dedication to Hobhouse, and xxxvi–xli.
54. Ibid., lx.
55. Ibid., xiv.
56. Minta, *On a Voiceless Shore*, 108, 113–114, 167–168.
57. As he remarked in notes compiled for the Second Canto of *Childe Harold's Pilgrimage*:

They are to be grateful to the Turks for their fetters, and to the Franks for their broken promises and lying counsels! They are to be grateful to the artist who engraves their ruins, and to the antiquary who carries them away! To the Traveler whose jannisary flogs them, and to the scribbler whose journal abuses them.

(As quoted in Artemis Leontis, *Topographies of Hellenism: Mapping the Homeland* [Ithaca, NY: Cornelll University Press, 1995], 2n1).

58. Byron, *Childe Harold's Pilgrimage* II, xi–xv.
59. Byron, "The Curse of Minerva," in *The Works of Lord Byron*, 138–141.
60. Byron, 1813 Preface to *Childe Harold's Pilgrimage* in *The Works of Lord Byron*, 174–175.
61. Trelawny, *Records of Shelley, Byron, and the Author*, 90–91. Byron knew better, as even Trelawny admits, 200–201.
62. Byron, *Childe Harold's Pilgrimage* II, lxxiii–xcii.
63. Ibid., xciii.
   For more on the Napoleonic campaign, see Said, *Orientalism*, 76–92, and *Culture and Imperialism*, 33–35, 118–119, as well as Russell Chamberlin, *Loot! The Heritage of Plunder* (London: Thames and Hudson,Ltd., 1983), 39–65, 123–148.
64. Pierre de Coubertin, *The Olympic Idea: Discourses and Essays* (Köln: Carl-Diem Institut, 1967), 106–107.
   See also C. P. Bracken, *Antiquities Acquired: The Spoliation of Greece* (London: David & Charles, 1975), 176–179.
65. This may be overstated a bit. Byron's involvement with various rival groups of Greek bands left him profoundly ambivalent about the possibilities for success in the war, as well as with a strong sense of the capacity for treachery that characterized all the klephtic groups. Byron's love of Greece was, ironically enough, not "romantic" in the least. See Minta, *On A Voiceless Shore*, 125–127, and Appendix One.
   For more on the Greeks' villainy, see Trelawny's self-serving account of his own affairs in Greece after Byron's death, *Records of Shelley, Byron, and the Author*, 247–283.

66. Byron, *Childe Harold's Pilgrimage* IV, lxi.
67. Ibid., clxxv.
68. Ibid., lxxviii–lxxxviii.
69. Ibid., cxlvi–clix.
70. In a letter to Hobhouse, written in Patras and dated October 4, 1810, he notes: "I have some idea of purchasing the Island of Ithaca. I suppose you will add me to the Levant Lunatics" (quoted by Tresgakis, in *Beyond the Grand Tour,* 100).
71. A telling clue appears in Herman Melville's 1850 classic, *White Jacket, or, The World in a Man O' War* (New York: Quality Paperback Book Club, 1996). Byron, it would seem, was *the* poet whom many a sailor could quote by heart in the mid-nineteenth century (14, 39, 261, 269, 341ff).
72. More even than *Typee* (1846) or *Billy Budd, Sailor* (1843, first published in 1924) or *Moby Dick* [1851], close attention should be paid to Melville's remarkable account of life at sea, published in 1850 as *White Jacket, or, The World in a Man O' War,* cited above.
73. Joseph Conrad, *The Mirror of the Sea* (Marlboro, VT: The Marlboro Press, 1998), 122.
74. Conrad, *The Mirror of the Sea,* 65.
75. Conrad, *The Mirror of the Sea,* 123.
76. Ibid., 64.
77. Trelawny, *Records of Shelley, Byron, and the Author,* 118–119.
78. Charles Sprawson, *Haunts of the Black Masseur: The Swimmer as Hero* (New York: Pantheon Books, 1994).
79. Sprawson, *Haunts of the Black Masseur,* 122–124.
    Oddly, this swim (along with Byron's three months in Turkey) is barely glossed by Minta, *On a Voiceless Shore,* 144.
80. Ibid., 102–105.
    For Byron's description of this swim in particular, see Jacques Barzun, ed., *The Selected Letters of Lord Byron* (New York: Grosset & Dunlap, 1953), 31–33, as well as "Written After Swimming from Sestos to Abydos," in *The Works of Lord Byron,* 58 (dated May 9, 1810).
81. Ibid., 117–121, 124–132.
82. Trelawny, *Records of Shelley, Byron, and the Author,* 56–58, 143–146; cf.28–29, 145–146, 218–222.
83. Sprawson, *Haunts of the Black Masseur,* 105, 120, 122.
    This was, in some ways, Nietzsche's definitive insight. The whole distinction between surface and depth, between superficiality and authenticity—with Nietzsche ironically privileging the surface over depth—is the leitmotif of *Twilight of the Idols,* surely the finest single summary of his mature thought. In 100 crisp, shocking pages, Nietzsche applies the taxonomy with a dialectician's razor edge, and with astonishing humor, to a wide variety of contemporary ideas: Socrates, the Greeks, the Romans, the Germans, as well as to various abstractions, such as reason, virtue, truth, and perhaps most scandalously of all, to women. I argue that Byron anticipates many of these Nietzschean moves in his letters and long verse.
84. Ibid., 111; Minta, *On a Voiceless Shore,* 202–205.
85. Sprawson, *Haunts of the Black Masseur,* 112–113; Trelawny, *Records of Shelley, Byron, and the Author,* 140–152.
86. For a rhapsodic modern treatment of the specialness of this Sea, see Predrag Matvejevic, *Mediterranean: A Cultural Landscape,* trans. Michael Henry Heim (Berkeley: University of California Press, 1999).
87. Byron, *Childe Harold's Pilgrimage,* IV, clxxix.
88. Ibid., clxxxii.
89. Ibid., clxxxiv.

1. In making this claim, I do not mean to suggest that Anglophone tourists in Greece today are simply recapitulating a newer version of the nineteenth century Grand Tour. Not at all. The rediscovery of Greece as a *modern* country, with a modern history, not simply as a museum full of fragments and antiquities—while having clear roots in Byron's own travels—seems to be a more deliberate creation of the 1930s. Lawrence Durrell and Henry Miller were instrumental in popularizing this, with a great deal of Greek assistance.

    See Avi Sharon, "New Friends for New Places: England Rediscovers Greece," *Arion, Third Series* 8.2 (2000): 42–62.

2. Edward J. Trelawny, *Recollections of Shelley, Byron, and the Author* (New York: New York Review Books, 2000), 251.

3. No greater spokesperson for that trend exists than Mark Twain. His 1869 classic, *The Innocents Abroad, or, The New Pilgrim's Progress* (New York: Airmont Publishing Company, 1967), describes the demotic sensibilities of these newer forms of travel, taking place as it does on a transatlantic steamer in 1867–1868. His alternately hilarious and poignant descriptions of Athens, and of Greece more generally, appear at 225–237.

4. Schliemann's own record of the excavations at Troy, originally published by John Murray of London in 1875, may be found in Philip Smith, ed., *Troy and its Remains* (New York: Dover Publications, 1994).

    A highly critical reading of Schliemann's career and its baser motives is David Traill, *Schliemann of Troy: Treasure and Deceit* (New York: St. Martin's Press, 1995). More balanced readings are provided by Katie Demakopoulou, ed., *Troy, Mycenae, Tiryns, Orchomenos: Heinrich Schliemann, the 100th Anniversary of his Death* (Athens: Ministry of Culture of Greece, 1990), and Susan Heuck Allen, *Finding the Walls of Troy: Frank Calvert and Heinrich Schliemann at Hisarlík* (Berkeley: University of California Press, 1999).

5. For more on this Egyptian campaign, see Edward W. Said, *Orientalism* (New York: Vintage Books, 1978) 76–92, and *Culture and Imperialism* (New York: Vintage Books, 1993) 33–35, 118–119. See also *Napoleon in Egypt: Al-Jabarti's Chronicle of the French Occupation, 1798*, trans. Schmuel Moreh with an Introduction by Robert L. Tignor and an Afterword by Edward W. Said (Princeton, NJ: Marcus Wiener Publishing, 1993).

    For the art-historical legacy of this Napoleonic looting, see Russell Chamberlin, *Loot! The Heritage of Plunder* (London: Thames and Hudson, Ltd., 1983), 39–65, 123–148.

6. For a fine discussion that serves to situate this Egyptian necrology, see Barbara E. Borg, "Faces of the Elite," trans. Glenn E. Most, *Arion, Third Series* 8.1 (2000): 63–96.

    For an intriguing sketch of the intellectual culture which contributed to such Egyptomania in the eighteenth and early nineteenth century, with specific mention of the Napoleonic campaign, see Martin Bernal's admittedly uneven *Black Athena: The Afroasiatic Roots of Classical Civilization* (New Brunswick, NJ: Rutgers University Press, 1987) Volume I: *The Fabrication of Greece, 1785–1985*, 161–188. Bernal's argument is that Egypt was gradually eclipsed among intellectual historians in the nineteenth century—first by India, then decisively by Greece—for complex reasons that include religious prejudice, racism, and Romanticism.

7. The Rosetta Stone, of course, is housed now in the British Museum, not the Louvre. When Lord Elgin was Ambassador to the Porte, he sent his personal secretary, William R. Hamilton (1777–1859), on a diplomatic visit to Egypt, specifically to oversee the French evacuation at Alexandria. Hamilton discovered that the French, in violation of their treaty agreements, had already prepared to ship the Stone. So he collected an armed escort, boarded the French vessel, and (re)confiscated it.

    The European Great Powers, amazingly, waged war with one another in the antiquities trade, as ferociously as they did in most other things. In the words of Major

General H. Turner, who accompanied the stone from Alexandria to Portsmouth in January-February 1802,

this artifact was a proud trophy of the arms of Britain (I could almost say *spolia opima*), not plundered from defenseless inhabitants, but honorably acquired by the fortune of war.

(As quoted in Brian M. Fagan, ed., *Eyewitness to Discovery: First-Person Accounts of More than Fifty of the World's Greatest Archeological Discoveries* [New York: Oxford University Press, 1996], 89).

For contemporary reflections on the meaning and scholarly relevance of the Stone, see Richard Parkinson, ed., *Cracking Codes: The Rosetta Stone and Its Decipherment* (Berkeley: University of California Press, 1999).

8. This story has been well told, if a bit too moralistically at times, by C. P. Bracken in *Antiquities Acquired: The Spoliation of Greece* (London: David & Charles, 1975).

9. For a nice analysis of the "museum tradition" and its essential linkage to Romantic Classicism, see Stephen L. Dyson, *Ancient Marbles to American Shores: Classical Archaeology in the United States* (Philadelphia: University of Pennsylvania Press, 1999), esp. 126–131.

See also Gerar Edizel, "Les ambitions dangereuses: How Art is Trying to Regain the Cultural Materiality It Has Lost," *Historical Reflections* 23.3 (1997): 331–347, an analysis which owes much to Hans Belting's definition of the nineteenth century as the "era of art," in *Likeness and Presence: A History of the Image Before the Era of Art,* trans. Edmund Jephcott (Chicago: University of Chicago Press, 1994).

10. See *The Works of Lord Byron* (New York: The Wordsworth Poetry Library, 1994) 59:

> Maid of Athens, ere we part,
> Give, oh give me back my heart!
> Or, since that has left my breast,
> Keep it now, and take the rest!
> Hear my vow before I go,
> *Zôê mou, sas agapô.*
>
> By those tresses unconfined,
> Woo'd by each Aegean wind;
> By those lids whose jetty fringe
> Kiss thy soft cheeks' blooming tinge;
> By those wild eyes like the roe,
> *Zôê mou, sas agapô.*
>
> By that lip I long to taste;
> By that zone-encircled waist;
> By all the token-flowers that tell
> What words can never speak so well;
> By love's alternate joy and woe,
> *Zôê mou, sas agapô.*
>
> Maid of Athens! I am gone:
> Think of me, sweet! when alone.
> Though I fly to Istambol,
> Athens holds my heart and soul:
> Can I cease to love thee? No!
> *Zôê mou, sas agapô.*

11. Interesting sketches of the Convent, with a view both of the Lysicrates Monument, and the Akropolis as scenic backdrop, may be found in Nicolas Revett and James Stuart, *The Antiquities of Athens, Measured and Delineated* (London: Society of the Dilettanti, 1762). This book was reprinted by the New York publishing firm, the Arno Press, in 1980.

12. Much has been written about Elgin's acquisition, which was of course also a theft, of the Parthenon marbles, though much of it is too polemical to be of much scholarly use. Several of the better treatments of the story are: Bracken, *Antiquities Acquired: The Spoliation of Greece*, 28–41; Chamberlin, *Loot! The Heritage of Plunder*, 13–38; Robert Eisner, *Travelers to an Antique Land: The History and Literature of Travel to Greece* (Ann Arbor: University of Michigan Press, 1991), 91–95; Hugh Tresgakis, *Beyond the Grand Tour: The Levant Lunatics* (London: Ascent Books, 1979), 44–50; Arthur H. Smith, "Lord Elgin and His Collection," *Journal of Hellenic Studies* 36.2 (1916): 163–372; William St. Clair, *Lord Elgin and the Marbles* (New York: Oxford University Press, 1967); and Theodore Vrettos, *A Shadow of Magnitude: The Acquisition of the Elgin Marbles* (New York: G. P. Putnam's Sons, 1974).

13. Chamberlin, *Loot! The Heritage of Plunder*, 13.

14. Quoted by Tresgakis, *Beyond the Grand Tour*, 45.

15. Smith, "Lord Elgin and His Collection," 255.

16. Byron, *Childe Harold's Pilgrimage*, II, xi–xv.

17. Dated March 17, 1811, and appearing in *The Works of Lord Byron*, 138–141, the poem was not published until 1828, posthumously.

18. Byron returned to the figure of Washington several times in his shorter verse. Here is how he concludes his "Ode to Napoleon Bonaparte" in 1814:

> Where may the wearied eye repose
> When gazing on the Great;
> Where neither guilty glory glows,
> Nor despicable state?
> Yes—one—the first—the last—the best—
> The Cincinnatus of the West,
> Whom envy dared not hate,
> Bequeathed the name of Washington,
> To make man blush there was but one!
> (*The Works of Lord Byron*, 72–74)

19. Bracken, *Antiquities Acquired*, 45; Chamberlin, *Loot! The Heritage of Plunder*, 31; Tresgakis, *Beyond the Grand Tour*, 105.

20. A great deal of material has been made available on Cockerell and his unusually long version of the Tour. There is no substitute for Cockerell's own later publications and drawings, both in Samuel Pepys Cockerell, ed., *Travels in Southern Europe and the Levant, 1810–1817* (London: Longmans, Green and Co., 1903), as well as *The Temples of Jupiter Panhellenius at Aegina and of Apollo Epicurius at Bassae Near Phigalia in Arcadia* (London: John Weale, 1860).

    In addition to this material, I have found the following secondary sources especially useful: Bracken, *Antiquities Acquired*, 106–136; Chamberlin, *Loot! The Heritage of Plunder*, 28–37; Eisner, *Travelers to an Antique Land*, 109–110; Tresgakis, *Beyond the Grand Tour*, 106–139; and finally David Watkin, *The Life and Work of C.R. Cockerell* (London: A. Zwemmer Ltd., 1974), esp. 3–37.

21. Cockerell had done some sketches of the marbles that Elgin had already managed to get to London, a collection that was housed in a famous house on Park Lane. William R. Hamilton, Elgin's private secretary in Constantinople and a close friend of the

Cockerell family, had written a letter of introduction on the back of some of these sketches to Giovanni Battista Lusieri, Elgin's point-man in Athens. Hamilton thus made all the necessary arrangements for the young Cockerell's trip; and so Cockerell later dedicated his 1860 publication of the Aegina and Phigalia discoveries to this old family friend.

See Smith, "Lord Elgin and His Collection," 298–300.

22. Cockerell, *Travels in Southern Europe and the Levant, 1810–1817,* 2:

> On the morning following my arrival, viz. April 16th, I embarked on board the vessel which was to carry me. She was a lugger-rigged despatch boat, hired by Government, named the *Black Joke.* She was very old, as she had been at the battle of Camperdown in 1797, but I was charmed with her neatness and tidiness. We had ten guns, thirty-five men, one sheep, two pigs and fowls. The commander's name was Mr. Cannady, and we were taking out 2000 young midshipmen to join the squadron off Cadiz.
>
> We did not sail till the 19th. . . .

23. His son troubles to mention three Teutons (Haller, Linckh, and Stackelberg), two Danes (Bronstedt and Koes), and three British (Graham, Haygarth, and Byron, but not Foster), as well as two ever-present Athenian noteworthies, the French Consul Fauvel and Elgin's aforementioned Neapolitan assistant, Giovanni Lusieri (*Travels in Southern Europe and the Levant, 1810–1817,* 44–46).

24. Information on notable British figures of this era may be found in the twenty-two volume reference work edited by Sir Leslie Stephen and Sir Sidney Lee, *The Dictionary of National Biography* (London: Oxford University Press, 1885–1901).

An entry for Foster may be found at VII, 499.

25. The work of reconstructing such biographies is advanced beyond measure on the German side by an astonishing two-volume reference work, Friedrich Noack, ed., *Das Deutschtum in Rom: Seit dem Ausgang des Mittelalters* [1927] (Darmstadt: Scientia Verlag Aalen, 1974), as well as by Hans Vollmer, ed., *Allgemeins Lexicon der Bildenden Künstler von der Antike bis zur Gegenwart* (Leipzig: Verlag von E. A. Seemann, 1929). Bracken's book, *Antiquities Acquired,* also offers a superb biographical appendix at pages 185–204.

Haller's correspondence with Cockerell is now housed at the Department of Antiquities in the British Museum. His Diaries and other letters were published in a variety of Leipzig publications, *Grenzboten* (1875,1876), *Kunstkritik* (1875), and *Zeitschrift für bildenden Kunst* (1877,1883).

Finally, see Hansgeorg Bankel, *Carl Haller von Hallerstein in Griechenland, 1810–1817* (Berlin: Walter de Gruyter, 1986).

26. Linkh's journals were also edited by P. Goessler as "*Jakob Linckh, ein Philhellene,*" in the *Münchner Jahrbuch der bildenden Kunst, Neue Folge* (1937/1938) Band XII, 149ff.

27. Pausanias, *Greek Walkabout* II.29.6–30.5. Pausanias mentions the Aeginetan highlights only: the shallow waters which serve to protect the island from invasion; the so-called Secret Harbor; and the major sanctuaries to Apollo, Artemis, Hekate, and Orpheus. He also mentions the local Aeginetan hero, Aiakos, with special appreciation, claiming that "it was on account of Aiakos and his exploits that I have laid out this memorial (*mnêmê*) to him" (II.30.5). It was Aiakos, he tells us, who first supplicated Zeus as god of all the Greeks (*tôi Panellêniôi Dii*) in order to lift a curse from the island (II.29.8).

But Pausanias's account of the sanctuary dedicated to the Panhellenic Zeus is confused. He tells us that "on Aegina, as you ascend the mountain of Panhellenic Zeus (*pros to oros Panellêniou Dios*), there is a temple of Aphaia (*Aphaías hieron*)" (II.30.3), and he provides an elaborate account of her mythic origins on—where else?—*Crete*. But then he refers to "the Panhellenion" as if it is a place (or is it the mountain, perhaps?),

which also contains "a temple of Zeus (*tou Díos to hieron*), but nothing else worth men-
tioning" (II.30.4). It is presumably this confusion which led our party of amateur archaeologists to identify this temple as belonging to Zeus, rather than to Aphaia.
Subsequent epigraphical evidence acquired during ensuing German excavations on
the site has proven this to be the sanctuary of Aphaia, not Zeus.

28. See Pausanias, *Greek Walkabout* VIII.41.7–9:

On the mountain is a place called Bassae, and the temple of Apollo the
Helper, made all of stone, including the roof. Of all the temples in the Peloponnese, this one may be placed next to the one in Tegea, for the beauty of its
stone and the harmony of its design.

29. Smith, "Lord Elgin and His Collection," 307–349, esp. 340–345.
30. Smith, "Lord Elgin and His Collection," 332.
31. Cockerell, *Travels in Southern Europe and the Levant, 1810–1817*, 51–56.
32. Cockerell, *Travels in Southern Europe and the Levant, 1810–1817*, 65–67.
33. Zante, which is an Italian name, had been a Venetian holding until Napoleon dismantled what was left of the Venetian Empire in 1797. The island passed over to the
French for two years, but was lost to the British in 1799. The French reoccupied the
island in 1807–1809, but then the British returned and organized the seven Ionian
islands into a loose confederacy, which lasted until Great Britain ceded the islands to
Greece in 1864. The island of Zante/Zakynthos would then be occupied repeatedly
in the twentieth century: by the French (1916–1917), by the Italians (1941–1943), and
by the Germans (1943–1944).
34. The *Academia dei Vigilanti Zacinthi* had been established by the Venetians in 1625. It was
reorganized as the Ionian Academy (literally "the Academy of the Free Ionian Islands,"
in Greek) in 1808, and quickly became a clearinghouse for looted Greek antiquities. As
Ambassador to the Porte in 1801, Lord Elgin had been very involved in debates about
the future reorganization of the Ionian islands. He left some of the Parthenon metopes
here at the Academy when he began transporting them, and Cockerell arranged for
both the finds from Aegina and from Bassae to be stored here as well.

While most of the archival records of the island of Zante were destroyed in the
massive earthquake and fire of 1953, I was able to locate references to *ho mêchanikos kai
archaiologos Kokorelês* as a faculty member in 1811, during a research visit to the island in
the summer of 1995.

35. Cockerell, *Travels in Southern Europe and the Levant, 1810–1817*, 58.
36. Ibid., 102–104.
37. Ibid., 104–126.
38. There is a large and growing body of material related to the extraordinary life and career of Johann Martin von Wagner. A collection of his letters, and discussion of his
Greek trip in particular may be found in the Bayerischen Staatsbibliothek in Munich,
as well as his personal archive which is located in the Würzburg Institut des Kunsts,
associated with Wagner's namesake, the Wagnermuseum at the University of
Würzburg. I have been especially instructed by the edition of Wagner's Diary, edited
by Richard Herbig in *Johann Martin von Wagners Beschreibung seiner Reise nach Griechenland
(1812–1813)* (Stuttgart: Verlag von W. Kohlhammer, 1938). The Wagner-Museum also
put together a show in 1989 (with narrative catalogue) entitled *"Auf nach Hellas heil'ger
Erde": Johann Martin von Wagners Reise nach Griechenland*. This book has some interesting
sketches made by Wagner in Rome and on the road. I am debted to Diskin Clay for
providing me with a copy of this catalogue.
39. There is a growing bibliography on the life and career of Bartholomew (Bertel)
Thorvaldsen as well. For my purposes, two sources are of special value: *Thorvaldsen in
Rom: Aus Wagners Papieren* (Würzburg: 20ten Programm zur Stiftungsfeier des von

Wagner'schen Kunstinstituts, 1887); and P. Kragelund and M. Nykjer, eds., *Thorvaldsen: L'ambiente l'influsso il mito* (Rome: L'Erma di Bretschneider, 1996).

40. I am indebted to the Wesleyan University Library which made this very rare book available to me in the Spring of 1994.

I have completed an English translation of Wagner's *Bericht über die Aeginetischen Bildwerke im Besitz Seiner Königl. Hoheit des Kronprinzen von Baiern* (Stuttgart und Tübingen: J.S. Gotta'schen Buchhandlung, 1817) which runs to some 200 manuscript pages, but have not yet found an interested publisher. This note may thus be read as a semi-shameless piece of self-promotion.

41. For a taste of Schelling's own "philosophy of mythology and religion," with special emphasis on *Greek* antiquity, see his "Treatise on the Deities of Samothrace," trans. and ed. Robert F. Brown (Missoula, MT: Scholars Press, 1974), as well as Edward Allen Beach, *The Potencies of God(s): Schelling's Philosophy of Mythology* (Albany: State University of New York Press, 1994).

42. The major names in this "school" are Kallon, Onatas, Glaukias, and Anaxagoras. All four of them seem too have been active between roughly 500 and 470 BCE—which is to say, precisely at the time of the construction of the Temple to Aphaia on Aegina. Pausanias is our main source for all of these figures, and seems especially appreciative of Onatas, whom he believes "we should rate below none of Daidalos's successors, nor even below those of the Attic school" (*Greek Walkabout* V.25.12).

An excellent summary of this material may be found in H. Stuart Jones, *Select Passages from Ancient Writers Illustrative of the History of Greek Sculpture*, ed. Al. N. Oikonomides (Chicago: Argonaut, Inc., Publishers, 1960), 40–50.

43. Several superb historical studies of the Glyptothek and its collection have been written. The most helpful are: Ludwig von Urlichs, *Beiträge zur Geschichte zu Glyptothek* (Würzburg, 1889); Adolf Fürtwangler, *Beschreibung der Glyptothek: König Ludwigs I zu München* (München: In Kommission bei A. Buchholz, 1900); Dieter Ohly, *Glyptothek München: Griechische und Römische Skulpturen* (München: C. H. Beck, 1980).

44. See Peter Murphy, "Architectonics," in Johann P. Arnason and Peter Murphy, eds., *Agon, Logos, Polis: The Greek Achievement and its Aftermath* (Stuttgart: Franz Steiner Verlag, 2001), 218.

45. Among Stackelberg's works, of special note are: *Der Apollotempel zu Bassae in Arcadien und die daselbst ausgegrabenen Bildwerke* (Frankfurt am Mein: Gedruckt mit Andreäischen Schriften, 1826); *Costumes et usages des peuples de la Grèce moderne* (Paris, 1825, no pub.), reprinted as *Trachten und Gebräuche der Neugriechen* (Berlin: Verlag von G. Reimer, 1831); *La Grèce: vues pittoresques et topographiques* (Paris: I. F. D'Ostervald, 1834); and *Der Gräber der Hellenen* (Berlin: Verlag von G. Reimer, 1837).

Of additional interest are: Carl Erich Gleye, ed., *Unveröffentliche briefe des archäologen Otto Magnus von Stackelberg*, in *Baltische Monatsschrift* 1913, Heft 6: 391–403, and *Aus Stackelbergs Nachlass* (Druck und Verlag Franzen und Grosse, 1859).

46. As quoted in Watkin, *The Life and Work of C. R. Cockerell*, xxi.

47. See Watkin, *The Life and Work of C. R. Cockerell*, xix–xxiii, 249–253, as well as Jane Turner, ed., *The Dictionary of Art* in 34 volumes (London: Macmillan Publishers, Ltd., 1996) VII, 502–505.

48. There is a large and growing bibliography on Aeginetan archaeology and history. The following is only a representative sampling. The Bayerische Akademie der Wissenschaften's Aegina-Kommission has published sixteen serial volumes entitled *Alt-Aegina* between 1974 and 1997. In addition, see:

Hansgeorg Bankel, *Der spätarchaische Tempel der Aphaia auf Aegina* (Berlin: Walter de Gruyter, 1993); Thomas J. Figueira, *Aegina and Athens in the Archaic and Classical Periods: A Socio-Political Investigation* (Ph.D. Dissertation at the University of Pennsylvania, 1977); Adolf Fürtwangler, *Aegina: Das Heiligtum der Aphaia*, mit Ernst R. Fiechter und Hermann

Thiersch (München: Verlag der K.B. Akademie der Wissenschaften, 1906) in two vols.; Otto Jahn, *Beschreibung der Vasensammlung König Ludwigs in der Pinakothek zu München* (München: Jos. Lindauer'sche Buchhandlung, 1854); Sonia di Neuhoff, *Aegina,* 3rd ed. (Athens: Apollo Editions, 1978); Dieter Ohly, *Die Aegineten: die Marmorskulpturen des Tempels der Aphaia auf Aegina* (München: C. H. Beck, 1976) in 4 volumes; Korinna Pilafidis-Williams, *The Sanctuary of Aphaia on Aigina in the Bronze Age* (München: Hirmer Verlag, 1998); Hans Walter, *Aegina: Die archäologische Geschichte einer griechischen Insel* (Deutscher Kunstverlag, 19); Anne Yannoulis, *Aegina* (Athens: Lykabettos Press, 1974, 1983).

49. I have discussed this material before, in *Afterwords: Hellenism, Modernism and the Myth of Decadence* (Albany: State University of New York Press, 1996), 45–53, but the crucial resource for this discussion is *Der Königsplatz, 1812–1988* (München: Staatliche Antiken-sammlungen und Glyptothek, 1991).

50. German excavators also discovered a number of other statues on site at Aegina, leading them ultimately to conclude that there were *three* pedimental groups, not two, at the sanctuary of Aphaia. This third pedimental group was presumably housed at ground level under a rooved portico, and may well have been the remains of a commissioned group that failed to win selection for inclusion on the temple. Such are the vagaries of artistic competition, then as now.

51. Albert Speer, *Inside the Third Reich,* trans. Richard and Clara Winston (New York: Macmillan, 1970), 3–79.

   For an intriguing analysis of the intellectual, aesthetic and moral culture of Munich in the pre-Nazi period—from the date of the completion of Ludwig's *Königsplatz* until the outbreak of the War—see David Clay Lodge, *Where Ghosts Walked: Munich's Road to the Third Reich* (New York: W. W. Norton & Company, 1997).

52. William J. Diebold, "The Politics of Derestoration: The Aegina Pediments and the German Confrontation with the Past," *Art Journal* 54.2 (1995): 60–66, esp. 62 and note 20.

   Diebold's article is a wonderful source of fascinating details, although I find his wholesale condemnation of the project of derestoration not only overstated, but actually self-contradictory at points. He worries so much about the erasure of the nineteenth-century layer of this collection that he fails to note the erasure of *antiquity* that Thorvaldsen's restorations, inspired by a particular kind of Romantic Hellenism, had managed. This, it seems to me, was what postwar scholars and derestorers were trying to address.

53. For more on this remarkably systematic and bureaucratic program of art acquisition, see Chamberlin, *Loot! The Heritage of Plunder,* 149–187. It is one of the many historical ironies implicit in these matters that Lord Elgin's former secretary (and Undersecretary of State for Foreign Affairs from 1809 until 1822), William Hamilton, had directed a similar project for the repatriation of art stolen by Napoleon, in 1815. (Chamberlin describes the Napoleonic project in *Loot!,* 123–148.)

   Finally, the Soviet armies of occupation proceeded to loot Germany after the War, under the aegis of recovering their own national treasures, as well as of "reparation." The most complex case proved to be that of "Priam's Treasure," removed to Berlin by Heinrich Schliemann in the 1880s, transferred to Moscow after the War, and now demanded by both Germany and Turkey for "repatriation." Debates about such matters have raged since the display of these rediscovered treasures in major museum exhibitions in Moscow and Leningrad in 1996. See Elazar Barkan, *The Guilt of Nations: Restitution and Negotiating Historical Injustices* (New York: W. W. Norton & Company, 2000), 65–87.

CHAPTER NINE

1. This is a complicated political matter, as such matters normally are. In 1967, King Constantine II left Greece with his family, after a failed attempt to seize power back

from a military junta known in Greek as the regime of "the Colonels." The royal family fled, instructively enough, to *Rome*. In 1974, when the Colonels were finally driven from power, a national referendum resulted over-whelmingly (with 69 percent of the vote) in the abolition of the monarchy and the establishment of a parliamentary republic in its place.

2. Pierre de Coubertin, *The Olympic Idea: Discourses and Essays* (Köln: Carl-Diem Institut, 1967), 110, emphasis mine.

3. It is worth reflecting that many of the languages we study for "religious" reasons— Hebrew, Greek, Arabic, and Sanskrit, to name only the most obvious examples—do not have a word that directly correlates to what we think of as "religion." Plato, as we saw in Chapter Two, wrote a dialogue on "piety" (*eusebeia*, which involved a set of *practices*), not on "religion" (which seems to imply a set of beliefs).

Some have even suggested that the very existence of the term, 'religion', ironically points to the increasing *secularization* of our conceptual frame—namely, by setting aside a separate space as the place where "religion" happens, and thus reinforcing the presumption that there is a realm outside of which it ceases to happen in any meaningful way. This terminology more subtly suggests that there is a great deal of public space which is *not* committed to the ideas allegedly served by "religion." And that is the concept of "religion" we have inscribed in our own decidedly modern politics and jurisprudence.

4. For Pierre de Coubertin's own admission of this devilish complication, see his essay, "The Olympic Games of 1896," *The Century Magazine* 53 (1896/7): 39–53, esp. 46.

5. For two wonderful introductory accounts of the genesis of the modern Olympic movement, with generous selections of archival photographs, see Davida Kristy, *Coubertin's Olympics: How the Games Began* (Minneapolis,MN: Lerner Publications Company, 1995) and Susan Wels, *The Olympic Spirit: 100 Years of the Games* (San Francisco,CA: HarperCollins Publishers, 1995).

6. For a humurously polemical and historical account of the development of these ideas, see David C. Young, "How the Amateurs Won the Olympics," in Wendy J. Raschke, ed., *The Archaeology of the Olympics: The Olympics and Other Festivals in Antiquity* (Madison,WI: The University of Wisconsin Press,1988), 55–75, as well as his *The Olympic Myth of Greek Amateur Athletics* (Chicago: The University of Chicago Press, 1984).

7. For a fascinating analysis of the modern permutations of this idea, beginning with Descartes (and, however unconsciously, with Montaigne), see Stephen Toulmin, *Cosmopolis: The Hidden Agenda of Modernity* (Chicago: The University of Chicago Press, 1990).

For the ancient ideal, see Martha C. Nussbaum, *The Therapy of Desire: Theory and Practice in Hellenistic Ethics* (Priceton: The Princeton University Press, 1994), especially 316–483 on Stoicism.

More recent attempts to rehabilitate Stoic ideas are Nussbaum's *Cultivating Humanity: A Classical Defense of Reform in Liberal Education* (Cambridge, MA: Harvard University Press, 1997), esp. 50–84, and Lawrence C. Becker, *A New Stoicism* (Princeton: The Princeton University Press, 1998).

8. See my "The Significance of the Scandal to the Modern Olympic Movement," *Soundings* (forthcoming 2002).

9. The, at best, partial success of the first Olympic Games was due in large part to their improbable and regrettable linkage to the alternative international spectacle of World's Fairs: in Paris, in St. Louis, and in London. In each case, the Fairs vastly overshadowed the Games. It was thus only in 1912, in Stockholm, that the modern Olympic revival established its full ritual autonomy . . . and then was nearly done to death by the Great War.

For more on these matters, see John J. MacAloon, *This Great Symbol: Pierre de Coubertin and the Origins of the Modern Olympic Games* (Chicago: The University of Chicago Press, 1981), 128–138.

10. There is perhaps no better indication of the deep-seated *political* rivalries built into the sanctuary at ancient Olympia, or the periodic and fairly frequent outbreak of violence even on the site, than the one Pausanias provides, especially at *Greek Walkabout* V.2.1–2.

11. The concept of political neutrality is a surprisingly underattended topic in Classical thought. One notable exception is Robert A. Bauslaugh's *The Concept of Neutrality in Classical Greece* (Berkeley: The University of California Press, 1991). Bauslaugh's analysis is of limited usefulness for my topic, simply because the concept of a "sacred truce" is so *under*determined in the Classical texts. Whatever notion of political and/or military neutrality was operative at the Panhellenic sanctuaries, it was just as fragile as all such political notions, and just as frequently violated (see pp. 38–43).

12. As we saw in Chapter Three, there are complex debates—involving the various and related disciplines of Archaeology, Art History, Classical Philology, as well as Classical and even post-Classical Greek history—regarding the alleged roots of these ancient Olympic festivals in the older, Bronze Age (Mycenaean, Helladic, and Minoan) Aegean cultures. Ancient testimonia do not help us here, since some imply that the Olympic festivals were *newly* founded in 776 BCE, while others insist that still more ancient Bronze Age athletic rituals were *revived* at that time.

     Be that as it may, *something* clearly happened at Olympia, something *religious*, in the ninth and tenth centuries BCE. The oldest cultic activity at Olympia dates from the Geometric Period, the so-called Dark Age of Greek antiquity (because we are so very much in the dark about it). Nearly 200 years later, an increasingly elaborate set of athletic rituals was stitched on to the essentially religious fabric of the sanctuary. That may have taken place initially in 776 BCE or later, but in any case the athletic activity was fundamentally restructured and the sanctuary-site itself was changed in the 680s BCE. It was *after* this that the Panhellenic Games at Olympia and elsewhere acquired the Greek shape that we tend to think of as essentially "Olympic" today.

     Debates about the relative continuity with Bronze Age athletic activity in mainland Greece, or Crete, or even the Near East aside, there is one essential aspect of the Olympic rituals which *cannot* be derived from earlier Bronze Age models—and that is their *Panhellenism*. The end of the so-called Dark Age was also the beginning of a whole new sense of identity, an infinitely larger if still unformed sense of *Greek* identity. In what did that unity, that sense of essential *Greekness*, consist? Here, quite suddenly, a whole series of independent eighth century Greek developments acquire significance:

     • first came *literacy*, the renewal of a set of writerly practices which had died out at the end of the Bronze Age palatial period.
     • one of the first poetic traditions to be set down in writing was the one we call "Homeric," a tradition which, if one considers the matter, tells the extraordinary tale of a truly Panhellenic expedition against Troy.
     • just as the *palaces* had been the root form of political organization in the Bronze Age, the *polis* emerged as the dominant political form in the eighth century, throughout the Greek world.
     • many of these newly founded *poleis* began to *colonize*, in places as distant as Sicily and southern Italy to the west, and the coast of Asia Minor to the east, not to mention the western coastal regions of the Black Sea, and sporadically along the coasts of Egypt, France and Spain.
     • finally, the sanctuary-sites at *Delphi* and at *Olympia* were re-organized on a model we now think of as emphatically Panhellenic in these same years.

     The elaborate ritualism of Olympia, and the emerging cult of *Panhellenism* that underwrote it, seem to be a product of this same extraordinary century. In much the same way, the modern Olympic revival, and Coubertin's *religio athletae*, are uniquely the product of a similarly disjunctive century: the nineteenth, in Europe.

For more on "the Panhellenic complex" of Olympia, Delphi, and the Homeric poems, see Gregory Nagy, *Pindar's Homer: The Lyric Possession of an Epic Past* (Baltimore,MD: Johns Hopkins University Press, 1990), 52–53; and *The Best of the Achaeans: Concepts of the Hero in Archaic Greek Poetry*, 2 Ed. (Baltimore, MD: Johns Hopkins University Press, 1999), 7–9, all of which builds on Anthony Snodgrass's *An Archaeology of Greece: The Present State and Future Scope of a Discipline* (Berkeley: University of California Press, 1987), 160–165.

13. The Baron Pierre de Coubertin emphatically presented his Olympic revival as an important promotion for what many Europeans were then calling "the cause of universal peace."

See Albert Shaw (Coubertin's close friend and editor), "The Re-Establishment of the Olympic Games: How International Sport May Promote Peace Among the Nations," *Review of Reviews* 10 (1894): 643–646. Tellingly, the long article immediately preceding this one is entitled "On the Threshold of Universal Peace" (635–643).

14. Leni Riefenstahl, "The Olympiad: Festival of the People" (Part I); and "Festival of Beauty" (Part II), dubbed in English (Timeless Video Inc., 1995). For an excellent account of the moral ambiguity of Riefenstahl's artistic career, see the documentary by Ray Müller, "The Wonderful, Horrible Life of Leni Riefenstahl," German with English subtitles (OMEGAFILM GmbH, 1993).

For further discussion of Riefenstahl's work at the Berlin Games, see Richard D. Mandell's fascinating but uneven study, *The Nazi Olympics* (Urbana,IL: University of Illinois Books, 1971, 1987), 250–274, as well as her own memoirs, *Leni Riefenstahl: A Memoir* (New York: St. Martin's Press,1992), 184–254.

The most compelling (if also overdrawn) case for Riefenstahl's essentially "fascist aesthetic" was made by Susan Sontag, in a now-famous essay, "Fascinating Fascism," in *Under the Sign of Saturn* (New York: Farrar Straus & Giroux, 1980), 73–105.

15. Coubertin, *The Olympic Idea*, 34, 92. See also "Why I Revived the Olympic Games," *The Fortnightly Review* 84 (1908): 110–111.

16. MacAloon, *This Great Symbol*, 138–139.

17. See David Constantine, *Early Greek Travellers and the Hellenic Ideal* (New York: The Cambridge University Press, 1984), 188–214, as well as the outstanding notes in Peter Levi, ed., *Pausanias: Guide to Greece, Vol. II, Southern Greece*, 317–318n94.

For Chandler's own account of his travels, see Richard Chandler, *Travels in Asia Minor and Greece*, rev. ed. Nicholas Revett (Oxford: Clarendon Press, 1825), and *Ionian Antiquities* (London: T. Spilsbury and W. Haskell, 1769).

18. In Coubertin's own words, we see reiterated the point which I made in the previous chapter: namely, that contests between the European Great Powers underwrote both the project of modern nation-formation, *and* of imperial spoliation:

On the 17th of August (1828), by virtue of an agreement concluded in London a month before, 14.000 men embarked at Toulon for Greece. They soon took Patras and occupied the whole of Morea. The expedition was accompanied by a scientific commission, which had the honor of being the first to ransack the spoils at Olympia. France was thus still more deeply pledged to the work of Greek emancipation. In her foreign as in her home policy, she showed herself, officially speaking, Liberal.

Coubertin, *France Since 1814* (New York: MacMillan Company, 1900), 74. See also Coubertin, *The Olympic Idea*, 107.

19. Coubertin, *The Olympic Idea*, 110–112.

20. For a representative example of some recent scholarship on this point, see Helen An-gelomatis-Tsougarakis, *The Eve of the Greek Revival: British Travellers' Perceptions of Early Nine-teenth-Century Greece* (New York: Routledge, 1990); G.W. Clarke, ed., *Rediscovering Hellenism: The Hellenic Inheritance and the English Imagination* (New York: The Cambridge University Press, 1989); David Constantine, *Early Greek Travellers and the Hellenic Ideal*; Vassilis Lambropoulos, *The Rise of Eurocentrism: Anatomy of Criticism* (Princeton: The Princeton University Press, 1993), and my review in "On Being Jewish or Greek in the Modern Moment," *Diaspora* 3:2 (1994): 199–220.

21. Coubertin himself refers to "the glorious battle of Navarino, which gave Greece her freedom, and threw new splendor on our Navy," at *France Since 1814*, 67–68 (see also 114ff). The British and Russians were, of course, also heavily engaged at Navarino.

22. See C.M.Woodhouse, *Modern Greece: A Short History*, ed. (Boston, MA: Faber and Faber, 1986), 125–156, and Paul Johnson, *The Birth of the Modern: World Society 1815–1830* (New York: HarperCollins Publishers, 1991), 673–701.

    For an instructive contemporary review of modern Greek history and identity, along with its singular problems and possibilities, see J. Irving Mariatt, "The Living Greek: A Glance at His Politics and Progress," *Review of Reviews* 11 (1895): 398–412.

    The borders and constitution of the fledgling nation were then drawn up in the "Convention Relative to the Sovereignty of Greece," signed in London on 7 May 1832 by the kings of France and Bavaria, and the Emperor of all Russia.

23. For the North American perspective on these and other matters, see Stephen Larrabee, *Hellas Observed: The American Experience of Greece, 1775–1865* (New York: The New York University Press, 1957).

24. Russell Chamberlin, *Loot! The Heritage of Plunder* (London: Thames and Hudson, Ltd., 1983), 39–65, 123–148.

    For a nice descriptive summary of the birth of the discipline and the gradual devel-opment of a method, see Brian M. Fagan, ed., *Eyewitness to Discovery: First-Person Accounts of More than Fifty of the World's Greatest Archaeological Discoveries* (New York: Oxford Uni-versity Press, 1996), esp. 70–71.

25. See *Napoleon in Egypt: Al-Jabarti's Chronicle of the French Occupation, 1798*, trans. Shmuel Moreh and intro. Robert L. Tignor (Princeton, NJ: Markus Wiener Publishing, 1993), with an "Afterword" by Edward W. Said (169–180).

26. Chamberlin, *Loot! The Heritage of Plunder*, 13–38.

27. For a representative Greek account of Elgin's work, see Theodore Vrettos, *A Shadow of Magnitude: The Acquisition of the Elgin Marbles* (New York: G. P. Putnam's Sons, 1974).

    See also Arthur H. Smith, "Lord Elgin and His Collection," *Journal of Hellenic Studies* 36.2 (1916) 163–372, and William St. Clair, *Lord Elgin and the Marbles* (New York: Ox-ford University Press, 1967).

    Finally, see some telling commentary in Elazar Barkan, *The Guilt of Nations: Restitution and Negotiating Historical Injustices* (New York: W.W. Norton & Company, 2000), 65–87.

28. See Charles Robert Cockerell, *The Temples of Jupiter Panhellenius at Aegina, and of Apollo Epi-curius at Bassae Near Phigalia in Arcadia* (London: J. Weale, 1860).

29. See the biographical note submitted by his friend and editor Albert Shaw, "Baron Pierre de Coubertin," *Review of Reviews* 17 (1898): 435–438, as well as MacAloon, *This Great Symbol*, 8–82.

30. See Chamberlin, *Loot! The Heritage of Plunder*, 17, and B.F. Cook, *The Townley Marbles* (London: Thames and Hudson, 1985).

31. For more critical reflections on this same idea, see George Steiner, *In Bluebeard's Castle: Some Notes Toward the Redefinition of Culture* (New Haven,CT: The Yale University Press, 1971), 110–111.

    Nietzsche's comments are also relevant here:

Where is the influence of antiquity visible? Surely not in language, not in the imitation of this or that, surely not in the perversity exhibited by the French. Our museums are crammed. I always feel nauseated when I see pure, naked figures in Greek style—confronted with this mindless philistinism that will soon devour everything.

(*Wir Philologen* 3[40])

32. For a somewhat heavy-handedly critical account of this Teutonic Neohellenism, see Eliza Marian Butler's *The Tyranny of Greece Over Germany: A Study of the Influence Exercised by Greek Art and Poetry Over the Great German Writers of the Eighteenth, Nineteenth and Twentieth Centuries* (New York: Macmillan and Company, 1935), esp. 3–8.

33. For further reflection on these institutional developments, see my "Hellenism on Display," *Journal of Modern Greek Studies* 15 (1997): 247–260, as well as "Classics at the Millennium: An Outsider's Survey of a Discipline," *Soundings* 82.1/2 (1999): 241–276.

34. Wolf's *opus* was his *Prolegomena to Homer* [1795], trans. and ed. Anthony Grafton, Glenn W. Most and James E.G. Zetzel (Princeton: The Princeton University Press, 1985).

35. Too few philosophers are aware of the fact that Nietzsche began his career as a Classicist and taught as one for ten years before poor health forced him to retire. See his unpublished notes for an essay entitled *Wir Philologen,* trans. William Arrowsmith in Arrowsmith, ed., *Friedrich Nietzsche: Unmodern Observations* (New Haven, CT: The Yale University Press, 1990), 307–387, as well as my discussion of the essay in *Afterwords,* 23–38.

36. For more on Winckelmann and his Neohellenic significance, see: Constantine, *Early Greek Travellers and the Hellenic Ideal,* 85–146; E.M. Butler, *The Tyranny of Greece Over Germany,* 11–48; and Kalman P. Bland, *The Artless Jew: Medieval and Modern Affirmations and Denials of the Visual* (Priceton: The Princeton University Press, 2000), 68–70.

37. Butler, *The Tyranny of Greece Over Germany,* 41–43.

38. The term is Edward W. Said's in his now-classic *Orientalism,* reprinted with an Afterword (New York: Penguin Books, 1995).

39. For the French dimension of these developments, see Olga Augustinos, *French Odysseys: Greece in French Travel Literature From the Renaissance to the Romantic Era* (Baltimore, MD: Johns Hopkins University Press, 1994); as well as Nina M. Athanassoglou-Kallmyer, *French Images From the Greek War of Independence, 1821–1830: Art and Politics Under the Restoration* (New Haven, CT: The Yale University Press, 1989).

40. Butler, *The Tyranny of Greece Over Germany,* 34–43.

41. Coubertin, *The Olympic Idea: Discourses and Essays,* 1.

42. G.W. F. Hegel, *The Philosophy of History,* trans. J. Sibree (New York: Dover Publications, Inc., 1956).

43. G.W. F. Hegel, *The Philosophy of History,* 223.

44. The Games were held from March 24 to April 3, 1896. The athletic programme was roughly as follows:

Track And Field
   100 meters
   400 meters
   800 meters
   1500 meters
   shot put and discus
   Marathon

Gymnastics: individual and team competition
   tumbling
   parallel bars
   rings

rope climbing

Military Contests
 fencing
 Greco-Roman wrestling
 riflery

Nautical Contests
 yachting
 skiffs
 yawls and outriggers

Swimming
 100 meters
 500 meters
 1200 meters

Cycling
 2000 meters
 10 kilometers
 100 kilometers
 the 12-hour race

Riding Events
Lawn Tennis
English Billiards/Cricket

For more, see Chrysaphê, *Oí Synchronoi Diethneis Olympiakoi Agones* (Athens: Bibliothêkê
tês Epitropês tôn Olympiakôn Agônes, 1930), 205–360, esp. 219–221, 224.

45. For the bitter struggle between Coubertin's commitment to the "ambulatory" character of the Modern Games and the Greek desire to keep them on Greek soil, see
MacAloon, *This Great Symbol,* 241–255.
   It is interesting that the two nations who did best at these first Games, the Greeks
and the Americans, were most supportive of their remaining permanently in Greece.
U.S. athletes won the most first place medals (cast in silver—such was Coubertin's desire to keep "gold" out of the Olympic arena), and the Greeks won the most medals,
overall. The final medal counts were as follows:

Individual First Place Medals (Second Place in Parentheses)
 USA 11 (6)   Austria 2 (1)
 Greece 10 (19)   Hungary 2 (1)
 Germany 7 (3)   Denmark 1 (2)
 England 5 (3)   Sweden 1 (2)
 France 5 (3)

Team Medals
 Greece 39   Austria 5
 USA 28   Hungary 5
 Germany 17   Denmark 4
 France 15   Sweden 4
 England 13

See Chrysaphes, *Oí Synchronoi Diethneis Olympiakoi Agones,* 341–343.

46. Alexander Gottlieb Baumgarten, *Reflections on Poetry*, trans. Karl Aschenbrenner and William B. Holter (Berkeley: University of California Press, 1954).

For more on Baumgarten's disciplinary legacy, see Hans Reiss, "The 'Naturalization' of the Term 'Ästhetik' in Eighteenth Century German: Alexander Gottlieb Baumgarten and His Impact," *Modern Language Review* 89 (1994): 645–648; as well as Elizabeth M. Wilkinson and L.A. Willoughby, eds., *Friedrich Schiller: On the Aesthetic Education of Man* (Oxford: Clarendon Press, 1967), xx-xxix.

47. Immanuel Kant, *Critique of Judgment*, trans. Werner S. Pluhar (Indianapolis,IN: Hackett Publishing Co., 1987).

48. Wilkinson and Willoughby, eds., *Friedrich Schiller: On the Aesthetic Education of Man*, Letter XIV, page 97.

49. For an abbreviated edition of Hegel's lectures, running to only one-sixth the length of the entire collection, see Henry Paolucci, ed., *Hegel: On the Arts* (New York: Frederick Ungar Publishing, Co., Inc., 1979).

50. MacAloon, *This Great Symbol*, 6–7, 194.

51. Edward J. Trelawny, *Records of Shelley, Byron, and the Author* [1858,1875] with an introduction by Ann Barton (New York: The New York Review of Books, 2000), 140–146.

52. The book which first alerted me to some of these complex developments was Gary Laderman, *The Sacred Remains: American Attitudes Toward Death, 1799–1883* (New Haven, CT: Yale University Press, 1996).

53. A third such diasporic figure is Dimitrios Vikelas (1835–1908) who happened also to be the first President of the International Olympic Committee. For a fascinating sketch of his life and its Neohellenic significance, see Artemis Leontis, "Mediterranean Topographies Before Balkanization: On Greek Diaspora, *Emporion,* and Revolution," *Diaspora* 6.2 (1997): 179–194.

54. I am indebted for much of this material to David C. Young, "Modern Greece and the Modern Olympic Games," in William Coulson and Helmut Kyrielis, eds., *Proceedings of an International Symposium on the Olympic Games* (Athens, 1992), 175–184.

55. In a wonderfully playful and self-conscious turnabout, Nikos Kazantzakis mastered the genre, turning the "imperial gaze" back upon northern Europe, reflecting on how places like England and Germany, among others, looked through the eyes of the modern Greek traveler. These remain, in my judgment, his most sophisticated literary works.

56. MacAloon, *This Great Symbol*, 45–60.

57. Shaw, "Baron Pierre de Coubertin," *Review of Reviews* 17 (1898): 435.

58. MacAloon, *This Great Symbol*, xi–xii, 134–137, 189, 262–269.

59. Alexander William Kinglake, *Eothen* (Marlboro, VT: The Marlboro Press, 1992).

60. Mark Twain, *The Innocents Abroad, or, The New Pilgrim's Progress* (New York: Airmont Publishing Company, Inc., 1967).

61. For more on the intellectual constellation of person and place, see D.S. Carne-Ross, *Pindar* (New Haven, CT: The Yale University Press, 1985), 1–39; and Frank J. Nisetich, *Pindar's Victory Songs* (Baltimore,MD: The Johns Hopkins Press, 1980), 1–21.

62. See my "Clio and Melpomene: In Defense of the Historical Novel," *Historical Reflections* 23.3 (1997): 389–418.

63. Georg Lukács, *The Historical Novel*, trans. Hannah and Stanley Mitchell (London: Merlin Press, 1962), 19.

64. In light of the imminent departure of the British from Hong Kong in July of 1997, many reflected on the poignant downward trajectory of the British Empire in the twentieth century.

For an extraordinary historical portrait, and the map, see Warren Hoge, "British Leave Hong Kong in Sour Kind of Grandeur," *The New York Times* (March 27, 1997).

65. Coubertin, *The Olympic Ideal*, 7–8, emphasis mine.

66. Robert Bellah, ed., *Emile Durkheim On Morality and Society* (Chicago: The University of Chicago Press, 1973), x.

67. Durkheim's masterwork was *The Elementary Forms of the Religious Life*, trans. Joseph Ward Swain (New York: Macmillan Publishing Co., Inc., 1915), a study which was based on what he called "the most primitive and simple religion which is actually known" (13), that of certain aboriginal Australian peoples, whose presence was advertised so dramatically at the 2000 Olympic Games in Sydney. What Durkheim emphasized, in any case, were precisely the practices of primitive ritual.

68. Bellah, *Emile Durkheim On Morality and Society*, x.

69. Durkheim, *The Elementary Forms of Religious Life*, 475–476, emphasis mine.

70. David C. Young is the scholar who has most clearly and passionately documented the modern Greek antecedents for the International Athletic festivals we call "Olympic." The Greeks had held Games of their own—most of them bankrolled by the Zappas trust—in 1859, in 1870, in 1875, and in 1889.

    See Young's, "How the Amateurs Won the Olympics," 55–75, and MacAloon, *This Great Symbol*, 151–153.

71. MacAloon, *This Great Symbol*, 128–131.

72. Ibid., 131–137.

73. Coubertin, *France Since 1814*, 174–175, 205–206.

74. Ibid., 238–239.

75. Coubertin, "The Present Problems and Politics of France," *Review of Reviews* 18 (1898): 193–194.

76. One reminder of just how novel and exciting this technological breakthrough appeared may be seen in Charles D. Lanier, "Two Giants of the Electric Age: Thomas A. Edison," *Review of Reviews* 8 (1893): 40–53.

77. Coubertin, *France Since 1814*, 260–261, 278.

78. Much recent work has been devoted to this extraordinary ritual event. See especially Stanley Appelbaum, *The Chicago World's Fair of 1893* (New York: Dover Publications, Inc., 1980).

    For some contemporary reflections on the significance of the Fair in the *American Review of Reviews* see: "The Progress of the World," *Review of Reviews* 7 (1893): 386–420; "Art at the Columbia Exhibition," *Review of Reviews* 7 (1893): 551–565; "The World's Fair Balance Sheet," *Review of Reviews* 8 (1893): 522; "A Closing Episode at the Fair," *Review of Reviews* 8 (1893): 633; and "The World's Fair in Retrospect," *Review of Reviews* 9 (1894): 198–199.

79. See Richard H. Seagar, *The Drama of Religious Pluralism: Voices From the World's Parliament of Religions, 1893* (La Salle, IL: Open Court, 1993), and *The World's Parliament of Religions: The East/West Encounter in Chicago, 1893* (Bloomington, IN: Indiana University Press, 1995).

    For some contemporary commentary on this event, see "The Chicago Parliament on the World's Religions," *Review of Reviews* 8 (1893): 252, and "The World's Fair Parliament of Religions in September 1893 in Chicago," *Review of Reviews* 7 (1893): 303–311.

80. It is important to recall how important a city Chicago had become, and how quickly. The re-organization of New York City as a massive, five-borough entity with an astonishing population of some 3.4 million was accomplished on May 4, 1897. It was conceived, in large measure, to counter the sudden emergence of Chicago as a premier, if not *the* premier, North American city after the rebuilding of 1871. See "New York City Celebrates a Century of Uneasy Unity," *The New York Times* (May 4, 1997).

81. So, for that matter, did Eugene Sandow, the British strongman who was displayed at the Fair as "the world's most perfect man." See Maria Wyke, "Herculean Muscle! The Classicizing Rhetoric of Bodybuilding" in *Arion, Third Series* 4.3 (1997): 54–55.

82. For more on this paradox, see Coubertin's negative assessment of "the religious policy" of Charles X which, so he argues, violated the Voltairean spirit of secular politics (*France Since 1814*, 71–74).

    For a cynical reading of the pro-Catholic sympathies of Louis Napoleon, see 200–202, 252–257. For the religious temper of the French people, see 228. For Louis Napoleon's exploitation of that Catholic sensibility, see 230ff.

83. MacAloon, *This Great Symbol*, 164–165.

84. Ibid., 138.

85. Coubertin, *The Olympic Idea*, 12.

86. For more on the complexity of this terminology, see my "Nietzsche and the (Choral) Birth of Tragedy" (forthcoming).

87. Much work has been done recently to heighten our sensitivity to just how pervasive this translational apprenticeship to the Classics became. In the words of George Steiner:

    > the classic wanes to the status of the academic or falls silent unless it is re-appropriated by translation, unless the living poet examines and affirms its relevance to the current idiom.

    The Penguin Book of Modern Verse Translation (New York: Penguin Books, 1966). A good glimpse of the contours of the field appears in Charles Tomlinson, ed., *The Oxford Book of Verse in English Translation* (New York: Oxford University Press, 1980) as well as *Eros English'd: Classical Erotic Poetry in Translation* (New York: Oxford University Press, 1992). See as well Adrian Poole and Jeremy Maule, eds., *The Oxford Book of Classical Verse in Translation* (New York: Oxford University Press, 1995).

88. See the crucial discussion of this Romantic idea in Charles Taylor, *Sources of the Self: The Making of the Modern Identity* (Cambridge, MA: Harvard University Press, 1989), 419–493.

89. Nietzsche, *Wir Philologen* 6[20], in Giorio Colli and Mazzino Montinari, eds., *Friedrich Nietzsche: Sämtliche Werke, Kritische Studienausgabe in 15 Bänden* (Berlin: Walter de Gruyter, 1967–1977) VIII, 105–106.

90. Pindar, *Pythian* 8, in Nisetich, *Pindar's Victory Odes*, 205. Here again is Pindar, on the site of Olympia itself (Ode #1):

    > Water is preeminent and gold, like a fire
    > burning in the night, outshines
    > all possessions that magnify men's pride.
    > But if, my soul, you yearn
    > to celebrate great games,
    > look no further
    > for another star
    > shining through the deserted ether
    > brighter than the sun, or for a contest
    > mightier than Olympia. . . .
    > (Nisetich, *Pindar's Victory Odes*, 82)

91. This is my main thesis in *Afterwords*, 23–24.

92. I am thinking of the Romantic myth of the modern swimmer, and a meditation on the oceanic in the construction of a human life, as described by Charles Sprawson in *Haunts of the Black Masseur: The Swimmer As Hero* (New York: Pantheon Books, 1992).

93. Frank M. Turner, "Why the Greeks and Not the Romans in Victorian Britain?" in Clarke, ed., *Rediscovering Hellenism*, 61–81.

94. See Bishop Kallistos Ware, *The Inner Kingdom* (Crestwood, NY: St. Vladimir's Seminary Press, 2000), 1–24.

95. See my "The Eastern Orthodox Churches of Atlanta," in Laderman, ed., *Religions of Atlanta,* 157–173.

96. MacAloon, *This Great Symbol,* 190.

97. Ioannes Gennadius, "The Revival of the Olympic Games," *Cosmopolis* 2.4 (April 1896): 74.

　　This essay has been republished by the Library which bears his name in "*Aphierôma ston Iôannê Gennadio,*" *The New Griffin Series,* No.4 (Athens: The Gennadius Library, 2001), 65–79.

98. See Norman Vance, *The Sinews of the Spirit: The Ideal of Christian Manliness in Victorian Literature and Religious Thought* (New York: Cambridge University Press, 1985). For a fascinating analysis of the complexity of the notions of masculinity and muscularity in the Victorian era, with special attention to the pre-Raphaelite Brotherhood and their confusion over how to depict the masculinity of Christ, see Herbert Sussman, *Victorian Masculinities: Manhood and Masculine Poetics in Early Victorian Literature and Art* (New York: Cambridge University Press, 1995), 111–172.

　　Finally, see Coubertin, *The Olympic Idea,* 103, and MacAloon, *This Great Symbol,* 51.

99. Coubertin, *The Olympic Idea,* 6–7.

100. Coubertin, "The Revival of the French Universities," *Review of Reviews* 16 (1897): 52–56.

101. Coubertin, *The Olympic Idea,* 38.

102. Ibid., 19, 45–46, 83, 103, 112, 132.

103. Ibid., 131. See also 108.

104. Ibid., 22, 107–108, 118, and MacAloon, *This Great Symbol,* 4–7.

105. Ibid., 118, and MacAloon, *This Great Symbol,* 20–21.

106. Ibid., 22.

107. Ibid., 2, 91, 115.

108. Ibid., 9.

109. Ibid., 9.

110. Coubertin, "Does Cosmopolitan Life Lead to International Friendliness?" *Review of Reviews* 17 (1898): 429–438. For a subtle analysis of this article and its main thesis, see MacAloon, *This Great Symbol,* 262–266.

111. See, for instance, Coubertin, "The Revival of the French Universities," *Review of Reviews* 16 (1897): 52–56.

112. Coubertin, "Does Cosmopolitan Life Lead to International Friendliness?" 431.

　　Interestingly, it became a virtual obsession of the Nazi organizers of the 1936 Berlin Olympics to see to it that each national team was provided with ample supplies of national dishes at each meal. See Mandell, *The Nazi Olympics,* 90–91, 139–141.

113. Coubertin, *The Olympic Idea,* 2–5, 31–32, 124.

114. MacAloon, *This Great Symbol,* xi–xii.

115. Coubertin, *The Olympic Idea,* 133.

116. Ibid., 134.

117. Coubertin, "Does Cosmopolitan Life Lead to International Friendliness?" 429–430.

118. The oath was a central and enduring concern for the Baron de Coubertin. See Coubertin, *The Olympic Idea,* 15, 34–36, 105.

119. Coubertin, *The Olympic Idea,* 116–118.

120. Ibid., 61–62.

121. Ibid., 7–8, 30–31.

122. MacAloon, *This Great Symbol,* 261.

123. Coubertin, *The Olympic Idea,* 12.

124. Ibid., 15.

125. See Henry Wysham Lanier, "In the Field of International Sport," *Review of Reviews* 12 (1895): 575–578; Charles D. Lanier, "The World's Sporting Impulse," *Review of Reviews*

14 (1896): 58–63; "English and American Sports," *Review of Reviews* 16 (1897): 73; "Sports' Place in the National Well-Being," *Review of Reviews* 18 (1898): 219–220; as well as Coubertin, *The Olympic Idea,* 8, on "the striking physical renaissance of the XIXth century."

126. For a stirring account of that explosive last year, see Lesley Chamberlain, *Nietzsche in Turin: An Intimate Biography* (New York: Picador USA, 1996).

127. Nietzsche, *Wir Philologen* 3[16], in Arrowsmith, ed., *Unmodern Observations,* 329.

128. Ibid., 345.

129. Ibid., 382.

130. Nietzsche, *Thus Spoke Zarathustra,* trans. Walter Kaufmann (New York: The Viking Press, 1966), "On the Vision and the Riddle," 155–160. See also James J. Winchester, *Nietzsche's Aesthetic Turn: Reading Nietzsche After Heidegger, Deleuze and Derrida* (Albany: State University of New York Press, 1994), 13ff.

131. Nietzsche, *The Gay Science,* trans. Walter Kaufmann (New York: Vintage Books, 1974), §125, "The Madman," 181–182.

132. Nietzsche, *Twilight of the Idols,* "'Reason' in Philosophy" §5, trans. Walter Kaufmann in *The Portable Nietzsche* (New York: Penguin Books, 1954), 483.

133. See my "Nietzsche, the Death of God, and Truth, or, Why I Still Like Reading Nietzsche," *Journal of the American Academy of Religion* 65.3 (1997): 573–585.

134. Edward J. Trelawny, *Recollections of Shelley, Byron, and the Author* (New York: New York Review Books, 2000), 32.

135. Coubertin, *The Olympic Idea,* 47–48. See also 39 and 85.

136. Ibid., 107.

137. Ibid., 6.

138. Ibid., 98, 106, 121, 129, 133, 135.

139. There was already worry about Coubertin's exclusivity before the Games were offically revived: "We note with regret that M. Coubertin does not allude to the considerable part played of late by women in athletic sports," *Review of Reviews* 10 (1894): 208.

It seems important to add that Coubertin was not entirely opposed to women's and team sports; he simply wanted to distinguish ritually between the center and the periphery of his Olympic revival, reserving the center—what he called "the moral Altis"—for the individual men's competition.

140. For more on these developments, see my *Afterwords,* 174–177, 192n65.

141. See Martha C. Nussbaum, "Transcending Humanity," in *Love's Knowledge: Essays on Philosophy and Literature* (New York: Oxford University Press, 1990), 372ff.

142. See Helene Foley, *The Homeric Hymn to Demeter* (Princeton: The Princeton University Press, 1994), 86–95, Jean-Pierre Vernant, *Mortals and Immortals: Collected Essays,* ed. Froma I. Zeitlin (Princeton: The Princeton University Press, 1991), 27–49, and Pierre Vidal-Naquet, "Beasts, Humans and Gods: The Greek View," in Johann P. Arnason and Peter Murphy, eds., *Agon, Logos, Polis: The Greek Achievement and its Aftermath* (Stuttgart: Franz Steiner Verlag, 2001), 127–137.

143. Coubertin, *The Olympic Idea,* 57, 113.

144. Athanasius, "On the Incarnation of the Word," in Edward R. Hardy, ed., *Christology of the Later Fathers* (Philadelphia,PA: The Westminster Press, 1954), 107.

145. Pausanias, *A Greek Walkabout* V.10.1.

146. For a stunning display of this thesis in the realm of philosophy proper, see Andrew Bowie, *From Romanticism to Critical Theory: The Philosophy of German Literary Theory* (New York and London: Routledge, 1997).

147. Ruprecht, *Afterwords,* 233–242, and MacAloon, *This Great Symbol,* xii.

148. Coubertin, *The Olympic Idea,* 114.

149. G. W. F. Hegel, *The Phenomenology of Mind,* trans. J. B. Baillie (New York: Humanities Press, Inc., 1966), 781–782.

150. Nietzsche, *The Antichrist,* in *The Portable Nietzsche,* 565–656.
151. Boxing, which is one of the few events to have been a major component of the ancient *and* the modern Games (although equestrian events were bigger in antiquity, and boxing has been in serious decline in the 1980s and 1990s), has not been a significant part of my story. Boxing held real significance for Coubertin, who noted that "[i]t is not so paradoxical to call boxing a 'pacifying sport'" (*The Olympic Idea,* 63).

   For a wonderfully rich and layered analysis of the way a sporting event like a boxing match maps out the cultural codes, aspirations and implicit values of the times, managed by focussing on boxing writer A. J. Liebling (d.1963) and Larry Holmes, who defeated Muhammed Ali for the World Heavyweight title in 1980, see Carlo Rotella, "Three Views of the Fistic Summits from College Hill," *South Atlantic Quarterly* 95.2 (1996): 281–320.

   For a similar analysis of the Joe Louis-Max Schmeling rivalry in the 1930s, see Mandell, *The Nazi Olympics,* 112–121, 289–290.
152. Mandell, *The Nazi Olympics,* 129–138.
153. MacAloon, *This Great Symbol,* 51–52, 59–70.
154. Ibid., 190–194.
155. Ibid., 96, 170.
156. Ibid., 93–97.